Decision Making
An integrated approach

Decision Making
An integrated approach

David Jennings
and
Stuart Wattam

PITMAN PUBLISHING
128 Long Acre, London WC2E 9AN

A Division of Pearson Professional Limited

First published in 1994

A CIP catalogue record for this book can be obtained from the British Library.

ISBN 0 273 60397 3

10 9 8 7 6 5 4 3

Typeset by ROM-Data Corporation, Falmouth, Cornwall.
Printed in England by Clays Ltd, St Ives plc

The Publishers' policy is to use paper manufactured from sustainable forests.

CONTENTS

LIST OF ILLUSTRATIONS

LIST OF FIGURES

LIST OF TABLES

PREFACE

Decision making is a broad subject that has a tendency to widen with time. The long-established contribution of the accountant has been joined by that of the management scientist, the strategist and the behavioural scientist.

Long-standing issues, such as the role of ethics and social responsibility, have recently enjoyed growing recognition of their significance, and new areas have developed, including chaos theory and the use of computers to model, simulate and support decision making.

With such a broad field the aims of a decision-making book have to be modest. Each of us has our own style of decision making, and the aim of this book is to provide an opportunity for understanding it in a wider sense and thus improving decision making in practice.

A large number of examples and case studies are provided throughout; these act as illustrations and opportunities to apply concepts and techniques. In reality decisions are often made in highly complex situations. The last chapter includes a case study that presents some of that complexity as an opportunity to practise the understanding of decision making issues that has been developed in this book.

Acknowledgements
This book owes its origin to the work of a group of staff at Nottingham Business School, colleagues from a variety of backgrounds who have helped develop each other's understanding of decision making. This book is also a collaborative effort with chapters contributed by Ray Lye, Alan Pizzey, James Stewart and Paul Whysall.

D.J
S.W.
4 February 1994

CHAPTER 1

Decision making

David Jennings and Stuart Wattam

MANAGEMENT DECISION MAKING

Decision making is an activity that lies at the heart of management. The assumption of a management role places an individual in the mainstream of an organisation's decision-making activity with authority to make decisions and to organise and develop the organisation's decision-making capability. To the extent that they are not the result of constraints imposed from outside, all of the actions of an organisation are, explicitly or implicitly, the result of management decision making. Decision making is a vital organisational activity.

It is unlikely that all decisions can be said to be 'good' decisions, providing the best possible choice for an organisation to follow. Organisations are complex and this complexity is often reflected in their problems. In many cases a solution that improves a situation is in itself a major achievement.

Our involvement in decision making often leaves misconceptions concerning the process that has taken place. Decision making bears the connotation of being decisive, yet many decisions are taken over long periods of time in which there are many starts and stops to the development of the issue and its resolution. Practitioners often overestimate how rational they have been. Given the complexity of organisations and the problems they face, together with the inability of any decision maker to obtain all the information he would like, it is unlikely we can be sure that the choice that has been made in fact represents the best possible alternative. In addition, those involved in the process often fail to perceive how the decision was made. Partly this is through not being involved in all parts of the process that lead to the decision. Some political aspects of a decision (in this context the term 'politics' does not refer to affiliation to a political party) will be inaccessible to most members of an organisation. Also participants have a biased view of the activities they have engaged in. The individual who feels that decision making is a matter of gaining the right data and applying analysis often does not recognise the range of group and organisational activity that their decision making has involved.

It can be argued that all organisations need to improve their decision making. This need arises because:

- In general, organisations face a scarcity of resources and the need to make the most effective use of the resources available to them.
- Increasingly both private and public sector organisations face competition, either from the rising pace of competition or through government exposing more organisations and their decisions to market disciplines.
- Issues such as consumer safety, pollution and employment practices, frequently raise public concern over the degree of social responsibility demonstrated by organisations in their decision making. Both public and private sector organisations often find

themselves open to examination by the wider society, not only for the results of decisions they have made, but also for how those decisions were arrived at.

Our academic understanding of organisational decision making is incomplete and managers are usually left reliant upon the skills and insights they have developed through experience. Decision making is such a vital and complex process that it justifies both academic study and critical examination by the practising manager. In order to make better decisions there is a need to be aware of what is in fact happening when we make decisions. What are the individual, group and organisational processes that are involved in decision-making activity? How can accounting and management science techniques assist decision making? How can the decision maker recognise and cope with the complexity and uncertainty that is a part of many problems?

TYPES OF DECISIONS

Organisations need a great many decisions to be made. Decisions are required so that an organisation can function, adapt, progress, take advantage of opportunities and overcome crises. The range of problems that an organisation faces is diverse. Many decisions are repeated several times during a working day while others occur infrequently and may take place over several years.

The range of decisions can be illustrated by considering a manufacturing organisation. Over a period of time the operations of a manufacturing organisation may require the following problems to be answered:

- which technology to employ?
- what scale of manufacture, how large a plant?
- how flexible should the plant be?
- where should the plant be located?
- how to finance and source the equipment?
- what should be the employment and training policies for employees?
- how much should be produced this year?
- where should materials be sourced?
- how much should be produced this week?
- what should be today's production schedule?
- how can that schedule accommodate the unforeseen requirements of a priority customer?

The list is not conclusive it merely illustrates the range of problems that are encountered by a manufacturing enterprise. A similar list could be derived for a service organisation, such as an airline or a charity or a public service organisation.

The problems facing a particular organisation differ in certain respects. The problems concerning technology, scale, flexibility and location are decisions that are taken infrequently. Some of those decisions are made only once in the life of the plant. Certain decisions, such as sourcing particular materials, are periodically open to reconsideration. Other decisions are made on a weekly or daily basis or even many times within a day. To a degree the decisions form a hierarchy. Decisions concerning such matters as technology, size and location, precede other decisions, such as training and scheduling. They shape the operating situation, the problems it will face and constrain the solutions to those problems.

These apparent differences imply a typology for problems and their consequent decisions, a classification scheme to highlight the differences between types of decisions. To the extent that decisions are *repetitive, routine or a definite procedure has been established for making the decision*, the decision can be described as *programmed*. Decisions are *non-programmed* to the extent that they are *novel, unstructured and consequential* (Simon, 1965). These decision types form extreme polar types, end points on a continuum of decisions.

This classification can be applied to the example of the manufacturing enterprise. Production schedules have to be developed for each day or week of operation. The decision is repetitive and a procedure will have been developed specifying who makes the decision and how the decision is made, whether that is by a formal technique, possibly based upon a set of decision rules that are run through a computer, or by applying informal rules and insights that have been developed and proven over time by the decision maker. The decision has become programmed; an efficient and effective way has been developed to solve the recurring problem.

Other problems may not have occurred before for the organisation. They may be regarded as novel and to that extent those who come to make the decision will not be able to recognise a familiar structure to the problem and apply a proven procedure to gain a solution. Such decisions are often consequential, not only by having a lasting effect on the organisation's performance and commitment of resources, but also through providing a part of the context for other problems and decisions.

The terms 'programmed' and 'non-programmed' decision refer to extremes on a continuum; there may be few decisions that are entirely programmed or non-programmed. All managers develop ways of dealing with problems, some of which can apply to novel situations. Even a non-programmed decision, such as a strategic decision, may have some familiar elements in its structure. This can be seen in the study of strategic decision making by Mintzberg (Mintzberg *et al*, 1976) which identifies a structured process for making strategic decisions.

Problems may also change their classification. Over time a supermarket group will have made numerous decisions concerning store location. When the location problem was first encountered by the organisation the problem would have had a high degree of novelty and the ensuing decision a lack of structure. Following a period of expansion the decision becomes repetitive, the organisation will have a clear understanding of the information that it requires to make the decision and will have established a procedure, possibly involving a computer model, with which to make the decision. The location decision will have moved towards becoming a programmed decision.

A decision may also move away from being a programmed decision to become more non-programmed. Seemingly routine decisions, concerning quality, customer relations, employee grievances, etc., have on occasion had extreme consequences for organisations and their market positions.

The most important decisions facing organisations may be described as closer to being non-programmed than programmed. The problems involved have a considerable degree of ambiguity. They may be continually redefined and highly interdependent with other important problems. Information concerning such problems is usually incomplete and a number of individuals and groups are likely to influence the decision. The decision itself may extend over a considerable period of time. A case study for such a problem situation is presented in Illustration 1.1. The case should be given careful consideration as it is referred to throughout Chapters 1 and 2.

Illustration 1.1 Taking stock at Schmorl Print

Schmorl Print is a medium-sized company manufacturing and marketing typesetting equipment and systems. The company has three principal groups of customers; newspapers, commercial printers (printing magazines, books, catalogues and calenders) and in-plant printers (large organisations undertaking their own in-house printing). The company's sales are divided 20% to the UK market, 80% to export (export countries including Greece, Spain, Portugal, Italy, Holland, Germany, Russia, the Middle East, Japan, New Zealand, Australia and South Africa).

In terms of profits systems are the most important part of sales. A system consists of an integrated network of computers and printers, the system is designed to customer specification and embodies leading technology. The ability of each new generation of system to provide customers with increased productivity, quality and flexibility gives Schmorl Print a basis upon which to build its sales. With the policy of being 'first to the market' with an innovation, Schmorl Print is able to charge a higher price than competitors and to stimulate the customers to replace existing equipment. Schmorl Print's competitive strategy is essentially driven by innovation.

Schmorl Print has a considerable amount of knowledge about its customers, both actual and potential. All of the main customer companies have been identified in each of the countries that Schmorl Print sells to. In addition, Schmorl Print has detailed information for each company's existing equipment (its age and capacity) and the organisation's broad operating requirements, together with estimates for the general state of each country's economy and the financial position of each customer. The information forms the basis for Schmorl Print's annual sales forecast. For each of the last few years the total of sales achieved has exceeded forecast.

As part of the sales agreement Schmorl Print undertakes to service all of its products, current and discontinued. While current equipment may be serviced with components from the production stores, a further 4000 different parts are held in the service store, none of these parts are employed in current models. In terms of value the service stock has doubled in the last two years. Most of the components are so new that failure rates have not been established and as yet no means has been found for determining an optimum level for the service store. To avoid large stock write-offs a stock obsolescence reserve has been established; this is charged to profits on the basis that if a new item to the service stock has not been required after twelve months, a 25% reserve is put on it, after two years 50%, and on to 100% after four years.

Customers invariably receive the newly developed system by the agreed date but final payment is often delayed by a period of 'de-bugging'. The development department has considerable status within the company and has been able to minimise its involvement in this process leaving the solution of customer complaints to the service engineers. For Mr Freeman, the Head of Hardware Development, 'once a system leaves development, its Production's pigeon and all information is to go to Production'. This policy results in conflict between Development and the Production Department but it does enable Mr Freeman's own engineers to focus upon the task of developing more advanced products.

Through the interaction between service and production engineers Schmorl Print modify the product, making it a cheaper and more reliable one. These modifications are built into future sales of the equipment. Often the modifications require further items to be added to the service store.

Mr Peters, the Financial Director, is becoming increasingly concerned with Schmorl Print's financial performance. Although sales are consistently ahead of forecast, rising in the last year by 30%, net profit is almost constant and liquidity is deteriorating. The accounting information clearly indicates that the service stock and its write-off against profit is a significant part of the worsening in Schmorl Print's financial results.

Schmorl Print has recently become part of a larger group of companies. The parent company is known to have an extensive set of policies and guidelines for various aspects of group performance but as yet the principles and aims by which Schmorl Print is to be managed have not been made clear to Mr Peters.

What should Mr Peters do?

In this case study, the identities of the company and of the persons concerned have been disguised.

DECISION MAKING: A NORMATIVE MODEL

How should a decision such as that facing Mr Peters be made? Is there a series of activities, a decision-making process, that can be undertaken in order to make the best possible decision?

The sequence of activities shown in Fig. 1.1 specifies a normative model of the decision-making process. The process provides a logical means for making a decision. The model is typical of the normative models that have been proposed in the decision-making literature of corporate planning and management science. A normative model describes how decisions should be made, rather than how they are made. The model is a proposal of how ideally to make a decision. The ability of this decision-making process to deliver 'best' decisions rests upon the activities that make up the process and the order in which they are attended to.

The normative decision-making process is based upon the organisation having a set of *goals and objectives*; the answer to the question of what it is we are trying to achieve with this organisation. For a business organisation such as Schmorl Print the organisation's objectives may include profitability, growth, gaining market share, excellence in service to the customer, and any other fundamental purposes that underpin the ultimate survival of the business and justify its continuation as a part of society. For a not-for-profit organisation, the goals and objectives may take the form of providing for the needs of various client groups through the provision of services such as housing and health care.

The goals and objectives of the organisation can be developed to provide *criteria*, clear definitions of how the objectives are to be measured so that the organisation can assess its progress in achieving the objectives it has set itself. Each objective may be measured by a variety of criteria, the intention is to develop a set of criteria that reflect the essence of the organisation's objectives.

Many criteria can be defined to measure profitability; for a company which emphasises its service to its shareholders the criteria will need explicitly to recognise the shareholders' interests.

Objective	*Criteria*
Profitability	Return on equity (the shareholder's interest in the company)

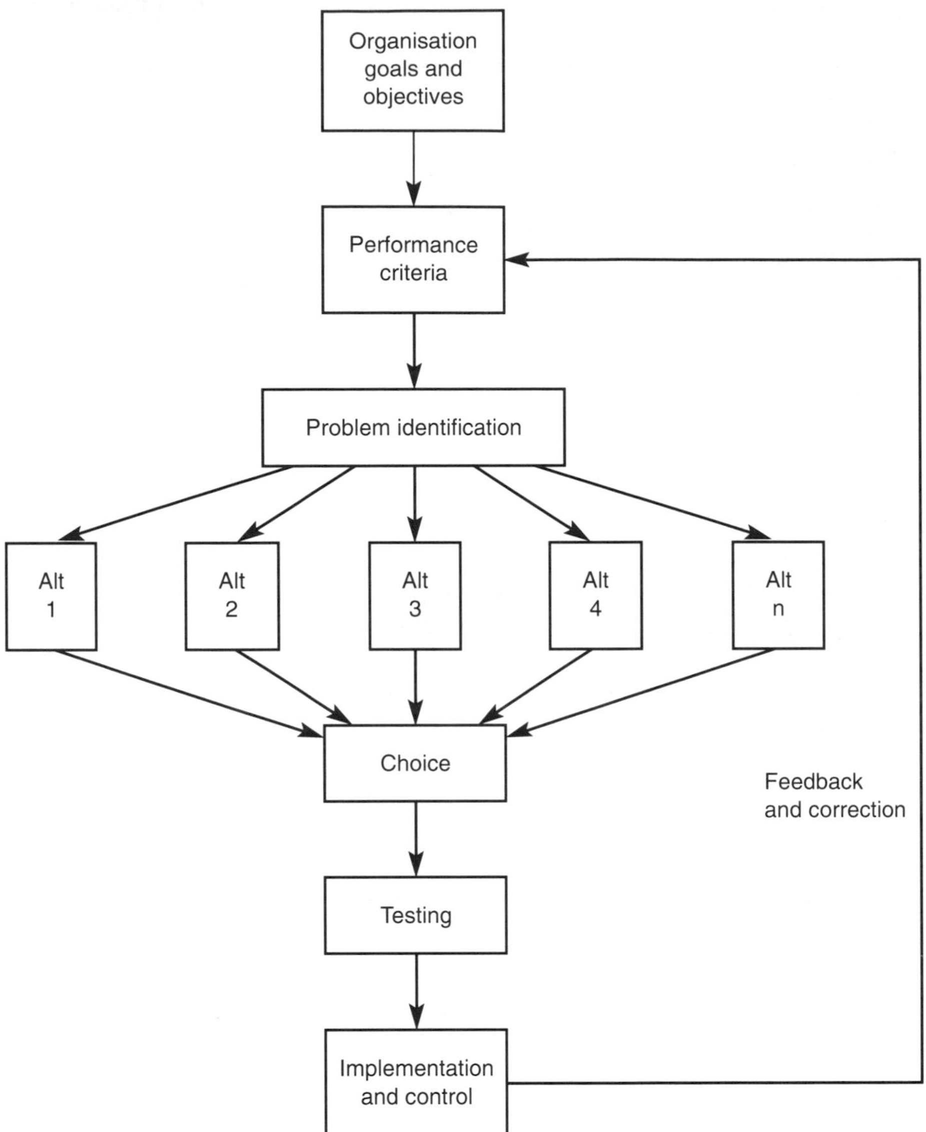

Fig. 1.1 The decision-making process: a normative model

The criteria become a part of the means by which problems can be identified. A target level can be set for an organisation's objectives and, by comparing that target to actual and potential performance, gaps in the organisation's performance can be identified, as shown in Fig. 1.2.

In the normative model of decision making the process of defining a problem is similar in nature to medical diagnosis. The performance gap is a symptom resulting from underlying problems occurring in the organisation's health. The causes of these symptoms may be explored in a logical fashion by structuring an enquiry and gaining evidence that supports or rejects competing explanations for the failure in performance. For a shortfall in profitability the series of decisions may form a sequence, as in Fig. 1.3.

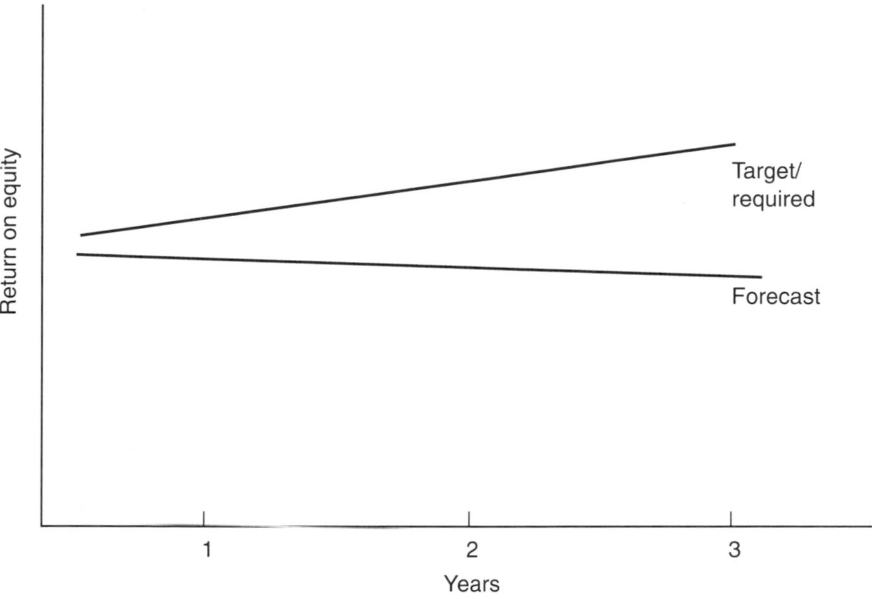

Fig. 1.2 Performance gap analysis

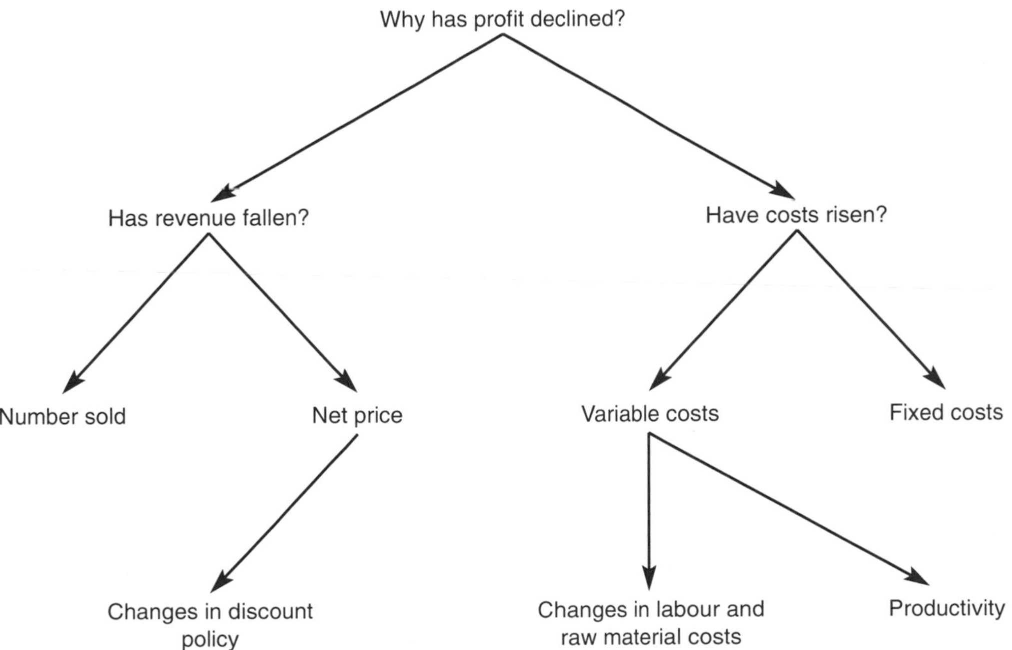

Fig. 1.3 Why has profit declined?

Identification of the problem is followed by a *search for alternative solutions* to the problem. Solutions may be found by a number of means. The decision maker may use memory, whether that is by seeing similarities between the problem and others that have been solved in the past by the decision maker or by other members of the organisation. Such a search process may extend to the active participation of other organisations and may include using consultants who are regarded as specialists in the problem area. It may be that alternatives will be sought not only through tapping organisational and personal memory but also by devising new solutions. Original solutions to problems can be found through dedicating individual and group resources to the creation of new solutions, techniques such as brainstorming and synectics can be employed to assist the process.

The purpose of this phase in the decision-making process is to seek the best solution to the problem. This may entail identifying a number of feasible solutions. The goals and objectives of the organisation continue to have a role in this phase of the decision-making process. The alternatives which the organisation is seeking must have the potential to correct the problem at hand and promote the organisation's goals and objectives. Its goals and objectives help to guide the search for appropriate solutions. Following the discovery and creation of a range of alternatives, the decision enters the *choice* phase. The organisation's objectives and goals are again relevant. The choice of a suitable solution is in part made in terms of the solution's ability to further the organisation's objectives.

The selected alternative may then be *tested* to evaluate the extent to which it remains the best choice under the range of possible circumstances that the organisation might face in the future. For Schmorl Print these uncertainties include the failure rate of components, the interest rate that will apply to future stockholdings and the rate of advance of technology.

With increased confidence that the selected alternative is the best choice under a variety of possible circumstances, the next phase is to *implement* the decision. Up to this point the decision-making process has been based upon information, knowledge and ideas. Only through implementation, with the organisation deploying and developing human and physical assets, does the decision become a part of the organisation's operations.

There is a need to see how the decision will work out in practice. Has the situation surrounding the problem changed to such an extent that the decision will need to be developed further? Does it need better resourcing in order to be effective? The final activity concerns *control*, monitoring the performance of the selected alternative to ensure that the shortfall in performance has been overcome, that the decision is effective in solving the problem. Without this activity the decision-making process would have no means of correcting an ineffective decision.

The control loop provides a continuing comparison between the performance which is being achieved and the performance criteria that have been set for the organisation. A shortfall in performance will, once again, trigger decision-making activity to define the problem and identify a further set of solutions. While the organisation's resources may be limited and the environment continually provides new opportunities and threats, the decision-making process maintains the organisation's pursuit of its objectives.

The normative model of the decision-making process provides a structured sequence of activities by which an organisation can identify and correct problems. However, following such a process can be difficult and Illustration 1.2 highlights some of the particular difficulties that are met in following the normative model of decision making.

Illustration 1.2 Corporate planning in a Local Authority

In the early 1970s a number of UK local authorities adopted a comprehensive corporate planning process, a Planning Programming and Budgeting System (PPBS). The methodology had been developed and applied in a number of areas of government in the USA and was seen as having great potential for improving long-term decision making in UK government at both a central and local level.

The PPBS methodology describes a number of stages for an annual process of planning and budgeting. The process begins with the definition of objectives, followed by development of alternative programmes, implementation and monitoring of the plans effectiveness.

In one particular Inner London authority a team of four planning staff were appointed, trained in the PPBS methodology, and given responsibility for implementing the system in the authority. A number of problems were soon encountered.

1 The local authority did not have a set of objectives that were both comprehensive and yet sufficiently specific to guide decisions on resource allocation. While the dominant political party's manifesto was comprehensive, and the elected councillors insisted that the manifesto stated their objectives, a costing exercise revealed that full implementation of those objectives would require resources far beyond those available to the authority. Over time such costing exercises and the activity of developing a comprehensive plan helped the emergence of a set of objectives that became a useful basis for directing analysis and evaluating the choices facing the authority.

2 A complex analytical process such as PPBS requires a number of years in which to become fully implemented. The local authority had to decide where the exercise would commence. The departments of the authority differed considerably in size and had varying amounts of influence over the authority's decision making. The large departments, such as Housing and Social Services, were able to argue the case for a phased approach to implementation that did not begin with consideration of their own programmes. The analysts recognised that they had to work not only within the constraints of their own resources but also within constraints set by the power structure of the authority. The initial implementation of PPBS was directed away from the major spending areas; the planning exercise began with areas such as Leisure Services, here the analysts were able to consider a range of alternative solutions, these included:

   Broadening the scope of the service to include wider groups and activities, such as subsidising the cost of television for relatively sedentary groups.

   Reallocating resources, selling playing fields and replacing them with year round indoor facilities

   These changes represented a radical departure from the existing use of resources.

3 In order to monitor programme areas and the effectiveness of the plan in meeting the needs that had been identified, the authority had to develop a more sophisticated information system, one that measured the achievement of objectives, rather than the use of resources. The new monitoring system had to capture relevant data and make it available to decision makers, and this required a considerable amount of investment.

Due to a variety of circumstances, within a few years most local authorities had abandoned the implementation of PPBS.

It may be extremely difficult to define objectives for an organisation that are sufficiently specific to be useful in diagnosing problems. In the local authority case the objectives seem to be intangible aspirations that groups and individuals are seeking, difficult to define, often unrealistic and open to change.

Information is the basis of decision making. Whether it is being used to identify and develop solutions or to monitor the effectiveness of a decision, the information requires collection, processing and evaluation. Clearly there are resource limitations upon the availability of information.

Further difficulties arise with the nature of organisations; the individuals and groups which constitute the organisation may differ in their perception of problems and the desirability of seeking new solutions.

In view of these issues it is difficult to envisage an organisation adhering to the normative model of decision making. Empirical studies of decision making have been undertaken and these are useful in providing insight into the process that actually occurs when organisations are dealing with novel and complex decisions.

THE STRUCTURE OF 'UNSTRUCTURED' DECISIONS

Mintzberg, Duru, Rasinghani and Theoret (Mintzberg, 1976) provide a study of 25 strategic decision processes drawn from a wide spectrum of organisations, including manufacturing, service and government agencies. On the basis of this field study, and a review of the literature, the authors identified a basic structure, or shared logic, underlying the decision making of the organisations in their handling of 'unstructured' decisions.

Three main decision-making phases can be defined:

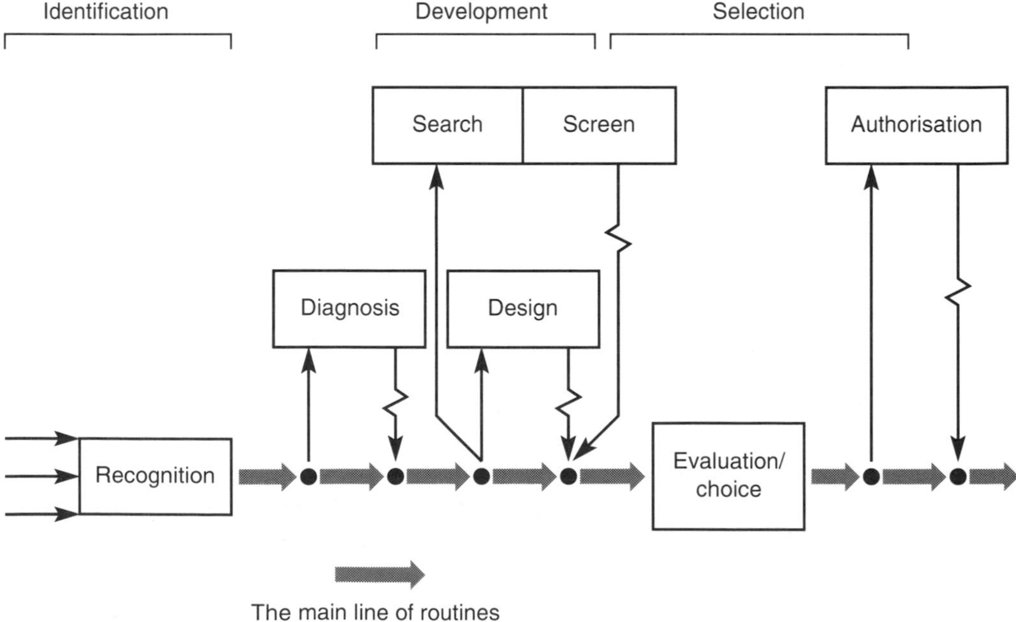

Fig. 1.4 A general model of the strategic decision process (adapted from Mintzberg et al, 1976)

- Identification
- Development
- Selection

Identification

This phase concerns decision recognition, the process by which situations that require a decision-making response come to be recognised. These situations include opportunities, situations that are problematic (in that the organisation would lose a potential benefit if it did not respond) and crises which threaten the organisation's survival. Recognition of the need for a decision is triggered by information, but that information forms a part of the on-going flow of communications originating both inside and outside the organisation. While recognition of a crisis may be triggered by a single stimulus, for example, loss of a key customer, other types of decision may only be recognised after a long period of time during which the situation has been indicated by a number of stimuli.

Individuals may receive information that indicates the need to make a decision, but that may not necessarily lead to decision-making activity. A decision maker is more likely to act if there appears to be a solution to the problem or the opportunity promises to help with a difficulty.

Having recognised the need for a decision (decision recognition) the decision maker is faced with 'an array of partially ordered data and a novel situation' (Mintzberg, 1976, p 254). There is a need to diagnose the nature of the situation. This may take place through a formal process such as a working party or task force, or through an external consultant providing an analysis of the situation facing the organisation. Alternatively, diagnosis may be an informal or implicit activity or, for an opportunity, simply recognition of the potential provided by the new situation.

Development

Mintzberg's study found that the greatest amount of activity was concentrated in the development phase of the decision process. This phase leads to the development of one or more possible solutions to meet the problem or crisis, or elaborates the choice of ways that are available for exploiting an opportunity. The development phase contains two basic routines: a search routine for locating ready-made solutions and a design routine to modify those solutions that have been found, or to develop custom-made solutions.

Search activity may be based upon scanning the corporate memory, the individuals and files that may be able to provide useful information. Search begins with those sources that are local or immediately accessible. If these are insufficient then the search may extend to other sources. Failure to find a suitable solution may lead the organisation to turning to design an original solution to meet the problem.

Design activity occurred in the majority of decision processes studied by Mintzberg. Design was used either to modify a solution that had been identified through search activity or to develop a custom-made solution. Design of such a solution appears to be a complex process, requiring subdivision of the solution as a basis for further search. Solutions are built up with parts of the solution being recycled until an acceptable solution crystallizes. The design of custom-made solutions is expensive and time consuming. Consequently it is unlikely that an organisation will fully design a range of alternatives. Typically the design phase produces a single proposed solution. Multiple alternatives are only considered when such choices become available, through ready-made or modified solutions being discovered by successful search activity.

Selection

In general it is not appropriate to describe selection as a single and final step in the decision process. Frequently the development phase requires the decision to be factored into a series of subdecisions each requiring a selection step. Selection may be intrinsic to the development phase of a decision. Typically selection is a multi-stage process, involving progressive deepening of the investigation of alternatives. Mintzberg's study identifies three routines that together make up the selection phase of the decision process, these are screening, evaluation–choice and authorisation.

A screening routine is appropriate to the extent that search has provided more ready-made alternatives than can be intensively evaluated. This process is an implicit part of search with ready-made alternatives being either accepted or retained as they are identified.

Similarly there is a low role for evaluation and choice activity. The functions of this routine appear, particularly in the case of a custom-made solution, to be implicit to the commitment required to design the alternative. The operation of choice activity on a larger scale encounters great difficulty in dealing with 'a plethora of value and factual issues ... many of them involving emotions, politics, power, and personality' (Mintzberg, 1976, p 259).

Authorisation to commit the organisation to a course of action is sought for a solution that is regarded as complete and has achieved the stage of evaluation-choice. The authorisation of a decision follows a path of approval through a tiered hierarchy within and, if necessary, outside the organisation, to parties that may have the power to block the solutions operation. The process is open to political influence and other forms of bias, including the biases of the individuals sponsoring the alternative. While the proposal may be presented as the result of analysis, the decision's sponsors will have developed an in-depth knowledge of the proposal that is greater than that of the manager whose approval is being sought. This may provide an advantage in gaining approval for the decision.

Time

Typically the decision processes in Mintzberg's study spanned long periods of time: 17 of the 25 decision processes studied spanned more than one year, 6 had lasted more than four years. The process of decision is 'recursive and discontinuous ... involving many difficult steps and a host of dynamic factors over a considerable period of time' (Mintzberg, 1976, p 250), a situation in which 'almost nothing is given or easily determined' (Mintzberg, 1976, p 251). This raises the question of how time is used when decisions are being made. In part the time is taken to operate the information and communication processes that make up the seven routines outlined in Fig. 1.4. Time is also required to manage the politics of the decision, to gain the involvement and support of those who can influence the decision and believe that they will be affected by the decision. The political context of a decision requires the development of a solution that accommodates political interests in and around the organisation. Political support must be achieved, even if this is through inviting powerful interests to be represented in the decision-making process.

Decisions do not develop along a path of steady and undisturbed progress. Problems are encountered along the way that have to be explored and, if possible, overcome. The decision takes place in the context of an organisation that exists in a changing environment with new priorities emerging. The progress of a particular decision may need to be speeded, slowed or even delayed as new issues are presented to the organisation and other decisions start to be developed.

Decision making in practice is in many respects different from the process described by the normative model of decision making. An organisation's objectives and goals do not form the basis of the decision-making process, nor do they provide an obvious guiding influence for the conduct of search and choice.

For non-programmed decisions the decision-making process is often both economical and protracted. One or only a few alternative solutions are developed and the process typically occurs over a long period of time, often encountering delays and the reworking of earlier stages. Decision making is a far more complex process than the normative model suggests but it is a process that has a structure and, like the normative model, addresses the issues of problem identification, solution development and selection.

INCREMENTALISM

Decision making is a process that often takes place over a considerable period of time during which a solution is evolved and accepted. Other studies of decision making confirm the lengthy nature of the process but instead of focusing upon the stages involved (identification, development and selection) depict decision making as *a process that uses time in order to gain knowledge and commitment through a prolonged process of exploration and learning.*

The incremental view of decision making is based upon the work of Charles Lindblom (Lindblom, 1959). Lindblom describes two approaches that may be adopted in making decisions, a rational comprehensive method (the 'root' approach) and a method of successive limited comparisons (the 'branch' approach).

The root approach is similar to the normative model of decision making. Following the root approach the decision maker is able to clearly identify the goals that are relevant to the decision and is able to identify the trade-offs that can be made between goals, the extent to which attainment of one goal compensates for lack of achievement, or sacrifice, of another goal. For example, by trading short-term profitability for increased market share. These trade-offs are in principle established before a particular problem has been encountered. Under this approach the decision maker is assumed to have an extensive knowledge of a range of alternative solutions that are relevant to the problem, together with a detailed knowledge of the consequences of those choices. On the basis of this knowledge a large number of alternatives are compared and the alternative selected which will provide the highest level of overall goal attainment.

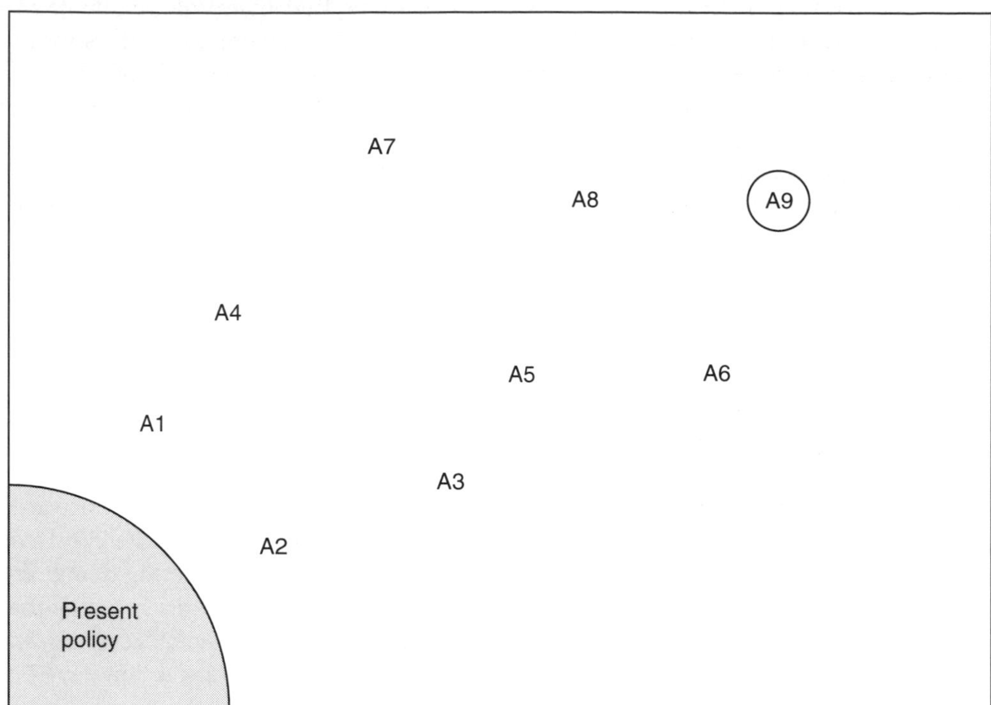

Fig. 1.5 The root approach to decision making

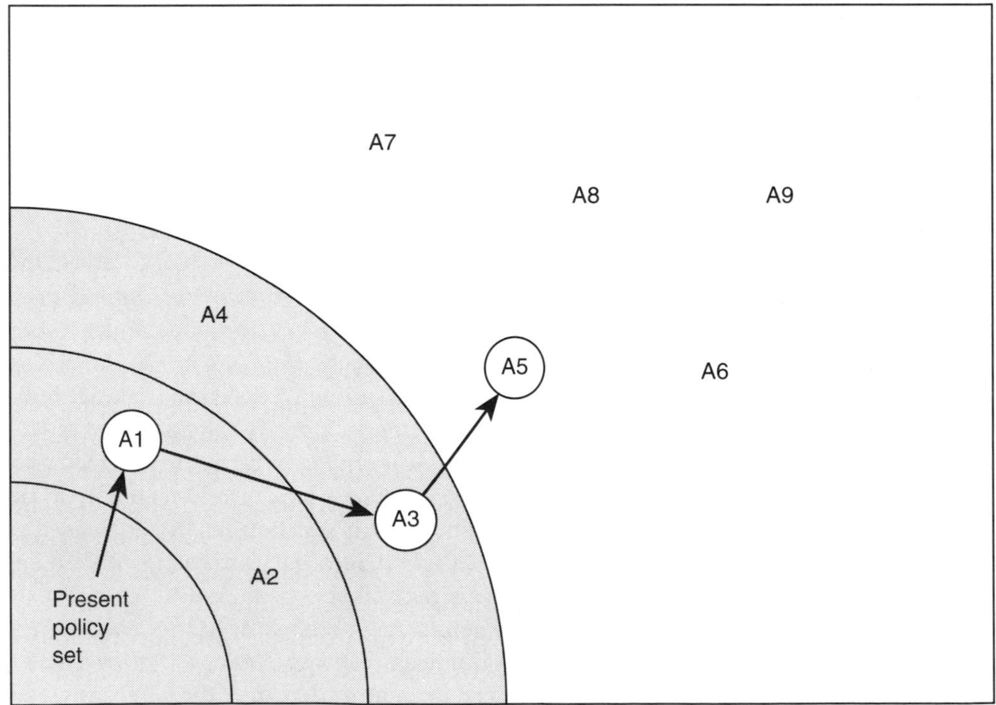

Fig. 1.6 The branch approach to decision making

This process is illustrated in Fig. 1.5. The decision maker has adopted and implemented a set of decisions, the present policy set. These decisions are manifested in the existing operations of the organisation. Faced with a problem, the decision maker is able to identify and assess a range of alternatives (A1 to A9) which vary in their similarity to the existing set of policies. Some of the alternatives are very similar, others differ markedly from the policies currently being undertaken. Nevertheless the decision maker has sufficient knowledge of all the alternatives and their implications to make an optimal choice, to select the alternative which optimises the attainment of the organisation's objectives (even if that alternative is very different from the present experience of the organisation, such as option A9).

On the basis of considering decision making in public administration, Lindblom proposed an alternative method of decision making, the method of successive limited comparisons or branch approach. Following the branch approach the decision maker identifies few alternatives and those that are identified are not radically different from the organisation's present policies and experience. Fig. 1.6 shows the organisation facing the same problem as under the root approach; the present policy set is the same and, given sufficient effort and creativity, the same set of alternative solutions (A1 to A9) could be identified and developed. However, under the branch approach the decision maker only identifies and considers a few alternatives: those that are readily at hand and are in many respects similar to the set of policies which the organisation has already implemented and has experience of. Following choice and implementation of the new solution there may be a need for further improvement. If that is the case then the process is repeated. Once again a limited range of alternatives is considered. The alternatives again are similar to the (developing) policy set of the organisation. It may be that a succession of decisions will take place (such as A1, A3 and A5), each one being made on the basis of a limited comparison of alternatives. A decision path evolves that takes the form of successive limited comparisons.

Lindblom considers the branch method to be a workable approach to decision making, an approach that recognises the decision maker's limited ability to identify and evaluate a wide range of alternatives, especially if some of those alternatives are far removed from present experience.

Not only does the root approach assist the decision maker by limiting the need for search and analysis, the approach is also less reliant upon a full understanding of goals. Instead of requiring the decision maker to be able to specify all relevant goals and the trade-offs between those goals before considering alternative solutions, the branch approach relies upon the act of choosing between alternatives to highlight the relevant issues concerning goals. Consideration of a specific alternative helps to identify the goals that individuals and groups are seeking. Similarly, as the decision maker considers the differences between alternatives and the potential of each alternative to promote a variety of goals, the trade-offs between goals can be identified and considered. For example, in the context of public administration, the consideration of a particular proposal, for example a housing project, helps councillors who are making the choice to recognise and articulate their objectives for that particular aspect of the authority's services.

Similarly in private life, the act of considering a particular choice of car helps to clarify and balance a complex set of preferences concerning speed, style, overall cost, trade-in values, etc., a set of objectives that may be very difficult to state and trade-off in an abstract way.

Lindblom recommends the branch approach as a practical way of decision making for complex problems, claiming that it is superior to a futile attempt at a more comprehensive consideration of alternatives and goals. However, the method can be questioned in terms of its dynamism. Will the series of decisions that the organisation adopts be sufficiently radical to match the rate at which a changing environment poses new challenges for the organisation?

LOGICAL INCREMENTALISM

A study of decision making by Quinn (Quinn, 1980) identifies a decision-making process that is similar to the branch method but provides a more proactive approach. Quinn's study is based upon case studies built up through interviews with executives from a number of large companies that had recently undertaken important strategic changes, non-programmed decisions. Strategic decision making is found to be a process directed and developed by the executives of companies in a conscious and purposeful manner.

In the companies studied by Quinn, the decision centres on an executive who has a broad vision of what he is trying to achieve through the decision. The decision is being made in a context where significant information necessary for making the decision does not exist. The novelty of the decisions that are being made ensures that much information concerning future markets, the operation of technologies and the cost structure that will be incurred cannot be predicted with certainty or even given probabilities. To some extent the future that is being considered is unknowable, consequently the precise form that the decision should take cannot be determined at a single point in time but has to be developed over time and through the building up of experience. The executive not only has to cope with a lack of information, he must also consider the political context of the decision, the need to win support for developments that may involve other individuals and groups who have power to influence the decision.

The lack of information concerning the precise form and viability of the development, and the need to build political acceptance, require a strategy for making the decision. The executive uses time to refine his understanding of the proposed development and to gain acceptance for the solution. Through this process a solution emerges and is developed over a considerable period of time, often three to ten years. The decision takes the form of a series of actions that explore and develop the solution while building a greater commitment of resources and a consensus to support the development. The decision to become committed to a particular strategy is in fact delayed while the issues involved are explored through feedback and the solution refined.

The usefulness of this approach to decisions can be seen by examining the case of a well known UK producer of hand cleansers whose main product was sold through distributors to industrial customers. The company achieved some limited diversification by developing a range of products but during the early 1980s began to recognise a case for further diversification. Many of the grounds for making this decision could be seen as based upon evidence that was uncertain.

- The recession of the early 1980s had resulted in a considerable reduction in the UK's manufacturing base and hence a loss of demand for hand cleansers; but would that decline continue?

- The product had been on the market in one form or another for several decades; was the market now in the decline phase of its life cycle?

If the company's main product was facing a long-term decline in demand, then further diversifications had to be considered. One of the alternatives was to use the company's knowledge of skin and surface cleansers to develop a range of products for use by hospitals, clinics and nursing homes, where the demands for greater health care, together with the needs of an ageing population, might provide an expanding market. The logic for such a diversification is a familiar one, providing a move from a focus on manufacturing to service industries, and from a business that generates turnover by selling products to one that meets specific customer needs and provides service as well as products. Yet again there are uncertainties.

- Could the company produce suitable products on an economic basis?
- Distribution would be by direct delivery using staff that would provide advice; would business build at a rapid enough rate to make it an economic form of distribution?

Facing a situation where so many fundamental issues cannot be known with certainty, a phased commitment to the development, using information derived from experience to refine the solution, offers the best way of handling the decision. While experience and understanding develop, the organisation's executives have time in which to change their basic beliefs concerning what brings success in their company and industry. In addition, as the new product gains in success the politics of the organisation may change to provide support for the innovation.

In the decision-making process identified by Quinn, goals have a role which reflect the uncertain and political context of the decision. The executives announced few goals to the organisation, those that were announced were broad and general in nature, with an avoidance of quantitative statements. Such goals do not primarily act as a basis for making choice; they have a broader role in assisting the development of the decision. The goals are used to help focus attention to important issues; they help to define problems, guide and stimulate problem solving and confirm actions that have been taken. The use of broad goals provides flexibility as the decision develops. Such goals help the executive to avoid precipitating internal resistance to change and, through their generality and wide appeal, facilitate the task of consensus building.

Compared to the normative model of decision making, logical incrementalism is a process that lacks a clear structure. The executives do not progress the decision by moving clearly through a series of discrete stages of decision making; progress is achieved through a developmental activity that shapes the solution and builds understanding and acceptance. The decision process is primarily concerned with that phase of decision making which Mintzberg describes as solution development. Development is achieved through the phased implementation and testing of the solution.

In the context of logical incrementalism, evaluation and choice are implicit in the development of the solution. The logical incremental process of decision making in effect only provides a single alternative. The selection phase of decision making is therefore a question of whether the solution continues through development and the timing of full commitment to the decision. This final act is delayed either until sufficient understanding and acceptance of the decision has been built or until events, such as competitive pressures or the clear perception of an immediate opportunity, precipitate full commitment and implementation.

EVERYDAY INCREMENTALISM

The use of an incrementalist approach to decision making need not be restricted to long-term, strategic decisions. The familiar management situation of a problem arising and 'landing on your desk' may be met by an approach that is essentially incrementalist. Even a seemingly clear-cut situation may not be what it seems. When a problem is first encountered we never know enough about it, not only in a factual sense but also how far we as individuals should or need become involved, and who else may have an interest in the problem. Often the way to proceed is as follows.

- Rapidly acquire information about the problem from a few reliable sources, such as immediate colleagues.
- Act immediately only on those parts of the problem that require urgent attention; recognise that time is available to explore the remainder of the problem.
- Discuss solutions with those who feel they have a stake in the situation.
- As far as possible if immediate choices have to be made select alternatives that leave room for later manoeuvre when more information becomes available.

Many of our best instincts when making decisions may be based upon an incrementalist approach.

DECISION MAKING: PHASES AND CONTEXT

In the case study (Illustration 1.1) it seems as if Mr Peters is about to recognise that a problem exists, that he has a responsibility to ensure that the situation is improved, and that he is going to initiate a decision-making process to bring about that improvement. From the discussion of the decision-making process it is apparent that the decision will involve *three phases*:

1 Identification
2 Development
3 Selection

Most of the time and activity will be concerned with the development of one or a few solutions, with commitment to the final decision being implicit in its continued development.

A decision can be examined as a process it can also be examined in terms of its *context*.

Figure 1.7 shows decision making taking place in a context that shapes how the decision is made, also the solution that will be developed and implemented. The relevance of these contextual variables can be explored for the Schmorl Print case study.

Organisational and group behaviour, and psychology

Schmorl Print's stock problem is made complicated by the fact that a solution to the problem will potentially affect other parts of the organisation. For that reason the decision-making process may be based upon the use of a group approach to explore the problem and to develop solutions. Groups can both help and hinder the decision-making process. They may allow information to be shared and new insights developed. They can assist creativity. Groups can encourage risk taking, they can also act as a conservative influence on decision making.

Fig. 1.7 Decision making: context and process

As in any organisation the decision will also be affected by the organisation's formal and informal features and its decision-making style, culture and politics.

A range of psychological factors will have the general effect of limiting rationality in information processing. Each of the individuals involved in the decision will have their own personal view of reality and, in part, the meaning and significance given to new information will be based upon that view.

Analysis and model building

Accounting techniques are relevant to a wide range of business problems and they have been used by Mr Peters to identify the deteriorating performance of the company and the cost of its stockholding policy. Management science techniques are also available to assist in improving and even optimising specific aspects of performance. In addition, there is the possibility of the organisation developing its own model to simulate the problem, using the model to develop and test solutions.

Some form of modelling may well be appropriate. The problem that Mr Peters faces is produced by a system. It arises from the interaction of a number of organisations, groups and individuals, from the technologies that are being used and the policies that are being followed. Some form of systems modelling would help to capture the complexity of the situation. The solution that is eventually adopted will become a part of the system, therefore the appropriateness of the solution needs to be assessed in terms of its effects upon the system. Would reducing stocks improve immediate financial performance at the cost of lost customer service and increased difficulties for the service engineers?

The problem that is identified will in part be determined by the role of the decision maker in the system. Mr Peters is the company's Financial Director; that role, his previous training and experience, may be decisive in how he views 'the problem'. Customers, the Development Department, the Production Department, Service Engineers, each would provide their own definition of the problem.

Strategic context

Mr Peters' problem exists in a strategic context. Schmorl Print has decided to compete for customers on the basis of supplying systems which are ahead of competing products, and which embody leading technology. This strategy, also the resulting products and their subsequent modification, causes the stock of service components held by the company to increase. The strategy, in fact, forms a part of the decision's context, a constraint on reducing stock levels. It may be that for strategic reasons Schmorl Print will have to continue to hold and develop an extensive service stock.

Goals, objectives and ethics

Schmorl Print is a private company, its primary objectives are to achieve a good return on the funds invested in the company and to increase its sales and assets. The values and objectives of the company are a part of the company's success but they are also part of the problem facing Mr Peters.

There is increasing interest in the responsibility of organisations and the ethics of their decisions. Schmorl Print's problem has an ethical dimension; in the pursuit of its objectives, is the company deceiving the customer? Schmorl Print are quite aware that there is a strong possibility that their customers will face delay before new systems operate in a fully satisfactory way. Should the company make the customer equally aware of the situation? The solution that Schmorl Print develops has ethical consequences which the company needs to understand.

Degree of uncertainty

Chaos theory suggests that many of our assumptions about the predictability of events are misplaced. Instead of an ordered world which becomes increasingly predictable as our knowledge increases, is the world in reality chaotic in nature? If so there is a need for decision makers to recognise the unpredictability of events. The stock problem involves uncertainty concerning markets and technology. Schmorl Print has a great deal of information concerning potential customers and their existing equipment but changes in economic conditions and the future financial condition of customer companies appear to contribute to a failure to accurately forecast annual sales. How can Schmorl Print's decision making accommodate the uncertainties that exist in the situation?

FRAMEWORK FOR SHORTER-TERM DECISION MAKING

So far in the chapter the framework used for the decision-making process has assumed that the time element for the decision is long term, i.e., longer than one year. Alternatively the problem is not urgent enough to warrant quick investigation, analysis and solution.

There are types of decisions made within organisations that are either short term or are extremely urgent. The shorter the time scale in which a decision is made the more responsive the organisation has to become. The shorter the time scale the more likely that the decision has to be made by the lower management structure of the organisation, conversely senior management will take longer term strategic decisions. Figure 1.8 illustrates the concept of layers of management decision making, a structure that is similar to an Army command and control structure.

The time span of the decision decreases the further down the management structure that decision has to be taken. In modern organisations the principle that senior management deals with strategic matters, middle management deals with tactical planning and lower management deals with operational control is still valid. A major development is

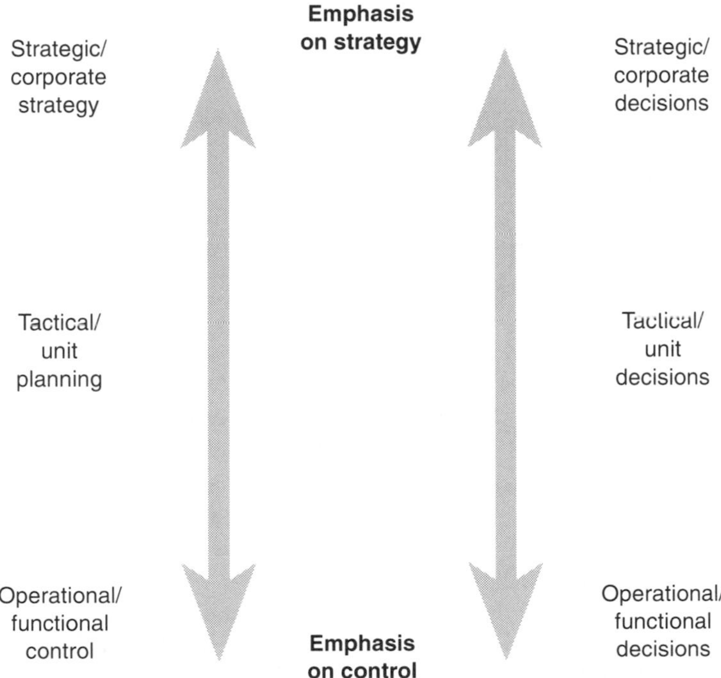

Fig. 1.8 Management level and decision making

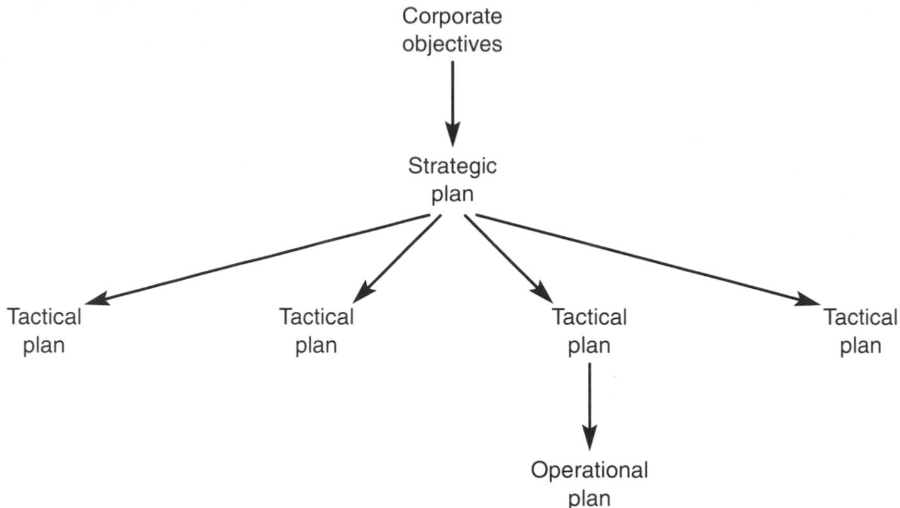

Fig. 1.9 Evolution of a strategy

that the traditional pyramid shape of the management hierarchy has been replaced by a flatter structure. The large organisations have tended to remove, or try to remove, the middle management layer, and give autonomy to functional or unit areas. These functional or unit areas have been given both responsibility, and a certain amount of authority to run their 'own show'. Typically the decisions covered by these autonomous units are less than one year, and will include decisions on budget spending, yearly production scheduling, market planning, number of staff, etc. The decisions previously made by middle management are now made on the autonomous unit's behalf by a 'managing director' of that unit assisted by a small staff of managers who may also have responsibility for operational short-term daily or weekly decisions, such as what machine to use for a production run, etc.

This does not mean that the type of decisions made are not important, they are. If the basic decisions are left unmade or are incorrect then the organisation will quickly find itself in great difficulty.

The management hierarchy exists to check on the 'health' or otherwise of the organisation, and to exercise control and action for the organisation. To do this, higher levels of management supervise lower levels, for which they need feedback. The feedback comes from basic information which flows around the organisational structure, essentially in an upwards direction. In turn, senior managers exercise control over subordinates. The feedback and control mechanism is therefore a fundamental part of the management hierarchy, with more control exercised at lower levels. Consequently more data for feedback is collected at these levels.

In a well run organisation the decision-making system will run efficiently and will be controlled and monitored by all levels of management. The ideal pattern is that strategic directions obtained from the corporate objectives are formulated by the organisation's board of directors in conjunction with senior management. These strategic directions are evolved into tactical plans by middle management who then expect lower management to execute them by developing and implementing courses of action which make up the

Table 1.1 Characteristics for decisions

	Timescale	*Nature of risk*	*Structure*	*Control*
STRATEGIC	Long Term	High	Ill Defined	Heuristic
TACTICAL	Medium Term	Moderate	Variable	Qualitative
OPERATIONAL	Short Term	Low	Well defined	Quantitative

tactical plans. The evolution of strategy into tactics, hence into operational plans, is shown in Fig. 1.9.

When a reorganisation occurs, as in the formation of 'business units', the large organisation splits into profit areas or functions. The process outlined in Fig. 1.9 does not alter but the time scale becomes shorter, and the responsibility, monitoring and authority is vested with the new units. This move to smaller subunits is in direct response to a rapidly changing environment; in general the smaller the unit the more rapid can be its reaction to change.

There is a real difference in the decision-making framework used at the lower levels of management, in that the process is more deterministic, hence less risky. The model presented in Fig. 1.7 can be seen to apply to all types of decision and at all levels of decision taking, be they strategic, tactical or operational.

Table 1.1 illustrates a set of characteristics for decisions taken at each level in the management framework.

Illustration 1.3 clearly identifies a change in strategic direction: a diversification from a one-product company into a two-product company, i.e., from kitchen manufacture and sales into a related but different product, fitted bedrooms.

The production units, and middle management levels (sales manager, production manager, marketing and accounts) would be required to develop tactical plans for the diversification decision, would lead ACME to be able to price, market and produce the new product range. These individual areas would then be investigated by functional areas to make operational plans such as machine allocation, store space, allocations of stock, etc.

The discussion so far has assumed that the decision takes place at the appropriate level, and that level has the correct amount of time to deal with the decision or problem area. Often critical situations arise when organisational decision makers have to make appropriate decisions quickly, and at the level that sees the problem first. (They have time enough for action but little time for passing the problem to higher authority.)

Time span, risk and information

The move towards flatter organisational structure, or novel organisational structures, has

Illustration 1.3 ACME Furnishings

ACME furnishing products, is a retail organisation that wishes to diversify into related products. They currently manufacture and sell fitted kitchens directly to the public. The board of directors, in conjunction with senior management, wish to start manufacturing and selling fitted bedrooms to the public via the same distribution and retail channels.

caused decisions to be taken in a shorter time period. This has been the result of the turbulent business environment, and the slimmed down organisational structure.

This reduction in time span of making any decision at whatever level will decrease the consideration given to that decision by the decision maker(s). This in turn increases the risk of making an inappropriate decision. The decision maker(s) will try to offset this by obtaining as much information as possible regarding the problem area. The purpose is to reduce the risk by knowing more. Unfortunately this often presents the decision maker(s) with an *information overload*, i.e., too much information, and hence an increase in complexity and percieved uncertainty.

There is also a secondary effect of the turbulent environment, and this is bureaucratic management. The senior managers will want to 'interfere' or take control of the shorter-term decisions. The belief that a decision is critical, and hence either at the least tactical or strategic, is common and causes the removal of autonomy for decision making. This in turn leads to tighter control of the decision-making process; the classical organisational hierarchy reinstates itself, and the organisation starts to suffer from inertia.

The other secondary, and possibly more devastating effect to organisational performance is called *fire fighting*. All decisions are made on a necessity basis, i.e., put things right when they go wrong. There is no plan strategically, tactically or organisationally. The organisation becomes reactive rather than proactive. Again the time span for decision taking becomes short due to the critical nature of all decisions, and hence the associated risk goes up. The information required to alleviate the risk is not gathered this time, because the organisation will not have, or has, no time to get it. The organisation is fire fighting, and has little time to think about strategy and tactics. Therefore decision taking moves to an operational level and becomes very short term and lacking foresight.

THE STRUCTURE OF THIS BOOK

The following nine chapters are concerned with exploring the context of decision making, through consideration of a range of concepts, theories and techniques that have been developed by a variety of disciplines. The chapters may be read in isolation from each other or in relation to the contextual model identified in Fig. 1.7.

Subject	*Chapter*
Organisation and group behaviour	3
and	
Psychology	4
Analysis and model building	2, 5, 6 and 7
Strategic context	8
Goals, objectives and ethics	9 and sections of 8
Degree of uncertainty	10 and sections of 6

The aim of each chapter, and of the entire book, is to enable us to:

- Develop a fuller understanding of decision making.
- Improve our decision making.

But first, an exercise to build awareness and insight into the decision-making process.

EXERCISE: EXAMINING A DECISION

In order to evaluate a decision it is useful to see how the decision was made. For a decision with which you are familiar insight can be gained by considering the following questions.

When was the problem first recognised?

How was it diagnosed?

What was the problem?

Was the problem redefined in the course of the decision?

Over what period of time did the decision take place?

Were there delays and hold-ups in making the decision?

Why did they occur? Did they change the decision?

What were the stages involved in making the decision?

Which were the most significant stages? Were all stages well handled?

Who was involved in the decision? Was it a single person?

Was a group involved?

How did the context provided by the wider organisation affect the decision?

Were several organisations involved? How did they affect the decision?

How well was the decision made in terms of meeting the problem and furthering the objectives of the organisation? Could the search activity have been better conducted to identify further feasible alternatives?

At what stage and how was the choice of a solution made?

How can you evaluate whether this was a good or a bad decision?

GLOSSARY OF MAIN TERMS

Branch method A step-wise, incremental method for achieving the development of a solution.
Choice Act of deciding between alternatives.
Diagnosis Identifying the causes of a failure in performance or the nature of an opportunity.
Goal A level of attainment for an objective, possibly specifying a time period for its achievement.
Incrementalism Making a decision by, over time, adopting and testing a series of subdecisions.
Normative A statement of what ought or ought not to be.
Objective A direction in which to develop organisational performance, e.g., improved profitability, less risk, higher quality.
Programmed decision A repetitive and routine decision for which a definite procedure has been established.
Root method A method of decision making based upon, consideration of all possible alternatives and evaluation of each alternative against a clear understanding of objectives or values to be achieved.
Search Investigation to identify existing solutions for a problem and/or to create new solutions.

REFERENCES

Lindblom, C. E. (1959) 'The Science of Muddling Through', *Public Administration Review*, Vol. 19, Spring, 79-88.

Mintzberg, H., Raisinghani, D. and Théorêt, A. (1976) 'The Structure of "Unstructured" Decision Processes', *Administrative Science Quarterly*, June, 246-275.

Quinn, J. B. (1980) *Strategies for Change: Logical Incrementalism*, Irwin.

Simon, H. A. (1965) *The New Science of Management Decision in Management Decision Making* (Eds. Welsch, L. A. and Cyert, R. M.), Penguin Books, 13-29.

FURTHER READING

Bass, B. M. (1983) *Organisational Decision Making*, Irwin.

Hickson, D. J., Butler, R. J., Cray, D., Mallory, G. R., and Wilson, D. C. (1986) *Top Decisions: Strategic Decision Making in Organisations*, Blackwell.

Johnson, G. (1988) 'Rethinking Incrementalism', *Strategic Management Journal*, Vol. 9, 75-91.

CHAPTER 2

Diagnosis and systems thinking

David Jennings and Stuart Wattam

SYSTEMS CONCEPTS

A system is *an assemblage or combination of things or parts forming a complex or unitary whole* (Beishon and Peters, 1976, p 15). A system forms a whole. This is achieved through the system not only having parts, elements or components, but through the interrelationship of these characteristics with each other. A range of systems can be identified.

A comparatively simple example of a system is provided by a timing device. The electronic and mechanical parts are in a relationship one to another that has been carefully designed to predetermine the behaviour of the simple dynamic system. The timer will behave as a clock. The behaviour of the system is predetermined because it is *a closed system*; the system exists in an *environment* but the system can be seen as not interrelating with that environment. The system at some stage contains energy, from a battery or through a spring mechanism, but will lose that energy over the course of time. In systems theory this phenomena is called *entropy*. Unless the timing system renews its energy by importing energy from outside itself the system will lose its ability to fulfil its function, in this case the transformation of energy into images of time passing. As entropy increases the system tends towards randomness, a loss of order, and its behaviour becomes increasingly erratic until it ceases to function.

The tendency towards entropy is a general property of systems. Heated metal will cool and by cooling become less distinguished from its environment. Similarly an organisation that does not sustain training inputs will experience a decline in the distinctive nature of its staff; the organisation's staff will lose their outstanding abilities, becoming more random and similar in their skills to those available in the organisation's environment. For a system to continue to be viable the tendency towards entropy has to be offset. This is achieved through the system being open to the environment in order to import energy, materials and information, imports that allow the system to sustain its functioning.

Human beings, forests, business organisations, charities, each of these can be analysed as *open systems*. Each requires inputs from the environment in order to continue their functioning. The inputs are transformed to become outputs back to the environment (see Fig. 2.1).

The ability of the forest to sustain itself is dependent upon characteristics that are inherent in each tree's genetic make-up. However ecology provides an understanding of a forest as a whole, as more than a collection of individual trees. The forest requires inputs: water, sunlight, nutrients. The debris produced by trees are nutrients that form the basis for the forest to continue its growth. Similarly, the exchange of carbon dioxide for oxygen enables the forest both to grow and to provide an output to the atmosphere that provides the carbon dioxide. The forest as a system can offset the tendency toward entropy. Much of the behaviour and health of the forest can be explained in terms of the cycle of input, transformation and output.

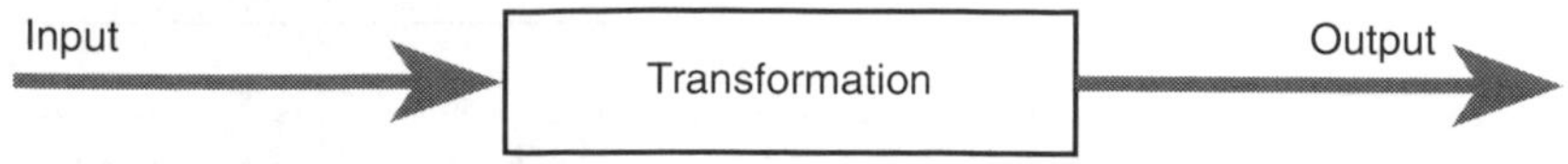

Input → Transformation → Output

Fig. 2.1 An open systems model

Some of the inputs received from the environment take the form of *feedback*, information which helps the system to adjust so that it can retain equilibrium. In a living organism a variety of feedback mechanisms allow the system to maintain a steady state, such as the cooling of the blood acting as a stimulus for the body's heat producing mechanisms. The visual feedback available to a driver of a car leads to the maintenance of a desired speed and position on the road. The information available to a cost accountant helps the organisation to follow its budget over the course of a year. Each of these examples is an instance of *negative feedback*, informational input which indicates when the system is deviating from equilibrium and should readjust its activities in order to move towards a stable state.

Illustration 2.1 provides an example of business failure that can be analysed by the use of systems concepts. Modern Leisure has failed to develop a cycle where its outputs are traded for further inputs.

Illustration 2.1 Business as a system: Modern Leisure

Modern Leisure is a company that produces and distributes videotaped courses. It is a small company that was established a year ago on the basis of a bank loan and the personal finances of its directors. The company engaged in some market research and, guided by that information, produced an aerobics video. The video has had disappointing sales and, through conversations with retailers and potential customers, the directors have come to realise that there is no longer a demand for that particular product; live classes have become readily available and potential customers prefer to visit those classes rather than follow a filmed course. Reluctantly the directors have realised that their company will have to cease trading.

1 Describe Modern Leisure in terms of inputs, transformation and outputs.
2 In a sense, a new business can be seen as similar to the emergence of a new species or mutation in biology. Following this analogy, and given further resource inputs, how could Modern Leisure adapt in order to survive and make its environment more supportive?

The aerobics videos are not given sufficient value by the environment (here the customer) to allow them to be traded for money that can be used to sustain inputs of energy, materials and knowledge. Without adequate resource inputs Modern Leisure experiences entropy. Eventually the components of the business – people, physical assets and financial resources – will no longer form the structure known as Modern Leisure; they will lose that ordered form and return to the environment.

The systems concepts:

- Closed system
- Open system
- Input

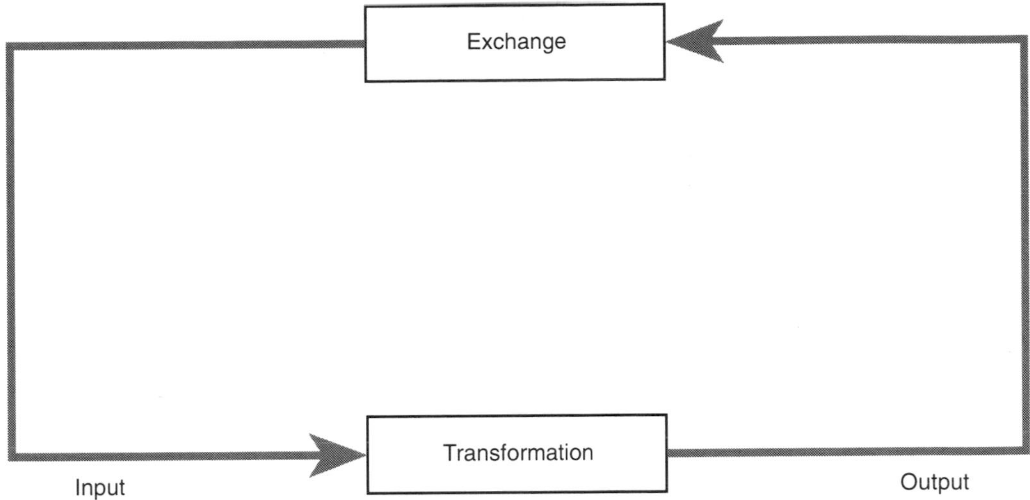

Fig. 2.2 A system as a cycle of activities

- Transformation
- Output
- Entropy
- Negative feedback

These concepts can be used to examine biological, social, mechanical and economic systems, in fact any system from a static closed system, such as a bridge, to the functioning of a developed social system. General systems theory provides a basis for understanding any system, it provides a set of principles which hold for systems in general, a metatheory of systems. The abstract nature of general systems theory can discourage its use in examining the problems encountered by organisations. However, application of systems concepts, and the drawing of analogies with other systems, can be rewarding. At a fundamental level the systems viewpoint helps offset the tendency for organisations to seek explanation for their failings by examining their internal operations to the exclusion of a concern for the wider system.

The use of analogies between business situations and other systems can offer useful insights. An example is provided by examining the operation of a thermostat, a control device which forms part of a system that operates on the basis of negative feedback.

In Fig. 2.3 the thermostat is part of a larger system, a central heating system. The boiler produces heat that is passed into the environment, the building. The boiler will continue to produce heat until it runs out of energy or is switched off. The latter is accomplished by the thermostat sensing the temperature of the environment and comparing that information to a pre-established goal, the intended temperature. Overproduction of heat by the boiler is countered by the thermostat's signal switching the boiler off until the temperature of the building has fallen to below the desired state – the temperature setting of the thermostat. A *negative feedback loop* is in operation by which a deviation in the system's behaviour (excessive heat) is countered by an opposing signal (to reduce heat). Through negative feedback the temperature of the building is kept above a minimum level.

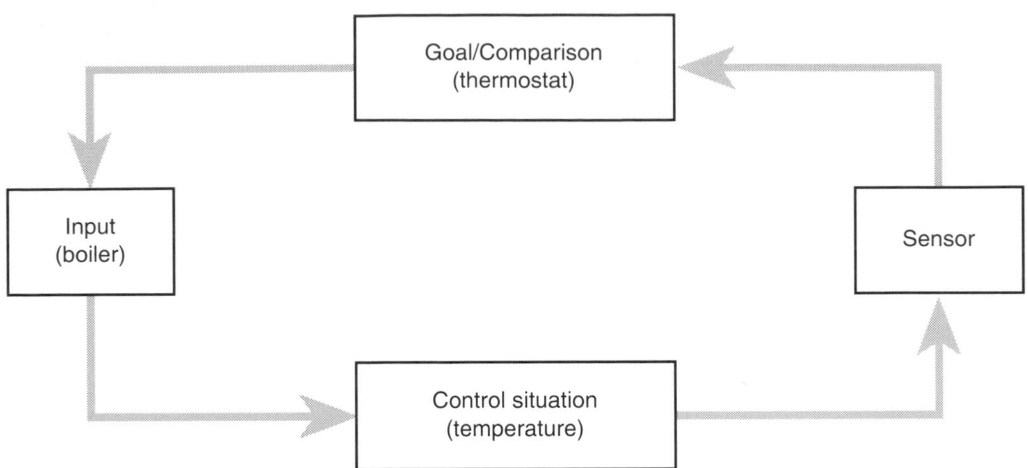

Fig. 2.3 A negative feedback system: central heating control

Control processes are a common part of organisations. Insight into many of the problems of cost control can be provided through examining the adherence of the cost control system to the principles shown in Fig. 2.3. Control activity may fail to maintain equilibrium because:

- The goal, the cost standard, may not be relevant. It may be based upon a study undertaken for production processes different from those now in operation.
- The management may be unable to act rapidly and effectively to correct deviations.
- The information providing feedback upon performance may be perceived and processed too slowly, by the time the deviation is understood it may have corrected itself or deteriorated further.

ORGANISATIONAL SYSTEMS

Organisations can be viewed as complex systems. The various parts of the organisation, the human and technological systems that make it up, interact and need to be considered in a holistic framework. In addition, organisational systems have the following characteristics (from Beishon and Peters, 1976):

> Social organisations are *contrived systems*. They are established by human beings to serve a great variety of purposes. The system is held together not by biological or mechanical linkages but essentially through psychology, social systems are anchored in the attitudes, perceptions, beliefs, motivations, habits and expectations of human beings. Such systems may have an indefinite life or dissolve overnight.
>
> The *boundaries between the social system and its environment are permeable*, the system is open and the boundaries unclear. For instance, a bank may be seen as part of a business's environment but the bank may also have a considerable and direct influence upon the organisation's decisions. A similar ambiguity can be found in the role of government and the influence of clients upon organisations. Such interactions are often highly desirable, assisting the organisation to adapt in order to maintain its viability.

Social organisations through acquiring resource inputs are able to offset the entropy process indefinitely, often to such an extent that the system develops towards increased order and organisation, a process of *negative entropy*, with the organisation attaining an indefinite lifespan. While a closed system must eventually attain an equilibrium state with maximum entropy, a social organisation may maintain an equilibrium through the continuous inflow of resources, energy and information, a *steady state or dynamic equilibrium* whereby it continues the process of input/transformation/output and is able to both maintain its subsystems and adapt to changes in the environment. The systems adjustment is assisted by feedback from its environment.

For a physical system, such as a clock, there is a direct cause and effect relationship between the initial conditions and the final state of the system. This is not the case for a social system. Following the concept of *equifinality*, organisations can pursue paths very different from each other in order to attain essentially the same final result. There is no one best way for an organisation to pursue its objectives. Organisations may adopt strategies, techniques and processes that are very different from each other yet attain similar results. Examples of these differences abound in all industries. Some organisations take the lead with technological change, others vertically integrate to control supply. Some seek advantage through size and others through experiencing the benefits of smallness and a rapid response to a focused set of customer needs. The concept of equifinality has profound implications for management decision making. Organisations can vary markedly in their decisions yet essentially move towards the same state.

SYSTEMS THINKING

General systems theory provides a set of concepts so general that they can be used to examine the nature and functioning of any system, whether it is mechanical, biological or social. Managers have numerous methodologies available with which to analyse and resolve the problems that arise in organisations. Management accounting provides a set of concepts and analyses which are widely used to identify and solve problems. Similarly strategic analysis and management science each provide a major set of techniques for resolving business problems. With so many specific methodologies available is there need for a general theory of systems?

The systems approach provides a distinctive, *holistic*, view of a situation and the problems that are associated with that situation. Organisations are divided into sub-groups by functions (such as marketing, accounting, personnel, etc.) and by hierarchy. By describing and analysing situations as systems an integrated view is developed where the effects of the various subsystems on each other can be identified.

It is common for business problems to be identified and treated as marketing or accounting or stock problems, or be given some other functional label. However a problem is often caused by a number of areas of the business. In addition, the failure to co-ordinate and integrate activities is often a significant part of an organisation's problems. The systems approach provides a means of considering the whole system and the linkages within it.

The solution to a problem has to take account of the systemic nature of the problem. It is possible that a solution can improve the performance of a system in one respect, only to initiate a deterioration in other aspects of the system's performance. The answers to problems can easily have the effect of appearing to improve the immediate problem while initiating adverse changes in the wider system. The solution may also help to make the

Illustration 2.2 Schmorl Print revisited

Schmorl Print is experiencing a marked and unwelcome increase in its stocks. Has Schmorl Print 'a stock problem'?

Labelling the situation as a stock problem will lead the managers to a closed and biased view of the situation that neglects the causes of the problem. The causes of increased stock levels at Schmorl Print concern:

The innovation policy of the company.
The company's development process.
The expectations of customers.
The company's lack of knowledge concerning the life of components.
The increasing level of stock is a result of the behaviour of a complex system.

Illustration 2.3 Stock reduction at Schmorl Print

If Mr Peters could implement a policy to reduce the future growth of the service stock, for example by placing a budget limit on future expenditure on stocks that hold the value of the service stock to its present level of investment, what effects would this policy have upon:

The company's customers?

The service engineers?

The stock of parts held by the company for manufacturing current products?

system more complex and difficult to comprehend. It can be a major achievement for a decision to be made that achieves an apparently modest improvement to the overall performance of a system. The temptation should be resisted of prematurely focusing on a subpart of the system that seems most clearly identified with 'the problem', then attempting to optimise the performance of that subsystem. The solution must address the wider system.

Systems thinking, using systems concepts to examine situations, improves both the way that decision makers define problems and the effectiveness of decisions. But care must be taken when using a systems viewpoint. A system is an abstraction that often, in a real-world sense, does not exist, or can be defined in alternative ways. An organisation can be examined as a system, yet that same organisation may not have a shared purpose and may lack integration between its subsystems. We may examine the organisation as an open system even though those within it regard it as closed. Despite the lack of a systemic nature in a particular organisation's functioning, it is useful to describe and analyse the organisation as a system, while guarding against the danger that the organisation is assumed to have a greater degree of coherence as a system than is in fact true. A system is an abstract mental construct, devised as a means of improving understanding of the real world.

DIAGNOSIS

Effective decision making requires good problem diagnosis. Unless a problem has been correctly identified the decision-making process will not be successful, inappropriate alternatives will be developed and the best choice will not be made.

The rational model of decision making, reviewed in Chapter 1, includes problem diagnosis. This is achieved through the use of pre-established objectives and performance criteria that are used to highlight areas where there is a performance gap, where actual performance has, or will, fall short of that which is required by the organisation's objectives. Identification of a performance gap is followed by a series of logical questions to identify the cause of the shortfall, the problem. Empirical studies of decision making support the conclusion that it is unlikely, especially for non-programmed decisions, that the rational model forms an accurate description of decision-making practice and the way in which problems are diagnosed. As a method of diagnosis the model faces the following problems.

- *Organisational goals* may not be comprehensive enough nor sufficiently specific to form a basis for fully diagnosing the problems facing an organisation.
- In the course of training, working in an organisation, and gaining experience, individuals develop a set of *beliefs and assumptions as to how an organisation should function* in order to be successful. These beliefs can be helpful or they can mislead the manager's perception and understanding of a situation. To the extent that the problem is in some respects similar to those encountered in the past the manager is assisted in making a correct diagnosis. But in other situations, for example for an industry that is experiencing change, prior beliefs and assumptions can be a barrier, preventing the manager from establishing a correct understanding of the new situation and the nature of the problem that has been encountered.

Empirical studies of decision making show that problems are often recycled. Failure to develop a suitable solution can lead to further consideration of the problem and a questioning of whether or not it has been correctly diagnosed. The use of an incremental approach to decision making offers the opportunity for the decision maker to re-examine the diagnosis of a problem. Through the process of developing solutions that are effective, the decision maker is able constantly to readdress the problem or opportunity that is driving the development. The environment of an organisation is continually changing and it is likely that the diagnosis stage of the decision will have to be returned to in order to redefine the nature of the problem.

THE NATURE OF PROBLEMS

The systems approach takes great care in examining the nature of problems. Problems do not have an existence that is separate from the people involved in them. Organisations are systems made up of a number of interacting individuals and groups. The definition of a problem varies according to the perspective of those involved or interested in the situation and it may be that a situation that appears to present a problem to one part of an organisation will not seem problematic to another. This principle can be illustrated through reference to the Schmorl Print case study. In the case various individuals and groups can be identified:

- Financial Director
- Head of hardware development
- Production department
- Customers

Each of these individuals and groups will perceive the situation at Schmorl Print differently.

- Mr Peters, the Financial Director, is concerned with the financial consequences of stock-holding and stock write-off. As far as possible he would like to reduce the costs of holding a service stock.
- Mr Freeman, head of Hardware Development, may not recognise Mr Peters' problem and may in fact wish to have no interest in the issue of stockholdings.
- The firm's customers, so far as they have an interest in the situation, would like to be assured that Schmorl Print is committed to maintaining the equipment they have supplied.

Each of the above have their own *world view* (sometimes referred to as Weltanschauungen), their own perspective on the situation. Problems do not have an existence that is independent of the people involved, the definition of a problem is based upon adopting a particular viewpoint of the situation.

Those involved in a problem situation may differ in their perceptions in two respects. There may be differences concerning the *facts* of the situation, i.e., what is. There may also be disagreement concerning *values*, i.e., what ought to be the desired state of affairs. The nature of problems and solutions is that both are mental constructs that reflect a particular viewpoint of the problem situation.

A further characteristic of problems concerns complexity. Problems interact with each other to produce a system of problems or 'mess'. These are problem situations where problems are so interrelated that it is inadvisable to attempt to treat each in isolation, 'solving' one problem at a time. Changes to one part of the system will have effects upon other areas of the system.

In summary, for many problems that occur in organisations, and probably those that are most significant:

- Definition of a problem is a question of perspective; definition will vary between the various individuals and groups involved in the system.
- Attention to one problem area requires consideration of the effects of those changes on other areas.

SOFT SYSTEMS ANALYSIS

For such problem situations it is unlikely that a solution can be found that 'solves the problem' in the sense that an optimal or best solution can be found and implemented that can logically be agreed to meet all aspects of the situation. The nature of the problem situation means that the solution will be a *process of improvement*, a process that helps those involved to share their perceptions and to engage in a debate from which agreed proposals for improvement will emerge and be implemented. Soft systems methodolgy, outlined in Fig. 2.4, provides such an approach.

Soft systems methodology (SSM) was developed by Peter Checkland (Checkland,

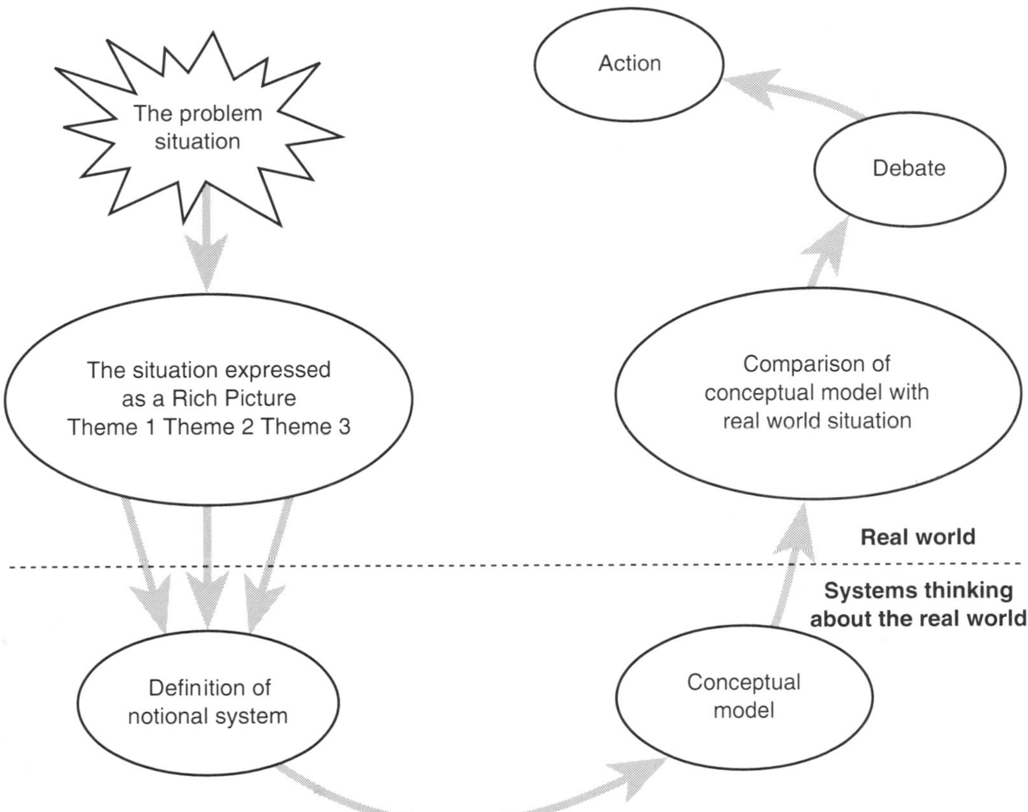

Fig. 2.4 Soft systems methodology

1981) as a strategy for analysing complex problem situations and identifying acceptable improvements that could be made to those situations. The methodology is complex and in the following account some parts have been condensed at the cost of providing a slightly less disciplined approach than that specified by Checkland. As with any methodology SSM requires a degree of skill from the analyst, and the analyst's ability improves with experience in applying the approach. The aim of the analysis is to gain improvement to the system; this is achieved through a multi-stage process of information gathering, description, analysis and debate.

The rich picture

Problem situations are complex both in terms of involving a variety of perspectives and also through interrelationships between problems. In order to capture as much as possible of the 'real world' situation a soft systems analysis begins with the analyst seeking a broad view of the situation. This information, gathered through interview, from documents and observation, is shown as a rich picture, a pictorial representation of the problem situation. A rich picture summarises all that the analyst knows of the situation. This summary contains hard information, facts, and soft information. The hard information may include the following:

- authority structure
- departments
- groups
- significant individuals
- reporting channels
- physical structure and assets
- products
- key activities undertaken
- statistics

Soft information is also vital to describe the problem situation, this may include:

- norms of behaviour
- social processes such as gossip and grapevines
- hostilities, conflicts, friendships and loyalties
- attitudes, motivations
- politics
- climate and atmosphere
- perceived status
- judgements of efficiency and competence

It is essential that the rich picture is an honest representation of the situation. In particular care has to be taken not to imply a greater degree of order than actually exists. All too easily the analyst may indicate linkages between activities or departments that should logically be present if the situation is to operate effectively as a system but which may not in reality be present, and can be a part of the problem. In addition, the analyst must acknowledge that he is also a part of the situation. The analyst has been invited in to examine the situation therefore he becomes a part of it and its politics. Consequently the rich picture needs to show the analyst's role and aims, and the relationship with the person who invited him into the situation.

The analyst has to be recognised as part of the real world that is being described. The analyst is involved in that real world but that involvement has to be disciplined. It is not the analyst's task to decide what is a suitable solution; those who are more directly involved need to make that decision. The analyst's role is to assist the development of a debate that will lead to the adoption of acceptable proposals for improvement. To promote that goal the methodology that is being used by the analyst should be explained to the participants.

Drawing a rich picture requires a degree of confidence; expressive pictures are not one of the standard ways of communication in an organisation. The purpose of using a pictorial, rather than a narrative, format is twofold. A picture can condense a great deal of information so that the results of many hours of information gathering can be shown as a whole, as a single complexity. In addition pictures are expressive, especially when soft material is included, and can capture the feeling of a situation. A rich picture is a way of summarising all that is known about a situation using symbols rather than words. As the analysis proceeds new information will emerge that can be added to the picture in order to develop understanding.

Before considering the rich picture in Fig. 2.5 it may be necessary to re-read the case study in Chapter 1 (Illustration 1.1). The picture can be interpreted as follows.

Products seem to flow out of the company, mainly to far away destinations. The

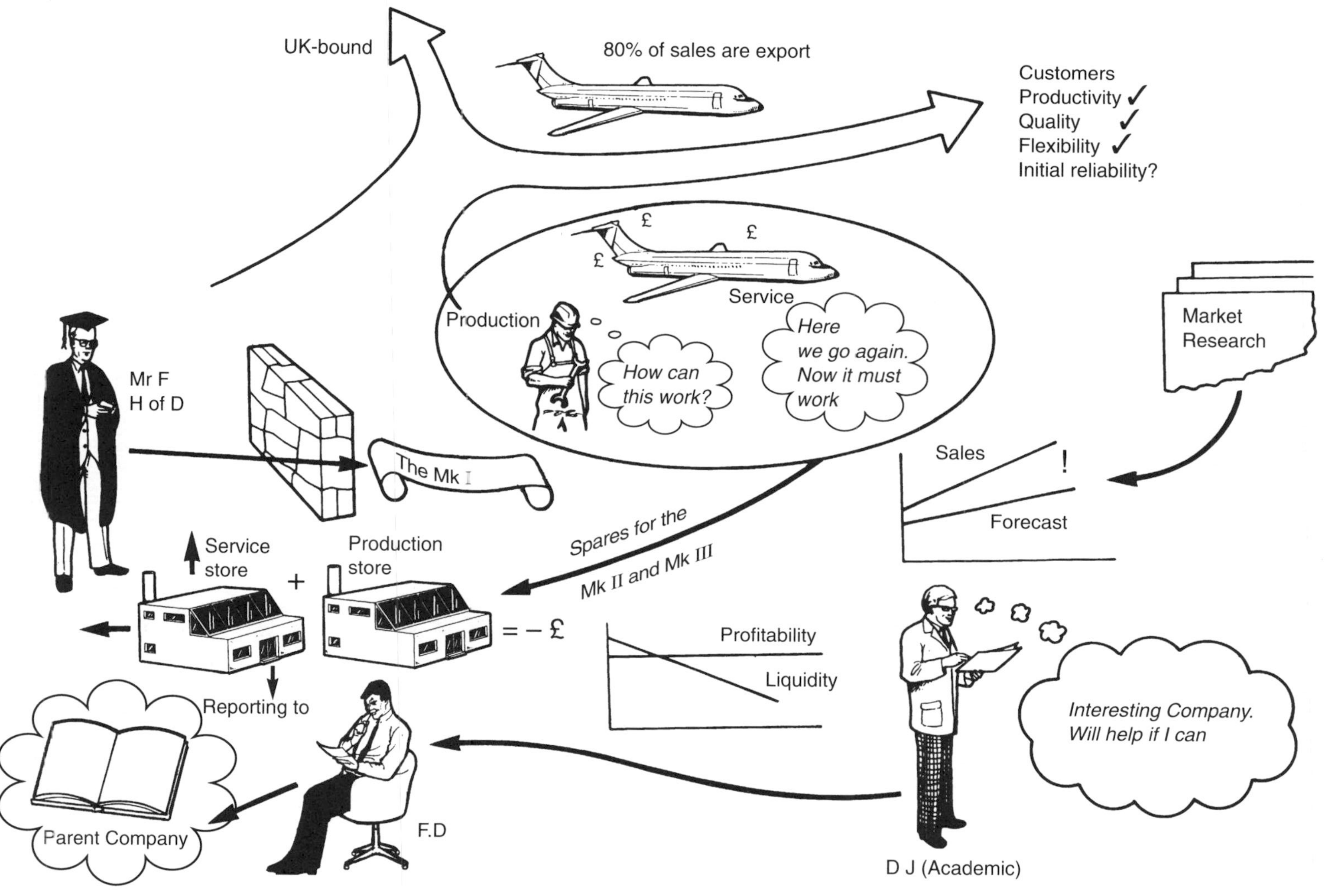

Fig. 2.5 A rich picture: Schmorl Print

customers have a set of requirements by which to assess Schmorl Print's systems, in terms of initial reliability Schmorl Print's products are questionable. Market research is gathered in a well-documented way but there is a surprising divergence between forecast and actual sales.

The flow of product originates from development and production. The Head of Development is represented as a somewhat academic figure who is central to the company. Production has a more practical character. Although there is a flow of plans and specifications from development to production there is a barrier, shown as a wall, between the two. Clearly the two have different orientations, and understanding between them is obstructed.

Production and Service form a subsystem, sharing the same concern for making the system work. The service engineer's jet seems to burn money. The stores for service and production add up to a loss of money, with the service store expanding.

In comparison to the Head of Develoment, the Financial Director is a less central and dominant figure. The Financial Director is concerned about the stores part of the business. The parent company is an entity outside Schmorl Print that the Financial Director reports to. It exists as an extensive book of rules.

The author has declared his interest in the company and made clear his relationship to it.

Analysis

After constructing the rich picture the analyst can reflect upon the situation it describes to come to an initial view of the *kinds of problem* that are present. Identification of the problem themes may be stimulated by questioning 'what kinds of problem seem important in this situation I have drawn', 'what general or endemic issues are depicted'? The question 'what is the problem?' is avoided in order to find general problem themes. A *list of themes* can be made, each theme subjected to further analysis.

To provide a clear insight into the selected problem theme the analyst requires a systematic viewpoint from which to examine the theme. This is provided by adopting a *notional system*, a system that would have some effect on the selected problem theme, *a relevant system*. The relevance of the system is dependent upon whether or not it is helpful in eventually developing improvements. The relevant system that is adopted by the analyst is hypothetical, it is not a proposal for implementation, its purpose is to sharpen the analyst's perception of the problem.

A number of such notional systems should be generated, each based upon either the *primary tasks* of the organisation or *issues* that face the organisation. The two types of system can be illustrated by reference to a partnership of doctors, a general practice. One definition of a notional system, based upon primary task, would view the practice as 'a system that provides primary health care services to meet the needs of a local population'. Another perspective is provided by defining the practice as 'a system that invests and manages human and financial resources'.

Systems definitions that are proposed on the basis of an organisation's primary tasks tend to be rather conservative. Further insight into the situation can be provided by adopting an issue-based definition of a relevant system. A relevant system for a general practice, suffering a lack of harmony amongst its partners, might describe 'a system to reconcile the conflicting professional interests of its members'. For a practice that fails to make the best use of resources a relevant system could be defined as 'a system to optimize the use of available financial resources'. Each relevant system is a hypothetical system proposed in order to develop the analyst's insight into the problem situation presented by the rich picture.

The remaining stages of a Soft systems analysis develop the logical consequences of viewing the situation from the perspective of each relevant system.

Illustration 2.4 Rich Picture exercise

Consider the rich picture in Fig. 2.5. If you feel it is appropriate add to and amend the picture. When you feel that you understand the picture, suggest relevant systems for Schmorl Print based upon:

The organisation's Primary Tasks.
The Issues present in the rich picture.

Conceptual model

A conceptual model specifies the activities or processes that must take place for a particular relevant system to exist. A flow block diagram can be used to show the set of linked activities logically implied by the system that has been described. The model is a representation of what is necessarily implied by the relevant system; it is not a representation of what does or ought to exist in the real world. The model simply outlines the activities which would have to be carried out, and the order in which they would be carried out, if that system were to function. The specification of activities concerns only what would have to be carried out for the system to operate, not how those activities should be undertaken. Fig. 2.6 is a conceptual model for the general practice seen as 'a system that provides primary health care services to meet the needs of a local population'.

Comparison and change

The conceptual model is a source of ideas for change. By comparing the conceptual model to the real world, the analyst is able to identify divergencies between the logically constructed model and practice. In reality certain activities may be missing, poorly performed or performed in a different order. Linkages between activities may be missing. The result of questioning the correspondence between model and reality is an agenda, a list of items that need to be discussed by those concerned, the actors in the situation. Care must be taken to develop an agenda that is concerned with *what* needs to be achieved rather than *how*. If specific changes are discussed before the need for change has been accepted the result may be that those involved in the debate will assume their traditional viewpoints on the problem.

Illustration 2.5 Conceptual model exercise

Take one of the relevent systems proposed for Schmorl Print and develop a conceptual model.

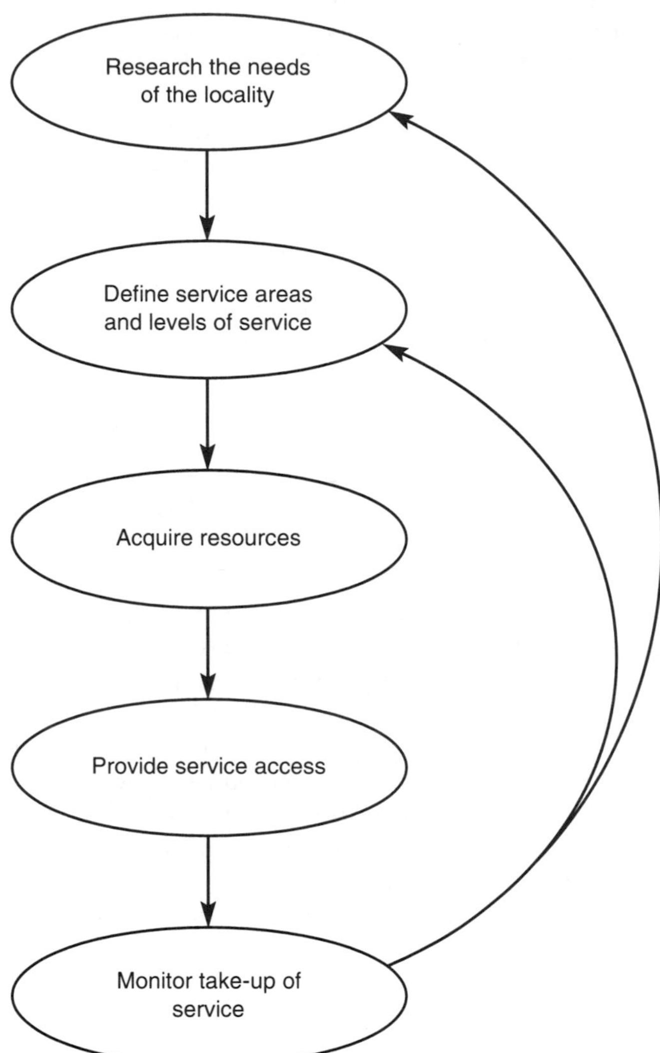

Fig. 2.6 A conceptual model for a general practice

The agenda forms the basis for a debate, a structured discussion with those people concerned with the problem situation, the actors. The aim of the debate is to identify those ideas which are agreed by the actors to be both *systemically desirable* (recognised as sensible changes when we realise that they will be a part of a system) and *culturally feasible* (in terms of culture, politics and behavioural norms) for that set of actors. Such changes have the best chance of being successfully implemented.

HARD SYSTEMS ANALYSIS

There is a range of systems-based methodologies that can be used to apply systems thinking to the resolution of problems. Among them is hard systems analysis (HSA). If we use HSA then our analysis of the system in question is linked closely with the organisation's objectives and goals. These in turn are expressed in a logical framework consisting of a set of requirements relating to the system that are intended to outline the boundary of the area that is to be considered. The boundary is also set by consideration of why the analysis is to be done, what is to be done during the systems study, and what time-scale, resources, and commitment are present. The type of system that is studied varies by organisational area and managerial level. Some systems are 'hard closed systems', such as production cycles, while others are 'open soft systems' such as customer care (Fig. 2.7).

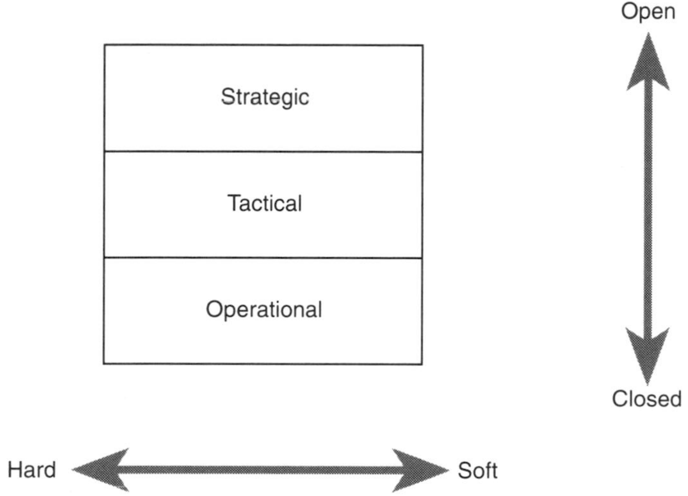

Fig. 2.7 Systems framework

For HSA the terms 'analysis' and 'design' have a specific meaning, as shown in Fig. 2.8. The process of analysis and design forms the iterative cycle represented in Fig. 2.9.

HSA: OVERVIEW OF THE ANALYSIS

Figure 2.7 illustrates the type of system and the applicable management levels. The management levels are those introduced in Chapter 1.

Strategic	Board level, long term, fuzzy knowledge.
Tactical	Medium term, middle management oriented, mainly qualitative data to support decisions.
Operational	Short term, low level of management, mainly quantitative data available.

The essence of the hard system approach is to assume that every system can be disaggregated into a number of subsystems and that the components of those subsystems

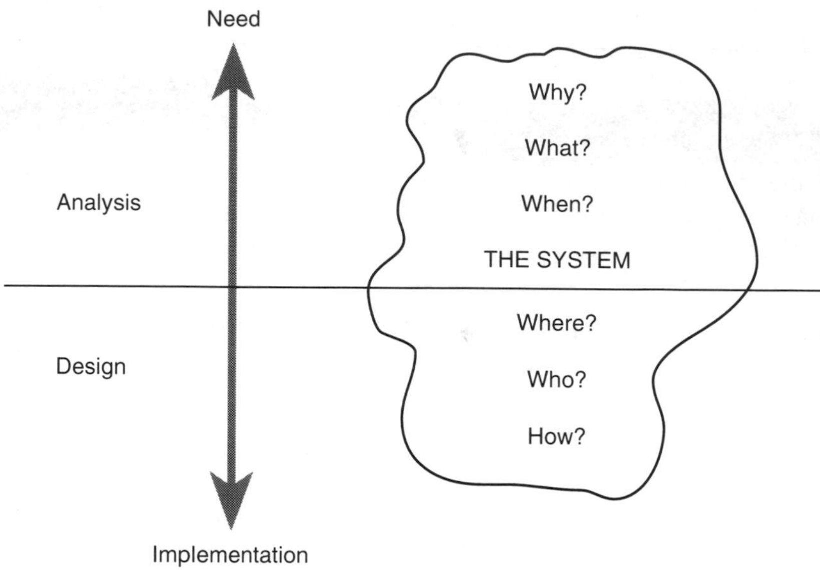

Fig. 2.8 Hard systems analysis and design

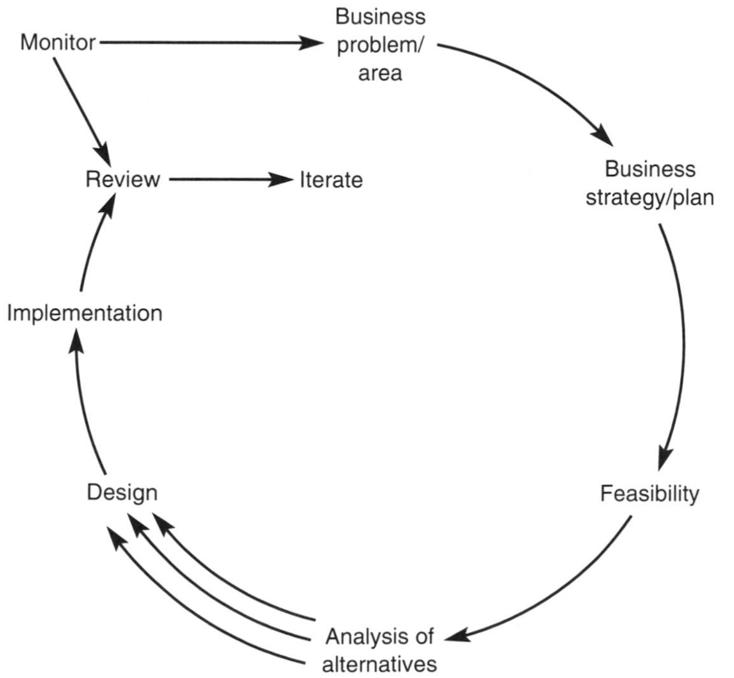

Fig. 2.9 Hard systems analysis: an iterative approach

can be identified and, as far as possible, quantified to provide an explanation of the workings of those subsystems. Added together the subsystems form the whole.

Each of the subsystems are examined in the light of the following:

- The properties of the subsystem in terms of purpose, definition, size and importance, e.g., by use of lists of inputs and outputs.
- The internal structure that transforms the system's inputs to become outputs, e.g., organisation chart.
- The processes that transform the inputs into the outputs as a series of logical steps, e.g., calculations performed on data, and manual actions to transfer data from one source to a destination.
- The communication of data, information and messages in and around the structure, and external to the system, e.g., the content of messages, reports and instructions in terms of the data they contain.
- Finally, the controls which are placed on the system, e.g., the performance limits that have been set for the system and the management instructions that act as control functions.

A variety of tools are used to describe and analyse systems. These include diagramming techniques, such as structured flow charts of the processes involved, and mathematical representations based upon the application of management science techniques. These techniques provide the basis of the system model.

In the following sections the various stages of a HSA are described. At each stage of the process consideration must be given to the system's owner and why the analysis is being done, as well as checking to see if what has been done is correct. Therefore the stages identified are intended to be self-checking, and iterative.

Awareness and commitment

This stage is of critical importance, and needs to be done properly in order that the system study is completed in the correct fashion. Unfortunately it is also at a time when little is known about the area under study. Therefore the first step is to develop an awareness of the nature of the problem. This begins with the analyst meeting the client and the team that he or she will be working with during the study. Agreement has to be reached concerning the purposes and the scope of the study and attempts will have to be made to define the problem. There is a distinction between knowing that a problem exists and accepting that it exists. The problem needs corrective action and an agreement to take the necessary action may be appropriate at this stage. The corrective action agreed in general terms leads to an outline view of the project's subsequent activities.

A selling job may be appropriate at this point to gain commitment for the next stages. Gaining the commitment of the problem or system owners, and of people who can stop the project, may not be at all easy. However, if the project is undertaken without this commitment it will fail.

Constraints, objectives and goals

At an early stage the analyst must identify the constraints and objectives that are relevant for the system that is being studied. The constraints are requirements and limitations from outside the system boundary that must not be violated, e.g., the treatment of stock in hand as a taxable asset by the Inland Revenue or the requirements of key customer groups.

The nature and direction of the organisation must also be established; this may be expressed in a number of statements that form a hierarchy.

- *Mission*: the organisation's long-range purpose or reason for existence.
- *Objectives*: the long- and medium-term direction of the organisation, leading to the accomplishment of the mission, e.g., to improve product quality.
- *Goals*: measurable steps to achieve an objective, e.g., registration of product with safety organisation by a given date.

Objectives may be expressed as formal statements, as part of a business plan or budget exercise; or they may be informal, the expectations and intentions of those who manage the system. Objectives may also take the form of quantified statements, e.g., a desired rate of sales growth, or they may be expressed in qualitative terms. (Chapter 8 provides a fuller consideration of organisational mission and objectives.)

Hard systems approaches are often characterised as being mechanistic. It is much more accurate to say that the hard systems approach is systematic as well as systemic. The emphasis should be on a disciplined, well structured approach to finding facts about the system, problems, opportunities and data at each stage of the process, until a single system is obtained, or the idea of a system is generated from a business area. Once this has been achieved a different thought pattern is needed, from one related to achieving a consensus view on system, problem/opportunities and objectives, to one concerned with alternative ways of achieving objectives.

Generation of alternatives

This stage concerns the generation, design and assessment of alternative paths to achieve the given objectives and goals. Each of the alternatives must not violate the constraints but must provide a feasible way to meet the objectives. If no such alternatives exist then an iteration will take place to reassess the system, its definition, mission and objectives, thus creating a review of what it is the analysis is trying to solve. It may be that even after considerable attempts have been made to generate a set of paths to the objectives no complete alternative is found, therefore an adequate, if not entirely complete, alternative is proposed. The alternatives are carried forward to the next stage for detailed assessment, modelling and evaluation.

Assessing alternatives

To carry the analysis further we must be able to measure the alternatives against a set of criteria that allow us to make a value judgement as to the effectiveness of the proposed paths for objective attainment. To do this a quantifiable figure or value is put on the objective so that:

- A measure of performance is established.
- A target level is set for that measure of performance.
- A time limit is established for the attainment of that target level.

Illustration 2.6 provides an example of an open objective and a goal. The objective has

Illustration 2.6 Hartree Trading: objectives and goals

Hartree Trading has just taken over a company that sells flat-pack furniture directly to the public (ACME Furnishing). They wish to supply the new company with own-label manufactured flat-pack furniture, but ACME have a reputation for supplying good quality furniture at an affordable price. Hartree would like to maintain this reputation, but also expand the outlets for their own brand. Hartree wish to provide 35% of ACME flat-pack furniture within the next two years.

no measures attached to it, the objective is just a statement of intent, i.e., 'wish to supply flat-pack furniture to ACME, but keep the reputation for quality'. This objective is closed, to become a goal, by putting quantitative values on the objective so that when the actions are taken to achieve the objective, a set of measures for intentions (the goal) can be compared against what is actually achieved.

Measures of performance can themselves be classified. This classification is sometimes known as the four E's.

- *Effectiveness*: does the selected alternative provide the best level of achievement of the goal and the minimum disruption?
- *Efficiency*: will the alternative be accomplished with the least use of resources, assets, money, time and people?
- *Equity*: will the costs and benefits be apportioned fairly and distributed correctly across the many claims?
- *Efficacy*: will the intended objectives be reached, and will the ethical consequences and responsibilities be acceptable?

One of the major criticisms of the hard systems approach is that it can fail to recognise the cultural and ethical aspects of the system under study. Care must be exercised when using hard systems methods to make certain that these considerations are not ignored in pursuit of the first three E's.

Model construction, evaluation, implementation

To model the system there needs to be a systematic description of it, its objectives, constraints, and measures of performance. There is a wide variety of modelling techniques to choose from, and some are discussed in Chapters 5 and 6.

Evaluation of the model allows the analyst to determine its credibility and to evaluate the alternative routes to the objectives. A third feature is communication to the problem/opportunity-holder. Being able to describe a feature in an abstract way is often part of a solution. The explanation must be in an understandable form and easy to explain to the decision maker.

A simplified approach

Figure 2.10 is an attempt to simplify some of the processes explained above and to provide what could be termed a 'quick and dirty' approach to analysis. Unfortunately the high-level mission, and the goals and objectives may still be a problem in that they must be known at least in outline prior to attempting the analysis. The quick method is encapsulated in the bottom four boxes.

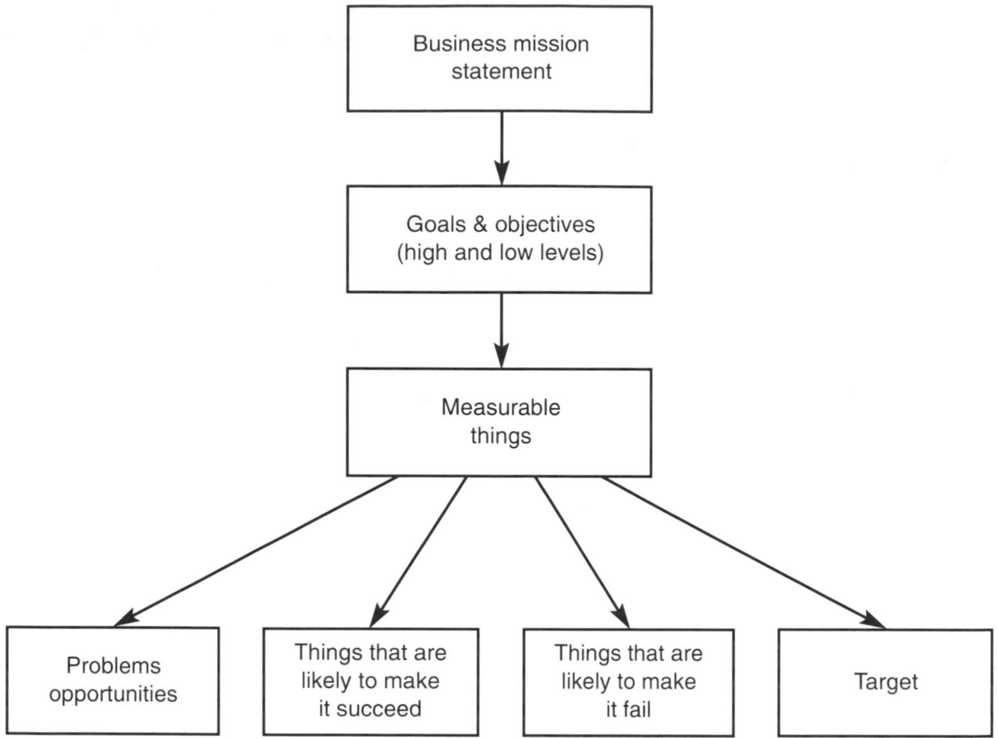

Fig. 2.10 A simplified approach

GRAPHICAL TECHNIQUES

The purpose of graphical techniques is to obtain an understanding of the *structure, processes* and *control* contained in the system. Graphical techniques are part of the 'language' of HSA, and are useful in understanding and communicating findings. There are several levels of diagrammatic or graphical technique; these are identified in Fig. 2.11.

There are many types of technique that can be used for the analysis of systems, in particular computer systems, but all have a structured method for producing their diagrams. To assist understanding of the main levels shown in Fig. 2.11 some examples of these techniques are described in the following sections.

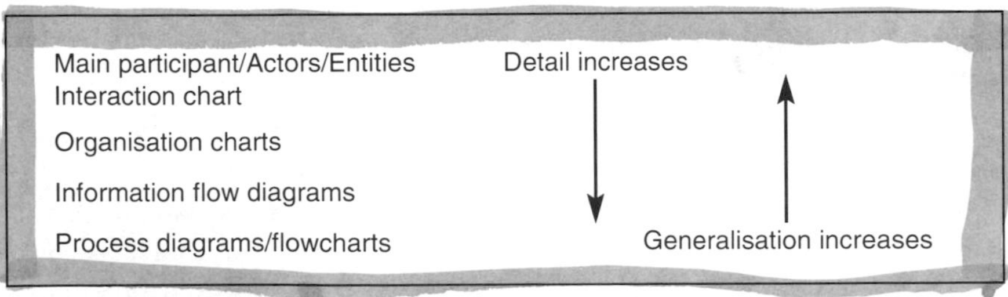

Fig. 2.11 Graphical techniques

Description of the structure of a system starts with establishing the context in which it exists, and the main influences on it or the problem area, also the main entities and actors. At this stage a tentative decision is made regarding which entities or actors should be included within the system boundary and which are external to it. When drawing up the chart all actors possible should be included so that all influences on the system, and hence the problem domain, can be identified.

Illustration 2.7 'Clearing'

Potential students apply to Higher Education establishments to join courses on the basis of their 'A' level passes or other examinations, and on the entrance requirements of particular institutions. If potential students fail to secure places due to inadequate examination passes they can go into a process called 'clearing', where alternative courses are offered to them, or alternative establishments. All institutions and the clearing house report the numbers of such students to the Department of Education.

Illustration 2.7 identifies an area of concern, the 'clearing house system'; the main actors and entities in the system are clearly identified in the text. The next step is to try to put the action of 'clearing' into the context of the other actors in the system as a whole.

Entity interaction/context chart

The shape of the boxes and style of arrows, or where the text is placed, are unimportant at this stage; indeed a pencil drawing is ideal for discussion with the problem owner as to whether or not the analyst has got the context correct. (Pencil is easily rubbed out.) What is important is that the diagram should contain the main actors or entities and their interaction with one another. This interaction could be in many forms – information, materials, energy and control. The different forms of interaction can be identified by different types of arrow if so wished.

One of the difficulties is that often entities also have entities within them, e.g., functional areas or departments in an organisation. The analysis can stop at this point if all that is required is to understand the context of the problem; or the diagram can be developed further to establish the internal contexts of each of the individual actors shown in the diagram. Task-oriented areas of process, such as customer orders, stock control, production scheduling, etc., can be used as a basis for obtaining the internal structure of an entity. Use can also be made of organisation charts.

In Figure 2.12 the entities 'clearing', 'institution', 'government' and 'student' are identified as being directly involved in the process known as clearing. The student is an individual, and the other three are organisations that will lend themselves to further analysis, for example by charting organisation structure, as in Fig. 2.13.

The organisation chart can go into further detail, if required, down to individuals in departments. The level at which the chart stops is dependent on the problem in hand or the decision that has to be made. Already the chart has thrown up some questions regarding computer services which serve two masters, the academic teaching in departments and the provision of administrative services to functions such as Estates and the Registrar.

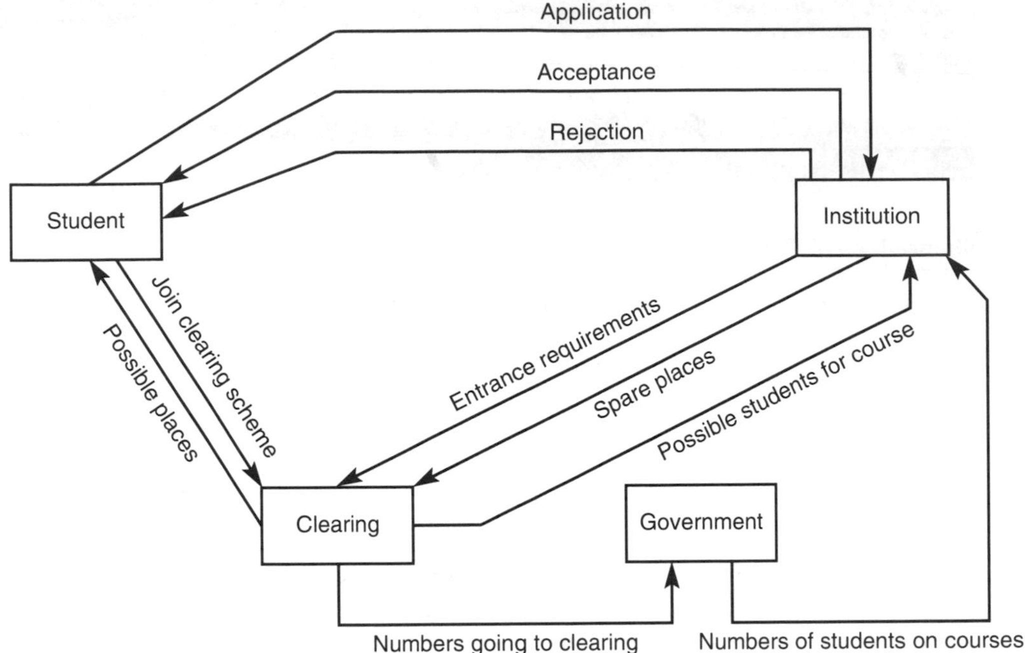

Fig. 2.12 The clearing-house context

The institution may wish to review the computerisation of its undergraduate administration. Again individual areas intended for computerisation need to be split up to reveal the structure, procedures, information flows and control within them. There are numerous types of diagramming technique. A lot of the diagramming techniques used in Computer System Analysis can be used to analyse problem solving.

Data Flow Diagramming is a useful technique for examining the interaction of administrative systems. This technique, illustrated in Fig. 2.14, shows the drawing of a boundary round the system, and the identification of inputs and outputs to externals. The boundary of the system is the course administration function and all other entities are external to this system. The next step is to break down the function further. If the problem is to monitor and evaluate the amount of data going into the function, also that going out, then there is sufficient information contained in the diagram to build a suitable model of the volume of, say, students asking for advice on course timetables, results, availability of tutors, etc.

Flow charts

These diagrams are used to describe the processes of problem areas in the greatest level of detail. Each step of a procedure is written down, together with the decision alternatives, the logical paths and the start and stop positions. Using the process of paying a mortgage, a set of processes can be identified as well as a set of logical alternatives. An example is shown in Fig. 2.15.

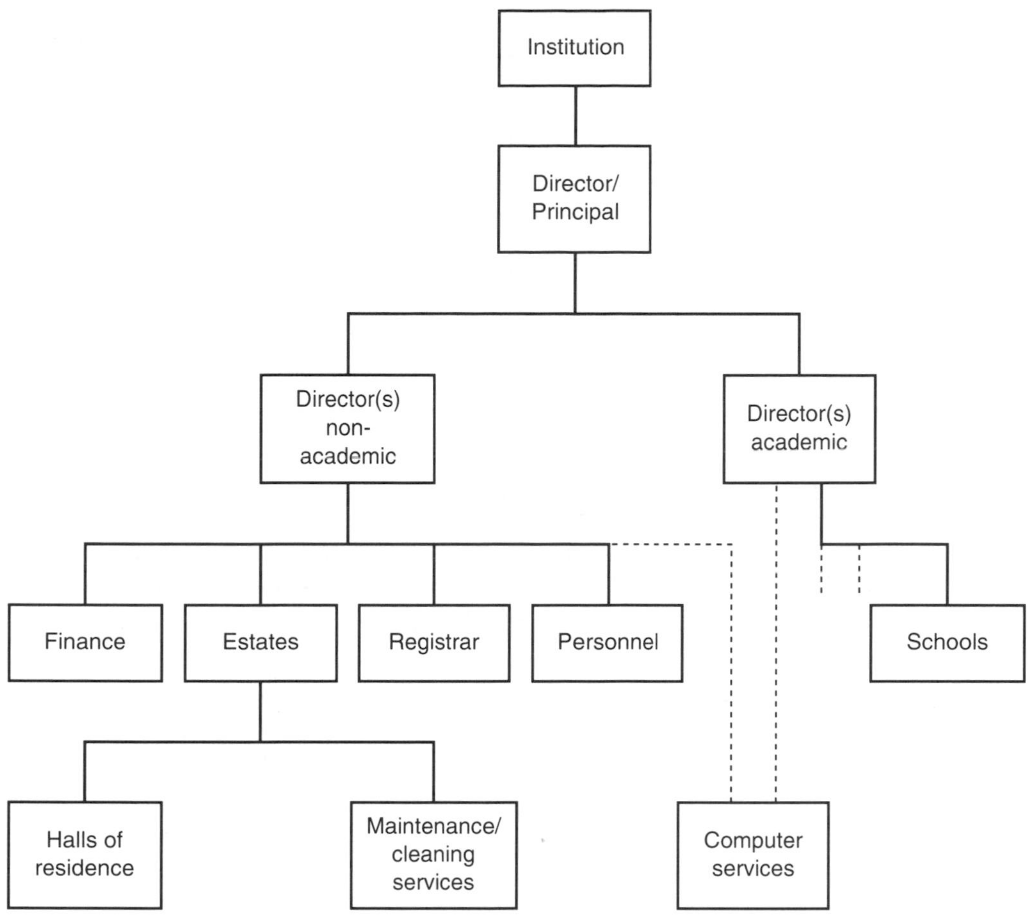

Fig. 2.13 Organisation chart for the 'institution'

THE SYSTEMS APPROACH TO DECISION MAKING

The examination of decision making in Chapter 1 revealed a number of problems in applying the normative model of decision making (Fig. 1.1), it also found decision making in practice to be a process that is largely concerned with the development of a single solution. Systems-based methodologies provide a practical approach to decision making that deals with complex problems in a disciplined and balanced way.

A systems approach pays considerable attention to the identification or diagnosis stage of decision making. A holistic view is taken of the situation and the diagnosis of problems is deferred until sufficient awareness, and examination of the situation, has taken place to avoid the error of imposing inappropriate solutions. Through the use of soft systems methodology the diagnosis stage of decision making is enriched, and all the information that has become available is considered by the analyst. Factual information is used alongside subjective insights. Commitment to a particular diagnosis is postponed in favour of developing awareness of problems.

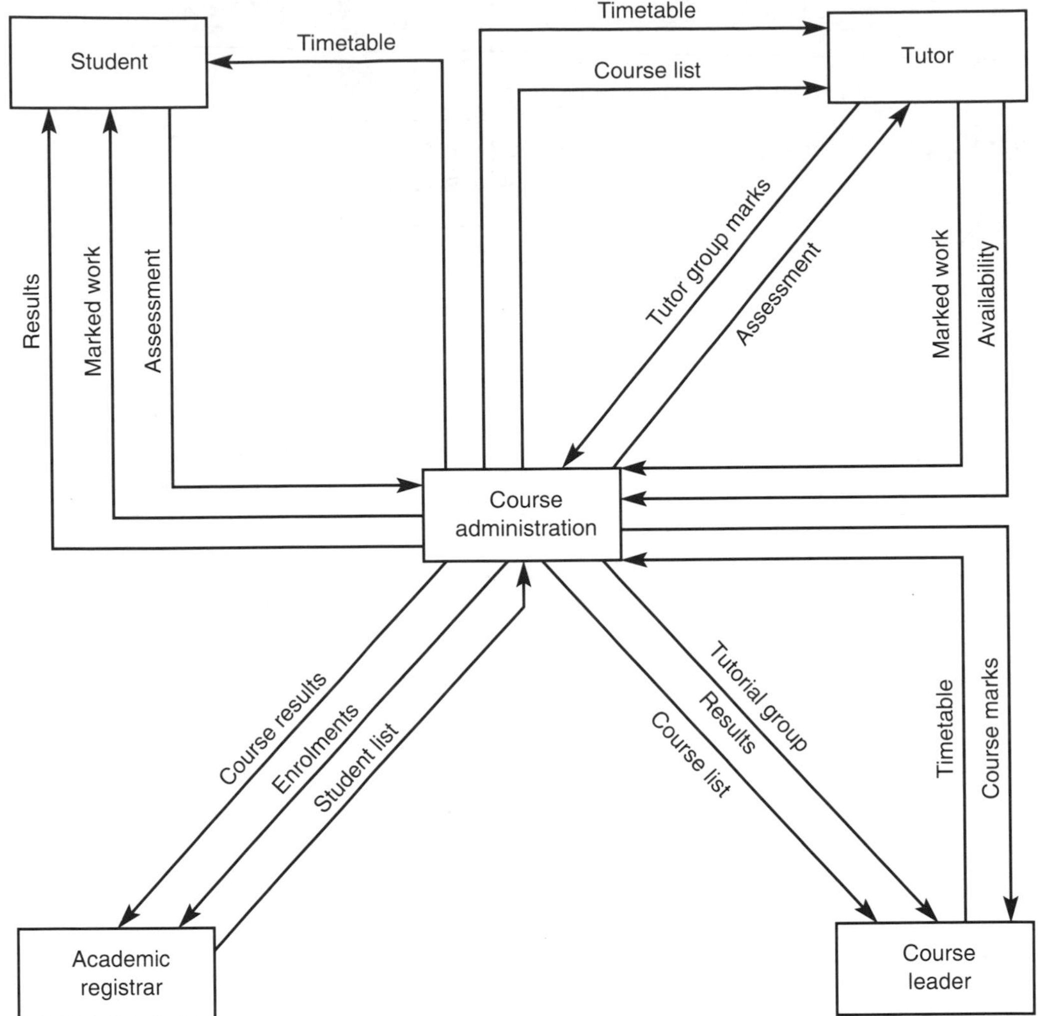

Fig. 2.14 Course administration

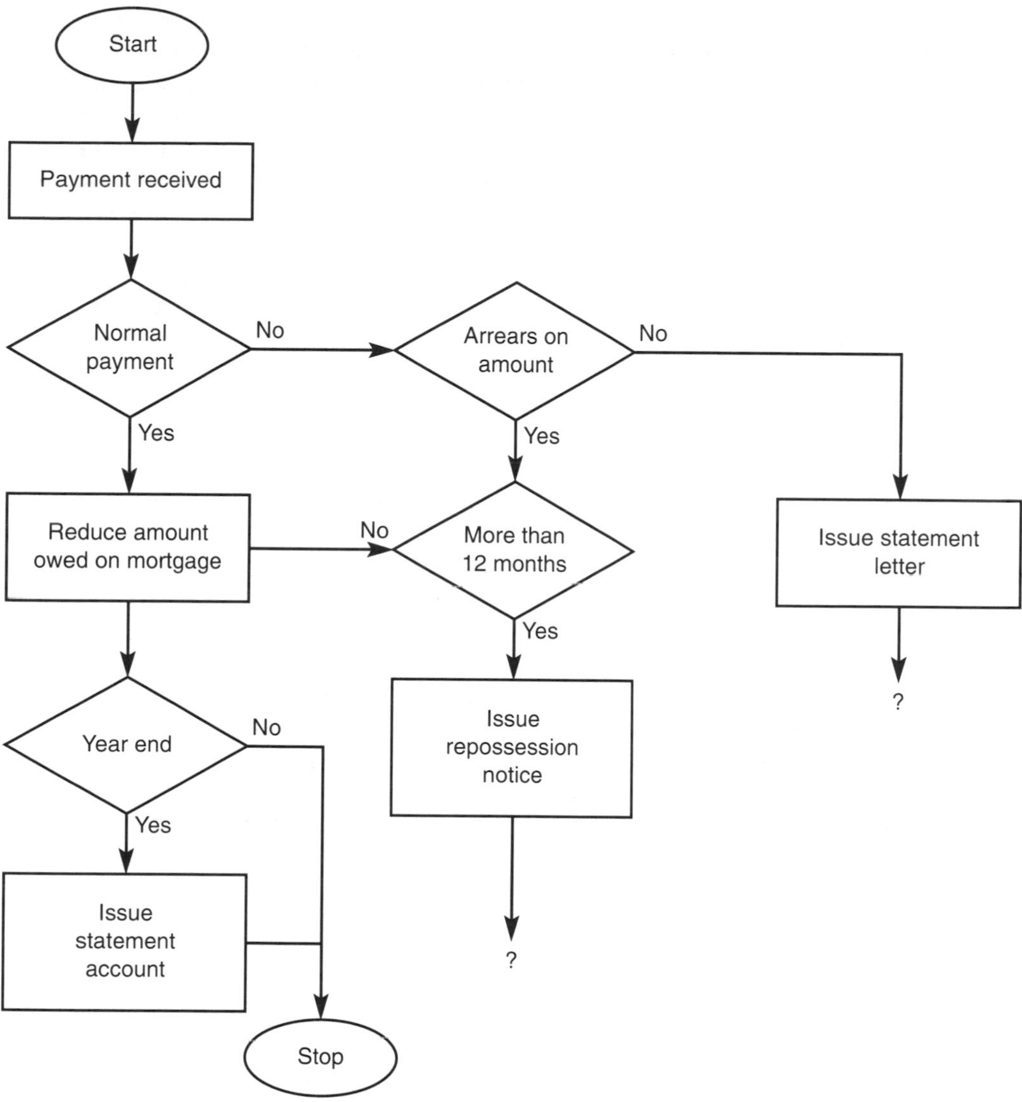

Fig. 2.15 Paying a mortgage

The following case provides material for an exercise in soft systems analysis.

EXERCISE: CRISIS IN THE HOUSING MARKET, A SOFT SYSTEMS ANALYSIS

During the early 1990s the UK experienced a period of recession. During that time many tens of thousands of house owners, unable to maintain their mortgage payments, faced the prospect of repossession. The number of repossessions for failure to maintain mortgage payments could have been far higher. For a variety of reasons the building societies made great effort to avoid making repossessions. They viewed repossession not only as a potential source of bad publicity, but also against their basic purpose.

The Council of Mortgage Lenders monitors the industry for its members the banks and building societies. The Council was concerned, not only by the level of repossession and its possible future trend, but also by the failure of information about an impending repossession to be shared among the various lenders involved. This concern led the Council to set up a working party that issued guidance notes on exchanging information. The Council concluded that it was unlikely for home-owners to face repossession through inability to maintain payments on their first mortgage (that granted to purchase the house). The incidence of repossession was mainly concerned with secondary loans: up to 60 per cent of home-owners borrowing from the Council's members possessed a secondary mortgage.

Many of the providers of secondary mortgages had few reservations against seeking legal redress for their debts. In a single year up to 30,000 home-owners lost their homes through a repossession order issued by a court following default on a secondary mortgage, a loan that had been obtained to pay for such expenditure as home improvement. In many cases the sum involved was small, a debt of a few hundred pounds. Many of the lenders seeking court action had only become established in the 1980s and, suffering losses during the recession, they were keen to recover as many debts as possible.

Other organisations were concerned about the situation including Shelter, a charity for the homeless, also many local authorities. Attempting to limit the call upon their own resources, local authorities advised owners faced with debt on how they might avoid repossession. At the same time the National Association of Citizen's Advice Bureaux called for a change in the 1974 Consumer Credit Act to improve the protection available for people obtaining loans secured against their homes.

The government was also becoming increasingly uneasy about the growing number of repossessions. Faced with the prospect of a general election within one or two years, it believed that a recovery of confidence in the housing market was an essential part of any broader economic recovery. Following discussions with leading lenders a rescue scheme was launched by which owners who were experiencing difficulty could transfer ownership of their property to the lender, or to a housing association, and stay on as tenants. Although many of the larger building societies set aside considerable sums of money to support the scheme (£100m by the Leeds Building Society) only about a hundred householders took advantage of it. The reason identified for the scheme's failure was attributed to the fact that people who choose to buy a house, rather than rent, will do all they can to avoid becoming tenants. In the few cases where home-owners decided to take adavantage of the scheme there were a number of problems with the transfer of the property. When banks or building societies approached housing associations to discuss a transfer of ownership, the associations often found that before a property could be legally rented the association would have to find a considerable sum of money for structural improvements in order to meet regulations concerning the state of properties under their jurisdiction.

Home-owners looked for some relief from a fall in interest rates, apparently kept high by Britain's membership of the European Exchange Rate Mechanism, but as rates fell the number of householders in arrears continued to increase. In part this anomaly resulted from the basis upon which many lenders calculated overdue debt. By dividing the total arrears by the current (lower) monthly payment the number of months of indebtedness was increased.

For 1992 it was expected that over 113,000 borrowers would be over 12 months in arrears. Some commentators suggested that in excess of 50 per cent of these would be repossessed, adding to the stock of over 68,000 repossessed homes that the building societies were trying to offload, often at a loss, onto an already depressed housing market. In some instances building societies helped the sale of such properties by offering cheap mortgages on repossessed properties.

Scenario: The circumstances described in the case study *Crisis in the Housing Market* have persisted and the building societies are anxious to improve the situation. As a consequence of this, the industry's trade association has commissioned you to act as a consultant to provide proposals for consideration by those involved. Use the various stages of soft systems analysis to develop a suitable set of proposals from the above case material. They are as follows:

- Rich Picture
- Notional Systems
- Conceptual Models
- Comparison

GLOSSARY OF MAIN TERMS

Entropy The tendency for a system to run down; loose order.

Equifinality The principle by which a system may achieve a final state from different initial conditions and through different ways.

Iterative The action or process of repeating a step or given set of steps to some pre-determined satisfaction or accuracy.

Negative feedback Informational input indicating deviation and the need to adjust to a new steady state.

Notional system A system that would have some effect upon a problem theme identified in a rich picture.

Open system A system that receives inputs, transforms those inputs and exports outputs.

Rich picture A pictorial representation of a problem situation.

System A complex whole.

REFERENCES

Beishon, J., and Peters, G. (1976) *Systems Behaviour*, Harper and Row Ltd.

Checkland, P. B. (1981) *Systems Thinking, Systems Practice*, John Wiley.

FURTHER READING

Hicks, M. J. (1991) *Problem Solving in Business and Management: Hard, Soft and Creative Approaches*, Chapman and Hall

Macro, A. (1990) *Software Engineering: Concepts and Management*, Prentice Hall.

Pressman, R. (1992) *Software Engineering: A Practitioner's Approach*, 2nd ed, McGraw Hill.

Shooman, M. (1988) *Software Engineering: Design, Reliability and Management*, McGraw Hill.

Wattam, S. (1990) *Software Engineering: A Dynamic Approach*, Sigma Press.

Wilson, B. (1992) *Systems: Concepts, Methodologies and Applications*, Wiley.

CHAPTER 3

Group and organisational decision making

Ray Lye

INTRODUCTION

Traditional approaches to decision making, such as that represented in Fig. 1.1, assumed the individual decision maker operated rationally and in isolation from any possible group or organisational influences. Group allegiances or departmental interests were not supposed to interfere with the single-minded pursuit of rational procedure. However any look at business decision making in practice will dispel the validity of this perspective. To understand decision making and to improve decision-making skills it is necessary to be aware of the group and organisational contexts in which decisions are taken.

Business decisions are increasingly being taken by groups. As matters become more complex and more specialists are employed it becomes less and less possible for the individual to take decisions in isolation. Even if a group is not the decision-making body, it is difficult to imagine the individual is not in some way affected by group pressures or interests. Similarly the organisational setting of a decision is likely to have a major influence on the decision maker. For example, the degree of centralisation or the strength of an organisation's culture have an impact on both how the decision is arrived at and the final decision itself.

In this chapter we shall look at the nature of both group and organisational influences on decision making and examine the ways in which these factors might be best utilised in arriving at effective decisions.

GROUPS AND DECISION MAKING

Modern organisations use groups for making decisions. The Board of Directors, the Senior Management Team, the Project Group, the Brainstorming meeting and the Social Club Committee are all examples of the tendency to believe that in some way 'two heads are better than one', and better decisions are likely to emerge from a group than from an individual. For some this belief appears to be based on hope rather than experience because we can all identify poor decisions that have been taken by groups but, overall, there is a marked trend towards group decision making in contemporary organisations, and there are likely to be some genuine reasons for this.

Why then are groups used in decision making? There appear to be five major reasons for this. The first of these is the issue of *legitimacy*. If an individual takes a decision the person may be perceived as acting autocratically, without regard to the interests and feelings of others, and implementing the decision by compulsion rather than by consent. If this happens the decision might be questioned in terms of its legitimacy. 'Nobody asked me so why should I feel bound by this decision' is a possible response. However if the decision is arrived at and agreed by a group it may well be seen as having a general legitimacy and even if someone does not concur with the decision it can always be said that they had their say and were directly involved in the process of deciding. Generally speaking it is reasonable to suggest that a group decision will gain wider support more quickly than a decision taken unilaterally by an individual.

Secondly, there is the question of the group and the *quality* of a decision. Of course a group may make a bad decision but overall there are reasons to expect the general quality to be better if decisions are taken by groups. Both intuitively and from research studies we can safely predict that a group will generate more alternatives than will the lone individual. By applying a wider range of experience, ability and expertise than the individual can bring, there will a greater awareness of both potential solutions and the potential problems and drawbacks of adopting a particular course of action. In general these factors will lead to groups producing higher quality decisions than can the individual.

Point three concerns *novelty*. In situations which require new ideas, or with problems that require original solutions, the group is seen as superior to the individual. Faced with a need to generate new ideas the group has been shown to be a significantly more prolific source. To harvest the benefits of the group in this regard techniques, such as brainstorming, have been developed and refined and are widely used in business situations that require originality and creativity.

Fourthly, where there is a *shortage of information*, getting a group to take a decision brings more information to bear on the decision than if matters are left to one, less informed, individual. By getting together a group of the best informed persons it becomes easier to access the most appropriate and complete information. The group cannot realistically always have all the information at its disposal but it does lead to a greater sharing of what information is available, and leads to a clearer understanding of what information is lacking.

Fifth and finally, there is the important issue of *morale*. Participation in group decision making is shown by many research studies to be positively related to morale and job satisfaction, and negatively related to matters such as occupational stress and career dissatisfaction. In groups, people will not only gain some social satisfaction from interacting with others; playing a role in decision making can enhance the person's status and self-esteem as well as providing opportunities for self-expression and personal development. The introduction of group decision making into situations where decisions have traditionally been imposed from above has almost invariably shown an increase in morale.

In the light of these arguments favouring group decision making one might wonder why there is not an even greater emphasis on harnessing the powers of the group in taking more and more decisions. Decision-making theory still tends to focus on the individual and, in practice, many managers are reluctant to become involved in more participative approaches. There are both good and bad reasons for this. On the negative side there are those who see group decision making as a threat to their personal power and prestige, who have difficulties coping with a diversity of views, who are autocratic by inclination and who generally show a lack of trust in their colleagues. People like this will seek to keep a tight hold on the reins of power and see decision making as simply their personal prerogative.

However there are some circumstances and some decisions where action is best left to the individual. These decisions are marked by characteristics such as:

(a) *Urgency*. The pressures of time may not make the relatively lengthy process of group involvement appropriate.
(b) *Unique knowledge*. Where a decision is based on the unique knowledge of a single specialist then group methods are not relevant.
(c) *Confidentiality*. In the business world there are secrets and confidential information which cannot be divulged to the wider group. Decisions associated with such information must rest with the individual who has access to confidential information.
(d) *Responsibility*. The former US president Harry S. Truman was said to have a sign on his desk saying 'the buck stops here'. Some individuals find themselves in positions where, when all other approaches to a decision have been tried, they have the ultimate responsibility and must take the decision alone.

It should be noted that these factors can be genuine reasons for not using groups for decision making, but they can also provide excuses for the manager who is unwilling for whatever reasons to become part of anything which seems too much effort or is a threat to personal power.

GROUP PROCESS AND DECISION MAKING

Groups have been the subject of many studies which have examined a wide range of their functions, processes and behaviour. Not all the studies are directly concerned with decision making. In this section we will examine some of the major processes of group behaviour which do have direct implications for successful group decision making.

First for consideration is the process of group formation. Tuckman (1965) suggests that in the formation of groups it is possible to recognise four distinct stages: forming, storming, norming and performing (see Illustration 3.1).

It is important to recognise, in the light of these four stages, that group methods can in the early stages appear to be a very unsuitable way of taking decisions. Early in its development the group is not focused on the decision and may even rebel against the task it is facing. The group only operates successfully after it has completed the first three stages and it is necessary to accept the apparently chaotic behaviour of the forming, storming and norming phases. These are crucial precursors for the effective decision-making group because they establish the atmosphere and relationships which make it possible for the group to work at all.

The next aspect of group behaviour to be examined is group norms and conformity. For a group to achieve goals, and control the activities of its members in pursuit of those goals, there will have to be some rules or norms which people will be expected to conform to and mechanisms, or ways, for the group to deal with those who do not conform. The norms which govern behaviour may be formal or informal. Some decision-making groups will have the formal rule of committee procedure as the framework for their behaviour. There are also likely to be informal norms which develop in the particular situation. One of the first observed set of informal norms shaping group behaviour was the Bank Wiring Room studies which formed part of the Hawthorn Experiments. The

Illustration 3.1 Stages in group formation

Stage of development	*Process*	*Outcome*
(1) Forming	There is anxiety, dependence on the leader, testing to find out the nature of the situation and what behaviour is acceptable.	Members find out what the task is, what the rules are and what methods are appropriate.
(2) Storming	Conflict between sub-groups, rebellion against the leader, opinions are polarised, resistance to control by group.	Emotional resistance to demands of task.
(3) Norming	Development of group cohesion, norms emerge, resistance is overcome and conflicts are patched up; mutual support and sense of group identity.	Open exchange of views and feelings, cooperation develops.
(4) Performing	Interpersonal problems are resolved, interpersonal structure becomes the means of getting things done, roles are flexible and functional.	Solutions to problems emerge, there are constructive attempts to complete tasks and energy is now available for effective work.

(Based on Tuckman, 1965)

group was an under-performing department of wiremen and inspectors whose behaviour was best understood in the light of four group norms.

(1) Don't be a ratebuster. You should not work too hard.
(2) Don't be a chiseller. You should not work too slowly.
(3) Don't be a lone wolf. Mix in with the group.
(4) Don't be a squealer. Do not tell tales about members of the group.

Since these pioneering studies many others have found similar kinds of informal norms governing group actions. There will be some standards of minimum and maximum ways of behaving together with rules which protect the integrity of the group. Such norms will impact upon the decision-making process in ways that can be either harmful or beneficial to good decisions. For example, norms which restrict the effort that might be made in the search for information would impede decision making while norms that emphasise quality and success would help.

The norms of a group must be enforced if they are to be meaningful. Groups have many ways of influencing the actions of their members, from physical force to humourous rebukes. People can be brought into line simply by questioning their own judgement when it is at variance with that of the group. Asch (1951) carried out a well known experiment into the influence of the group on people's judgement. The experiment consisted of asking a group of people to estimate which of three lines corresponded to the length of a standard line. Groups were shown a series of cards (as in Fig. 3.1). The experiment involved groups of seven people but only one of the seven was the subject of the observations. The other six participants had been briefed beforehand to give false responses. The unknowing individual was thus exposed to a set of responses which were totally at variance with his personal perceptions. The results showed that some 37 per cent of the naive subjects agreed with the group's judgement in preference to their own and that most subjects missed the feeling of being at one with the group. People experience an inner conflict which leads them to question their own judgement.

For decision makers, Asch's experiment shows how the group has powers to bring about a consensus in the group, but it also suggests that people's judgement in making a decision might be adversely affected by group pressures. The tendency to conformity in the group, with shared norms backed by pressure for conformity, could lead to a failure to consider the full range of options, and a willingness to discard any decisions that do not fit in well with the aims and aspirations of the group.

A study of group cohesion and teamwork provides a different perspective on the issue of group conformity. A group must display a level of cohesion if it is to act as a team. The cohesive group is the product of a wide range of factors:

Example of cards used by Asch

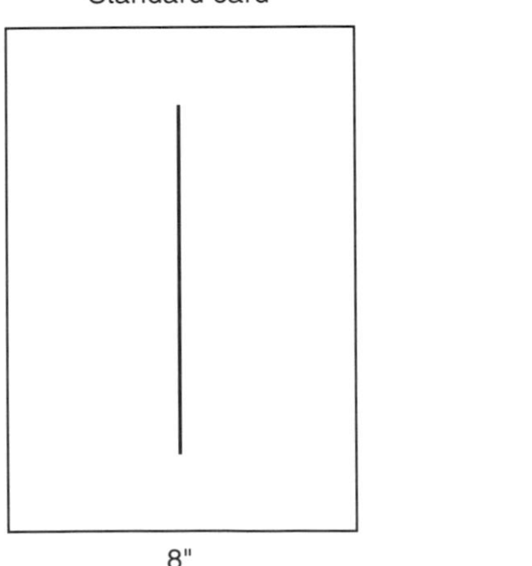

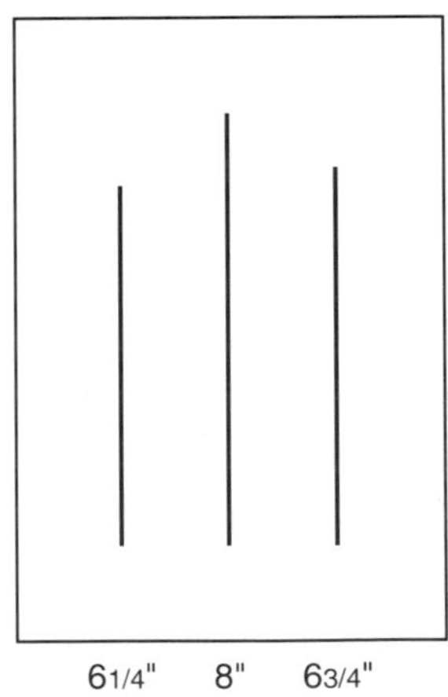

This is one of the stimulus presentations used in Asch's experiments.
The standard 8 inches is on the card to the left, the three comparisons on the card to the right.
The cards are shown 40" apart.

Fig. 3.1 Asch card experiment

(1) *Group size*. Beyond a particular size groups will be likely to fracture and cohesion will be lost as subgroups form.
(2) *Group status*. In general high status will lead to greater cohesiveness.
(3) *Success*. Generally speaking, high status groups show greater cohesiveness. However there is an exception to this when the low status group unites in the face of adversity.
(4) *Group goals*. One reason a person joins a group is that the group can help to achieve individual goals. Agreement over goals and the extent to which group goals complement individual goals will have an impact on group cohesiveness.
(5) *Stable relationships*. Groups with a continuously changing membership are going to be less cohesive than a group which has a constant, continuing membership.
(6) *Environment and proximity*. Where work is noisy and people are physically apart, the group will be less cohesive than in circumstances where working conditions are pleasant and people are close together.
(7) *Homogeneity*. The more similar the members of a group, the more probable that they will perceive common interests and be prepared to work to common goals.
(8) *Intergroup competition and conflict*. The existence of outgroups who are rivals and compete for scarce resources will lead to the ingroup demonstrating greater cohesion.
(9) *Intragroup competition*. This will, by definition, have negative effects on group cohesion.
(10) *Communications*. The cohesive group is marked by a complex and highly developed network of communication.

Group cohesion has been seen as wholly beneficial for decision making but, as we shall see later, this is not always the case and decision making can be harmed by groups that are too cohesive. However, any negative aspects of group cohesion can be set aside in any discussion of teamwork. By definition a team must be a cohesive group where individual members each play an effective role in helping the group reach its goals.

A team will consist of individuals who make a special contribution to the functioning of the group. A model for analysing the distinctive and necessary roles for the effective decision-making group is to be found in the writings of Belbin (1981). He identified eight roles that are needed in decision-making teams:

(a) The company worker who works to keep the organisation's interests to the fore.
(b) The chair who ensures that all views are heard and keeps things moving.
(c) The shaper who influences by argument and by following particular topics.
(d) The ideas person, or plant, who contributes novel suggestions.
(e) The resource investigator who evaluates whether contributions are practical and finds out where and how to obtain resources.
(f) The monitor/evaluator who assesses how valid the contributions are and the extent to which the team is meeting its objectives.
(g) The team worker who maintains the group by joking and agreeing.
(h) The completer/finisher who tries to get things done and suggests conclusions.

At different times each of these roles must be filled if good decisions are to be made by the team. Though a person may play more than one role in most persisting groups people tend to take on one particular role. What distinguishes a team from a group is the existence of these roles and Belbin has been responsible for the development of many training exercises which seek to identify people's capacities in playing these roles and establishing the appropriate membership for groups. Though this may be a rather mechanical view of the working of the effective decision-making team it is still important to note that, in groups, there is not one ideal decision maker but many in that people make distinctive and valuable contributions in their own way.

The next group process to be covered is that of group communications. The pattern of communication within a group can have important consequences for decision making and for the satisfaction of group members. Leavitt (1978) suggests that communication in groups can vary in terms of the number of channels available, the equality of information sharing through communication, and the degree of centralisation of the network (see Fig. 3.2). There is no right pattern. Certain patterns are seen as the best for certain

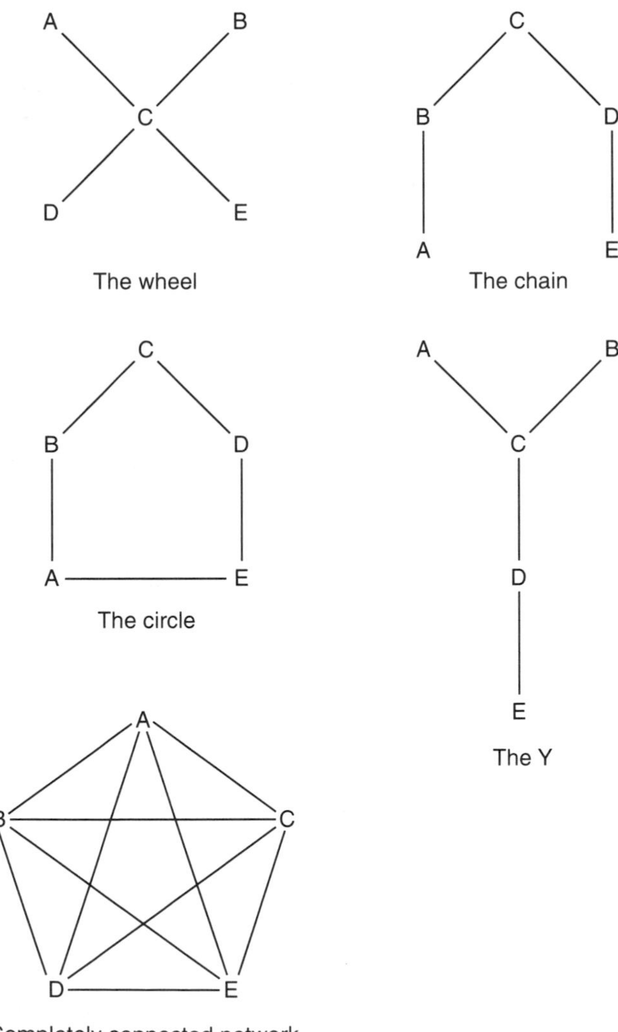

Fig. 3.2 Leavitt's communication paths

Illustration 3.2 Leavitt's communication patterns

The wheel	All communication has to go through the person C at the centre. This pattern provides quick answers to simple questions but A, B, D and E tend to be dissatisfied with their roles.
The chain	No one member is able to communicate with all of the others. Members are reasonably satisfied with the system of communication, but it can be slow and lead to errors.
The circle	By closing the chain each member can communicate with two others. This provides the highest level of general satisfaction and can be effective for dealing with complex problems.
The Y	This combines the features of the wheel and the chain in a centralised network.
The completely connected network	Each person can now communicate freely with every other person and all are satisfied with their roles. This can be effective in dealing with complex problems but is unsatisfactory in dealing with straightforward matters.

situations. A summary of Leavitt's analysis of communication patterns in groups is shown in Illustration 3.2.

It is the case that the prevailing communication pattern in a group will have a significant influence on the quality of decisions made and the way the group feel about those decisions. There is no one best pattern but it is crucial to have the right network to suit the decision. The conclusion here is that simple decisions are best suited to simple networks and that the complex pattern is most pertinent to complex decisions.

The final process to be examined here is the overarching notion of group participation which is particularly relevant to the student of decision making. Almost all writers on this subject praise the value of group participation in arriving at effective decisions. Not only is it viewed as technically efficient, it is also valued in human terms. Satisfaction is increased, stress reduced, and social responsibilities to employees are fulfilled. A cursory glance at contemporary business will find examples of quality circles, team briefing, project management and autonomous work groups which suggest that support for group participation is highly regarded by practitioners as well as by the theorist.

There are many well-researched examples of group participation in practice but there is not space here to consider the full range and variety. Instead one landmark study by Coch and French is summarised below.

Coch and French: overcoming resistance to change

In 1948 L. Coch and J.R. French carried out a classic study of employee participation. The research was carried out at the Harwood Manufacturing Corporation in Marion, Virginia, USA. The company manufactured pyjamas and was experiencing resistance from employees to changes in the jobs and working methods that had to be made in the light of increased competition. The decisions as to the nature and scope of the changes were taken by management and the methods engineer.

Faced with the problems of resistance to change Coch and French hypothesised that allowing employees to participate in the decisions and their implementation would make a significant difference in their acceptance of the change. To test this hypothesis they established three groups who would undertake the changes but with different degrees of participation. The groups were:

(1) *No participation group*
A group of eighteen hand-pressers who were required to change the way in which they stacked their finished work. They undertook the change in line with the established company procedure which allowed no participation and simply involved having the changes described to the workers.

(2) *Participation through representation group*
A group of thirteen pyjama pressers were required to adopt different methods of folding the trousers and jackets. The group were given a demonstration of the need to reduce costs and improve efficiency and then asked to send two representatives to work with the methods engineer in developing the new methods. The representatives then trained the rest of the group.

(3) *Total participation group*
Two groups of pyjama inspectors were required to change their inspection routine. They too were given the demonstration about costs and efficiency, then everyone took part in the design of the new job.

The performance of the groups was monitored for thirty working days after the change. The resulting performance is shown in Fig. 3.3.

(1) The 'no participation' group showed an immediate resistance to the change. They complained to the methods engineer and were aggressive and uncooperative with the supervisor. Some left the company while the remainder deliberately restricted their production. Such was the failure of this group that they were eventually broken up and given other jobs around the factory.
(2) The 'participation through representation' group showed a cooperative and permissive atmosphere in which the rest of the group worked well with the representatives. The efficiency of the group rose and no one chose to leave the company.
(3) The 'total participation' group showed the best results in that their efficiency rating rapidly rose to a much higher level than before the change. The group was co-operative and friendly and no one left the group.

Coch and French were able to conclude that employee participation, in decisions about changes in methods of work and their implementation, plays a major role in overcoming resistance to change.

THE DRAWBACKS OF GROUP DECISION MAKING

Despite the general support for group decision making from social scientists, there have been critics who claim that there are significant dangers; that under certain circumstances the quality of decisions, rather than being enhanced by group participation, may in reality be worse. Perhaps the phrase 'the camel is a horse designed by a committee' is the

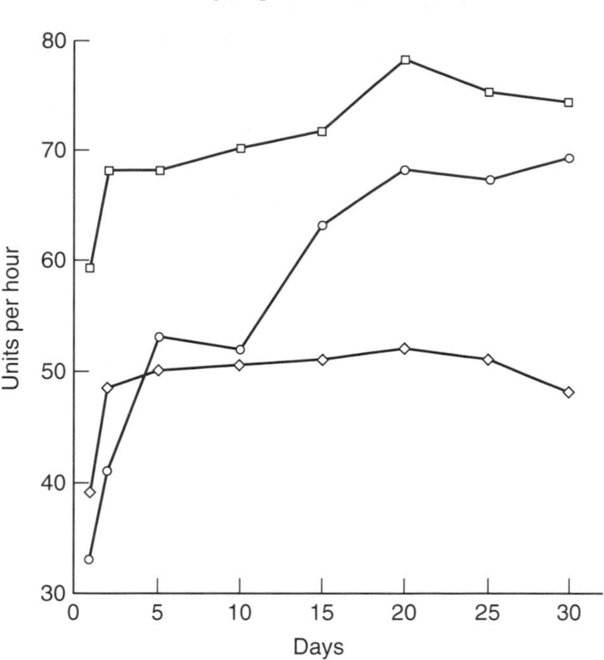

Fig. 3.3 Effects of participation

equivalent perspective of the layman who has serious doubts about the decision-making powers of the group.

Whyte (1956) in his influential book *The Organisation Man* presents a strident criticism of some aspects of the reliance on groups in decision making. He identifies the development in organisations of what he calls the Social Ethic. This is seen as a replacement of the traditional Protestant Work Ethic which stressed individualism, hard work, acquisition and achievement. The Protestant Ethic had been the driving force behind American business, providing a motivation which led to its great success. In contrast, the Social Ethic is based on the values of belonging, fitting-in and self-effacement in the light of the needs of the group. This concern for the group rather than the individual is seen to stem from two major causes. First there was the Human Relations

Illustration 3.3 Group participation

The example from the Harwood Manufacturing Company can be matched by many more. Group participation is seen as effective because people become 'ego-involved' in decisions in which they have had an influence. The decisions become their decisions and they develop expectancies to the effect that when decisions are successful they will experience such intrinsic rewards as feelings of competence and self-esteem. Because of this, they work to implement the decision even though no extrinsic rewards are involved.

movement in management thought. Originating from the Hawthorn Experiments it emphasised the importance of the group and abhorred conflicts which might weaken its solidarity. The second cause relates to the structure of the large business organisation. The pyramidal structure means that not everyone can achieve chief executive position and, realistically, a middle-management position is the ceiling to which the majority can aspire. Competing for promotion at this level is irrelevant and the Protestant Ethic can be seen as providing inappropriate motivation while the Social Ethic can possibly help people come to terms with their role. Thus we have the so-called 'organisation man' who puts aside personal aspirations and desires in the interests of the organisation.

Whyte gives many examples of the Social Ethic as it applies not only in business but also in such diverse areas of social life as family, religion, literature and education. A particularly relevant example of the relationship between the Social Ethic and the practice of decision making is to be found in Whyte's quotation from the *Bureau of Naval Personnel Handbook* which deals with taking effective committee decisions. It refers to 'good' and 'bad' members of a committee and tells us how to deal with the 'bad' type, the Aggressor. If encountered in a committee the Chairman's remedy is to

> Place Donald Duck on your left (the blind spot). Fail to hear his objections or, if you do, misunderstand them. If possible, recognise a legitimate objection and side with him. Object is to get him to feel he belongs. If he still persists in running wild, let the group do what they are probably quite hot to do, i.e., cut the lug down. They generally do it by asking Little Brother Terrible to clarify his position, then clarify his clarification, then to clarify his clarification of his clarification, etc., until our lad is so hot and bothered he has worked himself into the role of conference comedian. Then soothe his bruised ego and restore him to human society by asking him questions that he can answer out of special experience.

Amongst the 'good' people is the 'compromiser'. He

> may offer compromise by admitting his error by obviously disciplining himself to maintain group harmony or by 'coming half-way' in moving along with the group. This takes courage. Let him know he is appreciated. Give the occasional cigar. A fifteen center. He deserves the best.

The reader will be pleased to know that this handbook is no longer in use but it does provide a vivid illustration of how the Social Ethic can have negative effects on decision making. In this example, what if the aggressor has the best ideas and any compromise is likely to lead to failure? Clearly the Social Ethic puts group harmony before getting the best decision.

Overall Whyte criticises the Social Ethic on the grounds that it is:

(1) *Redundant*. There is a danger of a climate which inhibits individual initiative and the courage to exercise it against group opinion.
(2) *Premature*. It places the cart before the horse by seeing the means of taking the decision as supremely important rather than the content of the decision.
(3) *Delusory*. It appears to be kind and benevolent to everyone but in fact can lead to a sort of tyranny and lack of freedom for individuals.
(4) *Static*. There is nothing in the Social Ethic that will lead to change or innovation. These are likely to upset established group relations, hence it is always better to maintain the *status- quo*.
(5) *Self-destructive*. In the long run, attempts to maintain group cohesiveness at all costs will fail. People will react to the control and uniformity which will lead to more controls which will lead to more organised resistance and so on.

This critique by Whyte has had a significant influence on the development of management thought, and organisations, particularly in the US, have responded by seeking to avoid the dangerous consequences of a belief in the virtues of the Social Ethic. However, it still points to some of the ever-present risks of a total faith in the effectiveness of the cohesive group as the decision-making body.

The dangers of the over-cohesive group in decision making is highlighted in the concept of 'Groupthink' developed by Janis (1982). Groupthink occurs when the emphasis in the group is placed upon maintaining a pleasant atmosphere and maintaining morale rather than taking effective decisions.

Janis identifies the symptoms of groupthink as follows:

(1) *The illusion of invulnerability.* The group feels, unrealistically, free from any external threat. They overestimate their ability to succeed against high odds and extraordinary risks.
(2) *Collective rationalisation.* The group is not likely to spot any snags. When it is suggested that their plans are going wrong they spend a lot of time thinking of rationalisations for failure and ways to discount warnings.
(3) *Belief in the inherent morality of the group.* In the process of maintaining a high level of conformity, the group develop a conviction that what they are doing is correct, not only in the logical sense but also in the moral and ethical sense, thus making the group less aware of any questionable moral or ethical outcomes of their decisions.
(4) *Stereotypes of outgroups.* Victims of groupthink hold biased or simple stereotypes of competing groups.
(5) *Direct pressure on dissenters.* When there are signs of non-conformity in the group, strong pressures are brought to bear, both in reward and punishment, to bring people back into line.
(6) *Mindguards.* Just as bodyguards provide physical protection, mindguards provide some sort of intellectual protection for group members. Mindguards may, for example, discourage people from talking to others with different viewpoints or choose to filter information that people might disagree with.
(7) *Self-censorship.* The group pressures people not to express any misgivings they might have about a particular decision.
(8) *Illusion of unanimity.* Stemming from self-censorship and the operation of mindguards, the victims of groupthink share the illusion of group unanimity. Silence is taken as strong assent and lukewarm approval is seen for genuine agreement.

The net outcome of groupthink is poor decisions. The group does not realistically examine the risks of its proposals, ignores negative data and, when faced with failure, is less likely to consider alternatives. There will not be any contingency plans since the group is convinced of the correctness of its original stance. Ultimately these factors can lead to decision-making fiascos, examples of which are given by Janis (1982) in his book *Victims of Groupthink.* They are drawn mainly from American political and military history.

An instance is provided by the Kennedy cabinet-backed plan to invade Cuba with a view to bringing down the regime of Fidel Castro. Even though the news of the 'surprise' invasion of the Bay of Pigs was leaked, and printed beforehand in the *New York Times*, the invasion still went ahead. Further examples given are the lack of preparedness for the Japanese assault on Pearl Harbour in the second world war, the Johnson administration's rationalisation of defeats in Vietnam as setbacks, and President Truman's strategic errors in the Korean war. While the examples are from the political and military arenas it is no great imaginative leap to believe that groupthink is a phenomenon that can easily be found in any organisation.

If groupthink exists can anything be done to remedy it? Can strategies be adopted which will prevent groupthink from occurring in the first place? Illustration 3.4 shows a number of possible strategies that may be applied as means of combating groupthink.

The criticisms of group decision making that are implicit in the notions of the Social Ethic and Groupthink are both trenchant and relevant. However, they should not lead to a total disillusionment with the use of groups for decision making. Groups can be very effective and, as we have seen, there are many good reasons for choosing group methods. What we do see here is a set of potential dangers and weaknesses. The problem facing those engaged in group decision making is how to ensure that these dysfunctional aspects do not emerge, and to sustain the smooth and purposive operation of the group.

THE EFFECTIVE GROUP

Some groups are better at taking decisions than others. They operate more successfully and arrive at better decisions. Having looked at what can make a group ineffective it is now reasonable to ask the question: what is it that makes a group effective? It would be

Illustration 3.4 Preventing groupthink

Symptom	*Preventative Measures*
Illusions of group invulnerability.	Leader encourages open expression of doubt.
Collective rationalisation.	Leader accepts criticism of his or her opinions.
Belief in the inherent morality of the group.	High status members offer opinions last.
Stereotypes of outgroups.	Solicit opinions of other groups.
Direct pressure on dissenters.	Periodically divide into subgroups.
Mindguards.	Assign a member to be devil's advocate.
Self-censorship.	Get reactions from outsiders.
Illusion of unanimity.	Invite outsiders to join discussions periodically.

gratifying if there was a simple answer to this but, just as so many things can go wrong with the workings of a group, so many factors contribute to group effectiveness. To make matters worse, a small change in one variable can turn an effective group into an ineffective one. A poorly ventilated room or one absent member can make all the difference.

The first view of the effective group to be examined is that of Charles Handy. In his book *Understanding Organisations* (Handy, 1985) he divides the determinants of group effectiveness into three sets of factors:

(1) The givens – the group, the task and the environment.
(2) The intervening factors – leadership style, processes and procedures, motivation.
(3) The outcomes – productivity, member satisfaction.

The givens are largely unchangeable while the intervening factors can be changed to enhance group performance. Using the outline model in Illustration 3.5 we can look in more detail at these determinants.

The group size is likely to impact on effectiveness if it is either too small or too large. Too small and the necessary range of skills and knowledge will not be present, too large and the group will fracture into subgroups with conflicting interests. There are no magic numbers for group size though Handy suggests that the small group of five to seven seems best for high levels of participation and involvement, and that groups over twenty will be less effective showing lower morale and greater absenteeism. Membership of the group matters in terms of individual abilities and the general compatibility of the people. In any group there is a mixture of group and individual objectives being pursued. If these objectives conflict to any great degree then effectiveness can be lessened as 'point-scoring and 'politicking' come to the fore. As we saw earlier, groups go through certain stages of formation and will only become a really successful unit if these stages are negotiated.

The task is a variable in that groups may be required to take on activities that vary considerably. Some decisions are more amenable to group participation and others less

Illustration 3.5 Handy's approach to group effectiveness

The givens	*The group*	*The task*	*The environment*
	Size	Nature	Norms and expectations
	Member characteristics	Criteria for effectiveness	Leader position
	Individual objectives	Salience of the task	Inter-group relations
	Stage of development	Clarity of the task	Physical environment
Intervening factors	Choice of leadership		
	Processes and procedures		
	Motivation		
The outcomes	Productivity		
	Member satisfaction		

well suited. Just as tasks vary so will the criteria for effectiveness. A brainstorming group may be judged on the number of ideas generated while a production-planning group have to arrive at the single best plan. The salience of the task is significant in that if a task is felt to be important rather than trivial the group is more likely to be effective. Equally significant is the clarity of the task in that a clear, unambiguous task can be dealt with by structured leadership and clear direction. Less clear tasks will make greater demands on time, compatibility and supportive leadership.

The environment consists of a range of factors – physical, psychological and sociological. The norms and expectations of group performance will result from the ways in which organisations develop ways of working, styles of meetings, methods of reporting and mechanisms of co-ordination. Groups will tend to conform with these established ways whether or not they are most suitable to their operation. The leader's position here refers to the amount of power of the leader. The greater the amount of power the greater the freedom the leader has to adopt a particular style of decision making. Intergroup relations play a role in that the status of the group is significant. A high status is normally associated with a more effective group because not only does it mean that decisions are more likely to be accepted by those outside the group, it also means that high status improves morale and creates a strong desire for members to stay involved in the group. The physical settings in which the group operates should not be overlooked. Factors such as noise, physical proximity of group members, the isolation of the group and comfort are all variables that can aid or hamper group effectiveness.

The 'intervening factors' are as important as the 'givens' in determining effectiveness. In that they can be changed more easily than the givens they may be seen as more important to the person who wishes to improve the effectiveness of a particular group. Leadership style can be modified to meet the demands of the situation. Handy speaks of the 'best fit' approach – the need to adapt the leadership style to the task, to the requirements of subordinates, and the leader's own natural preferences.

The 'processes and procedures' relate to both the task the group has to undertake and the group maintenance functions which facilitate group operation. Task functions are seen as initiating, information seeking, diagnosing, opinion seeking, evaluating and decision making. Maintenance functions are encouraging, compromising, peace-keeping, clarifying, summarising and standard setting. These are necessary functions in any effective group. Motivation of individuals to feel like a team, think like a team and act like a team will contribute to effectiveness, and the absence of such motivation can only reduce performance.

The outcome for productivity, the degree to which goals are met and member satisfaction provided, the degree to which the members of the group achieve their individual and group objectives, these are not only significant as measures of group effectiveness they will also feed back into the future operations of the group and success will contribute more to future effectiveness than will failure.

A more qualitative view of the effective group is presented by Douglas McGregor (1960) and is given in Illustration 3.6.

Illustration 3.6 McGregor's analysis of the effective group

(1) The atmosphere tends to be informal,comfortable, relaxed.
(2) There is a lot of discussion in which virtually everyone participates but it remains pertinent to the task of the group.
(3) The task or objective of the group is well understood and accepted by members. There will be free discussion of the objective at some point until it is formulated in such a way that the members of the group can commit themselves to it.
(4) The members listen to each other. Every idea is given a hearing. People do not appear to be afraid of being foolish by putting forth a creative thought even if it seems fairly extreme.
(5) There is disagreement. Disagreements are not suppressed or overridden by premature group action. The reasons are carefully examined and the group seeks to resolve them rather than to dominate the dissenter.
(6) Most decisions are reached by a kind of consensus in which it is clear that everybody is in general agreement and willing to go along. Formal voting is at a minimum. The group does not accept a simple majority as a proper basis for action.
(7) Criticism is frequent, frank and relatively comfortable. There is little evidence of personal attack, either openly or in a hidden fashion.
(8) People are free in expressing their feelings as well as their ideas both on the problem and the group's operation.
(9) When action is taken, clear assignments are made and accepted.
(10) The chairman of the group does not dominate it, nor does the group defer unduly to him. In fact, the leadership shifts from time to time depending on the circumstances. There is little evidence of a struggle for power as the group operates. The issue is not who controls but how to get the job done.
(11) The group is self-conscious about its own operation.

McGregor's views stress the human dimension of group decision making. If the situation is right for the people then good decisions are likely to follow. This can be questioned in terms of the technical and procedural aspects of decision making but there is nonetheless value in McGregor's observations.

A third view can be found in the work of Hall (1971) who identified the behaviours which characterised effective teams and presented them in the form of decision rules shown in Illustration 3.7.

Consensus is a decision process for making full use of available resources for resolving conflicts creatively. Illustration 3.7 shows some guidelines for achieving consensus.

THE ORGANISATIONAL CONTEXT OF DECISIONS

In this section the focus is on the internal environment of the organisation and, in turn, we shall examine the significance of organisational structure, organisational leadership, politics and conflict in organisations, and the concepts of organisational climate and culture. Though all these factors have implications beyond the study of decision making the analysis here will be about the practical and theoretical relevance of organisational variables to the decision-making process.

Illustration 3.7 Effective teams

(1) Present your position as lucidly and logically as possible, but listen to other members' reactions and consider them carefully before you press your point.
(2) Do not assume that someone must win and someone must lose when discussion reaches a stalemate. Instead, look for the next most acceptable alternative for all parties.
(3) Do not change your mind simply to avoid conflict and to reach agreement and harmony. When agreement comes too quickly and easily, be suspicious. Explore the reasons and be sure everyone accepts the solution for basically similar or complementary reasons. Yield only to positions that have objective and logically sound foundations.
(4) Avoid conflict-reducing techniques such as majority voting, averages, coin flips and bargaining. When a dissenting member finally agrees, don't feel that he must be rewarded by having his own way at some later point.
(5) Differences of opinion are natural and expected. Seek them out and try to involve everyone in the decision process. Disagreements can help the group's decision because, with a wide range of information and opinions, there is a greater chance that the group will hit upon more adequate solutions.

Illustration 3.8 Fantasy Games

Fantasy Games was founded fifteen years ago to design, manufacture and retail games. The games are distinctive and a large part of their appeal arises from the figures that are used in the games. These are die-cast figures based upon a blend of themes taken from science fiction, medieval warfare and the occult. Sets of figures, elaborate rule books, gaming boards and, more recently, software, combine to provide a range of products for the games enthusiast.

A large part of the appeal of each game depends upon its figures. Overall the figures for the various games have a style that is distinctively 'Fantasy Games'. The figures require design work that is original and creative but follows the established themes and style of Fantasy Games.

The company is wholly owned by Ben Goodwin. Mr Goodwin founded the company, designed some of the first games and has managed the company's development and growth to its present size where it has over one hundred employees and exports to eight countries. Ben Goodwin views himself as a manager who, in a highly competitive industry, focuses upon continuing the company's commercial success.

All design work is carried out in-house. The designers are largely art school trained with a gift for the 'Fantasy' style. Overall the twelve designers were principally attracted to the company by the opportunity to use their skills. However, they are a mixed group. One or two are loners, rarely speaking to anyone at the company. Others share their social lives. While most wish to continue modelling for Fantasy Games others feel that their work is becoming repetitive and that their creative abilities are fading.

What advice would you give Ben Goodwin?

ORGANISATION STRUCTURE

Tall *versus* flat organisations

A basic dimension of the structure of an organisation is whether it is 'tall' or 'flat'. This refers to the number of levels of authority that exist in an organisation and can be seen in Fig. 3.4. It should be noted, however, that tall and flat are relative terms and perhaps it would be more accurate to talk of 'taller' and 'flatter' structures.

For the purpose of decision making, claims are made for the advantages of both the tall and flat designs. The high level of specialisation in the tall organisation should ensure that specialist skills and knowledge can be brought to bear; group decision making can be facilitated by the existence of small, homogeneous specialist groups; there is less likelihood of duplication of effort; and managers with fewer subordinates to manage will be able to focus their attention on the decision-making process. With clear lines of communication, information will be both accurate and accessible, making for speedier

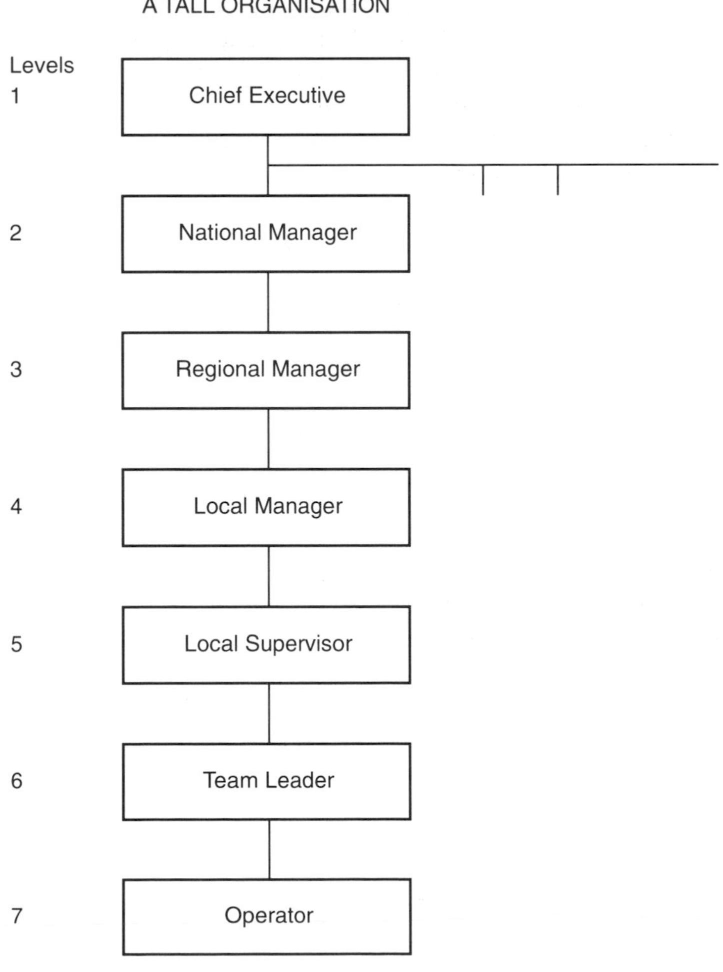

Fig. 3.4 A tall organisational structure

and more reliable decisions. These claims are not always found in practice where the problems of the tall structure have been the subject of greater comment than its benefits.

The tendency for the tall organisation to become over-bureaucratic and bogged down in red tape is well recorded. Communications, instead of being aided, are hindered as the status barriers in the organisation provide barriers and sources of distortion in the transmission of information. Specialisation, while it may aid specialist decisions, can impede the taking of more general or strategic decisions. There is a risk of people only being aware of their part of the problem and adopting a biased approach to the decision in hand. Bringing all the interested parties together for a decision can be a slow and expensive task. The tall organisation can create a wide distance between those at the top and those at the bottom of the structure creating, not only communication difficulties, but also problems of motivation and morale.

The flat organisation (Fig. 3.5) is perceived by many observers as providing a superior form of structure. The phrase 'a leaner, fitter, flatter organisation' has considerable currency among modern managers as they seek to gain the benefits of moving from a taller to a flatter structure. What are these benefits? Decisions can be made quickly by people who have a good general understanding of the issues involved. There will be a high level of delegation which will force decision making down the organisation to levels where appropriate expertise can be applied. More people will participate in a decision giving a higher degree of commitment to both the decision itself and its implementation. Morale will increase through greater involvement and the reduction in status barriers. Management will find it easier to stay in touch with the concerns and problems of

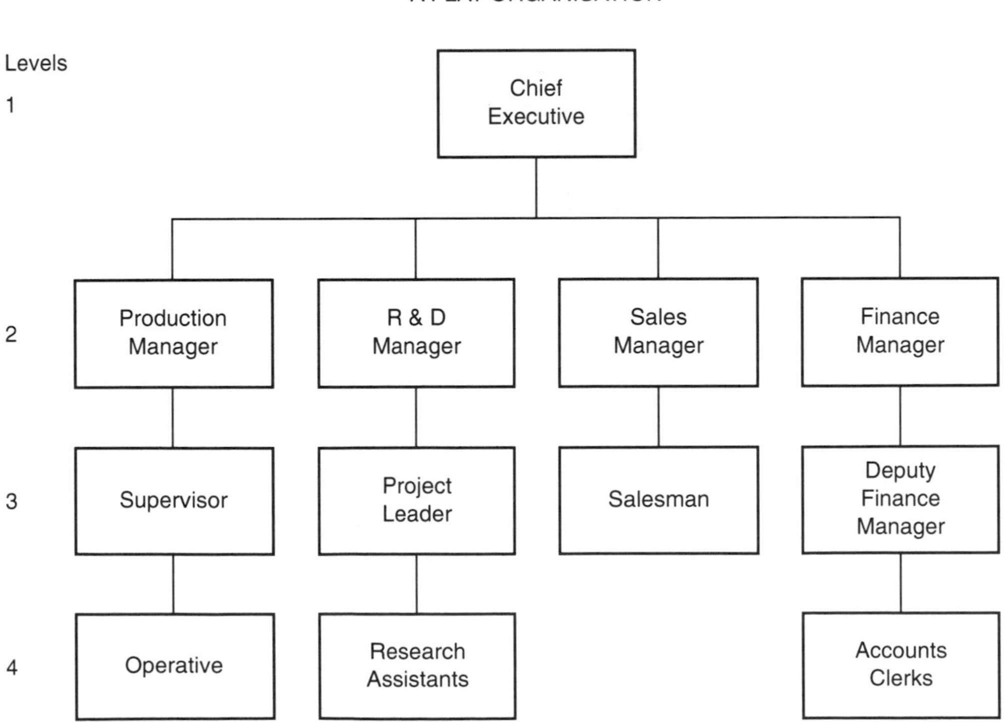

Fig. 3.5 A flat organisational structure

employees. Communication will be more face-to-face, which will minimise loss and distortion and give the benefit of speed and immediate feedback. Overall, the costs of decision making are reduced with fewer people involved and fewer problems from co-ordinating disparate groups.

Possible problems of the flat organisation are: the loss of specialist input to decisions and the increased pressure placed on the individual manager to keep himself informed and possibly to have to take decisions where there is less than a full understanding of the problem. If the motive for having a flat organisation is primarily one of cost then it is quite possible that savings might be sought in other areas, such as market research or computer software, which could impede the making of effective decisions. Morale might rise but this could be offset by higher levels of stress resulting from increased responsibilities. Such stress is likely to impede clear thinking and a logical style of decision making.

On balance, the flat structure does appear to have qualities which make it superior to the tall in the making of decisions. Decision making in terms of cost, speed, accuracy and the maintenance of morale will be facilitated by avoiding an excessive number of levels in the organisation. However the relative nature of the terms 'tall' and 'flat' must be borne in mind and there are certainly no magic numbers available to determine what is the optimum number of levels for any organisational structure.

Centralised *versus* decentralised organisations

A second, related, structural question is whether decision making is best served by a centralised or decentralised organisation. At first appearance the centralised organisation would seem to have advantages. It has the potential to make speedy and clear decisions which otherwise might be delayed and be the outcome of a compromise between diffused interests. The possibilities for specialisation are greater so that specialist knowledge and skills are available for decision making. Decisions are likely to be cheaper to take because of the economies of scale and a reduction in overhead costs. By preventing subunits becoming too independent, the centralised organisation can hope to minimise conflicts and 'politicking' between its members. The centralised organisation should find it easier to implement a standard policy so that decisions fit in clearly and appropriately with the overall mission of the organisation.

Despite these potential gains, many observers have stressed the dangers of over-centralisation. Centralised organisations will necessarily be taller rather than flatter and thus demonstrate the problems we examined earlier. In addition, there will often be a mechanistic style of decision, making the organisation less sensitive to the need for flexible responses. There is a great danger of remoteness and impersonality which can reflect in poor decisions which people will implement only with reluctance.

It is not surprising that the stress in modern organisations has been towards a policy of decentralisation. Firms such as ICI and Courtauld have in recent years been restructured so that they are now based on much more autonomous units than previously. The advantages of decentralisation are seen in terms of enabling decisions to be made much closer to the operational level of work where questions of both information and implementation can best be addressed. The skills of decision making are developed, through delegation, to a wide range of managers who benefit in terms of career development, motivation and involvement. The diseconomies of scale take over at a certain level of centralisation. The central body becomes too far removed from the day-to-day issues that concern managers in the subunits, and decentralisation becomes the obvious and necessary remedy.

Matrix *versus* line structure

The final structural aspect to be discussed here is the debate about the relative merits for decision making of the matrix structure and the line structure. The basic distinction between the two types can be seen in Figs. 3.6 and 3.7.

Figure 3.6 shows the simplest form of line organisation. This is relatively rare and will normally be found in some modified form in the larger organisation where staff functions are introduced into the structure to provide specialist support and advice to the line management. However the basic principles of the line structure still apply. There is a direct line of command from the top to the bottom of the organisation, direct lines of authority and responsibility, clear lines of communication and the functional arrangement of departments on a hierarchical basis.

The matrix organisation (Fig. 3.7), in contrast, is structured in such a way as to stress the integration of activities. It combines functional departments similar to those found in a line organisation with units which seek to integrate those functions. Thus a company such as Heinz will have Brand Managers who will co-ordinate all activities relating to their product or product group. In other organisations this integrating function may be filled by a Project Manager or a Territory Manager. In all cases the role of these managers within the matrix is, through planning and negotiating with functional departments, to achieve the particular objectives associated with their product, project, territory or whatever responsibility has been assigned.

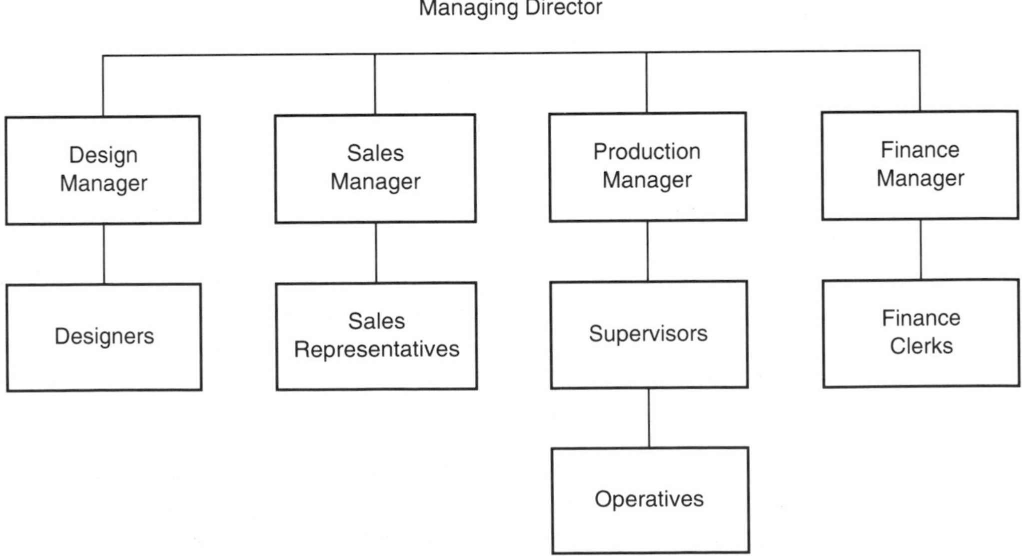

Fig. 3.6 A simple line structure

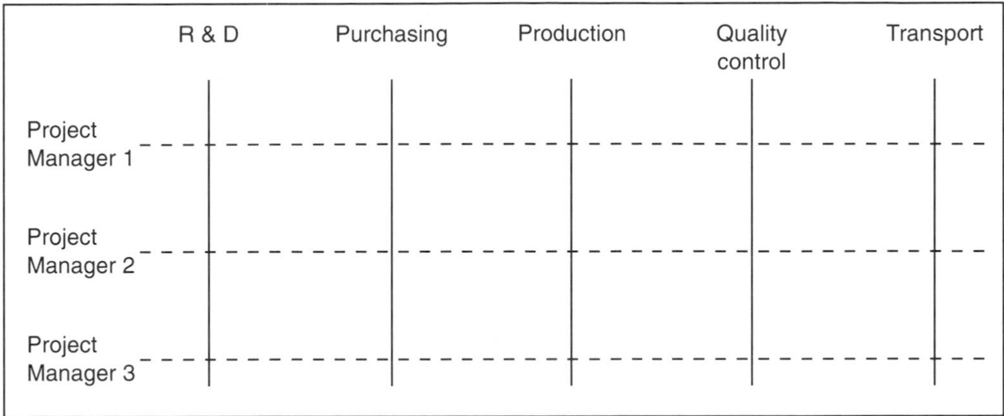

Fig. 3.7 A matrix structure

Line organisation offers the decision maker simplicity. Roles are clear, authority and responsibility are specified and, in theory, decision making should flow easily and effectively from such an arrangement. This is not always the case in practice. The degree of specialisation into purely functional departments is the most observed deficiency. The particular interests and knowledge of the department can overwhelm the more general interests of the organisation, its clients and customers. The criteria for a good decision can become simply 'does it serve the interests of the department?'

The matrix organisation is seen as a means of overcoming these limitations. It enhances integration and the sharing of knowledge providing a basis for good decision making. It becomes possible to take decisions in response to changing threats and opportunities through the necessary involvement of all interested parties. It is also claimed that the matrix form will lead to a greater willingness to accept and implement decisions.

These claims are not always realised in a matrix structure. Seeing it as complex and unwieldy Peters and Waterman (1982) state:

> People are not sure who they should report to for what. The organisation gets paralysed because the structure not only does not make priorities clear, it automatically dilutes priorities. In effect it says to people down the line, 'everything is important; pay attention to everything'. The message is paralysing.

It would appear, in the light of this criticism, that rather than bad decisions being made in a matrix organisation, no decisions would be made. The organisation would be consumed with the problems of internal co-ordination and, lacking clear priorities, decisions would be avoided. But despite these strong criticisms the matrix organisation is still to be found operating with success in project-based organisations.

The debate over line versus matrix continues. For decision making to operate effectively the stress must be on simplicity of form and to that end the basic line structure has advantages over the matrix in terms of the speed, clarity and control of the decision-making process.

The discussion of organisational structure and the question of the most appropriate form for decision making continues. Such is the nature of social invention that it would not be surprising to find new structures being developed and new exciting claims made for their effectiveness. However, we should not forget the importance of having an appropriate structure and the consequences of having a badly designed structure. As Child (1988) points out:

> There are a number of problems which so often mark the struggling organisation. These are low motivation and morale, *late and inappropriate decisions*, conflict and lack of co-ordination, rising costs and generally a poor response to new opportunities and external changes. *Structural deficiencies* can play a part in exacerbating all these problems.

ORGANISATION AND MANAGEMENT STYLE

Whatever structure an organisation has, the general style or approach to decision making will vary from individual to individual. Some managers will be autocratic, preferring to take and impose decisions themselves, others will be more participative and will defer decision making until everyone is consulted, and yet others will take a 'hands off' approach leaving decision making to their subordinates. These differences have led to a discussion of whether or not there is a right and a wrong style to adopt when making a decision. Can we identify an optimal style which will inevitably lead to better decisions being made? Does decision making style matter at all, or is it a key variable affecting the quality of the decision?

We will examine these questions by looking at three views of leadership in management which offer differing perspectives and have each been influential in shaping views on this subject. The first of these is referred to as the *Traitist approach* because it suggests that to be an effective decision maker the manager should possess certain basic traits of personality. Rather like the 'great man' theory of history it proposes that effective decision makers are born and not made. To those readers who wish to improve their decision-making abilities by reading this book this view offers cold comfort. You either have the traits or you do not. Training and education can only make a minimal impact on your abilities as a decision maker.

The popularity of the traitist explanation is probably due to its simplicity. The answer to the question of how to be a successful decision maker is to be found by looking at a series of historically successful figures, known for their decision-making abilities. By comparison and analysis of the traits that they have in common the recipe for identifying the good decision maker is revealed. Two such sets of traits are shown below.

Leadership traits
(Kirkpatrick and Locke, 1991)

Drive, achievement, energy, tenacity, initiative.
Leadership Motivation.
Honesty and Integrity.
Self-confidence (including emotional stability).

Cognitive ability.
Knowledge of the business.
Other traits of lesser significance: charisma, creativity/originality, flexibility.

(Stogdill 1974)

Adaptability.
Adjustment (normality).
Aggressiveness and assertiveness.
Dominance.
Emotional balance and control.
Independence (nonconformity).
Originality and creativity.
Personal integrity (ethical conduct).
Self-confidence.

The value of this viewpoint is perhaps more apparent than real. While it may be useful as a means of identifying potential, and recruiting putative decision makers, it also has its limitations. The basic objection to this approach is that it is just as possible to note the variety of traits among leaders. Some of the most successful leaders in history have been described as neurotic, insane, epileptic, humourless, narrow-minded, unjust and authoritarian. Other objections to the traitist view are its vagueness, the lack of a generally agreed set of traits, occasional contradictions, the bias in selection of examples of great leaders, and its inherently conservative tendencies. Once the traits have been agreed all future leaders and decision makers will be of the same ilk with no chance for those without the traits to show their abilities. In this way there is a danger of the traitist perspective being little more than a self-fulfilling prophesy.

The so-called *Behavioural* view offers a different perspective. Here the successful decision maker is seen as exhibiting a particular set of behaviours that lead to good decisions and *vice versa*. This behaviour is commonly referred to as leadership style or decision-making style. For example, a traditional means of classifying styles is:

(a) Autocratic.
(b) Democratic.
(c) Laissez-faire.

Though the behavioural approach recognises a variety of styles, nonetheless, writers have most frequently extolled the virtues of the democratic style. This has led to the idea that perhaps there is one best way of approaching any decision, and that style is the important variable.

A very influential example of this is to be found in the work of Likert (1961). As a result of empirical studies he was able to associate style of management with high and low productivity and suggested the need to adopt more participative styles of decision making. Likert classified behaviours into four styles:

System 1: Exploitative Autocratic
Here the manager has no trust or confidence in subordinates, imposes decisions, never delegates, motivates by threat and engages in little communication or teamwork with subordinates.

System 2: Benevolent Authorative
The manager has superficial, condescending confidence and trust in subordinates,

imposes decisions, never delegates, motivates by reward, and sometimes involves subordinates in problem solving though in a paternalistic manner.

System 3: Participative
The manager has incomplete confidence and trust in subordinates, listens to them but controls decision making, motivates by reward and some involvement, and uses the ideas of subordinates constructively.

System 4: Democratic
The manager has complete confidence and trust in subordinates, allows them to make decisions for themselves, motivates by reward for achieving goals set by participation, and shares ideas and opinions.

Likert's research shows that the effective manager adopts System 3 or System 4. Again the suggestion is that effective decision making is best served by a democratic style.

The strengths of the behavioural approach are its recognition of a variety of decision-making styles and the implication that people can learn to adopt a more effective style. In this way it does appear to be a significant advance on the traitist view. It can, however, be criticised on both practical and theoretical grounds. The active decision maker will often say that it is impractical in that the demands of the job make this approach too slow and cumbersome when faced by business realities. In theoretical terms, it is difficult to accept that all successful decisions must be taken in a democratic manner and that there is only the one best way. Both individuals and organisations choose to take decisions in particular ways and clearly success is linked with factors other than style.

A third approach seeks to overcome the limitations of both the trait and behavioural viewpoints. It is the *Contingency* perspective which, most simply put, suggests that the decision-making style must be tailored to meet the demands of the particular situation in which the decision is being taken. In other words there is no right person or right style for all decisions, it all depends on situational variables. The right personality traits and decision-making style can prove highly successful in one situation but disastrous in another. At one level this is a common-sense approach, for example, to go through the full democratic process when faced with a raging fire in a building is likely to add to the disaster rather than reduce it. On the other hand it is not always easy to recognise what are the situational or contingent factors that make one approach more suitable than another. Among the writers on contingency theory there is little agreement as to what these factors are. By looking at two differing classifications of what these contingent factors might be it is possible to see this problem.

Fiedler (1967), in his contingency theory of leadership, provides a way of analysing the situational factors which is focused on the manager's basic approach to managing people. To do this he measures their least preferred co-worker (LPC) score. This is obtained by asking mangers to rate how they view the person with whom they could work least well. Those who rate them negatively and do not see any redeeming features get a low LPC score and are seen as task-oriented. Those with high LPC scores are those who see positive values in those they dislike and are said to be relations-oriented. Their effectiveness as leaders is then seen as dependent on three sets of contingent factors:

(1) The extent to which the task is structured.
(2) The leader's position power.
(3) The nature of the relationships between the leader and follower.

To illustrate the relationship between the LPC scores and these factors Fiedler identifies three sets of conditions under which a leader may have to work.

Condition 1

The task is highly structured.
The leader's position power is high.
Subordinates feel that their relationships with the boss are good.

Here the task-oriented (low LPC score) leaders get good results. Conversely the relationship-oriented leader gets poor results. The task-oriented individuals are better suited because they will concentrate on performance knowing relationships do not require attention because they are good already. The relationship-oriented manager is inappropriate because, wishing to focus on relationships and finding them good, it is possible to take subordinates for granted and then concentrate on other, personal, objectives.

Condition 2

The task is unstructured.
The leader's position power is low.
Subordinates feel that their relationships with the boss are moderately good.

Relationship-oriented managers get the best results in this situation because of the importance of interpersonal concerns in achieving tasks. The task-oriented manager is likely to get poor results here.

Condition 3

The task is unstructured.
The leader's position power is low.
Subordinates feel that their relationships with the boss are poor.

Fiedler states that task-oriented leaders get the best results under these very unfavourable circumstances because they will get impatient, try to structure the task, ignore resistance from subordinates, reduce ambiguities in the work and hence get good performance. The relationship-oriented will tend to ignore important issues associated with the task and avoid taking what might prove to be unpopular decisions.

For the decision maker the implications of Fiedler's theory are that it is necessary to identify and analyse the organisational, contextual features and then adopt the decision-making approach to the particular context.

A similar approach to Fiedler can be found in the work of Kolb, Rubin and MacIntyre (1979) who suggest that in choosing any course of action the leader or decision maker must consider a range of situational variables or, as they call them forces, determining a leader's choice of strategy.

Before acting the leader should examine three sets of variables:

(1) Forces in the leader

The leader's value system
Leadership inclination

Tolerances of ambiguity
Assessment of own and the group's competence

(2) Forces in the subordinate group

Need for dependency or independence
Readiness to assume responsibility
Interest in the problem
Identification with organisational goals
Knowledge and experience
Tolerance of ambiguity
Expectations

(3) Forces in the situation

The type of organisation
The nature of the task
Pressure of time
General social, political and economic milieu.

Again the conclusion is that decision-making approaches must vary in line with different configurations of these forces. Though the contingency approach is capable of providing an explanation of why there is no one best way, and why effective decisions are taken in a widely different range of approaches, it also has its problems. It proposes that to adopt the right style of decision making the decision maker must be able to identify the relevant factors, make a correct analysis of them in their particular situation, and be flexible enough to respond exactly as the situation demands. As we see there is no great agreement as to what the factors are, analysis is likely to be a complex and lengthy process and people do not always find it easy to modify their behaviour constantly as situations change.

However, out of the three approaches we have examined the contingency approach is currently fashionable and does have advantages over the trait and behavioural perspectives. For decision makers it is valuable to note the requirement for some flexibility in their approaches to problem solving and the attendant decisions. It does rid us of the simplified 'one best way' approach, and presents a more realistic view of the challenges facing the decision maker.

CONFLICT AND ORGANISATIONAL POLITICS

There are many possible ways of explaining why a particular decision is taken. A perspective that is neglected in traditional approaches to decision making is the one which sees many decisions emerging as a result of conflicting interests and political behaviour in organisations. In some way decision making is seen as a rational and logical process above such things as departmental rivalries and personal quests for power. In practice these sorts of factors frequently play a role in decision making. As we shall see, organisations have a strong propensity for conflict and political behaviour, and many decisions would be unintelligible without an understanding of the part played by such factors.

Illustration 3.9 Leading Microsoft

Bill Gates was born into a well-to-do Seattle family; his father was a successful corporate lawyer, his mother a director on the board of a number of companies. Gates's intellectual abilities and commercial drive were demonstrated in his mid-teens through the successful start-up of a company selling software to help cities generate traffic statistics. A student of mathematics at Harvard, Bill Gates dropped out feeling that pure mathematics was a field in which he could not compete. 'I wasn't sure if after twenty years I'd make enough progress to feel really good about that'. 'There are some guys who have done mathematics through history who are even smarter than ... are just incredibly smart, relative to my abilities.'

As with any personality that becomes the subject of media interest, there are contradictions in what becomes known. A sense of humour, sentimentality, a normal guy. As a professional person a more distinguishing set of traits are apparent. Bill Gates possesses a high level of physical and intellectual energy. He has been described as a workaholic whose view of life is framed by an intensely competitive attitude, never-ending ambition and a single-minded drive for success. 'A bad personality and a great intellect' is the verdict of Tom Cheatham director of the Harvard Computer Center.

The success of Microsoft, the company that Gates founded, was based upon MS-DOS (Microsoft Disc Operating System), developed by the company for the IBM PC. In the following twelve years Bill Gates has become the richest man in America, with an office in Building 8 on the Microsoft campus at 1, Microsoft Way. The offices on the Microsoft campus have an informal atmosphere and are adorned with soft drink cans, mobiles and wind-chimes. Dress is informal and people may talk sitting on the floor or with their feet resting on the desk. An atmosphere that is a deliberate clone of the universities the employees have been recruited from.

Daily thousands of electronic messages criss-cross the campus, the globe and the organisation's structure, changing the meaning of the corporate meeting. The orientation to work is intense and demanding. Yet, in a software department that has grown by a factor of thirty or forty, turning out products on lean management assembly lines, Bill Gates, the Chairman, will still appear amongst the programmers, tackling technical problems, 'like a Michelangelo or an Einstein who happens to be working in computers'.

(Adapted from *The Sunday Times*, November 1992)

Conflict in organisations

Conflict occurs when individuals or groups perceive their objectives to be mutually exclusive to the objectives of another individual or group. Typically it can be described as a win–lose situation where if one party achieves its goals the other party must fail to achieve theirs. For example, if there is a fixed budget for new staff in an organisation and both the Marketing department and the Production department want all of the budget to increase their own department's staff, then clearly they cannot both get their wishes. Conflict, as in this example, normally occurs when there is a scarcity of some commodity. This commodity can be something concrete like raw materials, machines or rooms, or it can be intangible such as prestige, influence or status. Where there is a plentiful supply of such commodities, conflict is likely to be minimal. Where there is scarcity, real or imagined, the potential for conflict is great.

In the context of decision making, conflict can show itself in many ways and take a variety of forms. The following classification of types of conflict gives examples of how a particular form of conflict can affect a decision.

(1) *Hierarchical conflict*. This refers to any disagreement between superiors and subordinates which reflects their position in the formal hierarchy of the organisation. Thus a decision to alter the terms of employment by a management against the wishes of employees would lead to hierarchical conflict.
(2) *Functional conflict*. Conflicts between specialist departments or functions in an organisation are common. An example of this can be seen in the decision of a Quality Control department to reject a production batch when the Production Department wishes the batch to be dispatched to the customer.
(3) *Line/Staff conflict*. Due to the different organisational roles of line and staff departments, conflicts can easily occur, e.g., staffing decisions taken by a Personnel Department (a staff function) can be opposed by a Production Department (a line function).
(4) *Formal/Informal conflict*. Organisations develop ways of doing things through custom and practice that are at variance with the formal rules. When decisions are taken to enforce formal rules and override informal practices, disputes often arise, e.g., where the custom has been to allow a flexible approach to time-keeping and the decision is taken to strictly enforce the contractual hours of employment.
(5) *Institutionalised conflict*. If there are likely to be conflicts of interest between different parties, often policies, procedures and practices are established to enable those parties to live with the conflict. A grievance procedure is an example of this in many organisations.
(6) *Status conflict*. Just as in wider society people are concerned with prestige and the esteem of others, so organisations are affected by people's concerns about their status. A decision to reallocate car parking spaces may be perceived as a threat to status and conflict will follow.
(7) *Political conflict*. Decisions may have implications for the power of an individual or group in an organisation and, as we will discuss later, there is a political dimension to most decision making. Power is a scarce resource and when, for example, a decision is made to cut a Research and Development Budget, it may be seen as weakening the influence of the department, and considerable politicking will follow.

Having looked at the potential grounds for conflict and the range of forms it might take, it is reasonable to assume that conflict is likely to be an everyday part of organisational life. Though some early writers on management saw conflict as unnecessary, and an aberration in organisational activities, it is more realistic to see it as a normal occurrence. It is thus something which needs to be managed. Any notion that it can be eliminated and need never occur is not a feasible viewpoint and is a highly impractical approach for the decision maker.

For the student of decision making a vital question about organisational conflict is whether it is good or bad for effective decision making. At first sight it might appear to be largely destructive; it would distract the decision maker and distort outcomes. However, it might be said to aid decision making in that at least it highlights areas where decisions need to be made. This question can be examined in more detail by reference to Illustration 3.10.

Looking at the possible negative outcomes of organisational conflict it is clear that, at its worse, it can destroy an organisation. Where the parts cannot work together but consistently pull in opposite directions, this can lead either to no decisions being taken, or to such partisan decisions being taken that some parts of the organisation are undermined. An over-concern with conflict can be stressful, and a distraction away from the basic problems facing the organisation. The individual is less equipped to think clearly

Illustration 3.10 Decision making and conflict – the pros and cons

Potential benefits of conflict.	Potential harm of conflict.
Stimulate change and innovation.	Create stress and anxiety.
Identify problems and inefficiencies.	Distract from major goals.
Promote healthy competition	Cause destructive behaviours.
Create group cohesion.	Impair judgement through emotion.
Increase motivation.	Threaten teamwork and co-operation.
Raise standards of performance.	Make co-ordination of activities difficult.
Prevent complacency.	Make decisions too 'political'.
All leading to better decisions.	All leading to worse decisions.

about the issues and is likely to arrive at decisions with only a partial consideration of the evidence. Conflict can make people introspective, concerned with the internal affairs of the organisation, while changes in the external environment go unnoticed. Conflict can easily become personalised and personal enmities can develop where decision making becomes a process of defeating rivals and scoring points rather than of trying to arrive at the best decision for the organisation.

This examination of the dysfunctions of conflict might suggest that it can only damage effective decision making, but there is another side to the argument. Conflict can be claimed, not only to be inevitable but to be beneficial to decision making. Conflict is seen to be a necessary agent to stimulate change and innovation. Why bother to change when everyone is happy with things the way they are? Problems and inefficiencies in working will be highlighted by conflict whereas attempts to eliminate conflict can lead to such matters being swept under the carpet. Healthy competition and rivalry can lead to better decisions being made as attention is more clearly focused on the issues. Groups can become more cohesive and operate more effectively as teams, increasing both group and individual motivation. Standards of performance can rise as a result of a combination of these factors, and a commitment and concern to make better decisions will follow. Overall the risk of complacency and smugness is likely to be avoided.

The study of conflict has important implications for the decision maker. First, it is important to recognise its inevitability and the need to manage it rather than to try and avoid it. Secondly it can have significant harmful effects on decision making so that the control of conflict must be a part of the decision maker's role. Finally, and perhaps most importantly, the potential benefits of organisational conflict to the decision maker are great and, in managing conflict, it is vital to try and maximise those benefits.

Organisational politics

Increasing interest has been shown by decision-making writers on the form of conflict referred to as organisational politics. The normative model of decision making (Fig. 1.1) was based on a series of logical steps which were themselves based on rational analyses and procedures. The model ignored conflict in general and took no account of any political processes that might occur in arriving at a decision. Largely as a result of empirical studies of how decisions are actually taken in organisations, it is now commonly accepted that an understanding of political processes and behaviour is crucial to both decision-making theory and practice.

At a simple, intuitive level it appears that politics will play a significant part in decision making. Politics is concerned with the competition for power and power is a necessary attribute for any individual or group wishing to take and implement a decision. It is perhaps surprising that so little attention was given to this subject by early writers but contemporary authors show a much greater awareness of what is sometimes referred to as the 'micro-politics of organisational life'. (The term micro-politics is used to make the distinction between politics in the organisation and the 'macro-politics' of society at large).

In 1970 Zalenik wrote an influential article in the *Harvard Business Review* entitled *Power and Politics in Organisational Life*. In it he states: 'A sense of disbelief occurs when managers purport to make decisions in rationalistic terms while most observers know that politics and personalities play a significant if not overriding role'. Though people will seek to justify and explain their decisions as the outcome of a commonsense, rational approach, and deny the political dimension almost all studies of practical decision making have found some element of politicking in the decision-making process. Before going on to look at of some these studies and their conclusions it should be noted that there is a risk of going too far with political analysis. The view of organisational decision making in terms of individuals and groups, calculating and scheming for their own political ends, can lead to a rather paranoid perspective where the study of decisions is a continual digging away beneath the surface for plots and intrigues which may or may not be there. The concept of organisational politics is a metaphor based on general political behaviour and, as with most metaphors, there is a risk of over-extending it and it losing much of its value.

An early writer concerned with political manoeuvring in organisations was Dalton (1959) in his book *Men Who Manage*. This is an empirical investigation into conflict between managers, comparing and contrasting behaviour in two organisations. In particular, Dalton noted the political conflict between line and staff managers. Staff managers were younger than their colleagues in line management, frequently better qualified, but in career terms there were fewer levels in the organisation to which they could aspire. As a result staff managers tended to seek advancement through embroiling themselves in the politics of the organisation. A particular strategy Dalton noted was that of 'empire building' where staff managers sought to enlarge their own departments. Decisions were taken or avoided in terms of whether they helped or hindered this process of 'empire building'. Managers would intrigue, form alliances and coalitions in order to strengthen their power base. Dalton suggests that rational procedures were constantly subordinated to political interests.

An influential and important contribution to the discussion of decision making and politics is found in Pettigrew's book (1973) *The Politics of Organisational Life*. In it he looks at political conflicts between programmers and system analysts in a particular organisation. The programmers felt threatened by the new breed of trained system analysts and to deal with the threat they developed a four-point political strategy:

(1) *Deny the competence of outsiders*. Basically this consisted of saying that system analysts do not know what they are talking about and to get the real answers you have to deal with the programmers.
(2) *Protective myths*. For example, 'programmers cannot work under time constraints'. Based on other people's ignorance they were able to develop such myths which protected their status and working conditions.

(3) *Secrecy*. This simply meant keeping certain knowledge and skills within the programmers' group so that they would appear indispensable to the organisation.
(4) *Control of recruitment*. By recruiting like-minded people the cohesiveness of the group was maintained.

It is possible to generalise a conclusion from the study, that where a group feels threatened it will behave politically and develop a strategy which will either protect or expand its current power and status. The existence of such strategies has important implications for decision making. It provides one basis for understanding how certain decisions are arrived at, a way of interpreting deviations from the rational model, and helps to explain the popularity or unpopularity of decisions with different groups. Some would go further and say that to be an effective decision maker one must be politically active because to arrive at the desired decision one must navigate through these, often heavy, political waters.

Pettigrew, in a later part of his book, analyses the politics of a particular decision, the decision to purchase a new computer. The decision was technically the prerogative of senior management but the computer manager was able to ensure that the decision arrived at was to his liking, not by applying the traditional, rational model, but by politicking. In particular the computer manager was able to act as a 'gate-keeper' in the communication process. He controlled the flow of information to senior management, making sure that management saw data which supported his preferences and steered them away from alternatives. Though technically the decision rested with the senior management group, the decision was effectively taken by the computer manager through his manipulation of communication. They took their decision in the light of selective and filtered information and the final decision was due to the political skills of the computer manager rather than the outcome of the rational decision-making process.

Again there are important theoretical and practical implications in these findings. The rational model posits the availability of full and unbiased information if an optimal decision is to be reached. In reality it would appear that information is far from full and unbiased. Political interests and skills will cripple attempts to rely solely on the rational model. For the effective decision maker there is a need not only to be politically astute but also to make an interpretation of information rather than to take it at its face value.

Theorists have also played a part in bringing the political aspects of decision making to the fore. Though much remains to be done in incorporating the political dimension into a general theory of decision making there is, for example, a long tradition of seeing decisions as a product of a dominant coalition. March and Simon (1958), though not making political processes central to their theory of decision making, did recognise its significance. They saw the problems that arose when we talk of organisational goals and organisational decisions. People have goals and people take decisions so in any study of decision making it is vital to identify those individuals or groups who set the goals and make the decisions. They adopted the notion of the dominant coalition and viewed this group as the source of goals and major decisions in any organisation. This group is not represented on any organisation chart but emerges in the organisation as the result of a whole range of political processes. Groups with conflicting interests will compete, form alliances and cliques leading, at least temporarily, to the formation of a dominant coalition. The power to make decisions becomes vested in those who are most successful politically. This notion of the dominant coalition, though helpful, does perhaps miss out on the dynamics of organisational politics where there is an ongoing political process and continuing shifts in power. This means that decisions have to be seen not merely as the prerogative of the dominant coalition but also as strategies and tactics in the political game.

The study of political aspects of decision making is an important and traditionally neglected area. Not only do people act politically in the process of taking decisions but decisions themselves often have a political dimension. What may appear to be a technical decision, such as modifying a product or investing in new plant, can have a major effect on the power relationships between groups and individuals. To be an effective decision maker it is necessary both to possess the political skills to ensure acceptance of the decision, and to be fully aware of the political consequences of the decision when it is implemented.

ORGANISATIONAL CLIMATE AND CULTURE

In this final section on the organisational context of decision making the role of the climate and culture of the organisation is examined. They are both over-arching concepts which seek to generalise about the state of the whole organisation and the atmosphere or ambience in which decisions are taken.

Organisational climate can be defined as a set of attributes which can be perceived about a particular organisation and/or its subsystems that may be induced from the way that organisation and/or its subsystems deal with their members and the environment. More simply, using the meteorological analogy, climate is an attempt to describe the general conditions under which the organisation operates. Just as certain weather conditions are conducive to certain activities, e.g., snow for skiing or heat and sun for sunbathing, it may be possible to identify the organisational climate that is most conducive to effective decision making. Is there such a thing as a healthy climate for decision making?

Before we can try to answer that question it is necessary to look in more detail at what constitutes an organisational climate. Halpin and Croft (1962) identified eight factors:

(1) The consideration management has for people.
(2) The emphasis on getting work done.
(3) The emotional distance between managers and subordinates.
(4) The perception people have of social needs being met.
(5) The enjoyment people have from social relationships.
(6) The desire shown by management, through task-oriented behaviour, to motivate the workforce.
(7) The perception that people are merely 'going through the motions' to complete a task.
(8) The feeling people have of being burdened with busy work.

A more general approach is taken by Likert (1961) who lists six factors:

(1) *Communication flow*. How well do subordinates know what is going on? How receptive are superiors to communications from below? Are subordinates given enough information to do their job?
(2) *Decision making practices*. Are subordinates involved in the decision-making process? Is the know-how of personnel at all levels utilised?

(3) *Concern with people*. Does the organisation organise work activities sensibly, try to improve working conditions and show an interest in the individual's welfare?
(4) *Influence on the department*. Do low-level supervisors and employees with no subordinates have an influence on their department?
(5) *Technological adequacy*. Are equipment and resources well managed, and improved methods quickly adopted?
(6) *Motivation*. Do people in the organisation work hard for both extrinsic and intrinsic rewards, and are they encouraged to do so by the organisation?

From these two lists it is apparent that there is not a commonly agreed view of the detailed constituents of organisational climate. There are clear overlaps between them but also significant differences. This does inhibit any conclusions we might draw because different authors, while using the same term, are in fact talking about something different.

Another point to be noted is the inclusion of decision-making practices in Likert's list. The importance of this is that the relationship between decisions and climate is two way. Organisational climate will affect the way decisions are taken and it is also true that the ways of decision making in the organisation will have an impact on the sort of climate experienced. For example, to have a well-motivated workforce will aid decision making, but an autocratic style of decision making can weaken motivation.

What then constitutes a healthy organisational climate? Mullins (1993) suggests the following characteristics are typically exhibited by organisations with a healthy climate:

- The integration of organisational and personal goals.
- The most appropriate organisation structure based on the demands of the socio-technical system.
- Democratic functioning of the organisation with full opportunities for participation.
- Justice in treatment with equitable personnel and employee relations policies and practices.
- Mutual trust, consideration and support among different levels of the organisation.
- The open discussion of conflict with an attempt to avoid confrontation.
- Managerial behaviour and styles of leadership appropriate to the particular work situations.
- Acceptance of the psychological contract between the individual and the organisation.
- Recognition of people's needs and expectations at work and individual differences and attributes.
- Equitable systems of rewards based on positive recognition.
- Concern for the quality of life and job design.
- Opportunities for personal development and career progression.
- A sense of identity with, and loyalty to, the organisation and a feeling of being a valued and important member.

From these characteristics it is easy to see that the manner in which decisions are taken either will or will not contribute to a healthy climate. An authoritarian style will have negative effects and hardly represents the 'democratic functioning' and 'mutual trust' identified by Mullins. If an organisational climate is to be improved, attention must be given to all the factors and this will, of necessity, include approaches to decision making.

Will a healthy climate lead to more effective decisions being taken? The relationship here is more complex. First, we have to beware of the tautological answer which says good decisions are a part of a healthy climate and a healthy climate creates good decisions.

Second, the criteria for judging the effectiveness of a decision are dependent upon a range of potential factors such as: is it quite conceivable that effective decisions could be taken in an unhealthy climate? To this extent, it is not so much a problem of defining climate as being clear about what we mean by an effective decision. The third problem is concerned with the assessment of the healthy climate. There is no agreement as to how it can be measured and this makes it difficult to argue that the healthier the climate the more effective the decision.

Research shows that a healthy climate is no guarantee of organisational effectiveness, but that it provides a basis on which people can work together in a motivated, purposive manner, and will create a spirit of co-operation and trust on which good performance can be built. For the decision maker it will be easier to operate in an organisation with a healthy climate. People will be more forthcoming with information and support, more willing to accept decisions that they do not totally agree with and take a genuine interest in the decision-making process. This creates conditions that are very favourable to the decision maker, but to make effective decisions there is a need to add all the skills, knowledge and techniques of decision making to the situation if anything like optimal decisions are to be reached.

ORGANISATIONAL CULTURE

The term 'culture' has its origins in the work of social anthropologists and refers to 'the complex whole, including knowledge, belief, art, law, morals, custom and the many other capabilities and habits acquired by a person as a member of society'. The term was used to generalise about total societies, the external environment of organisations. However, it has become increasingly applied to organisations themselves where each organisation is seen as possessing its own distinctive culture which provides not only a basis for understanding organisational behaviour but is also a key factor as a determinant of organisational success. Decision-making practices can be observed as a part of an organisation's culture and, like the concept of organisational climate, the question is asked whether there is an appropriate culture for effective decision making?

There is no shortage of definitions of organisational culture. It has been described as 'the dominant values espoused by an organisation', 'the philosophy that guides an organisation's policy towards employees and customers', 'the basic assumptions and beliefs that are shared by the members of an organisation'. More simply, culture has been referred to as 'the way things are done around here' and 'it is what keeps the wagons rolling west'. Despite the variety of definitions, writers on organisation theory have found the concept of culture a valuable device for looking at what really goes on in an organisation.

In every organisation there evolves, over time, a culture of more or less shared beliefs about how things are and should be done, which gives the organisation its particular identity. Just as individuals have distinctive personalities, organisations have their own distinctive culture. One organisation may be friendly, relaxed and informal while another may be highly formal, hostile and aloof. A view of the main varieties of organisational cultures is offered by Handy (1985) who writes of:

(1) *The power culture.* Here there is only one major source of power and influence. This is most likely to be the owners in a small organisation or the major shareholders in a larger organisation. In this type of organisation there are few procedures or rules of a formal kind. The major decisions are taken by key individuals, using broad guidelines and knowledge of what has been done in the past. This form is seen as being very adaptive to changing conditions, though its success will be dependent on the abilities of the key decision maker. The power culture is most likely to be found in smaller organisations.

(2) *The role culture.* In this version of culture there is a formality of organisation structure, procedures and rules which determine what is to be done and how decisions are to be made. In the role culture people are required to behave strictly in terms of the role defined in their job description. The responsibility and authority of jobs are strictly delineated and boundaries are never to be crossed. Individual personalities are not important, it is the job that really matters. This culture is most often associated with large bureaucracies and though it may operate effectively in a stable environment it can have problems in surviving dramatic change.

(3) *The task culture.* Task culture is most often found in organisations where teams of employees operate together to achieve particular tasks. The teams exist until the task is completed and are then disbanded and their members assigned to other teams. This sort of culture makes the team the key decision-making body. It is to be found most often in rapidly changing organisations and is frequently associated with the matrix structure.

(4) *The person culture.* Less common than the other three types of culture, the person culture is characterised by the fact that the organisation exists to satisfy the requirements of its members, like a commune or co-operative. Decisions are taken in a highly participatory manner by all members who have a general interest and understanding of problems. It is most likely to occur in smaller organisations and will be a suitable culture if social objectives are seen, at least, as important as economic goals.

A different approach to analysing the culture of an organisation is to be found in Robbins (1990) who avoids a classification of types by suggesting that there are certain key dimensions of culture along which organisations can vary.

(1) *Individual initiative.* The degree of responsibility, freedom and independence that individuals have.

(2) *Risk tolerance.* The degree to which individuals are encouraged to be aggressive, innovative and risk taking.

(3) *Direction.* The degree to which the organisation creates clear objectives and performance expectations.

(4) *Integration.* The degree to which the units in the organisation are encouraged to operate in a co-ordinated manner.

(5) *Management contact.* The degree to which managers provide clear communication, assistance and support to their subordinates.

(6) *Control.* The degree of rules and regulations and the amount of direct supervision which is used to oversee and control employee behaviour.

(7) *Identity*. The degree to which members identify with the organisation as a whole rather than their particular workgroup or field of professional expertise.
(8) *Reward system*. The degree to which reward allocations, e.g., salary increases and promotions, are based on employee performance criteria.
(9) *Conflict tolerance*. The degree to which employees are encouraged to air conflicts and grievances openly.
(10) *Communication patterns*. The degree to which organisational communications are restricted to the formal hierarchy of command.

The approaches of both Handy and Robbins are useful frameworks for analysing the relationships between culture and decision making, though they carefully avoid a prescriptive element. The question remains as to what is the best form of culture for decision making to be effective. Given the wide variety of cultures that exist, it is likely to prove difficult to be confident about the 'right' one. This is made even more difficult by the fact that in most organisations there are subcultures which vary significantly from the beliefs of the main culture. In some circumstances, one can find counter-cultures opposed to the prevailing norms and values. There is an easy and erroneous assumption that cultures are uniform throughout an organisation. Clearly this is not the case and any attempt to introduce the 'right' culture will have to take account of this variety of cultures within cultures.

In the quest for an organisational culture which will best meet the needs of good decision making and organisational effectiveness, there are two key arguments. The first concerns the quality of the culture and proposes that organisations require a strong as opposed to weak culture. The second concerns the detailed beliefs and values of the culture and is best exemplified in the work of Peters and Waterman (1982) in their book *In Search of Excellence*.

A strong culture will be marked by strongly held and clearly defined beliefs which are shared by all members. Any deviation from the culture will be strongly censured by both formal and informal controls. There are reasons why this strong culture might be seen as an asset to an organisation and an aid to effective decision making. It, in theory, should provide a motivation and clarity of purpose which can make easier and more realistic the process of achieving goals. But there are drawbacks to a strong culture. The strong culture may not match the objectives and environment of the organisation and decisions may be ineffective. In a changing environment the persisting strength of a culture may well impede the organisation's capacity to adjust. If there is a merger of organisations, or some agreement to work together, a meeting of two strong cultures may promote difficulties. There is always the potential problem that a strong culture might inhibit different ways of viewing an issue, and impede innovation. At worst the strong culture can be seen as involving some form of brainwashing which manipulates people to take decisions and act beyond their personal judgement. Illustration 3.11 describes an attempt to introduce a new organisational culture at BP.

Illustration 3.11 Change at BP

At the beginning of the 1990s BP was the third largest oil company in the western world. The company was a multinational with over 120,000 employees and operations that covered all stages of production, from exploration through refining, to marketing and retailing. In 1990 BP appointed a new Chairman and Chief Executive, Robert Horton, whose aim was to make the company the most successful oil company in the 1990s and beyond. To that end the Chairman began a process of profound structural and cultural change (Project 1990) that was intended to affect the behaviour of the entire company, from oil rig worker to the Chairman himself.

A survey of 4,000 BP employees found widespread frustration with bureaucracy, the number of people, the amount of time and often the number of meetings that were required to make decisions. On the basis of the survey findings, the advice of management consultants, and the reports of teams working on the project, BP initiated a number of changes with the aim of developing a company that had the speed and agility of other, smaller, organisations.

The overall change was summarised in a company training brochure as a move from an old to a new, open culture.

Old culture	**Open culture**
Hierarchies	Teams
Boundaries	Connections
Internal focus	External focus
Smothering	Empowering
Second guessing	Trusting
Controlling	Supportive
Analysis	Action
Fear of mistakes	Calculated risk-taking

Some changes were already under way and fitted into the new scheme; amongst these was the move of corporate headquarters from its imposing location at Brittanic House. The number of managers engaged in corporate central management was reduced and over the whole company 8,000 jobs were cut. Twenty-seven committees were abolished. Teams were established that were disbanded on completion of their task, and a 'network' approach was introduced to integrate the organisation. Networking operated by all employees making the fullest possible contribution to a decision, regardless of their function or position in the hierarchy.

The changes were profound, not least for those individuals who had spent their working lives at the company. BP's employees were required to adopt, within a short period of time, a new culture and new ways of working with each other. An emphasis was placed upon 'people', 'teamwork' and 'empowerment'. New and explicit ground rules were established for meetings with an increased focus upon objectives. A new language and rituals were introduced, with group members able to declare 'a breakdown' when they felt a meeting had lost its way. Some of the language took a more concrete form with managers and group members using cards. A 'Right Foot' for showing approval for the exercise of trust or for networking. A 'Joker' for acting in the old way.

Project 1990 involved a number of risks. Would employees become disillusioned when change did not appear to reflect the views they had expressed as part of consultation? Would the new structure and culture work? Would individuals under pressure revert to their previous behaviour? The Director of Project 1990 believed that the majority of employees would accept the benefits of change. But if people did not change, then there was an argument for changing the people.

In 1992, after little more than two years in post, Robert Horton resigned following what has been described as a boardroom coup. Some commentators observed that Project 1990 had been foisted on the company's managers and workers in a way that violated its own ethos for cultural change. According to one consultant who had advised the company, Project 1990 had 'gone little better than nowhere'. One of the main aims of Project 1990, to make each part of BP talk to the rest of the company, still appeared to have a long way to go.

EXCELLENT COMPANIES AND THEIR SHARED VALUES

Peters and Waterman point to a need for a strong culture. They examined the culture of organisations that have performed consistently well over a period of twenty years in the United States. Their findings are summarised below.

Excellent companies

Amdahl	Dow Chemical	Maytag
Amoco	DuPont	Merck
Avon	Eastman Kodak	3M
Boeing	Emerson Electric	National Semi-conductor
Bristol-Myers	Fluor	Proctor and Gamble
Caterpiller	Hewlett-Packard	Raychem
Cheeseborough-Ponds	Intel	Revlon
Dana Corp.	IBM	Schlumberger
Data General	Johnson & Johnson	Texas Instruments
Delta Airlines	K-mart	Wal-Mart
Digital Equipment	Levi Strauss	Wang Labs
Disney Productions	Marriott	
	McDonald's	

Common values

(1) A bias for action
(2) Hands-on, value driven
(3) Close to the customer
(4) Stick to the knitting
(5) Autonomy and entrepreneurship
(6) Simple form, lean staff
(7) Productivity through people
(8) Simultaneous tight-loose properties.

Peters and Waterman's approach to organisations has been highly influential. They provide a simple guide, written in the language of management and copiously illustrated with anecdotes. The most obvious criticism of their work is the subsequent performance of the organisations they identified as excellent. If we look at IBM for example their recent results do not suggest excellence. Other limitations in their work are the American bias, the notion of only one excellent culture, and their rather uncritical support for strong organisational cultures. Nevertheless it is important to note that for decision-making theory and practice the approach has major implications. Decisions have to be seen in their cultural context. They will be affected by the norms, values and shared perceptions of organisation members. Decisions will be more or less effective as a result of the ways in which culture helps or hinders both the ends and means of the decision-making process. In trying to identify those cultural variables that will contribute to effective decisions, Peters and Waterman have at least raised a matter for further investigation and debate.

While the concepts of organisational climate and organisational culture should not be utilised uncritically, they do provide tools for the decision maker. They give a useful framework for understanding the particular organisational context of a decision; they also suggest a range of actions that may be undertaken to make that context more suitable for the execution of good decisions.

EXERCISE: SPRAY CODE

Martin Hughes is the MD of Spray Code, a company that produces bar-coding equipment. The product is based upon the use of ink sprays directed by computer software to provide the familiar bar codes that enable producers and retailers to control stocks and quality; they form an essential part of modern retail systems. Spray Code face a highly competitive environment. Established rivals contest for their customers and new, innovative, enterprises are constantly springing up, founded by employees who have left established companies and, occasionally, by ex-university researchers. The customers for bar-coding equipment include the whole range of enterprises, from the producers of globally-scaled products to concerns that operate in niche markets. In each category there are requirements, both for products that are based upon standardised designs, and for products that will operate under special conditions, or produce unusual patterns in the coding. The companies' sales are partly made up of standard products and supplies for past machines. But there are also adaptations of products, the provision of customised systems and one-off projects to meet a specific customer's requirements.

Spray Code has been a highly successful company. Based around a group of engineers and technologists, the company has grown rapidly and profitably. It now employs over four hundred people. The employees can be categorised as follows:

Managerial	15
Technologists and engineers	170
Administrators	18
Clerical and secretarial	63
Supervisors	21
Operators	126

For the last few years Martin Hughes has devoted most of his attention to expanding the company. The MD has relied on the original team nature of the company's employees to meet the need for organisation. He believes that most of the employees are sufficiently intelligent and well motivated not to require a clear specification of duties and formal relationships. Indeed, Mr Hughes believes that, faced with the constant need to innovate and the range of customer requirements, attempts to refine the organisation's structure could be counter productive. 'Spray Code can no longer be called a small business, but it still retains the human assets and original management of such a company'.

Asked to describe the company's organisation Mr Hughes can produce an organisation chart, but he admits that it is probably out of date.

Discussion

Spray Code is involved in a complicated process that involves software development, the incorporation of computer hardware, product manufacture and assembly, marketing and sales and servicing. Some of the activities and products take the form of projects, others have become

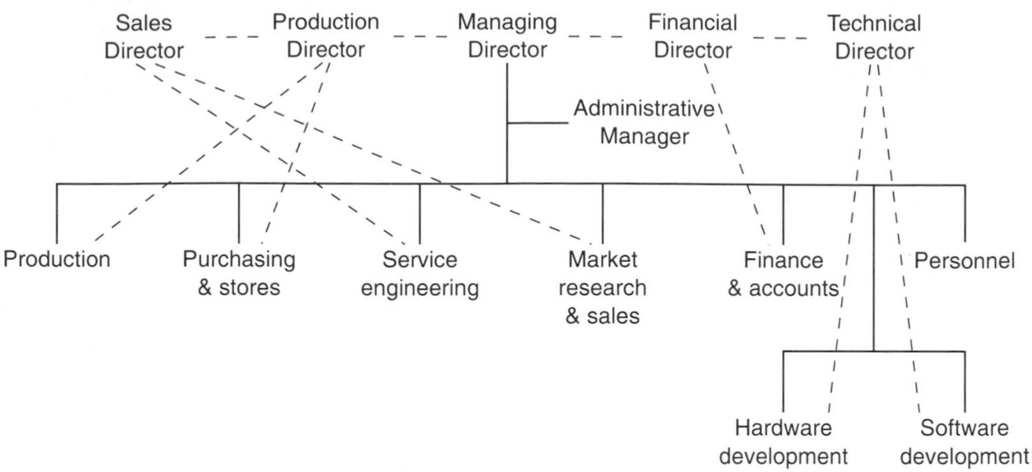

Fig. 3.8 Spray Code: organisation chart

standard operations. In each case successful delivery of the product to the customer is the result of numerous, co-ordinated decisions. Has Spray Code the correct organisation structure to facilitate those decisions?

GLOSSARY OF MAIN TERMS

Gatekeeper role The position in an organisation which by its nature provides the occupier with control of the upward, downward and lateral flows of information.

Group A collection of two or more people who, through interaction, share common perceptions, goals and forms of social control.

Group cohesion The degree to which the members of a group are prepared to pursue group interests as opposed to individual interests.

Group conformity The degree to which the behaviour of group members is identical.

Group norms Rules which may be both formal and informal which guide the actions of the group.

Group participation The extent to which decision making is shared amongst group members.

Leader The individual in a group who exercises the greatest influence, which may result from the power of the position, the skills of the leader or a combination of both.

Leadership The capacity to influence others without recourse to threats or punishment.

Line organisation A form of organisation characterised by a simple hierarchical structure where all positions are connected by a direct chain of command.

Matrix organisation A form of organisation which combines a line structure with units that integrate the various activities of the functional line departments, which may be based on a project, a product, product range or geographical areas, etc.

Organisational climate The generalised feelings members have and the evaluations they make about the overall state of their organisation.

Organisational culture The shared beliefs and understanding that members have about their organisation, acquired by the process of socialisation in the organisation.

REFERENCES

Asch, S.E. (1951) *Effects of Group Pressure on the Modification and Distortion of Judgements, in Groups, Leadership and Men* (Ed. Guetzkow, H.), Rutgers University Press.

Belbin, R.M. (1981) *Management Teams: Why they Succeed or Fail,* Butterworth-Heinemann.

Child, J. (1988) *Organisation: A Guide to Problems and Practice*, Paul Chapman.

Coch, L., and French, J.R. (1948) 'Overcoming Resistance to Change', *Human Resources*, Vol. 1, 512-32.

Dalton, M. (1959) *Men Who Manage*, John Wiley.

Fiedler, F. E. (1967) *A Theory of Leadership Effectiveness*, McGraw Hill.

Hall, J. (1971) 'Decisions, Decisions, Decisions', *Psychology Today*, November.

Halpin, A. W. and Croft, D. B. (1962) *The Organisational Climate of Schools*, Washington DC US Office of Education, Department of Health Education and Welfare, Contract No. SAE (8639).

Handy, C. B. (1985) *Understanding Organisations*, Penguin Books.

Janis, I. L. (1982) *Victims of Groupthink*, Houghton Mifflin.

Kirkpatrick S. A. and Locke, E. A. (1991) 'Leadership – Do Traits Matter?' *Academy of Management Executives*, May, 48-60.

Kolb, D. A., Rubin, I. M., and MacIntyre, J. M. (1979) *Organisational Psychology: An Experiential Approach to Organisational Behaviour*, Prentice Hall.

Leavitt, H. J. (1978) *Managerial Psychology*, University of Chicago Press.

Likert, R. (1961) *New Patterns of Management*, McGraw Hill.

McGregor, D. (1960) *The Human Side of Enterprise*, McGraw Hill.

March, J. G., and Simon, H. A. (1958) *Organisations*, Wiley.

Mullins, L. (1993) *Management and Organisational Behaviour*, Pitman.

Peters, T. S., and Waterman, R. H. (1982) *In Search of Excellence*, Harper and Row.

Pettigrew, A. M. (1973) *The Politics of Organisational Decision Making*, Tavistock Publications.

Robbins, S.P. (1990) *Organisation Theory: The Structure and Design of Organisations*, Prentice Hall.

Roethlisberger, F. J., and Dickson, W. J. (1939) *Management and the Worker*, Harvard University Press.

Stodgill, R.M. (1974) *Handbook of Leadership*, New York Free Press.

Tuckman, B. W. (1965) 'Development Sequence in Small Groups', *Psychological Bulletin*, Vol. 63.

Whyte, W. W. (1956) *The Organisation Man*, Simon and Schuster.

Zalenik, I. (1970) 'Power and Politics in Organisational Life', *Harvard Business Review*.

FURTHER READING

Arnold, H. J., and Feldman, D. C. (1988) *Organisational Behaviour*, McGraw Hill.

Dunford, R. W. (1992) *Organisational Behaviour: An Organisational Analysis Perspective*, Addison Wesley.

Huczynski, A., and Buchan, D. (1993) *Organisational Behaviour: An Introduction*, Prentice Hall.

Ivancevich, J. M., and Matteson, M. T. (1993) *Organisational Behaviour and Management*, Irwin.

Robbins, S. P. (1986) *Organisational Behaviour: Concepts Controversies and Applications*, Prentice Hall.

CHAPTER 4

The psychology of decision making

James Stewart

INTRODUCTION

The purpose of this chapter is to examine the decision-making processes of individuals as revealed by the science of psychology. Key psychological factors which influence and impact upon those processes will also be explored. The content of the chapter will include the following kinds of results of psychological research.

Descriptive theories
Explanatory theories
Prescriptive models

The first of these are attempts to describe the cognitive, affective and behavioural processes undertaken by individuals in decision making. The second are perhaps more ambitious in that they seek to explain those processes and thereby provide a basis for prediction and, potentially at least, control and manipulation. This latter point is at the core of the third item on the list. Prescriptive models provide what are claimed to be ideas which will have the effect of improving decision making by individuals. Thus they argue that if individuals adopt and implement these ideas, the quality of their decisions will be improved. It is in the adoption and application of the ideas contained in the prescriptive models that 'control' and 'manipulation' of decision-making processes and other significant factors occur. However, the prescriptive models are aimed at use *by* the individual *for* the individual; they are not therefore ideas which allow external agents, such as managers, to control and manipulate the decision making of particular individuals such as employees.

RATIONALITY AND IRRATIONALITY

It is appropriate at this point to highlight one of the central themes of this book since it is also at the heart of issues and debates raised in this chapter. This is the theme of irrationality. Psychological theories of decision making vary in the extent to which they attribute rationality to the processes engaged in by the individual. It is interesting to note that prescriptive models tend to imply a greater degree of rationality than many of the explanatory theories would suggest. However, there may be an argument within the prescriptive models that the ideas suggested will in fact impose a greater degree of rationality on what is essentially an irrational process. It may be argued that it is this imposed rationality which brings about an increased quality of decision making.

The degree to which such arguments are explicit varies between prescriptive models. The reader is recommended to be aware of the notion of rationality versus irrationality and the degree to which the concept is explicitly addressed as the chapter unfolds.

OVERVIEW

It is important to establish a context of psychological theory before examining specific theories and models. The next section, 'Perspectives in psychology', will therefore describe the main traditions and schools of thought within psychology. Some indication will be given of the influence and implications of these various perspectives for understanding individual decision making.

The following section, 'Rationality versus irrationality', will highlight key theories and models of decision making. These will allow a more detailed examination of the concept of rationality. This in turn will lead into an exploration of some critical psychological factors which affect and impact upon the individual's decision-making process. It is these factors which most clearly question the extent to which rationality can be achieved.

Having raised the question of rationality, the section following, 'Problems of perception' will look at the question of involvement of the individual in group and organisation decisions as a key factor affecting the degree of commitment held by the individual to such decisions. The section will be resonant of the previous chapter on group decision making. 'Involvement and commitment', important concepts in the context of individual decision making, come next; they illustrate the role of affective processes and therefore provide a contrast with the rational approach.

The penultimate section, 'Career choice decisions', will examine one specific context of individual decision making to illustrate some of the key themes and issues identified. The context of career choices has been chosen because of its general application to a wide readership. The final 'Summary and conclusion' points to applications within work organisations and the consequent implications for both students and practitioners of individual decision making.

PERSPECTIVES IN PSYCHOLOGY

It is worth starting with a brief look at what is meant by the term 'Psychology'. A very simple definition by Miller (1966) says simply that psychology is 'The science of mental life'. An immediate problem with this definition is that it seems to exclude, implicitly at least, phenomena outside the mind. But the definition does have the merit of focusing on the mind as a source of explanation for individual actions and behaviour.

A broader definition is offered by Ribeaux and Poppleton (1978):

> Psychology is the study of behaviour and experience pursued by methods the status of which is continually under review.

This definition encompasses the study of behaviour which, unlike 'mental life', is observable. The second part of the definition offered by Ribeaux and Poppleton also questions to some extent Miller's apparent confidence that psychology is a science. The reference to method is important in that the desirability of scientific status and its achievement through methodology has been a continuous source of debate within the discipline.

These definitional niceties are not without purpose. Two factors are critical to differences in perspective within psychology.

- The study of mental processes versus study of overt behaviour.
- The value and appropriateness of adopting the 'scientific method' developed in the natural sciences.

These factors to a large extent differentiate the perspectives described below and, consequently, partly explain the differing views each has of individual decision making. For our purposes, though, the following elements are those found in most generally accepted definitions and are significant for an understanding of the psychology of decision making.

- A focus on the individual as a source of explanation of human behaviour.
- An interest in cognitive, affective and behavioural factors.
- Research methods within the broad tradition of social science.

The range of perspectives

Different writers suggest different categorisations of traditions within psychology. Ribeaux and Poppleton (1978), for example, identify two broad perspectives, while Arnold *et al* (1991), in a more recent work, list five major approaches. We can discern four relevant traditions which have significance for decision making.

- Psychodynamic approach
- Behaviourist approach
- Cognitive approach
- Humanistic approach

Each of these approaches is described as follows.

Psychodynamic approach

Sigmund Freud, commonly acknowledged as the 'Father' of psychoanalysis and psychotherapy, together with his co-workers and students, founded what is known as the psychodynamic tradition within psychology.

The basis of this view is that individual human behaviour and psychological functioning is subject to biological influence through the operation of 'instinctive forces' (Arnold *et al*, 1991). These forces, also referred to as 'drives', act outside conscious thought and have significant effect on individual decisions and actions.

Early theorists in this tradition differed in their views on what drives exist and which are dominant in their influence. Freud himself emphasised the drive for reproduction and sexual gratification in much of his work. A further division, especially between Freud and Jung (Ribeaux and Poppleton, 1978), concerned the significance of interaction between biological forces and social experience. Currently, psychologists working within this tradition recognise a wider range of instinctual drives than originally suggested by Freud and also place greater emphasis on the role of life experiences in psychological development.

Freud's basic propositions remain influential both within and outside the psychodynamic approach. The propositions include three facets of the psyche.

- The Id — This facet is the basic source of energy supporting both physical and psychological actions. It is also the 'instinctual' or biological component which contains the basic drives. The id seeks immediate gratification without inhibition. Freud referred to this as the pleasure principle.
- The Ego — This facet develops in part as a result of experience. It seeks to restrain the impulses of the id through the reality principle which attempts to influence behaviour associated with instinctual drives in socially acceptable directions. The ego accepts the principle of delayed gratification.
- The Superego — The final facet represents development of a sense of morality and standards of behaviour. It is commonly referred to as the conscience. The superego develops during childhood and therefore, initially at least, its standards reflect those of the child's parents and aim to achieve perfection.

It is possible to find explanations for behaviour, and therefore the decision making of individuals, within this basic analysis. However, a further aspect of Freudian theory is even more informative for such questions. This suggests that these three facets experience continuous conflict. This conflict in turn causes the individual to experience anxiety, especially when the conflict is particularly marked. Anxiety itself is unpleasant and individuals seek to avoid or reduce it. They do this through various processes which Freud labelled defence mechanisms.

Three points of significance in understanding individual decision making arise from this tradition of psychology. First, decision making as identifiable behaviour is influenced by both biological and social factors, and by the interaction of the two as it affects a particular individual's psychological development and psychological state. Second, that a strong motivation governing choice between a range of action or behavioural options will be a desire to reduce anxiety levels arising from psychological conflict. However, since such conflict is, according to Freud, largely unconscious, the associated motivation is difficult to discover, even for individuals themselves. Third, many of the defence mechanisms suggested by Freud have the effect of denying the existence of objective factors and/or distorting reality in other ways. Therefore, a decision that appears irrational to an objective observer can be for the individual decision maker perfectly reasonable in the light of their interpretation of reality.

For our purpose, a major problem with the psychodynamic perspective lies in its application as therapeutic treatment. However, its continuing relevance as an explanatory framework of interest to understanding individual decision making within work organisations has been recently demonstrated (Kets de Vries and Miller, 1984). This work provides an analysis of individual and collective functioning of senior decision makers through application of a psychodynamic framework.

Behaviourist approach

The behaviourist tradition stands in contrast to the psychodynamic framework in two important aspects. First, in extreme application, behaviourists discount the internal workings of the mind, or psyche, as an area of study. Only that which can be observed and measured, i.e., overt behaviour, receives attention. Second, and related to this point, behaviourists are concerned to emulate the traditions of the natural sciences in their research methodologies and thus justify the status of psychology as a science.

From this initial perspective, the behaviourist approach views experience within the social and physical environment as being the primary or sole determinant of behaviour. Thus biological or innate causes are also rejected as explanatory factors. This latter point is less rigidly held among current psychologists working within the behaviourist tradition though it was central to the founders of the approach. Two particular psychologists generally acknowledged to have been instrumental in founding the behaviourist tradition are J.B. Watson (Ribeaux and Poppleton, 1978) and B.F. Skinner (Arnold *et al*, 1991).

Skinner's formulation of 'Learning Theory' provides an illustration of the basic elements of behaviourism. This formulation is known as operant conditioning which is a particular version of Stimulus-Response theory (S-R). Operant conditioning rests on the following propositions.

- Operant behaviour (of the individual) impacts on the environment and occurs relatively free of any particular stimulus.
- Such behaviour can and will become repetitive if subject to a reward, or reinforcement. (Note negative reinforcement is also possible).
- If specific operant behaviour is reinforced in the vicinity of a specific stimulus then the behaviour will become associated with that stimulus and therefore will tend to recur under similar circumstances.
- Behaviour is eventually 'learned' through reinforcement and becomes incorporated into the individual's conditioned responses to environmental stimuli.

What this means in simple terms is that the behaviour of individuals, including their approach to making decisions and the actual decision choices they make, is a function of what they have learned to do through experience. Therefore, according to this theory, individuals will make similar decisions through similar processes in response to similar external stimuli that they have made in the past. The implication is that, rather than being a rational process of seeking to 'maximise' or even 'satisfice' desired outcomes, decision making can often be the result of habitual and learned responses to environmental factors.

Operant conditioning is still accepted as a useful explanatory and predictive theory of human behaviour though it is now widely recognised as being only part of any possible full understanding. More recent developments within the behaviourist tradition accept a greater degree of conscious thought and action on the part of the individual (see, for example, Bandura, 1977, on social learning theory).

Cognitive approach

The third tradition has some similarities with the previous two perspectives. It shares with the psychodynamic approach an interest in and acknowledgement of the role of internal mental processes. In common with behaviourists however, cognitive psychologists also recognise the impact of the environment and social experience on individual behaviour. In fact, the basic idea of the cognitive perspective is the view that the individual is an 'information processor' (Ribeaux and Poppleton, 1978). Thus behaviour can be understood as the outcome of decisions reached by the individual as a result of taking in perceptual data from the environment and analysing the significance and meaning of that data. However, the mental activities of information processing which provide meaning to data, are themselves influenced by previous experience, and environmental data does not necessarily possess the properties of objective fact in terms of how it is perceived by a particular individual.

The two points made in the previous paragraph are critical when looking at decision making. The cognitive perspective is perhaps most relevant when examining rationalistic prescriptive models. However, as we shall see later in this chapter, cognitive psychologists have uncovered many limitations to a truly rational decision-making model, because of such factors as memory, perceptual bias and perceptual attention.

Two fundamental ideas developed within cognitive psychology contribute further to an understanding of the limits placed on rationality in individual decision making. First is the notion of 'maturation' developed initially through studies of child development undertaken by Piaget (Hilgard *et al*, 1975). This notion, more generally applied than in Piaget's initial work, suggests that an individual's capability to undertake mental tasks is dependent upon their first holding the prerequisite skills or abilities. The physical example that a person cannot run before they can walk illustrates the point.

The second idea is that of 'personal constructs' developed by George Kelly (Kelly, 1955). This suggests that individuals make sense of the world and manage their interactions with it (i.e., they process information and make decisions on how to act) on the basis of sets of concepts which they 'construct' and evolve through experience. A construct in Kelly's terms is a bi-polar concept such as 'warm – cold', 'love – hate', 'hard – soft', 'nice – nasty'. Constructs are developed for, and about, physical objects, people in the abstract and the particular, feelings and emotions, physical sensations, etc. They are also related and interrelated in systems of constructs which are unique to each individual. Thus the same 'objective' data will be interpreted as having different meanings by different individuals. This is complicated by constructs which relate to personal values, such as 'good – bad' or 'right – wrong'. For example, the construct 'warm – cold' can be applied to a person. Any two individuals could disagree on how they experience a given person on this construct (assuming they share such a construct in the first place!). Even if they agreed that the person is indeed 'cold', individual A may view this as being 'good' while individual B may view it as being 'bad'. Each would therefore behave very differently in response to the same act by the person in question.

The cognitive perspective is extremely important in informing understanding of individual decision making since it points to the existence of critical factors which limit rationality.

Humanistic approach

The humanistic perspective is within a broad tradition of philosophical as well as psychological thought which adopts a phenomenological view of reality (Arnold *et al*, 1991). This view contends that any 'objective' definition of reality is merely a widely held interpretation rather than recognition of an objective 'fact'. Such interpretations will never be universal and most events will be subject to highly individualistic and unique interpretations. Thus, the humanistic perspective can be said to go further than the cognitive school of thought in attributing unique 'world views' to every individual which are in effect representations of uniquely different realities.

There are two further significant factors associated with the humanistic approach. First, an implicit belief in a human property of 'free will' which provides the opportunity for (and responsibility of) the exercise of choice (Ribeaux and Poppleton, 1978). This view leads humanist psychologists to reject the determinism inherent in both psychodynamic and behaviourist theories. The second factor is that of motivation. Humanists believe that individual behaviour and decisions are motivated by a desire to fulfil their potential, i.e., to self-actualise. Two writers particularly associated with these central tenets of the humanistic perspective are Maslow (1962) and Carl Rogers (1970).

It should be clear that the general approach of the humanist perspective can be problematic in its application to the study of individual decision making. This is because it emphasises the uniqueness of each individual and their personal definitions of reality. However, the approach does have some value for our purposes. First, it confirms the appropriateness of viewing individual human beings as conscious decision makers capable of exercising free will. Second, in common with psychology in general, it views human behaviour as purposeful and goal directed. Third, it provides a general framework to aid understanding of that purpose which is the goal of personal growth and self-actualisation.

This section has provided a necessarily brief overview of the main perspectives within psychology. However, the overview does suggest some key concepts of relevance to understanding individual decision making. These are encompassed under the general factor of individual differences. In more detail, they include the following.

- Personality differences and their development
- Information processing activities
- The role of learned behaviour
- Motivation
- Exercise of free will

We shall take the last of these as our starting point for examining the validity and utility of rational decision-making models in the next section.

RATIONALITY *VERSUS* IRRATIONALITY

Rationality is commonly associated with notions of logic, reasoning and sense-making. When applied to decision making, two factors emerge as important. First, that decisions are the result of a logical analysis of available information. This would seem to fit with the cognitive perspective. Second, that the analysis evaluates alternatives against their expected value to the decision maker. This factor seems to have support from the humanist tradition in that the decision maker is exercising choice against the pursuit of personal goals.

Many prescriptive models seem to assume that these factors are indeed central to the decision-making process. They further reflect the humanist tradition in that they posit the decision maker as exercising free will. These points are apparent in the model of a rational decision-making process that was introduced in Chapter 1.

Figure 1.1 is representative of many rationalistic approaches to problem solving and decision making. Such approaches may *describe the actual cognitive and behavioural decision-making process* that an individual engages in. The models may also *seek to improve the functioning of the cognitive processes* by application of analytical techniques to examine causes and select solutions. These techniques in turn are derived from rules of logic and rational enquiry developed in philosophy and the natural sciences.

There are, however, problems with this view of decision making. First, it assumes awareness of some problem. This may not always be the case. As Jackson (1975) points out, there needs to be a process of problem detection. Jackson's suggestions on problem detection also highlight a second problem with rationalistic approaches. He recognises the role of the affective domain, i.e., feelings and emotions, as being significant in causing the 'discomfort' which activates problem formulation. Discomfort as a concept can be seen as similar to the 'anxiety' referred to by Freud.

The stages concerning problem definition and solution development raise further problems. We know from the psychodynamic perspective that individuals can and do distort reality as a means of reducing or avoiding anxiety. Limits on rational information processing are also evident from the notion of 'personal constructs' within cognitive psychology and the idea of unique 'world views' central to the humanist perspective. Therefore models which assume unencumbered rationality in decision making are likely to be limited in their application.

An additional problem arises with the choice stage, 'selecting the best solution'. Commonly, prescriptive models assume an objective truth to specifications of 'best' when examining decisions in work organisations. Or, at least, the existence of a wide consensus on what constitutes 'best' in terms of generally supported values. However, most perspectives in psychology would suggest that individuals vary significantly in their personal values and motivations. Therefore, what appears to be 'best' to one individual would not be viewed in the same way by others.

Recent work reported in Arnold *et al* (1991) goes some way towards understanding this dichotomy between 'rationality' and unique individuals. This work introduces the notion of 'subjective expected utility' (SEU). What this idea suggests is that individuals act in similar ways which can be viewed as 'rational' in that they make decisions on the basis of expected outcomes and the value they place on those outcomes. Thus choices will be made between alternatives according to the effects they are judged to have in terms of outcomes and according to the value the individual ascribes to the outcomes. What varies from individual to individual is the value placed on similar outcomes and the degree of 'expectedness' they are willing to accept. Both of these factors are subjectively defined by the individual.

The variation between individuals in their acceptance of degrees of 'expectedness' and the value they place on outcomes can be explained by the psychological perspectives described earlier. None would necessarily reject the existence of these variations, though each is likely to offer a different explanation. Such explanations do not form part of the purpose of this chapter. However, there are certain key concepts within psychology which may form part of the explanations but which are, more importantly, critical to understanding individual decision making. These are discussed in the next section. To close this section, Illustration 4.1 provides some examples to illustrate, from the viewpoint of psychology, the limitations of rational decision-making models.

Illustration 4.1 Rational decisions?

Example A
A medium-sized company decided to modernise its office equipment. Toni Campbell was tasked to determine a recommended supplier. She gathered information about the established manufacturers from their dealer networks and compiled a table listing the features of each of their products. Concurrently, she consulted the managing director, John Sanderson, and other senior managers and staff to determine decision criteria, including constraints imposed by budgets, etc., and performance specifications desired by users. From this information, Toni constructed a selection table using relative value scores for each supplier against the ranked criteria of performance specifications. Two suppliers were eliminated by constraints. Of the five remaining, one was a clear 'winner' in terms of its cumulative scores in the analysis.

Toni presented her recommendation to John Sanderson with the supporting analysis. 'Fine,' said the MD, 'but make sure it comes in black. I don't want any other colour. Go somewhere else if you have to.'

Discussion
You may wish to speculate why colour was such an important factor to John Sanderson when it was clearly irrelevant to performance and therefore 'irrational' in terms of those criteria.

Example B
A conversation between two students.

Kulveen: 'That presentation was really interesting. The lecturer was great, very enthusiastic. I think I will choose Human Resource Management as my option next year.'

Stephen: 'Interesting! He reminded me of my old man, going over the top about things that don't matter. Enthusiasm turns me off. I'm opting for marketing.'

Discussion
What reasons could there be for such different reactions to the same event? You could usefully think about how the cognitive and humanist perspectives might be applied to this example.

Example C
Hilda experienced difficulty in persuading her partner Earl to commit himself to buying a house they both liked and wanted. Earl had concerns about the size of the mortgage they would need, although Hilda was confident the repayments would not be a problem.

Earl believed the company he worked for would soon be making some staff redundant, including himself, and that he would have difficulty in finding a new job. Hilda, who worked for the same company, knew neither was true. There were no plans for redundancies and in any case Earl was well qualified in his work which itself was, currently at least, in high demand. Earl remained convinced however that their financial position was too precarious to take on a large mortgage.

Discussion
Earl was clearly anxious about the decision facing him. How might the psychodynamic perspective throw light on Earl's position?
(Note: These examples are based on true events which happened to real people.)

PROBLEMS OF PERCEPTION

Psychological research into perception has identified a range of factors which impact upon individual decision making and which generally have the effect of limiting rationality in information processing. They include the following.

- Attention
- Memory
- Heuristics
- Bias
- Person perception

Each of these is discussed separately though the probable reality is that they do not operate independently of each other and are likely to interact in significant ways.

Attention

It is useful to begin an examination of attention with a definition of perception.

> Perception is the active psychological process in which stimuli are selected and organised into meaningful patterns

What is obvious from this definition (Huczynski and Buchanan, 1991) is that perception is selective. The fact that perception has to be selective is also obvious if you consider the amount of stimuli we are all subject to in our everyday existence. Consider the stimuli around you now as you read these words. There will undoubtedly be sights, sounds and smells in your physical environment of which you are, or were, unaware until you gave them your attention.

You are too (probably!) wearing clothes, some of which are in direct contact with your skin. It is also likely that you recently ate or drank something which has left a residue in your mouth. You are, though, highly unlikely to be aware of the feel of your clothes or the tastes in your mouth. It is equally likely, however, that you were aware of the feel of your clothes when you put them on, and of the taste of the food when you were eating your meal. This is because you were, at those times, attending to those stimuli because they were relevant to what you were doing at that time.

Buchanan and Huczynski highlight the important distinction between sensation and perception. The former is the effect in the form of physiological responses that external stimuli have on our sense organs. Sensation is primarily a physiological and automatic response. We cannot consciously control it, and all our sense organs are continually experiencing a huge variety of sensations. Perception, though, is a psychological process which acts to select the sensations, and therefore the stimuli, which register in our conscious awareness. It is perception, therefore, which selects the stimuli that receives our attention.

The implications of this discussion of attention for decision making are fairly obvious: there are limits to the amount of data an individual can process at any one time. A further factor which acts to limit information processing and analysis is memory.

Memory

There are two features of memory which are relevant to perception. The first is to do with the storage of information. The second concerns access to and retrieval from the memory.

Three forms of storage are generally acknowledged to operate in the human memory (Ribeaux and Poppleton, 1978). The first is suggested to be a 'sensory memory' which stores sensations for a brief moment after they occur. The second is normally referred to as the short-term memory. This 'calls' and holds information from the sensory memory, although its capacity is thought to be smaller. The short-term memory holds information for quite short periods; for some information this can be as low as seconds. This period can be lengthened by 'rehearsal' which means, for example, continually repeating a telephone number. The third storage system is known as the long-term memory. This third element is probably what most people understand by the term 'memory': storage capacity. This is thought to be virtually unlimited and its duration permanent. So, once information enters the long-term memory, it is never lost or 'forgotten'.

The last statement is literal. In practice however individuals do 'forget'. Or rather we have problems 'remembering', i.e., retrieving and recalling information from the storage system. There are a number of theories which seek to explain why this is so. For example the psychodynamic perspective suggests the defence mechanism of 'repression' which operates unconsciously to block out of conscious awareness experiences and information which cause the individual discomfort. Understanding how memory works, however, suggests additional possible explanations.

Information which enters the long-term memory is not necessarily stored in the form in which it is first experienced by the sensory organs. It is first processed and compared with existing information in the system. This, in effect, means that the information is interpreted, then classified. In simple terms, the long-term memory works like a large filing system which stores information according to certain categories and thereby links different pieces of information together. In the system there is a wide range of different types of classification subsystems, therefore retrieval difficulties may occur because of searching for information under the wrong category, or in the wrong 'file'. This means that the appropriate question needs to be asked to activate the relevant subsystem before the information can be retrieved, i.e., remembered.

This discussion of memory reflects the word 'organised' in the definition of perception given earlier. Memory organises information into 'meaningful patterns'. A related concept to be discussed next is that of heuristics.

Heuristics

Heuristics are simple generalisations or guidelines that individuals use to reduce mental effort in processing information. They are broad categories which simplify and speed up the process of interpreting and classifying new information.

The concept of heuristics is particularly relevant to decision making since they are used by individuals to make both predictive judgements and choice decisions. An example of the former is in selecting someone for a job vacancy. Rather than a detailed investigation, the judgement is based on the person's similarity or otherwise to people already successful in the job. This is an example of 'representativeness' heuristics suggested by Kanhneman *et al* (Arnold, 1987). A heuristic applied to a choice decision involves formulating and applying rules which relate different factors together. An example is provided by a rule which combines the relative values to be assigned to price and quality in purchase decisions. Such rules, however, do not always have the intended or expected effects.

Heuristics as a concept has been developed in the cognitive school of psychology. It has relationships with the notion of 'personal constructs' discussed earlier and with the idea of 'schema' described by Hogarth (1987). A schema is a structure of knowledge and system of beliefs that an individual utilises to make sense of the world. Thus heuristics, personal constructs and schema, are all examples of 'ready made frameworks' (Arnold *et al*, 1991) that individuals apply to processing information. Such frameworks are means of classifying, organising and interpreting information. Hence they all present opportunities for introducing bias into the information processing system.

Bias

The *Pocket Oxford Dictionary* uses words such as 'predisposition', 'prejudice' and 'influence' to define bias. Each of these infers that information is not processed objectively. It is instead interpreted in a subjective manner according to the particular 'prejudices' and 'influences' of the individual or decision maker.

Bias can occur at any stage of the decision-making process shown in Fig. 1.1. A given situation or event cannot be said to be a problem in any absolute or objective sense. It will only be defined as such if one or more individuals perceives it to be a problem. Defining the problem, once its existence is accepted and agreed, will also be subject to bias. Given agreement say in an organisation that a particular situation is a problem, (for example falling profits) the marketing manager will be 'predisposed' to define the situation as a marketing problem, while the finance manager is likely to be 'predisposed' to view it as a finance problem.

Such predispositions, prejudices and influences will continue to operate throughout all stages of the process. Analysing the problem, developing alternatives, selecting a solution, etc., will all be subject to bias. Indeed, the 'best solution' can only be defined in terms of a particular perspective which is itself subject to bias.

Bias is often used as a pejorative term and as a label for something to be avoided. There are sound reasons for this to be the case. However, it is possible to view the concept of bias as being neutral and as a natural and inevitable occurrence. Our discussion so far confirms that perception is a subjective process. Linking this to the earlier discussion of main traditions in psychology supports the idea that bias is inevitable. The reader is recommended to think about those links and connections. However, there is perhaps one area where bias can be and often is particularly destructive and where attempts need to be made to avoid or, at least, control its effects. This is the area of person perception.

Person perception

Bias in the form of prejudice is perhaps more evident and more significant in its effects when operating on an individual's perception of other people. One example of this is the phenomenon known as stereotyping.

A stereotype is in effect a schema as defined earlier. It is a broad generalisation about what characteristics are held by a particular group or category of people. Examples of groups that are commonly found to be stereotyped are those categorised on the basis of criteria such as gender, age, class, occupation, race and ethnic origin. However, many other criteria are possible. Prejudice arises when a particular individual belonging to the general category is judged by another individual to have all or any of the characteristics associated with the general category, irrespective of any specific evidence. Stereotypes can be favourable or unfavourable and therefore the application of bias through prejudice can have favourable or unfavourable consequences.

A different but related (in its effects) concept in person perception is that of implicit personality theory. This is also referred to as 'prototypes' (Arnold *et al*, 1991). Each of us has our own implicit personality theory, that is, we utilise labels such as 'extrovert' and 'introvert' and have a view about the characteristics held by a 'typical' extrovert. Thus, when we classify an individual as introvert because of one characteristic, we then assume that the individual also has all the other characteristics that we attribute to our prototype, i.e., our typical introvert. This then influences our perception of the individual's actual behaviour and our judgements about the individual's expected behaviour.

Stereotypes and prototypes are both examples of how we utilise existing categories and classifications to process new information. They also illustrate how we then use those categories to form judgements and make decisions about future action. For example, when we meet someone for the first time we may apply a stereotype based on the immediate visual information of their obvious gender. How we then behave and interact with that person is influenced by the stereotype although we as yet know nothing about them as an individual. Based on a little more direct evidence, perhaps a brief conversation, we may then utilise our own implicit personality theory and apply a prototype. This then exerts an additional influence on our future interactions with and decisions about the person.

The obvious relevance of person perception in organisational decision making is in personnel selection decisions. The majority of the research carried out in this area confirms that the formal interview is the most common method used for such decisions (Bevan and Fryatt, 1988). Research into the validity and effectiveness of the selection interview consistently shows that it performs poorly as a decision-making device (see Ribeaux and Poppleton, 1978, for an overview). Research by Webster (1964), for example, indicates that interviewers form a favourable or unfavourable hypothesis about candidates in a very short time at the beginning of the interview and then spend the rest of the interview time searching for confirming evidence.

However, the selection interview is not the only context where person perception affects decision making. Any situation which demands interaction between individuals including, for example, multi-million pounds purchase decisions or group decisions on the part of senior managers, will be subject to the influences of person perception.

Other factors

Stereotypes and prototypes are not the only factors affecting person perception. There is a range of other factors which affect the whole of perception and which therefore apply, to differing degrees, to person perception. A useful indicative list is given below.

- Personality
- Motivation
- Previous experience
- Feelings and emotions
- Skills and abilities

This section has briefly described a number of key factors in the process of perception which limit rationality in individual decision making. A useful summarising notion is that of the 'Perceptual World' (Huczynski and Buchanan, 1991). This suggests that each of us possesses a personal and unique view of what is 'out there' and our place within it. As well as the factors internal to us listed above, our perceptual world is also influenced by our social and cultural environment, and by our physical environment. And it is not static. It changes as those internal and external influencing factors themselves change.

The conclusion from this section is therefore that decisions are not made on the basis of objective data. They are rather the outcome of both evaluative and predictive judgements which result from subjective perception of data. Subjective perception transforms 'objective' data into patterns of information meaningful to the individual. The meaning and significance attached to information is also in part at least influenced by the individual's feelings and emotions.

INVOLVEMENT AND COMMITMENT

A final stage in the rational decision-making model is that of implementation. In work organisations, this usually requires sets of individuals to do something new or do something differently. In other words, it requires individuals to change their behaviour.

When implementing a decision therefore the decision maker(s) are, probably unwittingly in most cases, presenting various other individuals with a decision of their own. The decision is simply whether to comply with the requirement to change their behaviour. In effect, the decision, or problem, being faced by those affected by implementation is whether to accept the initial decision. Illustration 4.2 provides some examples to further explain this point.

These examples are simplistic. The staff affected will in reality face myriad other decisions. However, their responses will be influenced by the degree to which they accept and agree with the initial decision (Stewart, 1991). And that will depend on their involvement in it. This argument is also advanced by other writers. Arnold *et al* (1991) suggest the following:

> Decisions made by groups can evoke greater commitment ... because more people feel a sense of involvement in it.

This quote supports a relationship between involvement and commitment. Research from the behavioural perspective provides further evidence and possible explanations.

Illustration 4.2 Implementation

Example A

A board of directors decide to adopt an aggressive sales strategy in their retail operations which requires sales staff actively to sell the full range of products instead of responding to customer requests.

The decision facing existing sales staff is whether to change the way they relate to customers.

Example B

A manufacturing company decides to install 'cellular' production processes in place of the established assembly-line method.

The decision facing existing production staff is whether to change the way they relate to their colleagues.

Example C

A service and distribution company decides to extend its operations into mainland Europe as a strategic response to intensifying UK competition.

The decision facing engineering service staff is whether to learn one more new languages.

Illustration 4.3 Involvement and commitment

Step one

(a) Select and describe three recent decisions which you made entirely by yourself and which affected only you, e.g., change your hairstyle or buy a new piece of clothing.
(b) Select and describe three recent decisions which you made in conjunction with others and which had consequences for you and those other people, e.g., attend university, selection of shared purchase.
(c) Select and describe three recent decisions taken by other people which had consequences for you, e.g., change in home location, a new work regime.

Step two

Rate each decision from Step one on each of the following scales.

Degree of involvement

Low									High
1	2	3	4	5	6	7	8	9	10

Degree of commitment

Low									High
1	2	3	4	5	6	7	8	9	10

Step three

(a) Examine your ratings for possible relationships between the nature of the decision, the decision process and the factors of involvement and commitment.
(b) Record your results and think about possible conclusions.

Kiesler's work (1971) suggests that public statements of agreement to a decision, made on the basis of exercising free will, creates commitment. The pre-condition of free will and public statements would seem to require involvement in the decision-making process.

However, it is not yet possible within psychology to draw firm conclusions. What can be said at the moment is that there is evidence to suggest that individuals will feel more committed to decisions they have been involved in making. This is because they will have an emotional investment in the decision. In turn, this is likely to lead to a higher probability of individuals adopting required changes in their own behaviour in order to implement the decision. This has obvious implications for the implementation phase of decision-making models.

Given the nature of psychology it seems appropriate to invite readers to engage in some self-reflection and analysis. The activity in Illustration 4.3 allows you to do this in terms of the issue of involvement and its relationship to commitment.

CAREER CHOICE DECISIONS

Career choice is an area which seems to offer the potential of examining decisions made by individuals. Sociologists would argue that there will be factors outside of the individual, arising out of the structure of society, which are equally important in determining career decisions. This is no doubt the case. However, such factors are likely to influence the range of choices available to an individual rather than determine the specific decision. Career choice decisions provide a valid example of individual decision making.

There is one particular general model of individual decision making which it is appropriate to describe here. The model is not specifically concerned with career decisions but, to the extent that it is a valid model, it will help explain how such decisions are arrived at. The model concerns the notion of decision styles.

Decision styles

Decision style refers to the existence of differences between individuals in terms of how they make decisions, and how the same person makes decisions in different ways according to the nature of the decision and the particular circumstances. As Arnold *et al* (1991) note, many models of decision style are based on personality types, and these in turn are generally devised from the personality theory devised by Jung, a co-worker of Freud. Thus the psychodynamic perspective provides insight into the processes by which individuals arrive at career decisions.

The work of Arroba on decision styles, also reported by Arnold, suggests a typology of six broad styles.

- No thought
- Compliant: (with external expectations)
- Logical: (careful, objective evaluation of alternatives)
- Emotional: (likes and dislikes most important factors)
- Intuitive: (the decision 'feels' right)
- Hesitant: (slow to build commitment to decision)

Interestingly, Arroba found that the logical style (nearest to the rational model) was used more often for work decisions than personal decisions. However, the emotional style was more common for important decisions and the intuitive style more common for very important decisions. This is an interesting finding, especially when put together with the finding of Nutt (Arnold, 1991) that top managers are more influenced by their decision style than middle managers. It has to be recognised, however, that the style typology devised by Nutt was different from that of Arroba.

Career choices

The notion of decision styles has been specifically applied to career choices. Phillips *et al* (Arnold *et al*, 1991) identified three broad styles applied to decisions on careers.

- Rational: (logical assessment of advantages/disadvantages of various options)
- Intuitive: (options are considered but choice made on which one 'feels' right)
- Dependent: (responsibility denied/avoided and other people or circumstances dictate decision)

This classification has some similarity with the more general style typologies. There are in addition other similarities. For instance, the work of Holland (1985) is one of the best known theories of career choice. This theory is firmly rooted in the notion of personality types as the key factor influencing career decisions.

Holland's theory suggests a match between personality and career choice. In other words, individuals choose careers according to which career will best suit their personality. The theory also goes on to suggest a relationship between the degree of match and eventual career success and satisfaction. Individuals will be more successful in, and will derive greater satisfaction from, careers which suit their personality. In brief, Holland's personality types are as follows:

- Realistic — An 'outdoor' type, who tends to prefer activities requiring physical strength and co-ordination. Also, a person who is comfortable with their own company.
- Investigative — A type more concerned with/interested in intellectual activities. Deals well with concepts and abstract thought.
- Artistic — An imaginative type. Expressive of feelings and ideas though not comfortable with rules and regulations.
- Social — As the term implies, a type most comfortable with other people, especially in helping relationships.
- Enterprising — A type concerned with action and with achieving objectives/results through other people. Enjoys leading and persuading.
- Conventional — A well organised type who prefers structure and order.

Holland does not suggest that any given individual will be a 'pure type', rather each person will reflect a combination of two or three types. It is also possible, according to Holland, to categorise occupations in terms of the six types. This has in fact been done in the USA, and Holland has also produced a self-assessment inventory which enables individuals to identify their type in order to establish which occupations may be appropriate for them.

Career anchors

Holland's theory reflects two perspectives in psychology. First, the psychodynamic approach in that it is rooted in personality theory which is resonant of the work of Jung. Second, the humanist approach in that the theory ascribes both the potential for exercising free will in making career decisions and the notion of personal growth through pursuing a personally satisfying and fulfilling career. A further view of career choice which bears comparison with Holland is the notion of career anchors developed by Schein (1978).

Career anchors are basically orientations towards work and occupations which influence the career choices and decisions of individuals. These orientations, or preferences, are the result of three factors.

- Attitudes and value systems
- Motives and needs
- Talents and abilities

Each of these factors is of course bound up to a greater or lesser extent with the personality of an individual. It is important to point out, however, that Schein emphasised that it is these factors as perceived by individuals themselves that produce career anchors. This self-perception will also be influenced to a great extent by experience of work in particular occupations. Indeed, the third factor, talents and abilities, requires some work experience, within or outside paid employment, before a self-perception can emerge.

The nature of each of the five career anchors suggested by Schein is described in the following list:

- Managerial — Primarily concerned with managing others. Individuals holding this anchor wish to be generalists rather than specialising in a particular occupation or function.
- Technical — In contrast to managerial, this anchor values expertise in specialist or functional skills.
- Security/Stability — A person with this career anchor usually makes a reliable employee. The concern is with a predictable work environment, therefore such people respond positively to organisation-defined career paths.
- Autonomy/Independence — The major feature here is having control over work activities and determining one's own pace and schedules. Individuals with this anchor are less likely to have ambitions about rising to the top.
- Creativity/Entrepreneurial — The final anchor is to do with creating a product or service, or indeed an organisation. Individuals place a high value on autonomy and on being managerially competent and on exercising their special talents.

Schein suggests that for most people it is clear which career anchor is dominant after a few years in work. Following that point, the dominant career anchor will be significant in career choices and decisions. In common with Holland, Schein suggests the probability of detrimental performance consequences for the organisation and psychological consequences for the individual if career anchors do not match work undertaken and career-development paths.

Psychological perspectives

The work of Schein is not dissimilar to that of Holland in terms of the underlying psychological perspectives. The components of career anchors as a concept reflect basic personality factors. The psychological effects of 'mismatch' because of the frustration of wants and needs are redolent of the anxiety caused by conflict between Freud's components of the psyche.

It is possible to postulate the influence of other perspectives in Schein's work. The notion of career anchor itself can be seen as a broad 'construct' in the way the term is used by cognitive psychologists. A career anchor can be seen as a view of work which is developed by the individual to make sense of their experience and as a means of interpreting and understanding the reality of engaging in a career.

Career anchors can also be seen as reflecting the behaviourist perspective. The idea of self-perception of talents and abilities obviously implies a learning process. The individual comes to a view of what these are through the experience of their behaviours and their effects in work environments. Indeed, Tyson and Jackson (1992) suggest that the career anchor itself is learned.

Other elements influencing career choice and career development identified by Tyson and Jackson are resonant of the behaviourist approach. For example, the notion of mentoring is discussed. In a broad sense, a mentor is someone who can, among other things, provide a role model for individuals. The concept of role modelling is an important part of social learning theory (Bandura, 1977).

Career choices and decisions is a relatively recent focus of research within psychology. It is, though, a growing focus. This section has described three models drawn from psychological research (decision styles, Holland's vocational personality types and Schein's career anchors) which throw light on individual decision making in relation to career choices. Each provides alternatives to a simple rational model. However, the latter two do suggest prescriptions which are designed to enable individuals and organisations to reach decisions on a more rational analysis of available information. This is particularly true of Holland's work.

It is possible that future work in the area of career development will provide greater understanding of decision making in general. This understanding may apply to both individual and organisation decision making. In the meantime, readers are invited to complete the activity which appears in Illustration 4.4, this may help to illuminate their own decision making.

Illustration 4.4 Evaluating career choice

Step one

(a) List your main characteristics as you see them. You may wish to check out your list with other people's perceptions of you. Include information on the following.
*Wants and desires
*Values, i.e., what is good and bad, right and wrong.
*Likes and dislikes, i.e., in relation to work.
*Strengths and weaknesses.
*Talents and abilities.

(b) List the main characteristics of the job or occupation you see yourself basing a career on.

(c) How close a match is there between (a) and (b)? Is there any relationship between your data and Holland's personality types and/or Schein's career anchors? Note your conclusion.

Step two

(a) List the factors which influenced you in your current career choice. Separate the items in your list into two sets: one headed 'Internal' (those to do with you) and one headed 'External' (those to do with other people or other circumstances).

(b) Analyse the two lists to see if they reveal anything about your decision style. Compare the lists with the decision style descriptions in this section. Note your conclusions.

Step three

Based on Steps one and two, think about how far the models described in this section help to explain your career choices. In addition, think about any ways in which applying the models may improve your decision making.

(Note: The results of this activity can be shared and discussed with others if you are part of a group studying decision making.)

SUMMARY AND CONCLUSION

This chapter has described the basic concepts and frameworks in psychology and has discussed their relevance to the study of decision making. In doing so, the chapter has emphasised the irrationality of individual decision making when it is viewed from a psychological perspective. The limitations on rationality imposed by factors such as the following have been highlighted.

- Psychological conflict
- Distortion of reality
- Personal constructs
- Individual and unique world views
- Problems in objective perception
- Influence of emotions and intuition
- Role of wants, needs and values

However, the conclusion should not be that all decision making is irrational for at least two reasons. First, one critical pointer from psychology is that it is highly unlikely that 'rational' is an objective concept. That is, the concept is an 'it all depends' concept. A decision which appears irrational to me or to other observers can be, for the particular decision maker, perfectly rational, given his/her perspective and the nature of the premise(s) on which that logic is built. Second, by being aware of the existence of the factors which limit rationality it is possible to overcome, or at least minimise, their effects. In some ways, this is the strength of prescriptive models. The general normative model of rational decision making described earlier, or the specific model developed by Holland for career decisions, are examples which have the potential of increasing the quality of decisions by dealing with the limiting factors. This is especially true of Holland since his work makes the factors explicit.

There are, then, two implications for the study of decision making in work organisations which arise from this analysis. In order fully to understand any given decision, and to understand the process which led to it, it is first necessary to have an understanding of the decision maker as a person. This is perhaps the most important lesson. What is required is first an understanding of the wants, motives, beliefs, values, experiences, constructs, etc., of the person in order to gain an insight into his unique world view. Only then will an insight into the 'rationality' of the person be gained. The second requirement is an understanding of the context from which the person draws data in order to process it into information which informs his decisions. From this will emerge an insight into the external factors which impact on the person's perception and which therefore influences what and how data is received. Putting an understanding of the person and an understanding of the context together in an analysis often reveals a logic which is missing from casual observation.

The second implication is that the quality of decisions in work organisations can only be improved if psychological factors are understood and taken into account. Rationalistic models of decision making are unlikely to have much validity as descriptive or explanatory theories. They do not represent reality, however defined, and therefore will have little if any predictive value. Mainstream psychological theories drawn from various perspectives, and those concerned specifically with decision making, are of much more value in describing and explaining individual decision-making processes. Hence it is these which need to be applied first of all. However, it is the case that rationalistic models are likely to have a value in application for the purpose of providing prescriptive advice. For, in implementing prescriptive models within a rational framework together with an understanding of psychological processes, it is possible to improve the quality of decision making. The detrimental effects of psychological processes such as perception, once recognised and acknowledged, can to some extent be negated by applying a systematic and logical framework.

The extended case study which follows has been written to enable the concepts and ideas discussed in this chapter to be applied.

EXERCISE: GIBSON'S CONFECTIONS LTD

Gibson's Confections Ltd (GCL) is a small-to-medium sized manufacturer of sugar based, boiled sweets. Until three years ago it was family owned, having been founded by Harold Gibson in 1901 to serve the local market of confectioners and grocers in what is now referred to as the West Midlands conurbation.

From those beginnings the company prospered and created for itself a niche within the total UK market for high-quality boiled sweets. However, from the early 1970s and through the 1980s, the market experienced a number of important changes. Key factors from the point of view of GCL were changing consumer tastes in confectionery products, the general trend in retailing towards supermarket shopping and bulk buying, and developments in production technology. The effect of these changes on GCL were to bring about decreasing performance in terms of both sales turnover and profit.

It was clear by the late 1980s that the company faced critical decisions if it was to remain in business. Major investment was needed to modernise the production process, product ranges required rationalising, marketing and sales strategies had to respond to changed and changing conditions. The then Chairman and Managing Director and, in effect, sole shareholder, Harold Baker III, decided to accept an offer from an American company to buy GCL. A major factor in this decision was that Harold Gibson III had never married and had no heir to pass the business to.

Thus, from 1989 onwards, GCL has been a wholly owned subsidiary of the US-based Stanton Corporation. The first act of the Stanton Corporation was to recruit a new Chairman and Managing Director, Mike Fox, who had had a successful background in retail marketing, and was appointed in June 1989. Investment funds were made available to him by Stanton on the basis of a five-year plan to increase market share, sales turnover and profit. A longer-term aim of the Stanton Corporation, agreed by Fox, was to utilise GCL as the base for exploiting the business opportunities afforded by the EEC and the opening up of the ex-Soviet Bloc markets.

Fox inherited a senior management team, some of whom are still in place. However, his early decisions concerned recruiting new people from outside GCL to senior positions. The current structure of GCL is as follows.

GIBSON CONFECTIONS LTD (GCL)
COMPANY STRUCTURE

Chairman and Managing Director
Mike Fox (43,3)

Company Secretary	Marketing Director	Production Director	Personnel Director
Jasif Rafiq	**Helen Wells**	**William Beatty**	**Toni Lennox**
(55,30)	(36,3)	(60,40)	(30,1)
Accounts	Marketing	Production	Personnel
Data Processing	Sales Office	Works Engineer	Training
Finance	Field Sales	Industrial Engineer	Industrial Relations
Administration	Key Accounts	Quality Control	
Services		Transport	
(40)	(55)	(220)	(5)

Notes:

1 The figures below the directors' names refer to their age and length of service with the company respectively. (NB Length of service does not necessarily mean in the present position.)

2 The figures under each functional area refer to numbers employed in those functions. These are expressed in full time equivalents.

It is clear from the organisation chart that GCL still adopts a traditional, functional structure. It is also clear that the Board of Directors constitute a mix and range of backgrounds, experience and, perhaps, ambitions.

Helen Wells was the first appointment Fox made. Prior to Wells, GCL did not have a Marketing Director. Helen Wells is a graduate with professional qualifications in marketing. Her experience before joining GCL was primarily gained in TV audio equipment and car manufacturing, so she has relevant knowledge of both production and consumer marketing. Since joining GCL, she has created Product Manager posts within the Marketing function and Key Account Manager posts within the Sales function. Wells is personable but clearly ambitious and does not hide her views on what she sees as the future for GCL.

Jasif Rafiq heads the finance and accounting function as well as acting as Company Secretary. He joined GCL shortly after qualifying and was part of the team under Harold Baker III. William Beatty was also part of that team. Beatty is very near retirement but remains committed to the company and its reputation for product quality. As Production Director, he has the responsibility for Industrial and Works Engineering, Health and Safety, Quality and also Transport. Beatty and his staff have been very important in planning and implementing changes in the production process and decisions affecting investment in capital equipment. Beatty strongly believes further investment is needed in these areas although available funds are at present limited. Both established directors favour continuing with the strengths of Gibson, as they see them, as a basis for expansion in the future.

Toni Lennox is Mike Fox's most recent appointment. As with marketing, personnel had not been represented at board level in the past. Lennox is the youngest member of the board. She is bright and ambitious and a little intolerant of those she views as not understanding the personnel function. Lennox has high-level qualifications in general management as well as personnel – a major reason Fox appointed her. Lennox does, though, have limited knowledge and experience of the sector since her career to date has been in public services.

The current situation in GCL is that performance is beginning to improve, though not at the rate demanded by the Stanton Corporation. Fox is under pressure to bring about speedier improvements and to develop a viable strategic plan to achieve the longer-term aims set by Stanton. Fox, Wells and Lennox have worked closely together over the previous 12 months to produce the basic elements of such a plan. These consist mainly of: adopting a strong marketing orientation in the company; rationalising both products and production processes (with consequent effects on both the customer base and staffing structures); introducing new approaches to the management of employees to increase labour flexibility and reduce unit costs; adopting and exploiting the advantages of new technology throughout all aspects of the business; and, finally, to bring forward the original timescales for extending the company's operations outside the UK.

Rafiq and Beatty have had little involvement in this work, though they are aware of its content. Both have expressed reservations concerning the appropriateness of the plan, and, in the case of Rafiq, its financial viability. These differences of view between the new and established directors is, to an extent, added to by the different outlooks of two different generations. There are also personality tensions within the board.

Mike Fox appreciates the caution being expressed by the longer serving directors. He also understands their reasons. He is, though, convinced that the basic elements are those required to ensure the long-term survival and success of GCL. Of more concern to Fox are the reactions and responses of others in the company. The vast majority of those in middle- and lower- management jobs are 'Gibson' people who have grown with the company. Most are unqualified and progressed through the ranks to their current positions. They have a loyal commitment to the 'Gibson Tradition'. This tradition places a high value on production which has previously been the dominant function in the company. Quality is another factor in the tradition. Standards set by GCL in the past have been more to do with internal criteria than with customer expectations or wants. Another factor of concern is that some of them are likely to lose their jobs through redundancy as Fox intends to reduce layers of management as part of the strategic plan. However, the plan will not succeed without active support from all levels of management.

Fox arrived at work today to find a fax waiting for him from the Vice President (European Operations) of Stanton Corporation. The fax requests a short paper from Fox outlining his medium-term plans for GCL. The paper is required for a Stanton Strategic Planning Group meeting to be held in three days' time. Mike Fox is in a dilemma. He does not have enough time to formalise agreement and support for his plan with the GCL Board. Neither can he gauge the nature of the response to the strategic plan from GCL middle managers in the time available. The decision facing him concerns the content of the paper he will send to the Stanton VP. Should it contain the details worked out by Fox, Wells and Lennox, and thereby commit GCL to that direction? Alternatively, should he send a 'holding' paper which will not meet Stanton's requirements? 'It's tough being an MD' Fox thought to himself!

DISCUSSION QUESTIONS

General

1 What psychological factors are having impact on each of the main characters in the case?

2 How will these factors affect each character in terms of their likely support or otherwise for the proposed strategy?

3 What are the key psychological factors influencing the MD's response to the Stanton Corporation's faxed request?

4 What do you think the MD will do, and why?

5 What advice would you give the MD in terms of how he makes his decision and in terms of what his decision should be?

Career choices

1 How can either Holland's personality types or Schein's career anchors explain the career history of each main character?

2 To what extent will the career anchor of each individual influence their support or not for the proposed strategy?

GLOSSARY OF MAIN TERMS

Behaviourist A psychological perspective which emphasises the role of life experiences and learned responses in determining individual behaviour.

Bias A predisposition or prejudice which acts to influence external data towards conforming with pre-existing interpretations.

Career anchors A classification of orientations to work and occupations which arises out of the interaction of self-perceived wants and needs, beliefs and values and talents and abilities. The career anchor held by an individual is a key influencing factor in career choices and decisions.

Cognitive A psychological perspective which focuses on the mind as an information-processing system which seeks to make sense of new experiences in terms of established understandings (See Personal Constructs).

Commitment The degree to which an individual feels an emotional or affective attachment to a decision and therefore is likely to support its implementation. May be a function of involvement.

Decision style Classifications of the range of approaches individuals can adopt to making decisions with approaches commonly being differentiated according to factors associated with established personality factors. Several typologies are suggested in the literature.

Heuristics Generalised 'rules of thumb' formed by individuals which provide simple guidelines for classifying and interpreting data and which can take the form of simple decision rules.

Humanistic A psychological perspective which views an individual as a responsible, autonomous entity exercising free will in pursuit of personal growth.

Implicit personality A term used to describe the predisposition of human beings to classify other individuals according to a personal specification of personality types and to ascribe all characteristics of the type to any individual displaying one or more characteristics of a given type.

Involvement The degree to which an individual participates in and is able to influence and/or determine a given decision.

Perception The active psychological process which selects and organises physiological stimuli into meaningful patterns.

Perceptual world A term used to describe the unique view of the world and their place in it held by all individuals.

Personal construct An idea within cognitive psychology which suggests 'frameworks' of knowledge and beliefs which are based on bi-polar concepts such as warm and cold, and which are utilised to make sense of the world.

Psychology The study of human behaviour which seeks explanations at the level of the individual through application of more or less scientific methods.

Psychodynamic A psychological perspective which emphasises the conflict between the Id, the Ego and the Superego, and the consequent anxiety as a cause of behaviour.

Rationality A concept concerned with logical and systematic processing of data which is seen to be objective in nature.

Subjective expected utility A concept which suggests that the value of outcomes, and the degree of expectancy of achievement considered acceptable, are subjectively defined.

Vocational Personality A classification of personality types specifically devised by Holland to support work in career guidance. Used to both explain and prescribe career choice decisions.

REFERENCES

Bandura, A. (1977) *Social Learning Theory*, Prentice Hall.

Bevan, S., and Fryatt, J. (1988) *Employee Selection in the UK*, Sussex, Institute of Manpower Studies.

Huczynski, A., and Buchanan, D. (1991) *Organisation Behaviour* (2nd Ed), Prentice Hall.

Jackson, K. F. (1975) *The Art of Problem Solving*, Heinemann.

Kahneman, D., Slovic, P., Tverskey, A. (Eds) (1987) Judgement under Uncertainty: Heuristics and Biases, Cambridge University Press.

Kelly, G. A. (1955) *The Psychology of Personal Constructs*, Vols 1 & 2, Norton.

Kets de Vries, M., and Miller, D. (1984) *The Neurotic Organisation*, Jossey Bass.

Kiesler, C. A. (1971) *The Psychology of Commitment*, London, Academic Press.

Maslow, A. H. (1962) *Toward a Psychology of Being*, Van Nostrand.

Miller, G. A. (1966) *Psychology: The Science of Mental Life*, Penguin.

Rogers, C. R. (1970) *On Becoming a Person*, Houghton Mifflin.

Stewart, J. (1991) *Managing Change Through Training and Development*, Kogan Page.

Tyson, S. and Jackson, T. (1992) *The Essence of Organisational Behaviour*, Prentice Hall.

Webster, E. C. (1964) *Decision Making in the Employment Interview*, McGill University.

FURTHER READING

Arnold, J., Robertson, I. T., and Cooper, C.L. (1991) *Work Psychology*, Pitman.

Hilgard, E. R., Atkinson, R. C., and Atkinson, R. L. (1975) *Introduction To Psychology*, Harcourt Brace Jovanovich.

Hogarth, R. M. (1987) *Judgement and Choice*, Wiley.

Holland, J. L. (1985) *Making Vocational Choices* (2nd Ed), Prentice Hall.

Ribeaux, P., and Poppleton, S.E. (1978) *Psychology And Work*, Macmillan Education.

Schein, E. H. (1978) *Career Dynamics: Matching Individual and Organisation Needs*, Addison-Wesley.

CHAPTER 5

Simulation and model building

Stuart Wattam

SIMULATION

The idea of simulation is nothing new. Most children mimic or simulate later adult life in their play. A practical definition of simulation may take the following form.

To mimic the action of a physical system by means other than that actually employed by the system.

Often quite complex situations and problems can be distilled into a few equations. The business problem can be approximated by a set of rules, equations and values that attempt closely to mimic the reality of the problem sufficiently accurately so as to make the simulation act almost like the 'real thing'.

The higher the degree of accuracy of simulation the more the simulation is attractive to the decision maker. The degree and level of accuracy is dependent on several factors; essentially the more accuracy that is required, the more expensive the simulation will become to develop. The trade-off in terms of cost is yet another decision which is associated with choosing to build a model in the first place.

The model of the problem area can be developed alongside, and at the same time as, the thought process of the decision maker. The simulation can be executed several times to test alternatives, or to allow for experimentation that would not be possible with the real problem area. The contraction of physical time into a few seconds of computation, using a simulation, can aid the decision maker to evaluate and test alternatives, without commitment of major resources, or the occurrence of major risks. The simulation can therefore be viewed as a luxury that a manager can afford to indulge in, since the consequences of failure are fateful only for the simulation, and not for the 'real' problem area. There are two principles of simulation, *time contraction*, and *what if* that we shall meet later.

The other basic ideas that must be defined are *problem domain* and *'problem requirements'*. Organisations may have problems that can be defined in general terms; for example, the sales figures may be variable and management are unsure of the reason why, but they know there is something wrong. The organisation has therefore defined the problem domain as being related to the sales figures, i.e., they have put a boundary around the area they wish to consider, and that area of activity within the boundary has a problem associated with it. The organisation can go further and say that it is not happy with the seasonal trend in the sales figures, and wishes to improve the nature of its sales. Thus the organisation has set a broad decision requirement that the study of the problem domain should lead to some ideas on how to improve the seasonal nature of the sales, if at all possible.

Alternatively the problem area may be viewed as the area of concern, and the problem requirements as the terms of reference and objectives of the study of the problem domain. The essence therefore of simulation is to provide a mechanism by which the decision

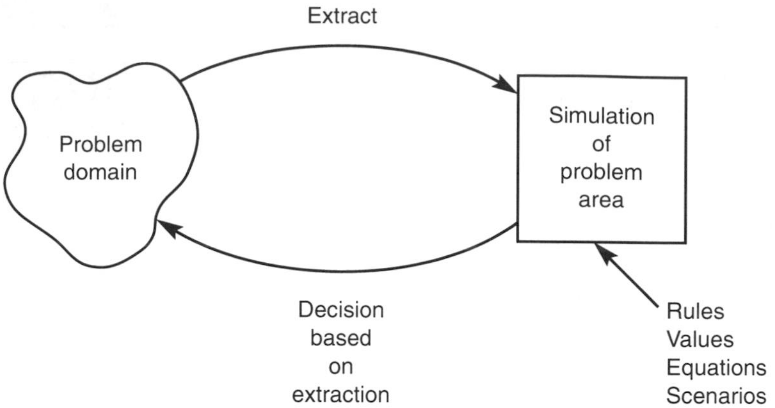

Fig. 5.1 Problem maps to a simulation

maker can do just that, i.e., make decisions, based on a finite set of criteria, simulated from the problem domain in a 'safe environment'.

The simulation can be quite complex or quite simple, but it will be a function of the problem domain. The more complex the problem domain the more 'noise' or confusion the decision maker will have to cope with. The 'noise' could take the form of interference from other projects, errors in information, or the influence of a lot of dependant actions, variables and characteristics. Extracting the critical characteristics, and the factors that drive the problem area, is one of the crucial things the model builder must do. The best types of simulation may also be approximations to what actually happens, so as to remove the complexity from the problem domain, and present the decision taker with a clear unambiguous picture of the problem. By simplifying the problem much of the 'noise' can be removed from the simulation. There is, of course, a price to pay in terms of accuracy of the simulation.

Essentially when we build a model we need some idea of why we are attempting the task. Table 5.1 explains a number of reasons why we build models. These are similar in many respects to the reasons why we try to simulate complex problems. In principle models and simulations can often be considered synonymous.

THE MODELLING CYCLE

The problem domain in business can also be quite expensive to simulate, and difficult to perform experiments and trials on. We must therefore ask ourselves a set of fundamental

Illustration 5.1 The flight simulator

Jumbo Jets

The flight simulator mimics the actions and physical feel of an aircraft for the trainee pilot; it is not a substitute for the actual aircraft or the experience of flight. The cost is often cheaper than the actual aircraft (not as expensive as allowing the trainee to crash a Jumbo). The simulator provides a good approximation to the actual task of flying.

Table 5.1

Why build models?
Inevitable There are no fixed or permanent dividing lines between facts about a system, and the beliefs held about a system or situation. Models are theories, laws, equations or beliefs which state things about the problem in hand, and assist in our understanding of it.
Economic The compression of a system into model form allows information to be passed, assessed and quantified, so that the ideas and beliefs contained within the model can be altered or modified at will. Thus, there is lower use of resources than when experimenting with actuality.
Simplification When we build a model, of necessity, we over-generalise and simplify. This is to make clear those complex areas within the task at hand. By simplification we can ensure a close examination of those parts of the system that may prove contentious, or those parts where an improvement in existing working is required.

questions about the problem domain. Does it require complex simulation? Does it lend itself to trial and experiment without detrimental effects?

To simulate the problem domain we need to define the essence of the problem, and distil this down to some form that can be manipulated, tested, experimented on and compared with actuality for confirmation of performance. Thus allowing the decision maker to test out the manipulations on the simulation prior to attempting to do so on the actual business area.

Figure 5.2 identifies the process as model building. The model itself simulates the actions and processes contained in the problem domain. The first pass may not simulate the problem domain accurately enough, therefore subsequent passes through the cycle are needed to refine, and redefine the model, and hence the simulation of the problem domain. Thus the decision maker may have to revise estimates, re-evaluate the rules, values and equations so as to modify the simulation several times.

Simulation of the problem domain and extracting the essence of the problem is akin to problem solving; we are building a model of reality which we can then manipulate to find a solution.

As an example consider the demand and supply chain. A product is supplied at a

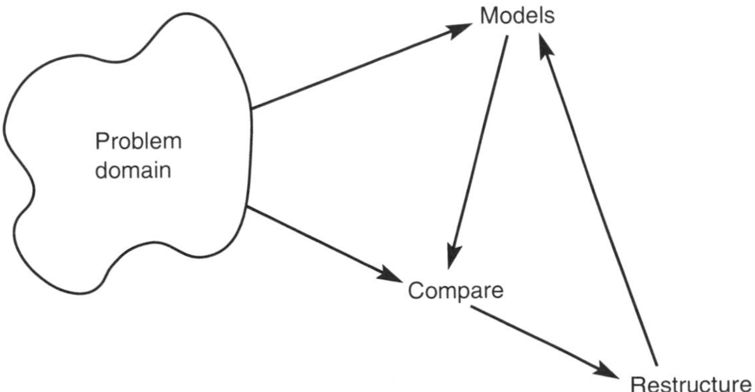

Fig. 5.2 Model, compare, restructure cycle

constant rate to the seller, but demand is patchy, and varies with no particular pattern only that it averages out over a given period of time (say one year). This we can average to monthly figures. The flow of supply and demand can be seen as analogous to the old mathematical problem of water running into a bath, and someone emptying it with a bucket.

- The water running into the bath at a given rate (volume) is equivalent to the supply of goods to the seller (supply side).
- The water being taken out via the bucket is equivalent to customers buying the product (demand side).
- The remaining volume in the bath is equivalent to 'stock in hand'.

We can even use algebra if we want and write down the following expression:

$$supply + stock >= demand$$

From this simple expression we can perform different types of experiment with the variables of stock, supply and demand. The supply of goods or services could be from several sources, not necessarily all supplying at the same rate. Similarly the stock carried can vary, and is dependant of the amount sold, also the supply rate.

For example, a company may expect a supply of 100 units from source A, and 200 units from source B. The suppliers never send exactly what is expected, but on average they manage 90 per cent and 95 per cent respectively. (These percentages are crucial, in that they determine what we can expect the supply of units to be.)

Supply can be expressed as

$$supply = (0.9 \times 100) + (0.95 \times 200)$$

Similarly we can obtain figures for stock and demand.

Assume that we want to obtain the best possible stock profile for the company. This means that at any one time we wish to keep the minimum amount of stock to satisfy the demand. This is illustrated in the following set of calculations that could be carried out using a computer spread-sheet.

First half of year:

	January	*February*	*March*	*April*	*May*	*June*
Supply A	90	90	90	90	90	90
Supply B	190	190	190	190	190	190
Total supply	280	280	280	280	280	280
Demand	300	290	280	270	260	250
Difference	-20	-10	0	10	20	30

Second half of year:

	July	*August*	*September*	*October*	*November*	*December*
Supply A	90	90	90	90	90	90
Supply B	190	190	190	190	190	190
Total supply	280	280	280	280	280	280
Demand	260	265	280	290	300	285
Difference	20	15	0	-10	-20	-5

Remaining stock level after one-half year is 30 units.

The model could be made more sophisticated by carrying forward the monthly difference in stock figures, so that the opening stock at each month reflects the position at the end of the previous month. However, even a simple calculation such as the above shows that for the year as a whole the company is either ordering too much, or not selling enough. To determine which it is would require further investigation. The problem can be viewed as over-optimistic sales forecasts, or the inability of the suppliers to produce enough of the units to the purchasing contract.

Chapter 2 identified some of the characteristics of a system, and outlined the way that systems concepts can be used to map the existing processes, tasks, or the organisations method of working, into a manageable set of statements.

To produce a model of a system in its necessary complexity, it requires the person or people who produce the said system, to thoroughly appreciate the workings and complexity of the system which they are building to mimic the actuality. The system model must reflect the reality of the problem area. This involves the constructor(s) in a learning phase: learning the language of the problem area, its workings, its interactions, and the people involved.

If the system is large then this task is extremely difficult. Most people tend to simplify and make generalisations or 'rules of thumb' when coming to terms with a new problem. Often, when that problem is large and/or difficult, we make a model of the system or problem so that we can simulate it, and hence understand its behaviour.

The economy of building such a model is obvious, since it will be on a smaller and more manageable scale than the actual problem or system, and all the proposed configurations, alterations and behaviour can be tested and simulated on the model.

The model forms the basis of discussion, measurement and simulation of the system rather than the system proper. This reduces costs, and improves the *reliability* and *functionality* of the decision making. The reliability of the decision-making process is improved by using the model as a basis on which to make the decisions. Since the model is a rational set of rules, values and variables, the decision is also based on these, and is therefore more reliable, free from error and more rational than one based on a guess, or on a less well-defined idea. Also, given the same or similar decisions at a later date, the model can be used again. The functionality of the model is dependent on how easy it is to change, and what spectrum of similar decisions it intends to cover. The more complex the model, the more functionality it will have, but it will be difficult to understand and modify, and may not be reliable because of these difficulties. There is a trade-off between these factors, the importance of the problem area and the reliability, functionality and cost associated with a model.

The idea of building a model of the system is a direct transfer from engineering, where the engineer will build a scale model of components and, finally, a prototype of the finished product for testing. These tests can be very comprehensive. Motor manufacturers not only test their designs on computer simulations of cars, but go on to test prototypes of the cars for endurance, crash resistance, vibrations, sales potential, etc. The behaviour of the prototype is then examined and set against the design criteria outlined in the original specification. The formulation of design criteria for engineering and software construction are similar.

Software construction can be viewed as a six-stage process as follows:

1 Statement of requirements, that identifies how the study is to be done, what the end

product is intended to achieve, and the resources allocated to the study.
2 Feasibility study which looks at the area for computer automation, and determines if the area is applicable for computerisation.
3 Analysis of alternatives, feasible solutions are determined for selection against the criteria set in stage one.
4 Design of selected alternative into a specification of hardware, software, and data structures. Also a detailed design, plan for construction and deployment of resources.
5 Implementation and training of the computer software and the people who are going to 'run' the software on the computer.
6 Evaluation of implemented software against initial criteria to see if the implementation meets initial requirements, or to see if any modifications or enhancements are needed.

The only difference between software models and those of engineering are that it is somewhat easier to put quantitative measures on reliability, performance and price on mechanical objects.

We can take the list above, and compare it with the model building or simulation process, and find that there is a marked similarity in approaches.

Inevitability of model building

The inevitability of building a model is closely tied with the method we use to build the said model. In an earlier chapter you were introduced to Soft Systems Methodology (SSM). SSM also has a few fundamental ideas regarding the structure and purpose of the problem-solving method, these are:

- *Purpose activity as a system (problem domain).* The problem domain in the real world defined in such a way that it is describable by the methods, tools and techniques of systems analysis (both hard and soft), complete with boundary, inputs, outputs, and it exists to achieve some sort of goal or set of goals.
- *Declaration of view or picture (Weltanschauung).* Every individual brings to the problem a set of knowledge understanding and experience of the problem situation which is unique to that individual. The crucial idea is to achieve a consensus of view in any team that is producing a model such that the model is agreed and understood.
- *Systemisity in the process of enquiry (method).* The process of developing a model needs to follow a known course, and when it deviates from that course this is understood and allowed for even though there may be several steps, iterations and loops round the set of steps, prior to a completed model being developed.
- *Outcomes of structure, process, flows, etc.* A well-understood 'language' that can be used to describe how the problem domain works and the influences on the domain. It can readily be understood, e.g., flowcharting using a graphical language and conventions.

The economies of model building

The 'cheapness' of the resulting model is a factor which should not be overlooked. The discussion of the problem domain, and the study of the complex problem area may not be possible without the use of a good model. The idea is to pass understandable information to the owner of the problem (the decision maker) and fellow analysts about what is happening in the problem domain. Clarity in understanding comes from the dissection of the problem into its component parts, and a description in a 'language', e.g., charts or diagrams, which are understandable for both the problem owner (the decision maker) and the modeller. These rules, facts, values and scenarios can then be assessed and understood by others who may be able to suggest alternatives and further ideas that may help with the solution. This can then lead to action with respect to the problem domain.

We can develop a model, using the example given earlier (see page 124), extending its development by allowing for the stock to be carried forward from one month to the next. The model's output is as follows:

	January	*February*	*March*	*April*	*May*	*June*
Supply A	90	90	90	90	90	90
Supply B	190	190	190	190	190	190
Carried forward	280	260	250	250	260	280
Demand	300	290	280	270	260	250
Difference	-20	-30	-30	-20	0	30

	July	*August*	*September*	*October*	*November*	*December*
Supply A	90	90	90	90	90	90
Supply B	190	190	190	190	190	190
Carried forward	310	330	345	345	335	315
Demand	260	265	280	290	300	285
Difference	50	65	65	55	35	30

This simple modification in the model shows that the required maximum stockholding is not 30, as suspected, but 65. The decision maker can handle this information in two ways. Either reduce the supply of both items of stock, or increase the sales. Further modifications of the model will improve the decision maker's information. Improvements in the model, by expanding and modifying its rules, form a circular self-modifying process. This process is the essence of model building, and should be seen as a necessary part of the process of actually understanding the problem domain, and acting on thc solutions that are proposed.

Simplification by model building

Simplification of the problem domain may at first sight be a difficult task, but we have to attempt this simplification in order to follow the system ideas in Chapter 2. However, by starting off with a few basic ideas, or adopting a method of investigation, a set of simple questions can be asked:

- Who does the tasks?
- What is the nature of the problem?
- Who is affected by the problem?
- Who is important in the given situation?

With the answers to these questions a start can be made to formulate some ideas of the complex issues that are involved in the problem domain.

In the case of the simple stock example above, the use of the model depends on who is looking at it. If, for instance, the Stock Control Manager uses the model the stock volumes will be a critical issue, i.e., he will be interested in the amount of stock the company must hold. Alternatively, the Sales Manager will be interested in the apparent seasonality of sales, as shown by the demand figures. The Purchasing Manager will be interested in the supply figures, and will wonder why there is a difference between promised supply, and items delivered.

The nature of the problem is that it is not associated with a single task area – stock, sales or purchasing – but an amalgamation of them all. It seems, from this simple example, that all three areas of the business need to be looked into to ascertain precisely what is happening, since all three are affected by the problem.

Certain problem areas are narrowly focused, and some are broadly focused such as this. The more narrowly focused the problem area the easier it is to model because questions and analysis cover only a small area of operation.

TYPES OF MODEL AND THEIR USES

We have a choice of model which we can create. The type of representation we choose is dependent on the system we are trying to model, and the purpose of the model. Table 5.2 gives a brief description of the types of model that can be constructed.

We can use many or all the types of model listed in Table 5.2 in the generation of a working understanding of the problem under consideration. There are, however, certain aspects that can be extracted from this table that help us to formulate a suitable model that can be used with effect in a decision-making methodology. The characteristics that we look for in our models are:

- a reflection in the representation of the real-world properties of the system and an accurate portrayal of the characteristics of the real-world system;
- that they are built in a standard and disciplined manner in accordance with some methodology;

Table 5.2 Types of Model

Descriptive models provide a qualitative description and explanation of the system we are considering, e.g., a word picture of the problem domain.

Predictive models are produced so that estimates of future performance, cost and accuracy of expected values, may be accessed, e.g., data collected over a period of time or area is analysed to produce the necessary guide values.

Mechanistic models are a description of the behaviour of the system, given its inputs, outputs and processing requirements. Such a model is provided by the analysis and design documents produced for computer systems.

Empirical/statistical models are obtained by fitting data to mathematical models from existing systems, e.g., regression analysis, finding average figures from groups of like figures, etc.

Steady state models model the system's average performance against time, e.g., as above in statistical analysis, but the data is dependent on time.

Dynamic models fully represent the fluctuations of performance with time, e.g., the model behaves exactly like the problem domain over the time span of the experiment.

Local models are a description of the individual subsystems that form the model and hence in the aggregate form the system.

Global models give descriptions of the whole of each model, and hence of the system.

- that the complexity of the model is handled by suitable tools.

MODEL-BUILDING STEPS

If we build a model we have an aid to problem solving, which is specific in terms of the decision-making environment it applies to. The following list is an outline to the task of developing a model. Most of the activity is concerned with obtaining the information required to understand the problem area, and then structuring it in an understandable way, so that the problem is amenable to the application of standard management science techniques, to be discussed in Chapter 6, or is developed so as to simplify and aid understanding. The information can be captured by using the tools and techniques described in Chapter 2, on systems, presenting them to the decision maker as a set of rules, analyses, scenarios and variables; these can then be developed further by the techniques described in Chapter 6. Model building is the essence of problem solving, and the use of a set of steps or methodology for model construction helps to enforce a structure to the solving of often unstructured problems. Each of the identified steps below can be subdivided as appropriate.

1 Classification of the problem area using the client's own internal knowledge, including any bias in that view. The model must try to reflect the way the decision maker thinks about problems, take into account his/her experience, and to use the same language and familiar techniques, or techniques that are appropriate for the problem's owner (the decision maker).

2 The encoding of the problem's elements into familiar concepts and ideas, e.g.,

   Supply is the percentage of expected deliveries from supplier A , plus the percentage of supplies expected from B. This can be expressed mathematically as

   $$S = M_1 \times X_1 + M_2 \times X_2$$

   where the X's represent expected supply, and the M's the percentages actually received. Some people will understand the mathematical equation, others will like the textual statement. It is best to include both in the model.

3 Formation of the problem's elements into structural patterns and representations rules, equations, scenarios, values, etc.

The steps are similar despite the problem area, or the type of model we are trying to build. There is a marked similarity between the model-building metaphor, and the process of simulation. Indeed the similarity is useful to the decision maker, in that the act of developing a model, and developing a simulation can be viewed as one and the same thing.

Figure 5.3 shows the broad outline of the model-building method. The management problem or system is the identified domain; in the example this was thought to be the amount of stock space or stock needed by a company. A model was built by looking at the monthly figures of supply and demand, which was checked against what actually happened. It was then found that stock was carried forward from month to month, and other factors, such as sales performance and supplier performance, should be considered.

The solution to the stock problem requires the analyst to bring together the three functional areas, and try to obtain a consensus for action for each of the areas concerned.

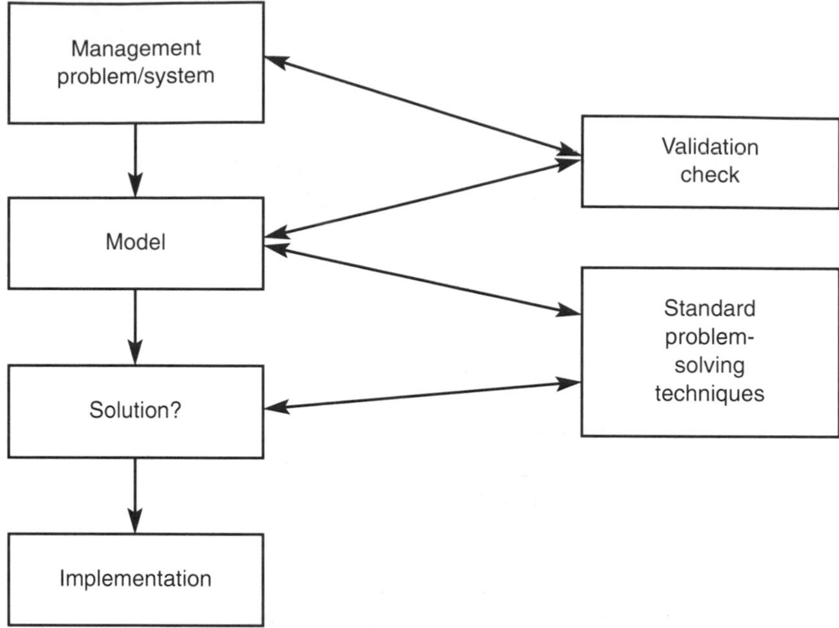

Fig. 5.3 Steps in model building

The model could be further developed to assist in the determination of these actions, e.g., by including market trends for the sales team, implementation of Just in Time for the purchasing, stock and sales functions, identification of alternative suppliers for the purchasing function.

CREATING A MODEL

The act of creating a model is an iterative and adaptive process. The model should contain all the desired information on a given system in a readable and usable form. The following set of documentation is suggested as a starting point.

- A description of the problem area, so that the domain can be identified. The domain is essentially the constraints of the model, i.e., the boundary that is arbitrarily drawn around the first rough model, and expanded or altered when more information becomes available.
- A consensus on the model requirements prior to the generation of a manipulable model. There may be more than one decision maker involved in the problem domain; often each has a different set of requirements, and the bringing together of a common set of requirements for the model may be the initial step.
- The viewpoint of the model must be flexible so as to encompass the set of processes that govern the problem area. This revolves around how easy it is to alter the contents of the model, add factors to it, alter rules, scenarios and values; manipulation of the model is critical to its usefulness.

What should be extracted from the problem domain?

First of all it is helpful if there is an identifiable mission statement, or an overall goal that can be identified and is associated with the problem domain.

Similarly the business's identifiable aims and objectives can be used as a set of targets or goals which we can include in our model building. These goals may be qualitative or quantitative in nature, and may take the general form of, for example, *increase sales by 10 per cent over the next year*. The problem, therefore, could be how to achieve this. Environmental factors governing the process of the business (such as the rate of inflation, bank rate, and so on), and hence the domain of the problem, can then be identified as influences on the business.

Entities, actors, and process in the problem domain – the identification of these can give a clearer picture of the model we are trying to build, and of the problem domain itself. These can be extracted by using Soft Systems Analysis.

Entity This is a person or item that has a set of characteristics attached to it, e.g., an order is an entity, and it has its own attributes or characteristics. It is created on receipt of a customer order and has certain values and data entries attached to it; acting together with others it has the properties of mass data such as average value.

Actors As in a play, these are the people who are in the situation covered by the problem domain. Following on from the stock example above, these would be the order clerks, and possibly the accountant.

Process The act of creating some artifact in the problem area, altering it or deleting it, e.g., the process of manufacturing the widget, will start from obtaining the raw material, and end when the widget is sold to a customer.

Figure 5.4 illustrates the use of a model of the problem domain to monitor the real-world problem. This enables us to assess the problem area and also any action or control function we wish to try on it prior to committing resources to the 'real world' situation.

The monitoring of the problem area is essential to establish performance criteria for it, and for the model which simulates the action. The qualitative and quantitative values obtained can then be collected for supporting the model, and for establishing the transformation mechanisms that can be applied to the problem domain.

Transformation mechanisms are the instructions, modifications to working practice, new markets, increased accountability, and other management decisions, instructions and ideas formulated by the management team. They are used to attempt the enhancement, modification and alteration of an organisation's actions, procedures and methods of working.

Essentially the model is mimicking the real world, and the manipulation of the model gives the decision maker the possibility of trying out new methods of working, new amounts of resources, alternative market trends, inflation rates, etc. The variables contained in the model can each be altered in turn to assess their particular influence on the model prior to altering them in the real world. When a successful combination of values, rules, variables and scenarios is obtained, these can be expressed as management decisions which can then be used to transform the operations, methods, resources and processes covered by the problem area. Remember though that when this is done the model will have to be altered to reflect the new set of 'real world' factors.

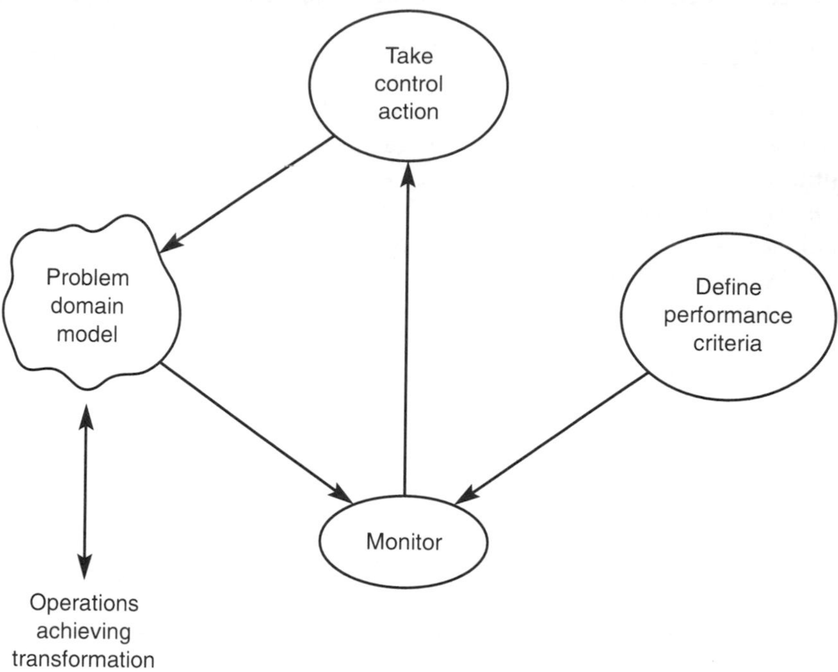

Fig. 5.4 Problem domain model and monitoring

MODELLING OF A 'REAL-WORLD' PROBLEM

When we build models, the form or format of the information which is used to convey the model's result is important. The example of the stock figures is worth examining again. Some people would like to view the results of manipulating the model as figures, and some as a graph; alternatively the decision maker may only be interested in the maximum and minimum values of stock level, and how these correspond to the number of people on the sales staff. The planning, directing and executing of the operations or activities involved in the selected methodology is important so that the correct data is displayed in the correct way to the correct decision maker. This allows the decision maker to make appropriate decisions based on effective data.

Of equal importance is the assistance that the chosen methodology gives in getting started, and in stepping through the development. The process of modelling is crucial to the quality of results. The system's methodologies should fully prescribe the way the analysis is done, right down to the number and type of diagrams used. Unfortunately when we build a model of a problem area there is no fixed method of working, only a set of general guidelines, tools and techniques which help with the solution of the problem.

Finally, it must be apparent when the process is complete. The solution of a particular problem may not be apparent; or the problem may be solved because in analysing the problem domain a greater understanding is obtained of the area, and the decision maker can make supposedly rational decisions based on that fuller understanding. This understanding may require one or more iterations through the modelling loop, or development of a set of rules which the problem domain displays leading to development of sub-problem areas for consideration in the same fashion.

The model itself must be in a concrete form; for example, it might be a table of expected values for the stock figures, or it can be an abstract declaration of behaviour such as 'the sales are seasonal: high in summer, low in winter'. The form the model takes will vary between these extremes, but should be a basis for understanding the *problem domain* and *decision requirements*, as well as the *essential properties of the system*.

The model representation can, therefore, be viewed as a set of languages, e.g., graphical, structured English, mathematical, that provide a representation of the system that we can think about and communicate to others, as well as modify and experiment with.

Traditional methodologies generate mathematical models of the existing systems. These are manipulated by the analyst to form a simulation which can then, if so wished, be coded into a computer. The mathematical model of the problem can then be developed incrementally by the analyst in conjunction with the decision maker.

Often, despite the implied interaction with the decision maker, the final product does not meet the requirements that are set by the decision maker. One critical reason for this is that the models we build must be manipulable, and accessible to the decision maker. Often the analyst and decision maker are the same person, however this principle remains the same.

Consider again our simulation of demand and supply:

$$supply + stock >= demand$$

As you are probably aware, if demand and supply don't match we have difficulty. The general rule is to keep the left-hand side as close to equality with the right-hand side as possible. Thus we have a simple model of demand and supply which we can manipulate.

It can also be described in English:

the supply of widget plus the stock of widget must be greater than or equal to the amount of widget we sell.

For instance, if we need to reduce the cost of storage of widget, the model says that the nearer we get to equality (supply equalling demand), the more we have either reduced the supply of widget, or reduced our stock levels of widget. Mathematically the expression stays the same, but the implications for the organisation of either reducing stock levels, or reducing supply can be far reaching.

We can also start asking some further questions of our simple model:

- How is the supply of widget made up?
- Which method of stock rotation is used?
- Is the demand showing any pattern?

The model can then be adapted to cope with the answers to these questions. It is therefore, accessible, and manipulable. By adding factors, and making assumptions, the simple model can become quite complex; the only problem is 'is it accurate?' This can be evaluated by testing the model's output against the actual supply, stock and demand figures over a given time. Indeed we may wish to use actual figures in our initial model. Our initial model may be based on averages obtained from previous years or months, inflated or deflated by known factors. As the current year progresses we insert actual figures into the model and see how the behaviour of the model, or the results of its numerical calculation, alter.

Essentially our ideas about solving the problem can be tested on the model prior to implementation in the real world. This reduces the risk of taking the wrong decision.

Figure 5.4 illustrates the process of using a model of the problem domain to monitor the real-world problem, and to assess actions which, by managerial action, attempt to control and manage the problem area in some way. To enable the model to assist the manager to make coherent decisions, the parameters which help the decision maker are set as criteria for performance (measures of performance), and are essentially the objectives of the simulation or model. These can be a mixture of qualitative and quantitative information collected to support the model and be of use when building it. As an example, consider the business requirement to increase sales by 10 per cent over the next year. Does this mean 'across the board', i.e., all goods sold by the company? Or does it mean 'in a specific market with specific items'? It may be that yellow widgets are easy to sell, and that the sales force needs to be reminded of this fact to achieve the required increase in sales. Alternatively the environment for selling the widget range might be difficult, and some investment in advertising or promotion may be needed as well as fresh commitment by the sales staff.

How, *who*, *why* and *what* are some suitable questions to ask when analysing a given problem domain. How is the set of tasks, jobs, processes or actions currently performed? Who does this set of tasks, jobs or processes? Why is the current area of consideration a problem? What are the set of actions, procedures, models that we need for a solution, or to aid our decision making? From the above can be generated the requirements for the problem solution, and the methods of how to meet those requirements in outline.

The next sections deal with the extraction of some of the factors that are to be considered in any model.

Qualitative and quantitative values

So far in this chapter the use of values, variables and factors, rules and scenarios has been used without much reference to what they are generically. Qualitative values are those expressed in 'soft' terms, e.g., 'The sales figures show an increase over the year'. Quantitative values will put a numerical figure to that increase, and provide an equation to analyse the figures.

The functional areas of the organisation or business need to be identified together with an indication of the managerial style, control structure, and problem owners. A variety of graphical techniques exist for drawing organisational charts; suffice it to say that any technique will do providing it gives the requisite level of detail.

Information is also required on products, people and control systems, e.g., the sales over a period of time, the number and cost of employees on the sales function, the type of targets set, and the time period concerned, such as yearly, monthly or quarterly. This information allows us to model realistic sales targets for a given sales team over a period of time.

Information is required describing the internal and external factors or variables which affect the organisation. These are invariably tied up with the economic climate, tax regime, competitor behaviour, customer and supplier behaviour. The model needs to be tied to the organisational strategy if it is to be successful. All of those environmental factors that affect strategy, positively or negatively, must be considered (see Chapter 8).

Historical information – what has happened in the past – may give an indication of what may happen in the future. The study of past behaviour of the market, customers, suppliers, products, and finance can be a rich source of ideas to put into a model, especially one that attempts to estimate the impact of any or all of these determinants.

Evidence should also be extracted from other sources to gain an insight into competitors, rivals and industry norms.

Factors can be prioritised and evaluated by manipulating the model and comparing its output against reality to see if it mimics the behaviour of the real-world problem. But remember it can be expected that they will change, as the model develops, or as more is found out about the problem situation. If the model is not dynamic then it should be treated with suspicion, especially if it is to be used for decision making rather than as a static illustration or explanation of a process.

Objectives and the organisation

The model builder should try to obtain a clear understanding of the objectives of the organisation. This in turn gives a good indication of the likely boundary of any proposed solution. The economic purpose of the business is usually a good guide in narrowing down the problem boundary.

A basic starting point for any model of a business organisation is to ask a set of questions related to the fundamental reason for the business or organisation's existence, e.g., the types of products sold or provided, the markets sold to, goals and activities of the business. (Similarly manufacturing, distribution, etc.) Ask also where the business or organisation sees itself in the environment in regard to its position, both at present and historically, and what it is that needs to develop. These questions can be classified as a set of items for consideration as in Table 5.3.

The difference between the two types of objectives in Table 5.4 is the qualitative nature of the general objectives, while the specific objectives have values and timescales attached. In Chapter 2 open and closed objectives were introduced; these are similar in that some quantitative values are attached to qualitative statements of intent.

POINTERS TO SUCCESSFUL USE OF MODELS

We start with something that may seem obvious, but which quickly gets overlooked in the heat of developing a model. It is summed up in the acronym KISS (keep it simple stupid).

Table 5.3

Achieving goals
achievement of a specific goal e.g., return on sales
maintenance of existing ratios e.g., financial capital gearing ratio
reduction in costs e.g., overheads, rejects etc.
increases in organisational goals e.g., increased market share
development of new areas e.g., diversification of products, markets, services

Table 5.4

Some typical organisational objectives
General objectives
To improve customer service.
To maintain our reputation of being a quality supplier of widgets.
To be the major supplier of widgets in Europe to the gnome-producing countries.
Specific objectives/goals
Increase the sales of widgets by 5 per cent over the next eighteen months.
Reduce our manufacturing costs by 2 per cent over the next year.

- The primary focus of the model should be to aid decision making, or problem understanding, and not to increase the complexity, accuracy, or elaborate nature of the model.
- The comparison of alternative models of reality must be clearly expressed in the developed model. Alternative ideas or viewpoints of the decision maker(s) may be expressed as a widening of the values, rules or scenarios that model the problem domain. The essence is to strike a balance between absolute accuracy and ease of understanding and use. The solution could have many trade-offs and assumptions, but these must be clearly understood and unequivocally stated.
- The procedures expressed in the model must be carried out in such a way that the explanation to another decision maker is as straightforward as possible, i.e., a common 'language' of description, identification, and explanation is found.
- Also the electronic computer is a desirable tool, but don't forget it is easy to get tied up in the idea of using a computer, without thinking about the problem in hand.

As an example of how to develop a more complex model, consider the existing example and the issue of product supply. Let us assume that the cost of processing at any given site is variable and dependent on several factors, and that to evaluate items produced in-house we need to assess the costs accurately. To do this we need to consider:

- The number of items passing through the individual machine centres, usually in batches.
- The length of time it takes to process each batch.
- The processing itself is actually three tasks:
  - (a) set-up time for the machine;
  - (b) actual processing;
  - (c) clean-up time.
- Each centre has a number of operatives using the centre – normally one, two or three people.
- For each location the amount spent on energy, water, rent, telephone, etc., is known.
- For each location the amount spent on administration is split equally.

Question:
What is a suitable expression for the cost of producing a given batch at a given site, on a given machine using given people? The answer is:

variable costs + fixed costs + raw material costs + waste cost

Both the variable and fixed costs can be allocated *pro rata* to the individual centres.

Care has to be taken since the difference between the two types of cost is a grey area, especially when considering individual production units. The more we can treat all costs as 'variable' the more accurately an assessment can be made of the cost of producing a given batch. More significantly, the performance of individual centres can be monitored against a set of criteria as identified above. A comparison of one site against another can be made for the operational costs of the items they produce. This would take the form of 'a measure of performance' such as the cost of producing product A at site A against the cost of producing it at site B.

The model produced is flexible enough to determine if it is feasible to produce the items in-house, at either site, or both, or, alternatively, purchase them as bought-in items. The use of the model does not stop at the decision to purchase or make; it can be used to monitor performance if it is fed with data relating to actual timings, costs, etc., thus enabling the productivity, costs and 'profitability' of each site or indeed each machine to be assessed.

DEVELOPMENTS IN MODELLING SOFTWARE FOR BUSINESS

A powerful set of tools is available for modelling complex situations. These vary in their usefulness to decision makers at all levels in an organisation, in terms of their understandability, functionality and ease of use. Different organisations and different individuals will have different requirements and be at different stages in their use of models and decision-making techniques. What seems old-fashioned to a person in one organisation may be new and exciting to another.

The mathematical approach to modelling has its foundations in operational research (see Chapter 6), and many of the techniques of operational research can be updated and used accordingly. The use of computer software in organisations has led to an explosion of software related to business, from statistical analysis through to report and printer handling programs, as well as the standard accounting, payroll and stock-control systems.

With the advent of the PC (Personal Computer) most people would instantly think of using the PC as a tool in the modelling and decision-making process. The PC is invaluable when undertaking a mathematical model of any complexity, it is also useful for storing text, figures, graphs and data relating to the problem in hand. Software packages of all kinds are freely available for PCs and they are moderately easy to use for the purposes of modelling a business problem. They range from specific computer languages, such as SIMULA, to general-purpose tools, such as spread-sheets, and, in between, there are data-storage packages, desk-top publishing, and a multitude of other software packages at the user's disposal. Having said that there is a lot of software available, the use of the software does not stop us having to think before we commit ourselves to using electronics in our modelling.

One of the most popular packages for the PC is the spread-sheet, and this method of mathematical modelling is both practical and flexible. The results of the analysis can be developed, modified, and displayed many times, thus testing the model, and collapsing the time element of our decision making. Remember that the analysis is only as good as the model, and if the underlying model is inaccurate, all we obtain from a computer is inaccurate results faster.

The analysis of data for insight into what is happening in the organisation is of critical importance. A large number of organisations have data in abundance, and don't do anything with it apart from storing it 'just in case'. This data is a valuable resource in its own right. The recent trend has been to pull information from the data produced by the individual functional areas into a meaningful whole, and to provide access to it either by generation of special reports and graphs or by accessing the data directly to provide accurate and up to date management information. These systems are generically called Management Information Systems (MIS) and can vary from simple data manipulation through report writing to complex statistical analysis of the data.

Other computer systems are available that may be of use to an organisation's decision makers, such as Executive Information Systems (EIS) and Decision Support Systems (DSS). EIS systems are the culmination of the development of an integrated view of the corporate data. They provide key executives with data in a variety of ways, from overall aggregate data on an organisationally wide basis, such as across a group of subsidiary companies to show performance of the group as a whole, to highly detailed data, e.g., the number of sales achieved at a particular shop. It is this ability to take different views, or slices of data, and present them in a form to the executive that is understandable that makes EIS powerful. Executives can aggregate, average, search sort, analyse and tunnel down data sets in any way they wish, to provide information on which to make a decision. There is an overlap of what is meant by MIS, DSS, and EIS. These characteristics are that they hold data in detailed form, but can present it in a meaningful way, by the application of the correct user commands. They have highly flexible interfaces with the user of the system, and can be altered to suit particular organisations, individuals and situations.

The final area that needs to be introduced is the expert system (ES). The ES can be used to make decisions instead of a highly skilled human decision maker. The ES has been around for a considerable length of time, and until recently has not met its potential. The use of ES in decision making is only useful if the decision area is well known and the data fairly stable, i.e., if the data and decision rules are static and don't change over the lifetime of the decision analysis. The ES would typically scan large amounts of data for trends, patterns and rules in much the same way as would an expert when scanning data.

Illustration 5.2 Purchasing patterns

Multiple furniture industry

The company sells self-build furniture directly to the public from large warehouses and needs to attract custom by providing discounts and attractive bargains; it also needs to make 35% margin on any sale to the public. Management also wish to look for trends in the purchasing pattern of the customers to determine future developments such as more 'wood' finishing on chipboard basic flat-pack furniture.

Typically, as in Illustration 5.2, the ES would cover a small area of expertise, where this expertise is expensive to obtain from human experts, or is repetitive, or liable to be lost due to retirement, etc. Any business area lends itself to the application of ES, e.g., analysis of sales figures of a company over a given time period may be difficult to do, so the model of the sales figures could be built using one of the techniques described in Chapter 6, and an ES built on top to interpret the results of the analysis. The development of an ES follows a similar path to building a model, as discussed in the Chapter 6.

SUMMARY

The formulation of a model facilitates the understanding of the problem itself, and gives pointers to its solution. It enables the decision maker to build a powerful tool with which to test facts, data, assumptions, ideas, and alterations to the problem area. The decision maker can use the model to simulate the problem area, test out new ideas, and monitor the behaviour of the problem area.

A variety of tools, techniques and methods can be used to develop the model; the essential mechanism is one of reduction to a set of facts, data, rules, values and ideas which map out the problem area. This is done in an iterative fashion by evaluating the model, or simulation, against reality so as to ensure accuracy of the analysis.

EXERCISE: W.M. STEEPLE

The following case is included along with a few pointers for producing a model of the organisation. It is based on a business that has been in existence for nearly 100 years, and has remained on the same sites since it was founded in the later part of the last century. It has also remained in the control of the original founder's family for that period. It has started suffering most of the problems of a company that has remained little changed. The case illustrates a number of typical problems, all of which have a variety of solutions which can be explored in the model-building exercise.

W.M. Steeple is a medium-sized company based on two sites. The two-site operation of the business lends itself to physical separation of the company's interests: basic seed provision for agriculture, seed for genetic research, and milling for specialist grain and seed. The company has a turnover of around £10m that has been growing at around 10% pa. Sales are seasonally affected.

It is noticeable that over the last few years the trend of profits has been going down, and projected five years hence the margin will be such that, due to competition and inflationary pressures on costs and operations, W.M. Steeple will be operating at a loss.

The first site contains the head office, and small-volume, high value production facilities; it is sited in Teasle.

The second site, Arbour Low, contains the high-volume production facilities for growing some of the basic seed stock such as fodder peas.

A number of areas of the business can be identified which need to act across both sites, these include:

Accounting and Management Information.
Production Control.
Stock Control.

To obtain full and flexible control, a member of senior management is in daily contact with the Arbour Low site.

The company has only the basic accounting information, and a rudimentary order, stock and invoicing system currently in operation. They have made a gesture to the modern world by purchasing a computer on which to 'word-process' letters, but it is indicative of the atmosphere of the company to say that the directors still stop for a glass of sherry at around 11 o'clock after the morning board meeting, and prior to lunch. It is therefore a matter of urgency that the typical business functions of accounting, stock control, and costing of production be brought up to standard as soon as possible. The current directors are getting near to the age of retirement, and the designate managing director is young and willing to modernise the business in line with current thinking; he also wishes to control the business more accurately.

There are other important sources of information that need to be considered in addition to accounting, stock levels and cost; these are transport, certification, subsidy moneys and mechanisms for applying for subsidy moneys. The UK membership of the EC has brought a considerable administrative load to the company due to the requirements of the EC regarding payments for the growing of genetically 'correct' seed.

W.M. Steeple have a small vehicle for short distances and small loads. Transport of purchases from the farms or suppliers is normally done by employment of an outside contractor. Similarly the shipment of finished product. The apparent savings provided by subcontracting transport include staff wages, maintenance of vehicles and vehicle running costs. The hire of vehicles from outside the business reduces the total of maintenance for the number of vehicles left. This fleet consists of five cars, one medium-size lorry and a van, too small a fleet to have a maintenance team on site. If a larger fleet was deployed the drivers' labour could be used in busy periods. (Remember the seasonal nature of the business.)

The transport of goods needs to be monitored by keeping records of the cost of transport, the material transported, the quantity, and packaging, the distance involved, and the haulier used, both incoming and outgoing. The offer of site sales at a small discount to people who wish to purchase directly from either site is encouraged since this causes the purchaser to incur the transport cost. Following some monitoring of the take-up of the offer, the current discount scheme could be extended from the present £3.50 per ton for 20–25 miles radius. There is no reason why a standard accounting package should not offer discount rates to people who elect to collect from W.M. Steeple.

The cost of transport is normally shown as inclusive to the cost of goods but it would be to W.M. Steeple's advantage to allow an invoice to show transport cost either as a separate or an inclusive item on the invoice.

Certification of seeds, the payment of money to the government, and the offer of the certification of seed to farmers all require careful handling. Again, there is a need to put standard charges and fees into either the accounting package, or into the stock control/job costing package to allow for the inclusion of these items in any invoice.

> £50 is required per certification for seed produced for genetic research, or as first-produced seed of guaranteed yield (the higher the guaranteed yield the more expensive the seed; first-grown is guaranteed 100 per cent germination on subsequent planting, known as A1). This fee is normally paid in advance, the year before the crop is in the field.
>
> Royalties and levies are handled by variety of seed and quality, e.g., A1 (100% germination), A2 (90% germination),etc.
>
> A fee for registration of genetic stock seed to the farmer of £15 is handled in the same way, and is paid when the seed is in the field.
>
> Cleaning, bagging, and other services to farmers, are priced on a standard system and added to invoices.

Existing accounting information is just about adequate to meet legal requirements, but needs to be improved. It is hoped that the current study will help that development. There is no rationalisation of the stock numbers used by the sites, nor is there any detailed costing, resource measurement or accounting attempted because of the lack of standard job costing codes. Therefore the management of Steeple believes there must be an immediate attempt at formulation of suitable job-costing codes for such things as seed preparation and packaging, transport in and out, royalty, certification and handling/storage fees.

To achieve the first of these Steeple's management has investigated the stock system, and the machining operations, and they have some ideas on improving the systems that are in place.

Stock control

A stock control system is nominally in operation and is typical of a trading business which handles commodities. The idea is to reduce the amount in stock, but increase turnover so that any stock held does not remain unsold for a long time. Seed kept for a long time does not germinate successfully, and a strict stock policy is needed to avoid this happening.

The use of old seed to bulk new certified seed is catered for by removing the old stock and stock number, and creating a new stock number for the certified material. To remove part stock, the number of bags is adjusted accordingly. Purchased weight and finished weight can be accounted for by comparing weighbridge tickets of incoming material and finished machining weights. This has to be written separately and no mechanism exists to write selected fields from the purchase order and the stock file to a printed report for comparison. This leads to considerable difficulties in the reconciliation of purchases to sales, and therefore the tracing of certified seed.

Numbering and identification of seed and seed type is important. This facilitates the production of the standard reports obtainable from common accounting systems.

Machining operations

The processing centres at Steeple write down the source of the incoming seed, the time processing starts and the time it finishes. After the seed is bagged, there is no method of determining which machine centre actually processed a particular batch, unless the shop supervisor can determine it from his memory, or from the notebook in which he records where a particular batch of seed comes from, where it was processed, and by whom. Each machining centre should keep a record of the type of crop, the processes done on the material, the start time and date, the finish time and date, and the down time to clean between material, for each machine centre.

For the purpose of assessing costs the following machine centres have been identified.

At Arbour Low

Plant Number 1

Contains the following items:

Boswell Pre Cleaner, Bowby Clean all, Kip Kelly gravity separator, two pea pickers, followed by three Sortex (photo-electric separators).

Plant Number 2

Contains the following items:

Boswell Pre Cleaner, Bowby Clean all, Kip Kelly gravity separator, two pea pickers, followed by four Sortex (photo-electric separators).

Plant Number 3

Contains the following items:

Boswell Pre Cleaner, Bowby Clean all, Kip Kelly gravity separator, cylinder (seed picker/separator).

Plant Number 4
Bowby Clean All, De stoner, two cylinder (seed separator/picker).

Plant Number 5
The Spice Mill.

Plant Number 6
Two mobile chemical treatment plants that can be added to the above plant. The cost of chemical treatment can be worked out from the number of litres used on the amount treated from the following table:

9 litres of A/Combi treats three tons
1 litre of Thiram treats one ton
2 litres Prelude treat 1 ton
20 litres of HY TL treat 12 tons

The table above will be added to from time to time as further chemical treatments become available, or others are removed from the permissible treatment list.

At Teasle

Plant 7 (known as 'No' 3 at Teasle)
Contains:
one cleaning plant, two mixing (consisting of blending and dressing functions) machines, one of which is used for chemical dressing.

Plant 8
Consists of:
a small bagging unit normally used for bagging kale.

People/operatives

At Arbour Low there are six operatives and one supervisor. From time to time a contract maintenance man is employed as are two casual staff in busy periods, which last about six weeks or 30 days per year; these are paid for on a cash basis. The number of operatives required are assessed on the number needed to process material on a given plant. The hours and approximate costs for the supervisory, casual and contract staff are aggregated over the whole year.

At Teasle there are two operatives and also office staff. A similar process could be used. Each batch of material or seed purchased would be given a unique number. This would form the basis of the stock number. The batch number could be based upon one of 150 varieties currently handled by W.M. Steeple. The seed could then be classified into five different categories: Pre basic, Basic, A1, A2, Commercial Crop. From then on, individual bags of seed could be identified by using the last three digits of the bag label number for certified seed if so wished.

Brief

Your task is to construct a suitable model to help Steeple gain an insight into its processing costs, and assess the profitability of each of the machining centres, and the sites.

Reasoning and pointers to a solution

By collecting data on the material and processing (machining), the cost of goods sold can be worked out. This is dependent on location, seed, quality, process and time taken. This data will allow comparisons and correct margins to be monitored and altered accurately. The names and detailed operation of the machines are not important, but the centres and sites are.

The provision of the job costing codes allows a cost-of-goods-sold structure to be built up that includes processes used, machine centres used and resources allocated, together with services and overheads. Similarly, fees paid to W.M. Steeple in the form of levies, buy-back or intervention, can be accounted for if they each have a unique code by which they can appear on reports or invoices. The only difference between moneys in and out should be the sign of the amount. (This is not possible at the moment; it is not possible uniquely to identify some batches of seed due to the mixing process.)

The following modules suggest themselves for an IT system:

Sales Ledger for sales to customers. Purchase Ledger for purchases from suppliers of goods or services. Nominal Ledger which combines the Sales and the Purchase ledger to provide the basic management accounts such as Profit and Loss statement and Balance Sheet. Invoicing to customers for goods and services sold by Steeple. Job Costing of the individual bulk seed amounts through the machining process. Payroll for the payment of salary, wages and casual labour. Stock Control to make it possible to ascertain the levels of stock at both sites and to control the incoming and outgoing of seed and processed material.

The costing method should be based on Activity Based Costing (ABC), rather than Standard Costing. Essentially ABC provides a more accurate assessment and allocation of costs than standard costing techniques. The essence is that everything is treated as a variable cost, which is accumulated by the product or service as it moves through the system. Therefore, in W.M. Steeple's case the material is seeds, to which are added costs in a variety of ways, at various levels, before that seed is sold, and the added profit margin is passed on to the customer.

The basis of this costing technique is to accumulate costs for:

Materials	Seed and seed types, bags
Labour	People, wages/rates and time
Office	People, salaries, technology
Processing	Machinery and chemicals
Sites	Number of sites and cost of sites
Utilities	Gas, water, electricity, etc.
Transport	Distance, quantity, direction

These can all be allocated a cost initially based on collected information, or on previous figures from the company's books if available. They can be adjusted when the appropriate information has been collected.

For the purpose of W.M. Steeple, the only costs that can be apportioned across the whole product or material range should be utilities and office costs.

Under the new system each batch of material or seed purchased will already have been given a unique number. This forms the basis of the stock number; it will also be the purchase order number, which is, in turn, linked to the supplier. The batch number, can be added to by one of 150 varieties currently handled by W.M. Steeple. The seed can then be classified in five different categories: Pre basic, Basic, A1, A2, Commercial Crop. From then on individual bags of seed can be identified by using the last three digits of the bag label number for certified seed if so wished.

Therefore, we have the following structure for the full stock code:

Four digits represent the batch number
Three digits represent the seed type
Two characters the classification
Two characters the location
Three or four digits the bag number if required

For example, the number 3509111A211 would represent the following when decoded:

batch 3509, seed 111 (these need to be decided, i.e., 001 peas, etc.), A2 classification, held in location 11 (all locations at each site to be numbered).

Alternatively the stock code could be four digits, as at present, and, in separate fields, the certification number, seed type and location. The main advantage of this method is that it is similar to the existing one, but reference can be made to the other codes for reporting and enquiry purposes.

Returning to the example of supply and demand developed in this chapter, the company obviously has a season-driven business. Most people will buy in the winter months the seed they are to plant in the spring. However the company can source the seed from home markets, and from the continent and, on certain occasions, from world wide. This means that they are not tied to the European growing and harvesting seasons for supply.

- The supply does not necessarily come in during Autumn.
- The supply will be obtained in the country of origin's currency, e.g., US dollars.
- Seed which is kept deteriorates, i.e., germination from old seed is at best erratic, and its use for bulking is limited.
- Processed seed keeps better than non-processed seed.

Building a model for this situation

The model can be started from two basic statements, and can be added to in the same way that the supply and demand model was added to in the chapter.

supply = amount of seed at any given time (fluctuates)

demand = highly seasonal, peaks in months January to March

The raw material cost is dependent on the weight and the currency in which the seed is bought. The supply of seed in the supply side can therefore be expressed as a set of variables.

supply cost = raw material cost + machining cost

The machining cost can be modelled as a table, the outline of which is given below. It summarises for each machine centre the costs accumulated per hour, or per item processed.

The machine centres are those specified, and the other two columns are costs associated over the time that each machine centre is utilised, which will normally be less than the actual times the sites are open. The final column is the same costs averaged over the items processed on the machine centre including set-up and cleaning times. In addition to these costs there are basic material costs as listed above.

The data collected at each site for each machine centre – the material processed, labour used, start and end times, set-up time, processing time, and clean-up time – can be used to calculate the required averages above. In turn this data can be analysed to find the highest rate of return from

Machine centre summary costs

Machine centre	*Per hour*	*Per item*
Labour		
Office		
Chemicals		
Energy		
Water		
Transport		

the materials processed. In fact the data can be split several ways, and analysed to find labour used/cost, set-up time, actual processing time, clean-up time, and site as well as material type.

The stock of seed can accumulate over the buying period, and space, time and effort must be expended to look after it. A good measure of the time we have to keep stock is 'stock days', e.g., the amount of time it takes to clear all the goods from a given batch to a set of customers from the storerooms or warehouses of a company.

Tracing a batch of material, from being purchased, processed and put into stock, to being delivered to a customer, gives a number of days. By doing this over a period, the average of the 'stock days' can be calculated.

The stock held is defined by length of stay, the site, and other attributes. If the stock deteriorates then a First In First Out (FIFO) policy might be in order so that the stock is turned over in strict rotation.

For the Steeple case the following can be identified:

The domain	The processing and costing of processing at the two sites, on the different machines.
Actors	The incoming director, the process workers, the accountant, the supervisor.
Entities	The machining centres, the seed.
Rules	New seed germinates better than old seed. Genetically pure seed is very valuable and a premium can be obtained for it. The spice mill needs complete cleaning between processes. Old seed can be used to bulk new seed to guarantee a percentage germination.
Variables	The amount of resource used to process the seed, seed, time, machine centre, labour, transport, overheads, seasonality, currency movements, etc.

QUESTION

Develop the above discussion to provide a model of the business using the supply and demand equation. Take into account the different factors which affect the main variables.

Here are some other figures to assist you:

- Average supply load 20 tons, average purchase load 1.5 tons.
- Sales price for the grade of seed is as follows: A1 £500, A2 £350, A3 £200 per ton. Genetically pure seed can be sold for £500 per sack of 50lb.
- Work on a standard dressed seed to waste ratio of 80:20. Remember that net profit is 9.5 per cent of turnover and that Steeples have been growing at approximately 10 per cent each year, but the profit margin has dropped from 20 per cent to the current 9.5 per cent in five years.

GLOSSARY OF MAIN TERMS

Accuracy The level of exactness possible for achieving the given objective, not that which is theoretically possible.

DSS Decision Support Systems. These give the basic facts, figures, and information on which managers can make rational decisions. They may or may not be computer based.

ES Expert System, development of the DSS.

Effectiveness One of the three E's: the action has the desired result.

Efficiency The second of the three E's: to produce or do something with the minimum input, but obtaining the maximum output; the achievement of total efficiency might be illusory.

Efficacy The last of the three E's, to deliver a solution that is justified as a means to an end.

FIFO First in first out, a stock control model. The first items received into the stock area are those that are delivered to customers first.

KISS Keep it simple stupid: try to make models that are understandable to a novice.
Method A process of working which maps out stages, tools and techniques.
Methodology The process of following a method laid down, or practised.
MIS Management information system, again not necessarily computer based.
Model The area of concern or domain mimicked or copied to extract essentials of behaviour, size, characteristics, and hence study the model rather than actuality directly. The model can thus be an exact or scaled replica of the area of concern/domain.
PC Personal Computer.
Problem domain An area of an organisation that is under consideration; that area of activity within a boundary which has one or more problems associated with it.
Qualitative Difficult to measure factors that are important to a given problem.
Quantitative Numbers and values attributable to a problem area variable.
Simulation Driving a model of a problem through a set of state spaces in a shortened time scale.
Tools The set of techniques or procedures used to analyse a given problem area.
Techniques The method of actually using a given tool.

FURTHER READING

Higgins, J.C. (1979) *Information Systems for Planning and Control: Concepts and Cases*, Arnold.

Pidd, M. (1992) *Computer Simulation in Management Science*, Wiley.

Rosenhead, J. (1989) *Rational Analysis for a Problematic World*, Wiley.

Wagner, H. M.(1975) *Principles of operations research : with applications to managerial decisions*, Prentice Hall.

Williams, H. P.(1992) *Model Solving in Mathematical Programming*, Wiley.

CHAPTER 6

Management science approaches

David Jennings and Stuart Wattam

INTRODUCTION

Management Science can be viewed as providing 'tools' for the analysis of problems. Often the use of the 'tool' is attempted before any serious work is undertaken on understanding the problem in hand. This is a result of the natural human reaction to a problem, i.e., we try and rationalise, qualify and quantify it in such a way as to try and categorise the situation into a set of like problems we have met before. This is not to say that the management science approach to problem solving and decision making is not valid in its own right. Management science, or rather the set of techniques it provides, must be used in conjunction with other knowledge to formulate a complete picture of the problem domain and hence provide the decision maker with the complete 'picture'.

Management science has its roots in the early conversion of the means of production from craft-based industries to those organised to produce. The advent of World War II showed *en masse* a flowering in this area and produced a lot of new ideas and findings that were tried both in America and Europe by the expatriate operations researchers who were taught their craft in America. It is the relationship between operations research, and management science that has been crucial to the development of quantitative techniques. Operations research was used extensively during the 1950s and 1960s to try and improve the productivity of manufacturing industry. It is now much more than this. When other techniques are added to operations research it extends from a tool that is only useful when examining those decisions that take place in the lower management structure, i.e., the operational decisions, to a valueable aid the decision maker can use at all levels of management.

Management science has a broader context, even though some of the techniques it uses come from operations research, mathematics, statistics and systems thinking. The broader context is applicable when used under a methodology for looking at a 'problem domain' or an area of concern. In Chapter 5 the methodology of model building was discussed, which in turn was based on the ideas and methods of systems theory explained in Chapter 2. This can be compared to a Russian Doll where one doll is inserted into a larger one and so on. The context of management science for the decision maker must be as part of a model-building exercise which is, in turn, part of an examination of a system.

The essence of this triple skin is to obtain knowledge regarding the problem domain in terms of a model, optimise the model, and then quantify the output to enable the decision maker to make rational decisions. The more uncertain the area of concern the more structure has to be imposed by the outer layers, conversely the more certain the area of concern, the more structure is already there. This does not mean that there is a need to dispense with the examination of the problem area in terms of a system, and a model of that system. This analysis, if done correctly, aids understanding and provides the decision maker with a set of viable alternatives on which to perform more analysis using the techniques of management science.

The chapter is split into two sections: modelling under certainty and modelling under uncertainty. This division should not be taken as absolute, some of the techniques can be used in both situations providing the analyst and decision maker are aware of the limitations and applicability of the techniques.

Part 1: Modelling under certainty

THE LINEAR PROGRAMMING MODEL

Linear programming (LP) is one of the major methodologies available to the management scientist. The methodology has found application in a wide range of business and economic situations to answer project-based questions, for example, the development of industrial facilities, and as a part of routine decisions, such as scheduling orders to gain the best use of production capacity, the least-cost mix of animal feed, and the minimisation of materials waste in production. Applications include scheduling, inventory, routing, waste reduction, blending, and any problem of allocating limited resources among competing activities in an optimal way. It is likely that applications have been made in all industries, including agriculture, chemicals, airlines and foods, as well as areas of government such as health care and the military.

Linear programming provides an optimal solution to the problem which has been modelled. The two essential requirements are that:

(a) Each of the variables included in the model behave in a linear fashion over the range relevant to the model, and
(b) The number of feasible solutions is limited by constraints on the solution.

Methods for achieving manual solutions are covered in a number of excellent texts, and computer packages for solving linear programming problems are readily available. Consequently the computation of LP models will not be dealt with here. The treatment provided by this book will focus upon the assumptions that are required by the LP model, the issues that may be encountered in formulating a problem as an LP, and interpretation of the data that the LP model generates. Illustration 6.1 provides an exercise in formulation.

LP EXAMPLE: RAMSEY CLOTHING

Formulation

The problem in Illustration 6.1 can be formulated as follows.

The three types of product can be represented as variables

x_1: number of Product 1

x_2: number of Product 2

x_3: number of Product 3

Illustration 6.1 Ramsey Clothing

A medium-sized manufacturer of industrial clothing has lost a major customer, with the effect that the company is now faced with excess productive capacity and the immediate need to make profitable use of that capacity.

Manufacturing consists of three key processes; cutting, making up and inspection. Packing and distribution are bought in as required. The spare capacity in each area can be summarised as follows:

Process	*Available time (hours per week)*
Cutting	100
Making up	320
Inspection	80

Fortunately the company has a number of products that could use the capacity and have a ready market, but it would not be possible to meet all potential orders as that would exceed the company's total capacity.

Each product requires the following production time:

	Process minutes required per unit of product		
Process	*Product 1*	*Product 2*	*Product 3*
Cutting	5	5	4
Making up	45	35	30
Inspection	4	4	2

The sales potential and unit profit for each product are as follows:

	Sales potential (units per week)	*Unit Profit (£)*
Product 1	300	5
Product 2	800	3
Product 3	(in effect unlimited)	2

Ramsey's managers have decided to use linear programming to help identify which products should be produced and in what numbers.

There are six constraints that the solution to the problem has to meet.

1 Total cutting time used has to be less than or equal to the cutting time available. In terms of the three products this implies that

$$5x_1 + 5x_2 + 4x_3 \leqslant 6{,}000$$

Since cutting time required is expressed in minutes, the cutting time available, 100 hours, is also expressed in minutes.

2 The amount of making up time used may not exceed that available, 320 hours (19,200 minutes).

$$45x_1 + 35x_2 + 30x_3 \leqslant 19{,}200$$

3 Similarly the constraint for inspection time available must not be exceeded.

$$4x_1 + 4x_2 + 2x_3 \leqslant 4{,}800$$

The next two constraints concern market demand for two of the products, Product 1 and Product 2. Demand for Product 3 is, as far as Ramsey's output is concerned, unlimited.

4 The sales of Product 1 must not exceed 300 units a week

$$x_1 \leqslant 300$$

5 Sales of Product 2 must not exceed 800 units a week

$$x_2 \leqslant 800$$

The final constraint is that Ramsey cannot produce a negative quantity of any product so that x_1, x_2 and x_3 must observe the following condition:

6 All variables are non-negative.

$$x_1 \geqslant 0$$
$$x_2 \geqslant 0$$
$$x_3 \geqslant 0$$

Ramsey's overall aim is to maximise the profitable use of its resources. For the model that aim can be expressed as maximising the total unit profit (contribution) that can be gained from producing and selling a mixture of the three products.

$$\text{Total contribution} = K = 5x_1 + 3x_2 + 2x_3$$

The problem is to find the optimal values for x_1, x_2 and x_3, the quantities of the three products that would maximise total unit profit while keeping within all of the constraints.

Overall, the model for Ramsey's problem is as follows:

$$\begin{array}{llllllll}
\text{Maximise } K = & 5x_1 & + & 3x_2 & + & 2x_3 & & \\
\text{Subject to} & 5x_1 & + & 5x_2 & + & 4x_3 & \leqslant & 6{,}000 \\
 & 45x_1 & + & 35x_2 & + & 30x_3 & \leqslant & 19{,}200 \\
 & 4x_1 & + & 4x_2 & + & 2x_3 & \leqslant & 4{,}800 \\
 & x_1 & & & & & \leqslant & 300
\end{array}$$

$$
\begin{array}{lllcr}
 & x_2 & & \leqslant & 800 \\
x_1 & & & \geqslant & 0 \\
 & x_2 & & \geqslant & 0 \\
 & & x_3 & \geqslant & 0
\end{array}
$$

The problem can be solved manually or by use of a computer package. The solution to the problem is as follows:

$x_1 = 300.00$

$x_2 = 162.857$

$x_3 = 0$

Maximum value of objective function = 1,988.572

In view of the large numbers in the solution it is reasonable to ignore the decimals (part completed garments). The solution therefore is to produce

300 units of Product 1 per week;
162 units of Product 2 per week;
not to produce Product 3.

For those levels of production the total of unit profit is, approximately, £1,988. A precise figure would be £1,986, ((300 × £5) + (162 × £3)).

THE L P MODEL AS A MODEL OF THE PROBLEM

The linear programming model contains a great deal of information concerning Ramsey's circumstances including a definition of their objective in making the decision.

Goals and objectives

In making this decision the goal of Ramsey's managers is to maintain the profitable use of Ramsey's resources. The goal appears in the linear programming model as the maximisation of the total unit profit that can be earned from the products.

In linear programming the criteria upon which the decision is being made is called the objective function. In many ways the objective function is similar to the other constraints that the decision maker has recognised; it is a requirement for the solution to meet. But this requirement is not fixed; it is to be maximised.

Alternatives

The three products are alternative activities; alternative uses for Ramsey's production resources. The model identifies the most profitable combination of alternatives which the constraints will allow the firm to achieve. The alternatives are those specified by the modeller. There may be alternative uses for the production resources beyond the three products that the management have specified in the model. If there are existing products that make use of the same resources those other uses can be evaluated by inclusion in the model.

It may be that the physical facilities have an alternative value through their being sold as assets. The linear programming model can be extended to include all product areas in order to help determine whether continuing production is preferable to disposal of the assets.

Constraints

The figures for capacity available and market demand are constraints upon the decision. Without constraints the answer to Ramsey's problem would be obvious: to produce only the product with the highest unit profit. It is the interplay of constraints that give complexity to this decision.

Technology

The process times required by each product are technological requirements. They are a specification of the inputs of each resource required by each unit of output. In a more general sense they are input-output coefficients: the amount of resource input required to provide a unit of output. The size of the coefficients reflects the efficiency of Ramsey's labour force and the machinery that it uses. If Ramsey were able to improve their production efficiency each unit of output would require less input. The result of this change would enable the firm both to produce more units and, through reduced unit costs, achieve a higher profit for each unit produced.

Market conditions

Market factors are taken account of by the linear programming model in a number of ways.

Unit profit, usually referred to as contribution, is calculated by deducting direct costs (in this case labour and materials) from the net selling price. For Product 1 the following price and cost data were used in calculating the product's unit profit.

	£ per unit
Net selling price	24.00
Labour	3.60
Materials	15.40
Unit profit	5.00

Product 1 has a net selling price of £24. At that price the market will buy up to 300 units of the product per week. The data for price and demand are a pair of co-ordinates from the products demand curve, Fig. 6.1.

Unless the price and demand data used in the linear programming model are based upon reliable estimates of market conditions, the firm will either over-produce, for example by assuming too high a price, or under-produce, through underestimating the product's market potential. (Chapter 7 includes further discussion of the role of contribution in decision making).

LINEAR PROGRAMMING ASSUMPTIONS

The use of any model is dependent upon the model's assumptions being met. In deciding whether to apply the technique to a particular decision, the characteristics of the problem must be examined to see how far the technique's assumptions are met and whether a linear programming model would be a satisfactory representation of the problem. There are four assumptions.

Proportionality

This assumption requires that each unit of Product 1 that is produced will use the same amount of resources for cutting, making up and inspection, and that each unit will also contribute the same amount to total profit.

Cutting	5 minutes
Making up	45 "
Inspection	4 "
Unit profit	£5

It may be that the firm's production function is not strictly linear in form. A long run of producing a particular garment will result in improved efficiency, lower costs and the capability to produce a greater volume of output. The assumption in using the model is that linear production and profit functions are a reasonable approximation to describe that part of the firm's operation.

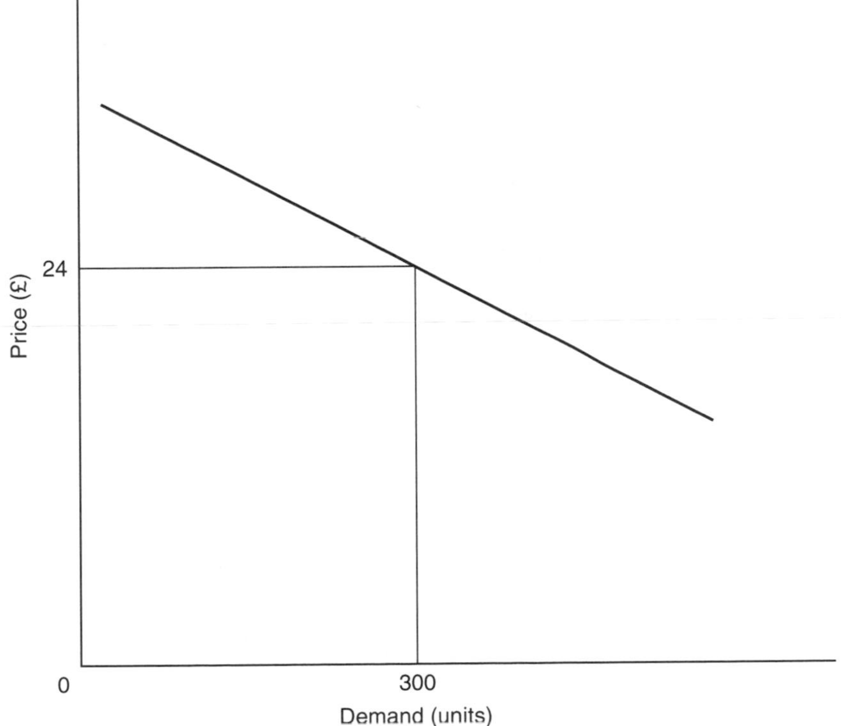

Fig. 6.1 Demand curve for Product 1

Additivity

For functions to be linear a further assumption has to be met, additivity. Additivity is achieved if the activities represented in the model do not interact with each other to change the total usage of resources or their total effectiveness, net profit. If efficiency in the production of a garment varied with the mixture of garments produced then the additivity assumption would not apply. Similarly if the products complemented or competed with each other, so that the prices that were achieved depended on the sales mix, then this would also mean that additivity could not be assumed.

Divisibility

The linear programming model for Ramsey provides a solution that includes fractional values for some of the garments. Decision variables often only have significance if they are integer, e.g., a part of a garment may have no market value. For Ramsey's decision the fractional garment can be ignored, the solution is to produce a large number of items. Not producing a part of one garment will not represent a significant shift from the optimum solution.

For decisions where assuming an integer solution would run the risk of adopting a suboptimal solution, such as decisions concerning investment in plant, the formulation of the model can be amended to provide integer solutions.

Certainty

Certainty refers to the assumption that all the parameters of the model are known constants. This assumption is seldom met precisely. All decisions refer to a future period of time when the decision will be implemented and the outcomes of that decision will occur. Those future conditions cannot be fully known in advance.

The future is not knowable but the consequences of a range of possible future conditions can be explored through sensitivity analysis. The model can be rerun on the basis of alternative values that may occur in the future. For each variable the range of possible values should be explored and the models values calculated for combinations of changes. For example the effect of alternative future prices may be combined with variations in input-output values and changes in constraints. The aim of sensitivity analysis is to identify future sets of circumstances that would lead to a new solution, being adopted by the decision maker. Before adopting a particular solution the decision maker may decide to gain further information concerning the critical variables that have been identified by the sensitivity analysis.

The Ramsey case is essentially an example of using linear programming to make a short-term decision. The production facilities already exist and the decision is how to make the best use of them. Although the case study concerns the use of modelling on a project basis – to make a one-off decision concerning spare capacity – it is apparent that the firm could extend the linear programming model to include the full product range and use the model to support the recurring decision of production scheduling.

SHORT-TERM AND LONG-TERM APPLICATIONS

The use of linear programming to make short-term decisions is common and has a number of advantages. For an application such as determining weekly production levels, it is usually reasonable to assume that the estimates included in the model are reliable. If the model is used repeatedly, those values that prove to be wrong can be refined by gaining further information.

Linear programming models can be expensive to construct; repeated use of a model helps to make the technique a cost-effective way of making decisions. As experience is gained in using the model, and the model itself is refined, the model's output can become the decision rather than an input into the manager's decision making.

Long-term decision making is usually of a project nature and concerns the one-off use of the model. Such linear programming applications require a consideration of the costs of developing a model and the benefits that can be achieved through the model's contribution to the decision. Illustration 6.2 describes a long-run decision concerning plant closure. In the case study a linear programming model is developed that can be adapted to support other decisions, including short-term decisions concerning scheduling. Linear programming is a flexible technique and once constructed, a particular model may have many uses.

Illustration 6.2 British Steel Corporation

The British Steel Corporation, later to be privatised as British Steel, was created in 1967 by the Iron and Steel Act. As a result of the legislation the corporation became the sole owner of Britain's fourteen largest steel producers and their 200 subsidiaries. At nationalisation the corporation's plants were divided into four broad groups based on geographical location.

The Problem

After nationalisation, four light section mills located very close together at Skinnigrove, Cleveland, Britannia and Cargo Fleet, which had previously been competitors, became part of the BSC. These mills all produced similar ranges of section sizes and after nationalisation all were working below full capacity. A BSC working party recognised that there might be a case for rationalising production at the four mills so that one of them could be closed. The problem was passed to the division's Operations Research group (Northern and Tubes Group, Iron and Steel Division) with a request for a quick answer. The Northern and Tubes Division was a large producer of structural steel sections with nine finishing mills.

Defining the problem and capacity

The study group decided to formulate an L. P. model in which the productive capacity of the four mills was expressed in terms of time. For the model, capacity was based upon a thirteen-week period. A close study was made of the mills to determine the maximum number of hours that each could work, after making allowances for maintenance and other production-restricting activities. A maximum work week was established for each mill, and the problem was defined as minimising the total time for producing all the required tonnages with the necesary frequencies in three of the four mills so that their maximum work weeks were not exceeded.

The number of steel section sizes was close to 100. With each size of section having a different production rate, the tonnage capacity of a mill was partly determined by the mix of sizes rolled.

Input-output data

Performance data was collected for each size rolled at each mill, this was based upon:

(a) The normal production rate (rolling rate); allowing for normal stoppages such as mechanical and electrical breakdowns, broken bars and meal breaks.

(b) An allowance for changeover time, the fitting of rollers for the required shape of section and a trial period of rolling to ensure the correct section shape.

The following sample data is for four sections of steel produced at each of the four mills.

(hours required per '000 tonnes of steel produced)

	Section 1	2	3	4	Maximum mill hours per week
Mill 1	72	60	56	84	120
2	50	48	50	90	140
3	84	65	54	76	80
4	76	70	62	80	100

Demand

Demand estimates were based upon the pattern of past orders expressed as quarterly demand:

(total quarterly demand '000 tonnes)

Section	1	2	3	4
	15	25	10	12

Model development

The model was developed to include all section sizes and used to provide a recommendation on closure. The working party that received the report was critical of the assumptions upon which the model had been run, particularly the thirteen-week period which had been used to obtain a typical pattern of orders. The working party also wanted to know the effect of a 100 per cent increase in those orders upon the closure decision.

On the basis of these changes in demand conditions together with studies of the social results of closure and the likely cost savings resulting from a closure the working party decided to retain all four mills.

The O.R. group proposed that the model should be further developed to include all of the division's section making activities with cost of production as the objective function. The expanded model could be used for a number of purposes including rationalising production within the division, determining where capital investment would be most beneficial, evaluating the effect of new plant and its technology and the short-term scheduling of orders.

(Source: based upon case study 'British Steel Corporation', IMEDE, 1971.)

LP EXAMPLE: BRITISH STEEL

The Problem

In the British Steel case study the OR group were required to provide a quick answer to a problem that had been defined for them. The group were given the task of examining the case for rationalisation among the four mills. It is unlikely that the solution to that problem would be the optimum solution for the wider problem of rationalising the division and British Steel. While they were building the LP model the decision makers moved on to recognise the wider problems of rationalisation. But the exercise did produce a model that was capable of aiding a number of short- and long-term decisions.

Measurement

When constructing a model great care must be taken to achieve consistency in defining the variables that make up the model. In the British Steel case both the demand and capacity constraints need to be based on the same thirteen-week time period. The input-output data and the objective function also need to be consistent. That can be achieved by measuring both of them in terms of time per 1,000 tonnes of steel. Inconsistencies in the definition of variables will lead to an LP model producing entirely misleading information.

The model

The problem can be formulated to take the following form.

Mill 1	Mill 2	Mill 3	Mill 4	
				) Section
				)
				) Demand
				)
				) Constraints
				)
				) Mill
				)
				) Capacity
				)
				) Constraints
				)

Objective function, minimise total hours of production

Each mill is capable of producing four sections of steel, consequently there are sixteen variables, x_1 to x_{16}. Using the data from the case study the linear programming model is as follows

Mill 1	Mill 2	Mill 3	Mill 4	
x_1	....	....	....	x_{16}
1	1	1	1	= 15
1	1	1	1	= 25
1	1	1	1	= 10
1	1	1	1	= 12
72, 60, 56, 84				≤ 1,560
	50, 48, 50, 90			≤ 1,820
		84, 65, 54, 76		≤ 1,040
			76, 70, 62, 80	≤ 1,300
72+60+56+84+	50+48+50+90 +	84+65+54+76 +	76+70+62+80	Minimise

The first four constraints ensure that output of each type of steel meets demand. The other constraints concern capacity in terms of mill hours available per thirteen-week period. For constraint number five, 120 hours × 13 weeks = 1,560 hours.

Information generated by the model

The computer solution provides the following information:

Optimal value of objective is: –3,449.76
Original variables are 1 to 16
Slack variables are 17 to 20
x_2 = 2.71
x_3 = 7.63
x_5 = 15
x_6 = 22.29
x_{11} = 2.37
x_{12} = 12
x_{17} = 970.24
x_{20} = 1,300

Range of right hand side constraints:

Constraint No.	Lower Limit	B(i)	Upper Limit	Shadow Price
1	12.4	15	30.53	-62.5
2	22.3	25	41.17	-60
3	2.37	10	27.33	-56
4	6.58	12	13.68	-78.8
5	589.76	1,560	Infinity	0
6	1,043.81	1,820	1,950	0.25
7	912	1,040	1,452	0.04
8	0	1,300	Infinity	0

Interpretation and use of output

The output provided by the computer package gives a great deal of information on which to make decisions concerning the mills. The first step in using this information is to identify the variables to which the output refers.

The original variables are the sixteen combinations of mill and section; the aim of the model is to find how much of each section to make at each mill.

The slack variables refer to capacity constraints and the degree to which the capacity of each of the four mills is fully used in the optimal solution.

The constraints. Constraints 1 to 4 refer to demand for each section of steel, constraints 5 to 8 to capacity at each mill.

The solution to the linear programme is as follows:

The demand requirements can be met with the use of 3449.76 hours of mill time.

Production should be allocated to the mills as follows:

		Section ('000 tonnes)			
		1	2	3	4
Mill	1	0	2.71	7.63	0
	2	15	22.29	0	0
	3	0	0	2.37	12
	4	0	0	0	0

Not all of the available capacity is used. The slack variables show spare capacity of 1,300 hours at Mill 4. The mill is totally unused and may be closed. There are also 970.24 hours of spare capacity at Mill 1. The remaining mills are fully utilised.

The *shadow price* information shows the effect of being able to relax the constraints on demand and capacity. Mill 4 (constraint 8) is not used. If further capacity was made available at Mill 4 that additional capacity would have no effect in reducing the total hours required to meet demand (the value of the objective function). Similarly there is spare capacity at Mill 1. If capacity could be increased at Mill 2 or Mill 3 there would be a reduction in the value of the objective function. Each additional hour at Mill 2 would reduce the total production time, the value of the objective function, by 0.25. The value of that improvement is constant up to a total capacity of 1,950 hours. If Mill 2 were to lose capacity, the effect would be to increase the overall total hours required for production by 0.25 for each mill hour lost.

Similarly the values for the demand constraints (constraints 1 to 4), show the reduction in total hours of production if the demand for a section of steel was reduced by 1,000 tonnes. The most beneficial marginal improvement would result from a reduction in the demand for section 4 steel. A reduction of 1,000 tonnes would reduce the total hours required for production by 78.8 hours.

The output from the linear programming model provides the decision maker with the optimal solution and its value, also a range of information with which to investigate either the sensitivity of the solution to errors in the model's data, or marginal improvements that may be achieved through being able to relax the model's constraints.

In the event the British Steel working party decided against closure. A range of factors influenced that decision, they included uncertainty concerning demand, the need to evaluate the social costs of closure and, possibly, a growing belief that rationalisation decisions should be based upon a wider consideration of all British Steel plant. Rejection of the advice provided through a modelling exercise does not mean that the exercise was without value. The model helps to structure the problem and leads to the development of information on the choices that have been identified.

The decision not to follow the optimum choice indicated by the LP model is not in itself illogical if that decision is based upon considerations that are not present in the model, in this case the social costs of closure. In such a case the model may still serve a useful role by providing a benchmark (the value of the optimal solution) against which to measure the 'loss of benefit' that arises from allowing other factors into the decision and consequently adopting another course of action. For the British Steel decision the value of social considerations has to, at least, equal the value of the production hours that could have been saved through closure.

Part 2: Modelling under uncertainty

RISK ANALYSIS

Some of the simulations we build are based on probabilistic models. They contain random, or seemingly random, behaviour. In the past they have been associated specifically with those models and simulations that have financial outcomes, but they can be applied in a much wider context.

The measure of uncertainty of events is a measure of the likelihood of a given situation or occurrence; the converse is also true. If the likelihood of an action succeeding is 0.5 then the likelihood of it failing is also 0.5 (1.0–0.5). The risk of a particular action failing can also be given a probability; the higher the probability the greater the risk. The analysis of likely courses of action, and the risk involved, is called risk analysis. Actions or courses of action are of course never simple, and often the risk is compounded at each stage.

Illustration 6.3 Will it rain?

In the recent weather forecasts the likelihood or probability of rain occurring has been given a 70% chance. This is another way of saying there is a probability of 0.7 that it will rain. An absolute certainty has the probability of 1.

Given the information in Illustration 6.3 it would be prudent to take some form of protection against the rain.

Probability also plays an important part in risk analysis and, hence, decision making. For instance, given two possible scenarios *a* and *b*; *a* is a product that has recently been developed in your organisation, and market research has shown that it has a good chance of success when offered to the public. It has a risk factor of (1–0.7) and *b* has a risk factor of (1–0.5), 0.3 and 0.5 respectively. This is also a product which has been developed, but the organisation is sharing the cost of development, and hence the risk, with a partner. Which one would you back?

Let's examine the last statement more closely:

Scenario *a*	chance/probability of success	0.3
	chance/probability of failure	0.7
Scenario *b*	chance/probability of success	0.5
	chance/probability of failure	0.5

On the above basis one would choose *b*. However, it is not as simple as that; what happens when we take the payoff into account, and the number of possible repetitions of the payoff (the same return may be possible on each attempt)? What would then be the correct choice? Assume that the expected payoff for *a* is 10 times the initial cost, and the expected payoff for *b* is 2 times the initial cost; which one is the best scenario to follow?

Let's work it out! The initial cost is £1; for the sake of argument we use each case 10 times. The cost for scenario *a* is £10 and similarly for *b*; on average the return from scenario *a* would be £10 and from *b* £40 minus the original cost.

Often in business we don't have the luxury of trying things several times to get a return; all we have is just one shot at getting a good return on our investment. Are there any ways of improving our chances of getting a good return on initial investment when we are dealing with uncertain outcomes?

Even simple situations like the two scenarios above give rise to complex questions regarding which investment is the best policy. The key word above is 'on average'. This means that all things being equal we shall have the expected outcome, but what happens when there are several steps (decisions) to a given outcome as in Illustration 6.4, and each has different probabilities of various outcomes. Average probabilities are realised over a large number of decisions or trials.

Illustration 6.4 Purchasing profile of a travel wallet

A company wishes to invest in a product to sell to the general population. In a market survey they have found that it is likely to sell in equal quantities to both men and women. Seventy per cent of men would choose the blue version, and 30 per cent the red, while for women it is 50:50 red, blue. The product comes in two forms; form A clips onto a belt or a pocket, and form B fits inside a purse or a pocket. The market research revealed that the following results occurred in a response of 400 people questioned about form of product 'clip-on or pocket':

Choice of Product
%

Number		*Number*		*Number*		*Number*	
Male	*Red*	*Male*	*Blue*	*Women*	*Red*	*Women*	*Blue*
A	B	A	B	A	B	A	B
75	25	80	20	90	10	75	25

On the basis of the information in Illustration 6.4, a diagram can be drawn which helps to clarify the information. What is the likelihood of a sale going to a man purchasing a clip-on red form of the product?

The diagram in Fig. 6.2 is drawn by taking the chances of each particular occurrence (probability). People who buy the product (probability of 1.0) are equally split male and female (0.5, 0.5 or 50:50). These are the first two positions on the diagram. After this stage there are two outcomes, the choice of red or blue.

To answer the question, we follow the decision tree down the path that gives us the result:

$$0.5 * 0.3 * 0.75 = 0.1125$$

In other words, 11.25 per cent of the sales will be made in blue clip-on style. Similarly we may calculate the other percentage of sales for the other types of products.

When the article is in production, the predictions given by the above probability model can then be checked against the sales returns.

The illustration does not tell the whole story. Often, even after a good market survey, a product or service will fail to come into existence because of other factors; some are

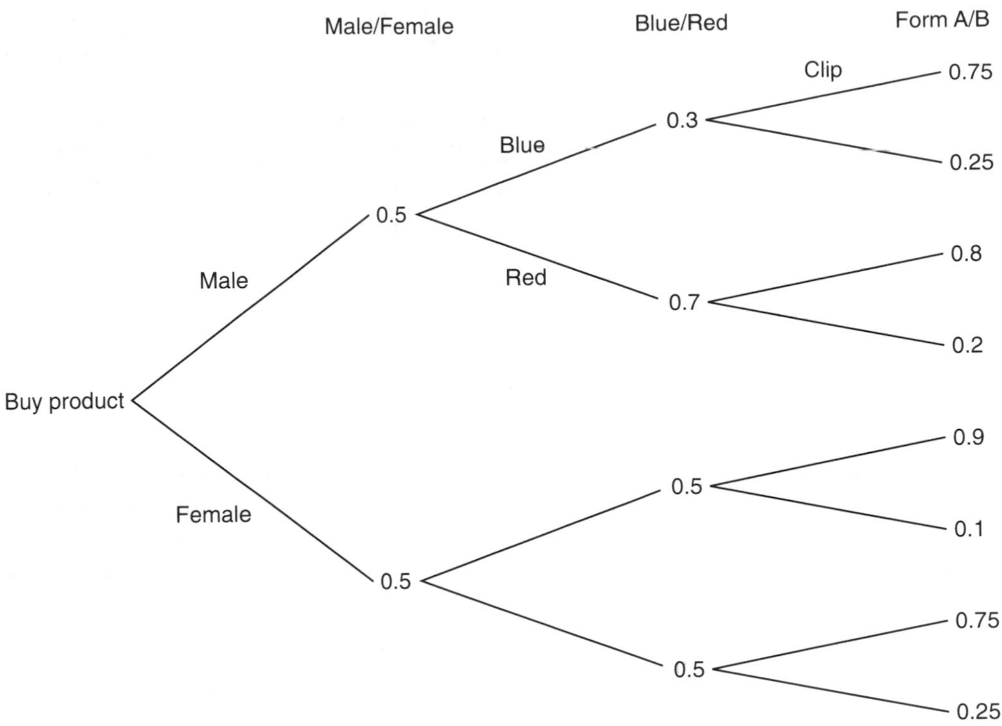

Fig. 6.2 Decision tree

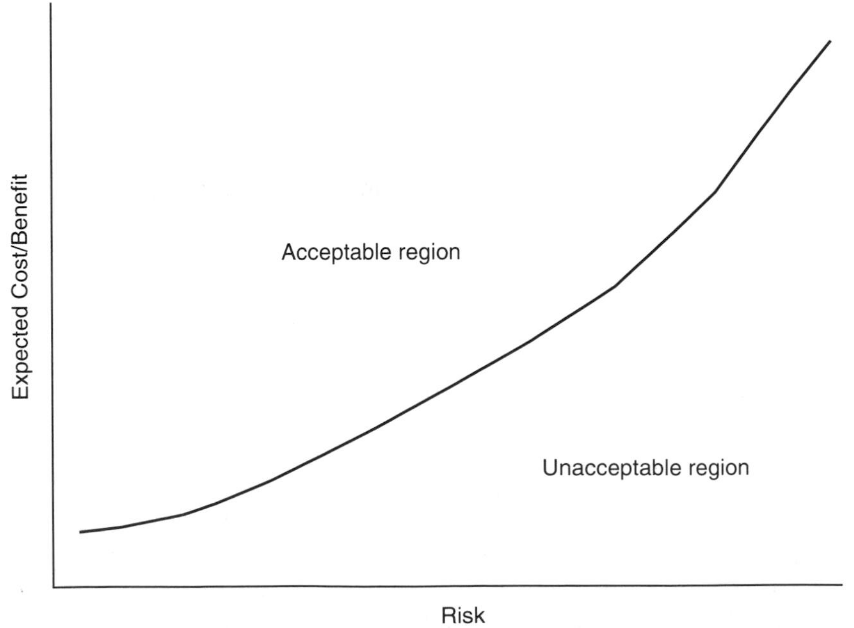

Fig. 6.3 Expected cost/benefit against risk

related to the technical abilities of the organisation, and others to commercial factors caused by inflation or political or social characteristics of a particular market.

The analysis in Fig. 6.2 results in the manager being able to ascertain what is a good project/investment, and what is a risky one. There are many criteria for guiding the decision maker through the process, and most of the literature cited will give a variety of different assessment methods. Remember that these methods are only as good as the data that are fed into them (for further discussion of these methods see Wagner 1975, Sincich 1993).

By analysing the probabilities of a given set of actions the expected cost/benefit to the organisation can be weighed against the associated risk in taking those actions. A relationship between cost/benefit and risk can then be developed (see Fig. 6.3). The frontier between what is a good risk, and what is not is not straightforward, and will be further convoluted the more factors that are taken into account. After completing the analysis, the decision maker(s) is in a better position to assess the risk associated with a given investment. The analysis in Fig. 6.2 shows that most people prefer the clip-on variety no matter what the colour. If development of the product is costly, or the projected benefit (profit) is marginal it may be wise to limit production to the clip-on variety, then extend it to others at a later stage.

STATISTICAL ANALYSIS

Often the data for any statistical analysis, from the height of people, to people's shoe sizes is hidden in preliminary results of investigations. These must be analysed to provide statistics. However, following on from the statement about good data (garbage in, garbage out), we may say that 'statistics are the last refuge of the scoundrel'. This means that statistics must be used where they are applicable, and where they are valid in determining the options available. Careful manipulation, where that manipulation is understood, will reap dividends too for the decision maker. How then can we reduce the risk of uncertainty by using statistical analysis wisely?

Firstly a 'population' must be identified. The 'population', for the analysis to be correct, is the potential number of individuals, or things, that can be examined, e.g., the adult population is all people above the age of 18 in the UK. By questioning that population, or more correctly a sample of that population, a statistical set of results can be obtained, a preference for 'Green Beer' for instance. Some of the sample will like the idea, some will be uncertain, and some will positively dislike the notion, and some will not give an answer. These groups can be expressed as a percentage of the sample providing, for example, the probability of a member of the adult population as a whole liking the idea of 'Green Beer'. The critical point is that by taking a statistically significant sample an idea of how the population as a whole will respond can be found. The following illustration shows some of the considerations a simple market exercise will concern.

Illustration 6.5 Will it sell?

A Blue Ice company wishes to test the viability of a new ice cream. For a trial they want to test the new product at several locations in the UK.

For a correct test:

- The population sample must be of the right size to be statistically significant for the population; approx 1,500 people in the UK may be chosen to represent the population as a whole.
- The location must include a wide spread of possible demographic areas, so that the test is equitable.
- The product must be offered over several seasons to determine any seasonality or otherwise.

Why go to all this trouble?

To reduce the risk of producing a product that no one wants.

The basis on which the test is run is the normal distribution, which is a statistical device that tells us the majority of the population lies between certain boundaries, e.g., the average shoe size, for instance, may be size 7 (UK) but when males are separated from females the average male shoe size will be found to be 10 and the female 5.5. The average or mean will fall between two markers that determine where 90 per cent of a population fall. These markers are twice the standard deviation from the mean. The Standard Deviation is the average distance from the mean. Figure 6.4 illustrates the concept.

The mean is the average value of the population, the mode is the most frequent value of the population, and the median the exact middle of the population.

As an example, consider the following figures: 18 male sports enthusiasts between the age of 18 and 30 were asked to run 80 metres; these were their times:

Sprint Times Seconds		
11.3	Average	11.90555
12.2	SD	0.304543
11.9	Mode	12
12.5	Median	11.9
12.3		
12.4	Avarage	$= x/n$
11.8	SD	$= \frac{(x\text{–}average)^2}{n}$
11.6		
12	Mode is the most common	
11.7	Median = (maximum-minimum)/2	
11.8		
12		
12		
12		
11.5		
11.6		
11.8		
11.9		

Apart from the fact that one or two of them have very good times, it shows that the mean, mode, and median of actual figures do not necessarily coincide; they are, however, similar. If all male sports enthusiasts between 18 and 30 were asked to do the same test we would get a wider spread of times, and the mean, mode and median would coincide.

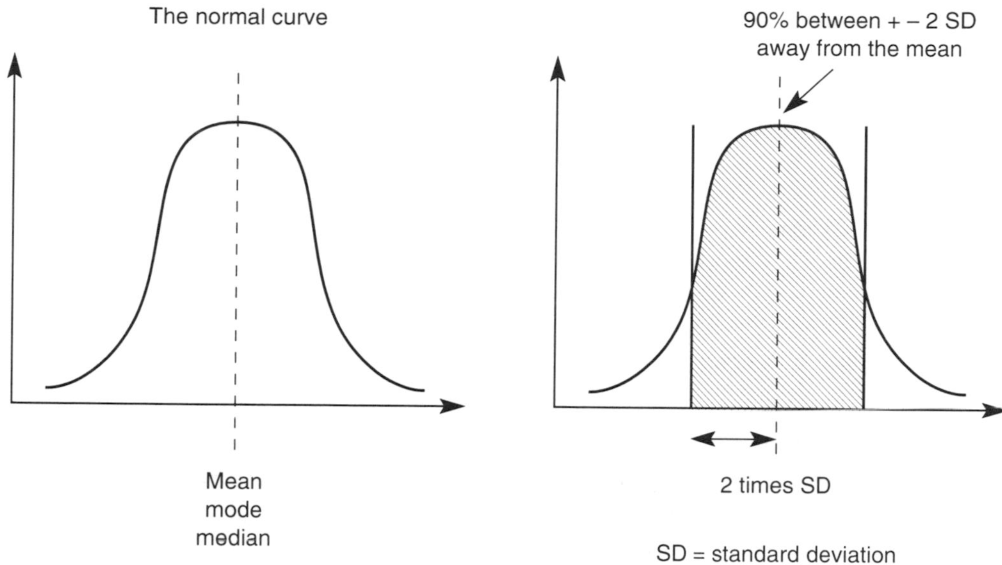

Fig. 6.4 Normal distribution

Statistics: worked example

The figures in Illustration 6.6 show the year's annual sales from a bakery.

Illustration 6.6 Annual sales for Bunn (000)

	1991	*Moving Quarterly Figures 1991*	*1992*	*Moving Quarterly Figures 1992*
January	1,090		1,200	1,180
February	1,050	1,063	1,160	1,170
March	1,050	1,087	1,150	1,190
April	1,160	1,117	1,260	1,220
May	1,140	1,173	1,250	1,280
June	1,220	1,187	1,330	1,300
July	1,200	1,198	1,320	1,313
August	1,175	1,205	1,290	1,326
September	1,240	1,215	1,370	1,337
October	1,230	1,223	1,350	1,353
November	1,200	1,203	1,340	1,333
December	1,180	1,193	1,300	
Year Average	1,161.25			1,276.666
Std Dev	63.38128			70.74995

The moving average is calculated from three figures, i.e., January, February and March is the first quarter. The average moves on by one month, i.e., February, March and April. They illustrate the following concepts:

- That raw figures displayed as a table do not provide much useful information.
- That the graph of the monthly sales (Fig. 6.5), although showing annual highs and lows, does not show the whole story.
- The quarterly moving average sales does show some important information: Bunn has fairly low bread sales in January, February and March, and high figures in August, September and October.
- The average yearly figure again does not tell us much, nor does the standard deviation from the average yearly mean, shown in Figs. 6.5 and 6.6.
- By examining the graphs it looks as though there is an overall trend, which is up. Can this be real or merely apparent?

Monthly sales figures do not tell the 'whole story'; there is an underlying trend apparent when we plot the figures. Secondly there seems to be a variance between figures for the sales of bread in different parts of the year. Often even if figures are plotted on graphs these trends and variances are not apparent to the eye.

To test if there is an overall trend we need to analyse the data over a fairly long time-scale. The time-scale must be sufficiently long to remove some of the variations

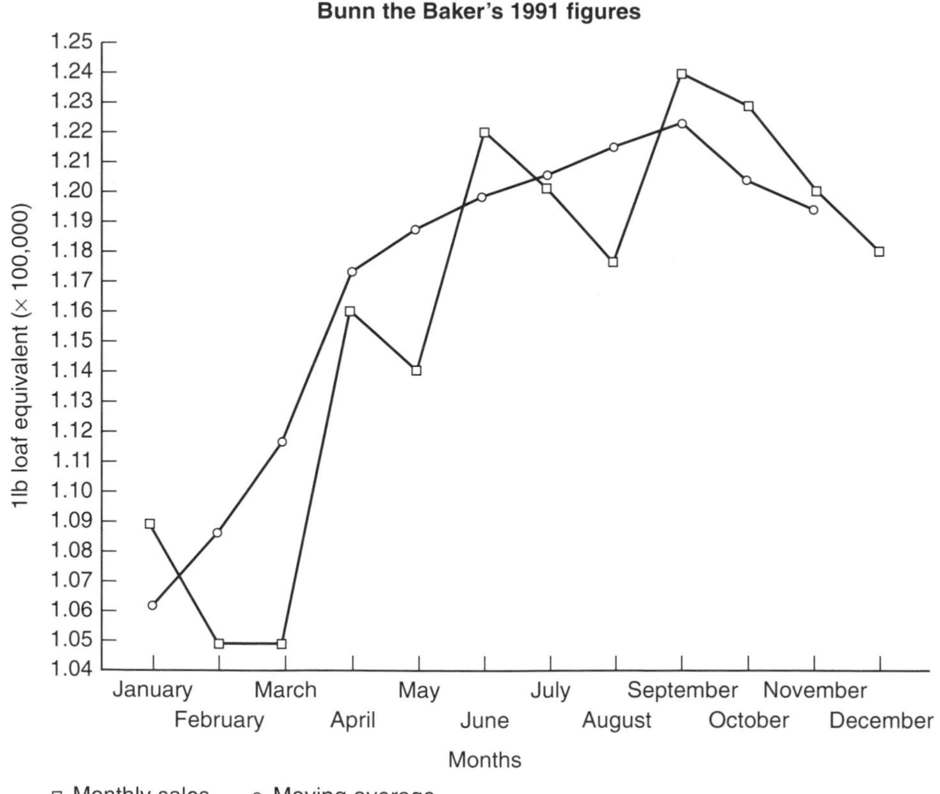

Fig. 6.5 Bunn's 1991 figures

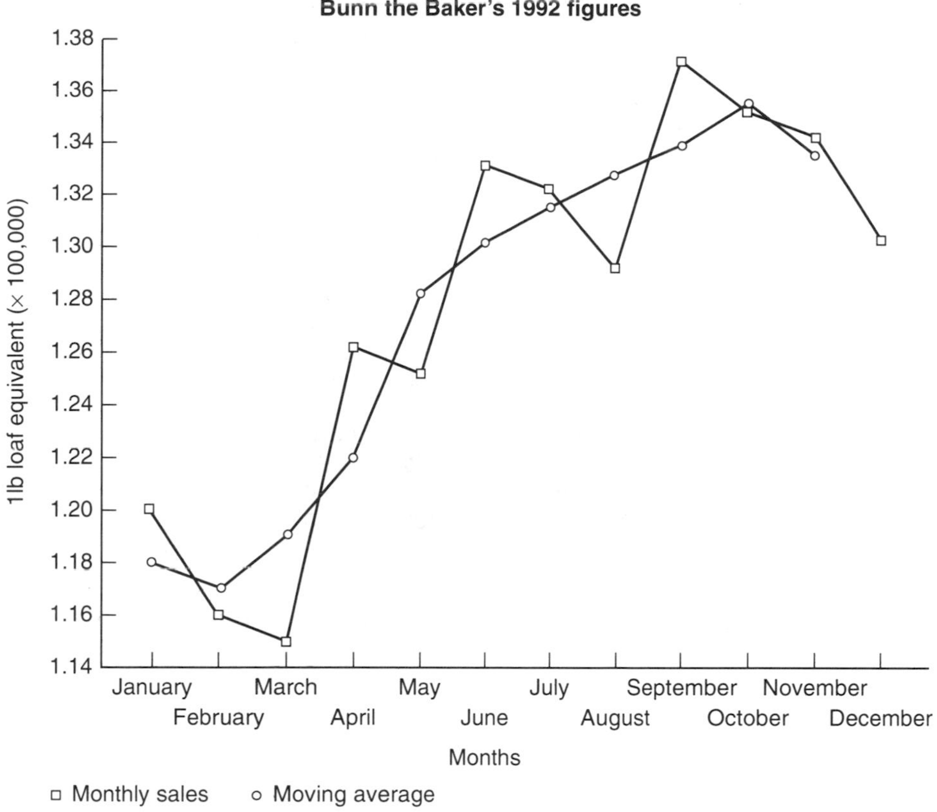

Fig. 6.6 Bunn's 1992 figures

shown in the graph. Three to five year's figures would be sufficient; this is to allow any noise (such as novelty value of a new product) to be reduced. But, since we only have two years to work on, can the overall long-term trend be extracted from the data? And what is the error going to be in our attempt at determining the trend and possible annual fluctuations? The trend can be used to assess the future production requirements of Bunn the Baker in the year 1993.

Regression analysis and prediction

There are several types of mathematical manipulation of data we can do to calculate the sales trend.

Here, the straight-line probabilistic model, one dependent variable and one independent variable, is needed; in our case sales of loaves, and months of the year (24 in all for two years).

To determine the best fitted straight line the method of *least squares* is used. We need to generate the *independent variable* since normally this is a number. The independent variable is one that is not dependent on any of the factors present in the problem, but can be determined as having other variables dependent on it. For the sake of our calculation,

January sales 1991 are given the number 1, and December 1992 sales the number 24, the other months are given the numbers between 1 and 24.

Table 6.1 Bunn's sales figures

	1991	*1992*
January	1,090	1,200
February	1,050	1,160
March	1,050	1,150
April	1,160	1,260
May	1,140	1,250
June	1,220	1,330
July	1,200	1,320
August	1,175	1,290
September	1,240	1,370
October	1,230	1,350
November	1,200	1,340
December	1,180	1,300

To calculate the regression on the figures given in Table 6.1 we can construct Table 6.2. The columns can be calculated using a computer spread-sheet, or a calculator.

Table 6.2 Regression calculations

	Sales (y)	*Month (x)*	x^2	x×y
	1,090	1	1	1,090
	1,050	2	4	2,100
	1,050	3	9	3,150
	1,160	4	16	4,640
	1,140	5	25	5,700
	1,220	6	36	7,320
	1,200	7	49	8,400
	1,175	8	64	9,400
	1,240	9	81	11,160
	1,230	10	100	12,300
	1,200	11	121	13,200
	1,180	12	144	14,160
	1,200	13	169	15,600
	1,160	14	196	16,240
	1,150	15	225	17,250
	1,260	16	256	20,160
	1,250	17	289	21,250
	1,330	18	324	23,940
	1,320	19	361	25,080
	1,290	20	400	25,800
	1,370	21	441	28,770
	1,350	22	484	29,700
	1,340	23	529	30,820
	1,300	24	576	31,200
Totals	29,255	300	4,900	37,8430

x^2 is the square of x

To calculate the totals or sums for the columns:

Σx, Σy, Σx^2 and Σxy

Σ is the sum of the variable

$$ssxy = \frac{\Sigma xy - (\Sigma x)(\Sigma y)}{n}$$

$$ssxx = \Sigma x^2 - \frac{(\Sigma x)^2}{n}$$

$$m = \frac{ssxy}{ssxx}, \; C = \bar{y} - m\bar{x}$$

$ssxy$ is the sum of x multiplied by y minus sum of x multiplied by the sum of y, all divided by n (the number of variables -1). $ssxx$ is the sum of the x's squared minus the sum of x all squared divided by n.

m is the gradient of the straight line, and C the intercept on the y axis, y and x are the means (averages) of the dependent and independent variables respectively.

Regression Analysis on the two years reveals:

Constant	1,080.452
Standard error	46.22401
R squared	0.750229
X coefficient	11.08043
Std error coef	1.363071

The constant (C) is where the fitted straight line crosses the Y axis of the graphs. The standard error in this crossing point is 46.22401. R squared is a measure of how well the data points fit the calculated straight line; the nearer to 1 R gets the better the fit. X coefficient (m) is the gradient of the fitted line (slope), and the error in the calculated gradient is 1.363071 (the gradient is 11.08043 +/– 1.363071). Most spread-sheet packages have special built-in functions that will calculate these values automatically for you, after inserting the data.

From the equation of a straight line

$$y = mx + C$$

Sales of Bunn's loaves for month 25, i.e., January 1993, can be calculated by putting the values of X coefficient as m, the gradient of the fitted straight line, and the Constant as C.

$$\text{Sales} = 11.08043 \times 25 + 1{,}080.452 = 1{,}357.46$$

Just by examining the history of sales and looking at the January sales figures we can see that for the first quarter of the year the seasonal trend is downward. A prediction for January 1993 of 1,357 loaves is probably on the high side. Even if we take the step of using the errors, this still leaves us with a questionable estimate for January 1993 of:

x	*Constant (C)*	*Gradient (m)*	*Loaves*
25	1,034.22	9.72	1,277
25	1,126.68	12.44	1,438

We know from experience of other years that January sales figures are slightly higher than those of December, so 1,357 loaves is not a bad guess. What happens when we use the regression for February and March 1993?

February = $11.08043 \times 26 + 1{,}080.452$
Sales = 1,368.54

March = $11.08043 \times 27 + 1{,}080.452$
Sales = 1,379.62

The predicted sales are still on the increase, when we know from experience that Bunn's seasonal low is in the first quarter of the year. Is there a better way of predicting the production requirements for each month? We could simply use graphs and our experience to look at the figures. This method is open to errors, but if we are cautious, and use the possible minimum figure each month, i.e., take away twice the standard deviation figure (not the error figures) of 140lb loaf equivalents each time. The predictions we would make are as follows:

January	February	March
1,217	1,228	1,239

e.g., February estimate of $1{,}368.54 - 140 = 1{,}228$.

The estimates are still going up, but at least we know we are being cautious! It may sometimes be meaningless to look so far ahead in this way, and to use these figures to accurately predict what Bunns are going to produce. Where it is of value is when Bunns can negotiate a supply or sales contract that gives them a discount or a premium respectively on guaranteed requirements or sales.

We can go through the exercise again, this time using moving averages, but we still come across the same problem in that the prediction still increases when we know from experience that demand falls. The figures are usable only as a guide to what to expect and, if we allow enough for discrepancies and inaccuracies, perhaps we may be able to use the method of regression to help when we are presented with a similar problem in future.

Time series

Is there a way of making allowances for seasonality, or periodic variance of a set of figures? We can use a type of statistical analysis that determines the effect of cycles, seasonality, or movements in figures. This statistical method concerns Time Series. There are four different extractions we can perform on a given set of figures: *secular trend*, *cyclical fluctuations*, *seasonal variation* and *residual effects*.

The *secular trend* is the straight line average over several time periods; these time periods can be days, years, seconds or other linear time measurements. The last example was indeed a secular trend for Bunn the Baker over two years, or 24 months.

The *cyclical effect* is the oscillation or wavelike behaviour of the data, and could be attributed to economic, business or other influences, at the time in question. The *seasonality* of the data is seen as a marked difference between seasons of the year, e.g., toy manufactures traditionally show a 60 per cent increase in turnover from September to January.

The *residual effect* is what remains of the time-series data after the secular, cyclical and seasonal variation has been removed from the data.

If we use a regression analysis on the data it is difficult to predict with any certainty any values beyond the fitted portion of the straight line. This uncertainty is not only related to the mathematics of the fitting routine, but to factors such as change in business environment, politics or economics. (The figures concern the past, and are as far as known, based on truth.) Because forecasting always involves risk we must balance the risk against the expected returns of getting a better guess at what is going to happen. The risk associated with the forecast is in getting it wrong: if the forecast is too large, then more is produced than is wanted; if too small then not enough is produced. In both circumstances Bunn will lose money.

To fit a straight line through the time series we assume that the errors in the data (i.e., movement away from the line) are zero, and that one of the variables is independent of the other. This is often violated when the data shows short-term trends, such as a stock process, or as in Fig. 6.7 between months 12 and 14. Notice that the sales of loaves fall in the early months of the year and rise in the later months, August through September.

Time series models have been developed specifically for the purpose of making forecasts for the data when the 'errors' are known to be correlated with one of the variables, i.e., they show rises and falls at fairly standard times or periods of measure-

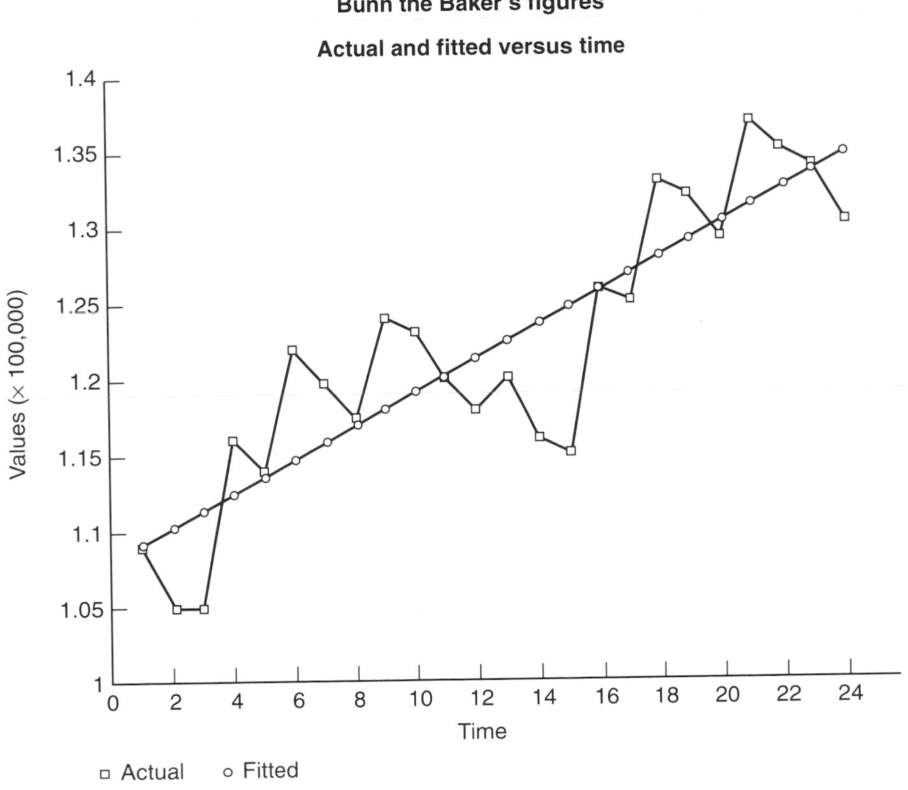

Fig. 6.7 Bunn the baker: regression analysis

ment. These models include terms for the contents of a typical time series; secular, cyclical and seasonal variation along with what is called the 'autoregressive term' (the tendency of the data to follow a straight line) for the 'errors' correlated with one of the variables. From the figures for Bunns the 'errors' are not really errors in the correct sense, but are movements away from what was expected to be a straight line of sales of loaves. The variable nature of sales ensures that the actual sales will vary from what is expected, in this case this variability looks as though there is a seasonal characteristic. The seasonal characteristic does not mean that the figures vary or fluctuate chaotically; they all appear to cluster around the straight regression line that was plotted. The 'autoregressive term' is often associated with the residual component of the time series (the clustering around the fitted regression line). The cyclical (in this case the seasonality of the sales of bread) effects can be determined and included with the deterministic (the calculated line) portion of the model as follows.

$$Y_t = A_t + B_t + C_t + E_t$$

A_t Secular trend	C_t Seasonal Variation
B_t Cyclical trend	E_t Random Error or Autoregressive error

The interesting part here is that the secular trend can be a trend fitted to the data which may be any polynomial of *t* the time greater than order 1. A polynomial is an equation which has the variable *t*, say, multiplied by a power, and is related to another variable *A*. Some examples of polynomials are straight lines (polynomials of power 1, quadratics polynomials of power 2), such as

$$A_t = m_0 + m_1 t$$

for a straight-line function such as may be used in LP problems, or in the equation for a regression line,

$$A_t = m_0 + m_1 t + m_2 t^2$$

for a curve, or a line that bends, such as the resultant demand supply curve.

For most business and economic time series there is a tendency to have positive and negative runs over time, i.e., consecutive figures tend to go away from the fitted straight line, turn, and go back towards it to cross before turning again to go down, as in Bunn's case. Most data collected in conjunction with business-related phenomena will follow a straight line regression rather than a *curvilinear regression* (curve). We shall return to *curvilinear trend* in the next section. Curvilinear means that the data does not all cluster around a fitted straight line, but is clustered around a curve, the equation of which is a power series, as above (this type of regression is classed as non linear). Considering the figures of Bunn the Baker, and removing the trend, the residual data is shown in Fig. 6.8.

Note that the neighbouring residuals tend to have the same sign, and therefore appear to be correlated; it is this effect that we are looking for when we analyse business and economic data. We can actually prove that there is a positive autoregressive correlation between the sales of loaves and the month, if we so wish, by some further statistical analysis.(See Sincich 1993 for a discussion on time series analysis.)

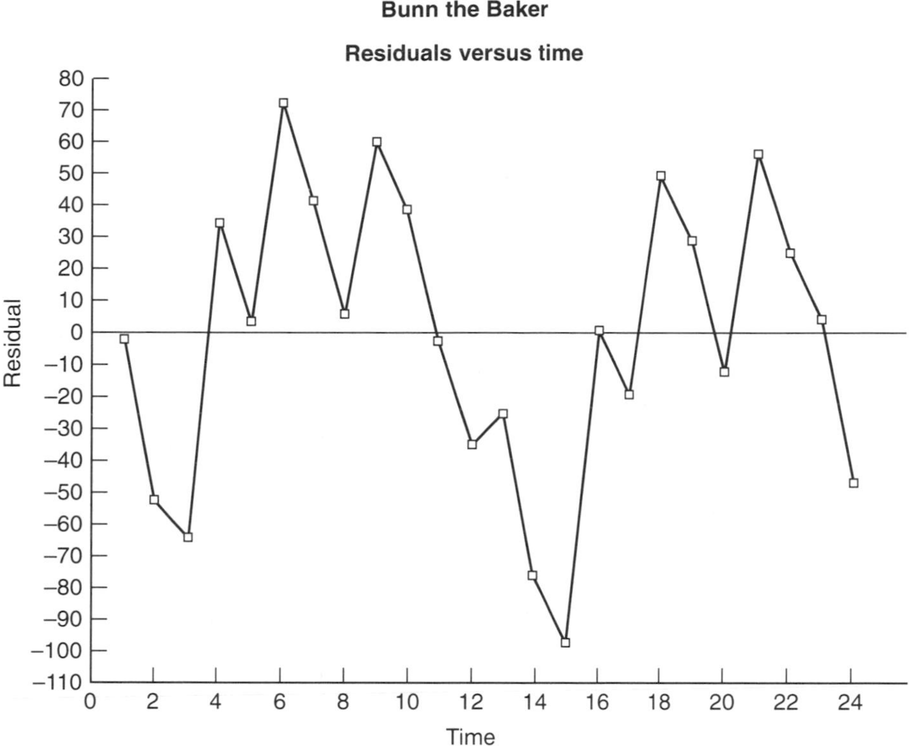

Fig. 6.8 Residual data for Bunn the baker

CHAOS AND COMPLEXITY

So far we have looked at linear systems: those that we can express as a simple straight line, for instance in the case of LP calculations, or those that are dependent on just a few parameters. The real world is not like that and we tend to extract from it the essence of what we think is the problem solution, or the explanation of the problem domain as a simplification of the area of concern (problem area). There has been a hint in Chapter 5, and also in the sections above that, once more than a few variables have their parameters manipulated, we quickly gain problem complexity. The isolation of the main parameters, and hence the driving forces on a particular problem, is itself a difficult and complex task.

> 'We can't help but disturb the Universe,' as T.S. Eliot almost said. The whole is almost always equal to a good deal more than the sum of its parts. The mathematical expression of that property, to the extent that such systems can be described by mathematics at all, is a non-linear equation: one who's graph is curvy. (Mitchell Waldrop 1992)

The description of non-linear systems is nothing new, indeed the mathematics has been known for quite a while (non-linear systems are expressed, if at all, with curvy lines). They are what the physicists call dynamic systems. These systems don't move with straight determination; they progress by what may be a circuitous route. The relationship between what is called linear behaviour and chaotic behaviour can be expressed as

$$\text{ORDER} \rightarrow \text{COMPLEXITY} \rightarrow \text{CHAOS}$$

The order of a system can be expressed by a fairly mundane set of equations, rules probabilities, scenarios and a simple model. The complexity of a problem becomes apparent when these multiply to such an extent that they are unmanageable and stagger towards chaos. Alternatively we can explain the above equation by what happened on 'Black Monday', when the stock market collapsed in 1987. Although a lot of people had a feeling that this may happen, the stock markets around the world kept growing, and became over valued, this led to a loss of confidence in the markets, and hectic selling triggered off a collapse of the value of shares. The precise reason for this happening is not totally known. We can attempt to explain it via chaos, linear programming etc., but it was these and much more. The act of a few individuals in the far east unloading stock probably set it off. There was a rumour that something was going on; the automatic algorithms in the dealers' computers took over, issued sell instructions to the dealers in the west and, as a result, the market crashed. The crash was dramatic, and not very predictable in so far that we could precisely tell the day.

The problem is that the Stock Market may operate within a small number of rules, but the outcome of applying those rules is infinite. In the language of complexity the state space is infinite.

The properties of a given set of fundamental simple rules, condition, characteristics, 'emerges' from the data in much the same way as we discern the shape of a building, then possibly the light, windows, doors, and individual bricks, as we come at it out of the fog.

> Complexity is the science of emergence, i.e., consumers and corporations, acting individually, group together to form economies which have different emergent properties to the individuals. (Mitchell Waldrop 1992)

It can also be viewed from a different context from that with which we are familiar. Consider the keyboard on which this book was written. It's called a 'QWERTY' keyboard from the first six characters of the top row of alphabetic keys on the keyboard. Most people will tell you that this is the standard layout of keyboards in the west, but why did it get to be the standard, when there are so many other alternatives? The answer is closely tied in with the buying behaviour of the consumer, individual preferences, what is available at the time, and factors such as ease of use, support, etc. The QWERTY keyboard is not the most efficient layout of the keys possible, there are other more ergonomic layouts; it's just that it is the dominant standard which was designed to be slow enough for mechanical typewriters.

Illustration 6.7 Chess

Consider the game of chess. There is a finite number of pieces, each of which has a set of rules associated with its movement, and the game itself has a few overall rules which govern its conduct.

However, no two chess games are quite the same. The end games are infinitely varied despite the simplicity of the game.

The basically simple game of chess illustrates that from very simple situations a great degree of complexity can develop, leading to an unpredictability of outcome.

Using the Stock Market analogy once again – the economists may believe that it can be modelled as a perfectly rational market, i.e., economic agents are perfectly rational, therefore all investors are perfectly rational. This means that the price of stocks should be perfectly predictable, its net present value projected into the future. The conclusion to this is that stock markets are quiet places where not a lot happens, and when it does it's been predicted beforehand, so nobody bothers turning up to see. In reality of course the floor of any stock market in the world is a barely controlled riot, where there are bubbles, crashes, euphoria, depression and mob rule, its behaviour almost becomes that of a 'living thing'. The statement 'The market is confident' might well equally apply to a living entity.

What has all this to do with business? Well, simply speaking, all organisations have to operate in a world that is not linear, and does not behave in a totally rational manner. Therefore, one should treat predictions, analysis and plans with more than a little suspicion.

The whole purpose of examination of techniques, and of using them to assist the decision maker, is to improve confidence in the decision and, hopefully, the quality of the actual decision itself. In recent years, due to the development of the computer, there has been a parallel development in 'artificial' decision systems. The automatic algorithms mentioned above were an example of this development. Computers are powerful enough, and sufficient is known about certain problems, for them to become electronic assistants to the decision maker. The next two sections cover the use of the computer in decision making. Remember, however, that the computer is only as good as the data, the program (algorithm) and the person using it.

EXPERT SYSTEMS AND AI

To some extent the use of AI (Artificial Intelligence) has had a varied acceptance as an aid to decision making. The use and availability of higher power desk-top machines has enabled some developments, which would have been difficult to support even on large business machines a few years ago, to be considered as viable aids to the decision maker. Secondly there has been some worry that the machines will 'think' for us. To a limited extent this is true, in so far as it enables most of the calculative work to be done by the machine, and allows the decision maker to be more creative or heuristic about the decisions. Expert Systems (ES) are also a type of Decision Support System (DSS) in much the same way as are other programs and systems. The differences, similarities and characteristics are discussed in the next section. Expert systems are, however, sufficiently different from the usual computer system to warrant further study.

Expert systems have a long history, almost as long as computing itself: indeed one of the milestones of AI was a chequers-playing program written by Arthur Samuel in machine code on the IBM 701 (the first IBM digital computer). The expert system behaves differently from models, simulations, LP and other types of computer program in that it has the ability to adapt and learn from its use, as well as its development.

Table 6.3

	'Behaviour' of an Expert System
Behaviour	Performs a task, simulates a consultation with an 'expert', explains results, and learns and adapts as it is used.
Project Management	Development via knowledge engineering and prototyping, sometimes using an expert system shell over two life cycles. The shell is the support program that allows development of the knowledge database which keeps the rules and values associated with the set of knowledge. There are two development cycles to manage: one concerning elicitation (obtaining the rules), the other concerning use.
Development Team	Expert whose knowledge is embedded in the system, and a knowledge engineer.
Skills	Novel programming languages, knowledge engineering, consultancy, high interpersonal skills. Because of the close interaction between the developer(s) and the expert the developer must be more adept at asking questions, and relating to the other person than is normally the case with computer development personnel.
Risk	High development costs, typically twice as much as standard computer systems, and possibility of failure.

As can be seen from Table 6.3 the development of an expert system is not to be undertaken by the faint hearted. The expert's knowledge has to be extracted, and presented in a form that is understandable to the computer program that supports the system, and finally to the user who wishes to consult the ES.

The importance of knowledge elicitation and consultation are not to be underestimated. The expert's knowledge normally consists of a set of rules, values, parameters and heuristics for applying the knowledge to certain circumstances.

Illustration 6.8 Know your potatoes!

Two people just bought a house, and with the house has come a plot of land on which they wish to grow vegetables. They wish one of their main crops to be potatoes, and have asked you to advise.

Contents of the knowledge base:

Varieties of potato
Diseases of the potato
Cultivating methods for the potato
Facts about the ground and climatic conditions

The reduction of the problem presented in Illustration 6.8 is a distillation of the set of rules, heuristics, guesses and intuitions based on the expert's ideas. These in turn are associated directly with the set of questions raised and answered in the mind of the expert by the elimination of possibilities as the expert goes through the process of using 'expert knowledge' to assess a given problem or area of concern.

Therefore, when deciding on the knowledge we wish to represent in the system, we must choose the area of knowledge by two overall criteria.

- First, the knowledge must be representable as a set of rules, patterns, heuristics and methods.
- Second, it must be on a specific small area of the total knowledge, i.e., the rule set must be moderately small.

This allows the knowledge to be represented in the machine in an understandable way, both to the developers and to the users.

The development cycle elicits the expert knowledge as a set of 'rules'. The rules are expressed in the *Knowledge Base* as an internal representation of the knowledge. Working alongside the knowledge base is an *Inference Engine* which acts as an interpreter of the rules, and as guide to the user in the consultation phase. It also allows the expert system to adapt by interaction with both the development team, and the user. Typically it 'learns' new 'rules' from the developers, and new ways of consultation from the user. Again the exact mechanism of how this is done is dependent on the problem that is to be addressed, the accuracy needed, and the method of consultation. The whole process can go through several cycles during development and use. The important idea is that once the development team has finished, the expert system is not static, and can develop through use. The rules are changed and added to when the existing stored set of rules differ from the experience of using the system. This process is handled by the system shell which allows access to the rules and the underlying knowledge base. The system shell can be purchased for most makes of computers: Leonardo, and Crystal are PC-based expert system shells; there are others that may be more suitable for a particular application so careful choice of system shell is necessary prior to development of the expert system.

There is a similarity between the Expert System Development Methodology shown in Fig. 6.9 and the Hard Systems Development Methodology shown in Chapter 2. The difference lies with the elicitation phase of the development, and the extension of the system through its use. The improvement of the ES via use is its real essence and value; it develops as it is used. The user consults the ES, it comes to a conclusion, via a search of the knowledge base, and this is presented to the user. The user can then interrogate the ES to ask for explanations as to how it reached the conclusion, and the steps it took

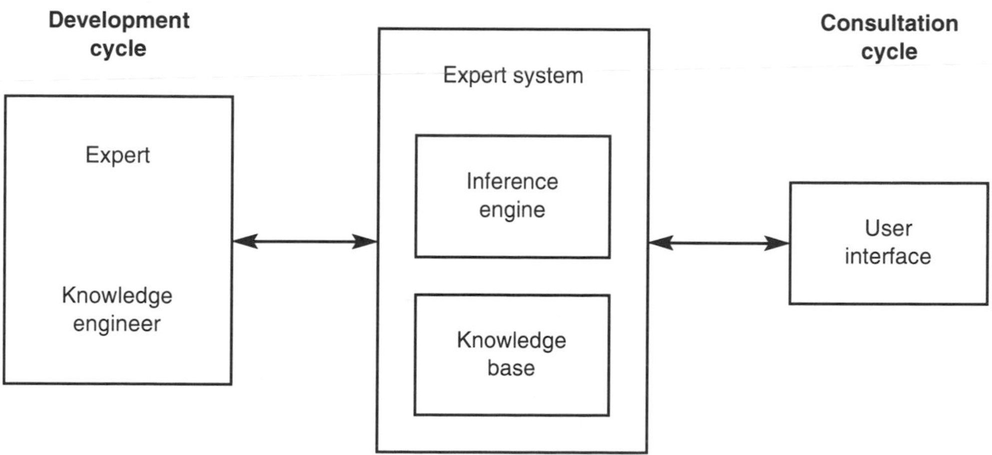

Fig. 6.9 Expert system development

to reach the conclusion. In this way the decision maker can then follow the reasoning behind the conclusion reached.

However, a word of warning here. The ES is only as good as the knowledge expressed. It will also, of necessity, be narrowly focused, and concentrate on a particular area of knowledge that can be expressed as rules, e.g., the Capital Gains Tax rules for companies is a good example of an area of knowledge that would lend itself well to a basic ES.

A typical example of the sort of thought process that could be represented in an ES consists of hard facts such as, for the location of a depot, separation of outlets, ports, railways, etc., which can be adequately modelled using the LP techniques mentioned earlier in the chapter, as well as heuristic information such as the preference for a market town rather than a village or a town without a market. The market town is a good environment for a depot, all the other factors being taken into account. (This type of rule is sometimes known as a 'rule of thumb'.) It is often these rules that are difficult to obtain from managers making decisions about investments, employment, etc. Sometimes such decisions are based on irrational rules or 'prejudice' of the individual managers concerned.

How can a manager's decision-making rules be extracted? The rules are extracted using the tools and techniques discussed so far, and the parameters of the problem identified. The inference engine is then used as the repository for the rules of thumb, and as the interface between the user and the knowledge base. When the rules contained in the inference engine significantly alter the major set of rules held in the knowledge base, they may be added to the knowledge base. This allows the expert system to adapt to new data. In the example of potato-growing in Illustration 6.8 we can assume that a new variety of potato has been released on to the market, and our garden owners are keen to try it out. However, they must first find out if it can be grown by the domestic gardener, what soil is best suited to it, how it is cultivated, and what conditions it requires. Even if these facts don't exactly fit the situation the landowners may wish to go ahead because of the taste of the potato. Therefore a rule which say's *if the taste of the potato is good then*

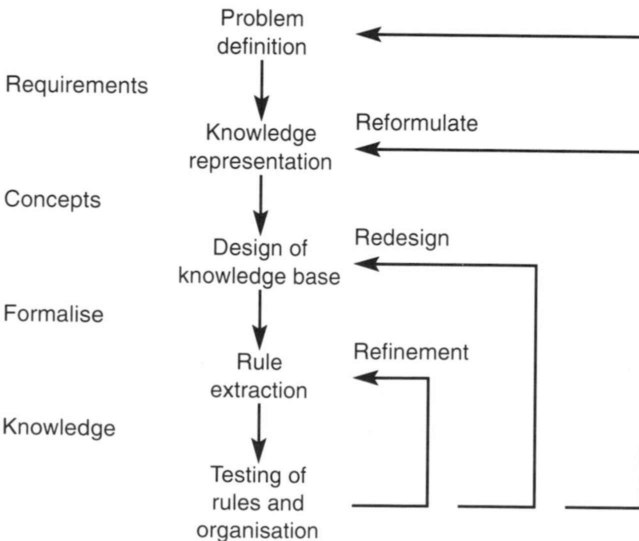

Fig. 6.10 Expert system development methodology

try out a crop should be added to the knowledge base for future use. The inference is that if other criteria are marginal, the criteria of taste may then be significant to the decision to grow or not.

DECISION SUPPORT SYSTEMS

Decision Support Systems (DSS) are systems that are intended to help and support the decision maker; they may be formal developments, such as computer systems, or informal networks of communication used by the decision maker.

The use of computers in this part of management science has been invaluable. They are not only useful in terms of the analysis that can be done on them, as we have discussed in this chapter, they can be used to process data in such a way as to make that data relevant for the manager to make timely decisions. For example, if the manager is making a decision on purchasing an item from a supplier, relevant information will consist of the number of items left in stock, the state of the account, and how many the business expects to sell. For the sake of argument we shall call these computer-based tools DSS. One difficulty that will be faced is that they can be called different things by different people, but there is a body of work which attempts to characterise the behaviour and properties of these systems (Saberherwal, 1989). Saberherwal's paper identifies and characterises the types of DSS, and presents them in a coherent fashion. Table 6.4 is adapted from the paper.

In Table 6.4 *problem homogeneity* (PH) is related to how well the problem domain or area is integrated into a systematic whole. The lack of relationships between separate parts of a problem cause difficulties for the analysis and subsequent modelling of the problem.

Table 6.4 Problem characteristic/development matrix

Problem	*Homogeneity*	*Knowledge*	*Duration*	*Predictability*
Intelligence	1	2	3	4
Design	5		6	
Choice		7	8	

Key to Table 6.4:

1 Low problem homogeneity makes intelligence more difficult.
2 Low problem knowledge makes intelligence more important.
3 High problem duration gives more time to structure problem.
4 High problem predictability makes it easier to structure.
5 High problem homogeneity facilitates ready-made solution.
6 High problem duration facilitates custom building while low-problem duration necessitates ready-made solution.
7 High problem knowledge facilitates analysis and bargaining, while low problem knowledge necessitates judgement.
8 High problem duration facilitates analysis and bargaining, while low problem duration may involve judgement.

Problem knowledge (PK) is fundamental to the understanding of the domain, and the more is known about the domain the more a rational analysis of the domain can be made.

Problem duration (PD) is a measure of the time taken, or time available for a solution to be found, which is in turn related to the type of decision, and the management level associated with that decision.

Problem predictability (PP) is associated with the certainty or uncertainty involved in the attempted solution, or how the problem domain reacts to analysis. The more uncertain the problem area the more error prone and, hence, risky the analysis done.

There are areas in the above matrix which are unaffected to any extent, and these are shown in Table 6.5. The development step has to be carried out anyway, despite the characteristics of the problem. This makes the development coherent, and not dependent on the problem.

Table 6.5 Properties of the problem

Effect of problem type

Problem	Homogeneity PH	Knowledge PK	Duration PD	Predictability PP
Intelligence	*			
Design		*		*
Choice				*

NB * means 'does not affect', i.e., PH does not affect intelligence.

On the basis of Saberherwal's analysis the ease of transfer of the problem area to computer-based models can be determined in Table 6.7.

Explanation/Notes for Table 6.6

1 *Scope or aggregation level of information.*
Similar problems have been encountered in the past, and the information search is narrow. Similarly high-problem knowledge means that less information needs to be used. A longer duration to the problem allows greater data search than does a shorter duration. It relates to whether the information used is broad and superficial or narrow and detailed.

2 *Form of information.*
Low PK means that a broad information search needs to be applied, and that the information is qualitative, and non-financial in nature (if financial information, or indeed any numerical data, is present, that part of the problem, or the whole problem, becomes a category PP problem). The form of the information can therefore be soft and qualitative to hard and quantitative.

3 *Format of information.*
In the case of high PH, there is a likelihood that formal channels of communication already exist. High PH thus implies greater use of formal data. In the case of high PK, managers tend to ignore formally reported data because of its inability to help identify relevant indicators. The format may range from verbal and/or informal to tables, charts, and graphs, etc.

Table 6.6

Problem type: NOTES

Note	PH	PK	PD	PP
1	High PH leads to narrow and specific information search	High PK leads to narrow information search	High PD results in broader information search	
2		Low PK leads to use of more qualitative data		
3	High PH implies a greater use of formal data	Low PK leads to use of informal or verbal data		
4		Low PK implies a decision structuring focus		
5	Low PH implies use of an adaptable MIS or use of generalised support	Low PK implies greater model variations	Low PD implies use of generalised support	
6	Low PH implies greater data orientation	Low PK implies greater data orientation		High PP implies greater use of models
7		High PK means quick response times	High PD means that a slow response time is often alright	
8	Low PH implies *ad hoc* or flexible access	Low PK implies *ad hoc* enquiries		High PP means scheduled access likely

4 *Level of support.*
In the case of high PK, decision-structuring support is of little value and decision-making support must be provided. It may range from retrieval and display of raw data to a suggested solution, or definition or solution to the problem.

5 *Decision range.*
Low PK means greater model variations are implied, and therefore generalised support. PD is important also in that high PD allows the generation of computer-based systems formally, while low PD implies generalised support. Low PH causes adaptable systems to be developed, and low PH implies greater generalised support. The support system is either generalised or institutional, or data oriented (data retrieval and analysis), model oriented (simulation and suggestion)

6 *Data model orientation.*
High PH suggests that models are tailored to fit, while low PH implies a greater data orientation. High PP makes it easier to build models, and low PP means that more support must be offered.

7 *Response time.*
High PK means that a quick response time is desirable or necessary; alternatively low PK means that the decision maker needs a slower response time. High PD means slow response, short PD implies quick response. Slow batch to quick on-line access.

8 *Access restrictions.*
Low PH implies flexible *ad hoc* access, similarly low PK and PP. High PP means that regular and scheduled access may be needed. This relates to the difficulty or otherwise of gaining access to computer facilities, and to whether those facilities exist to support the activities.

The dimensions and suitability of problems for computer-based support for the decision-making process are summarised in Table 6.7.

Table 6.7

Factor as in Table 6.6	*Spectrum of computer support* *From*	*To*
1	Broad and superficial	Narrow and specific
2	Qualitative and 'soft'	Quantitative
3	Verbal and Informal	Tables, Graphs, Charts, etc.
4	Retrieving and displaying of data. Focus on decision structuring	Suggesting or selection of solution. Focus on decision making
5	Generalised General Adaptable models with many variations High flexibility	Particularised Institutional Fixed models with few variations Low flexibility
6	Data oriented	Model oriented
7	Slow(batch)	Fast(on-line)
8	Slow periodic Low accessibility	Unscheduled *ad hoc* High accessibility

In terms of the decision maker the more flexible and responsive the model the more useful it is. The popularity of spread-sheets illustrates this concept; the spread-sheet is both flexible and responsive when the commands are known, and numerical models can be manipulated at will to show the results of decisions on those values. Non-numeric data is difficult to manipulate on the spread-sheet, so that there has been a growth of other types of software that manipulate this type of data, e.g., databases. The flexibility of the software is affected by the quantity of data; the greater the quantity of data required the more complex the software becomes. Adding flexibility to software that handles large amounts of data is expensive, and large MIS (Management Information Systems) as well as large basic software systems, such as Sales Order Processing systems, can cost a lot of money in terms of purchasing the software and input of data.

SUMMARY

The use of managerial science, and the associated mathematical techniques, can be very useful to the decision maker. However care must be exercised in constructing the mathematical model that represents the reality of the real-world problem. Remember that the model has to be a sufficient representation of what is happening in the real world, and the data fed into it must also have reasonable accuracy.

Finally, all the analysis in the world will not give the decision maker the answer; after considering all factors, including analysis, decision makers must exercise judgement for themselves.

EXERCISE: ICI share price

As an illustration of some of the techniques in this chapter, consider the share price of Imperial Chemical Industries over fifty trading days beginning 5 May 1992 and ending 13 July 1992. It was a period when the stock market was generally falling, and ICI was not alone in its fall.

The stock market is known for its variance, and its movements in prices, and ICI is similar in that its share price is a function of the general sentiment of the market, and the state of the company. If a regression line is fitted to the data, and the residual values are calculated from the equation of the straight line given by

Constant	1424.675	R squared	0.943678	Standard error	0.200098
Standard error	19.80870	*x* coefficient	-5.61524		

The result is Figure 6.11. It can be seen from this graph that although we have a good correlation,

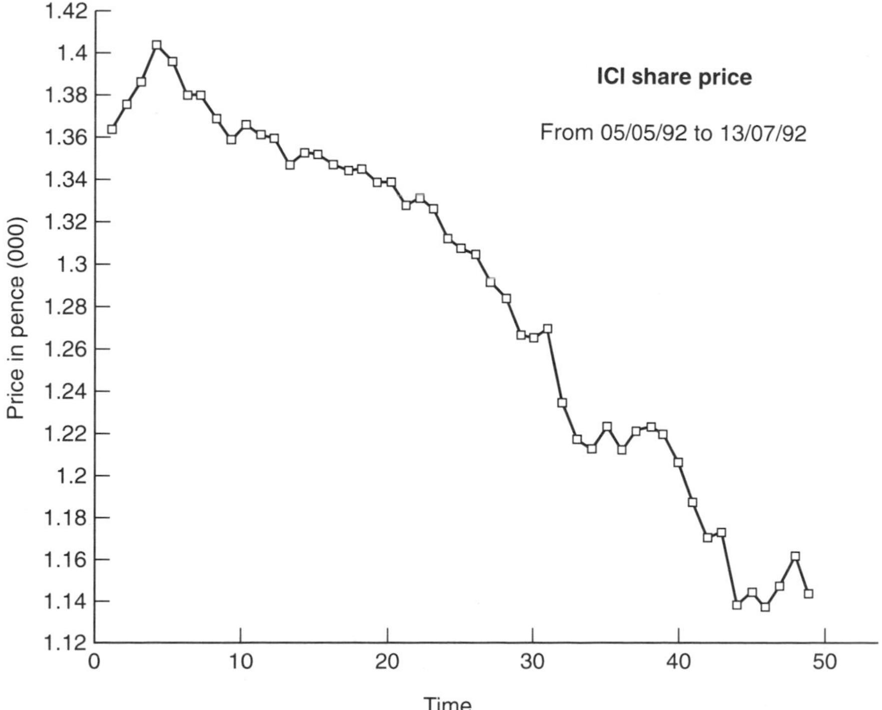

Fig. 6.11 ICI share price

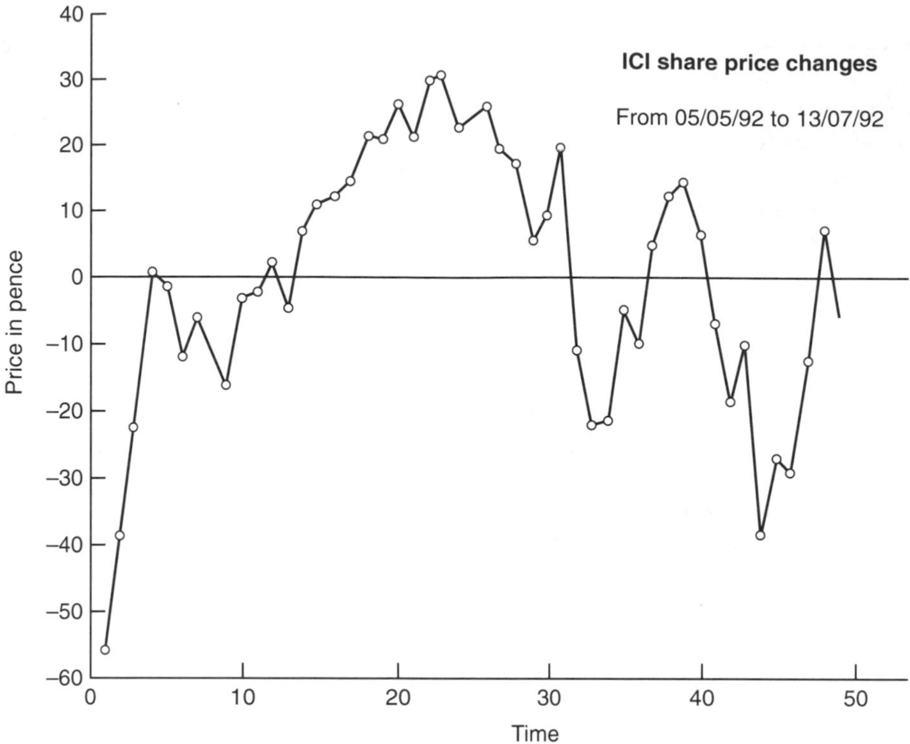

Fig. 6.12 The difference between the fitted values and actual prices

there does not seem to be a corresponding time series relation in the data. Therefore, there is no possibility of spotting trends in this simple way. Can the next few values be predicted from the equation of the straight line?

Price= date × gradient + constant
= 50 × (-5.61524) + 1,424.675
= 1,143.9

Price for days 51 and 52 can be calculated in a similar way and are as follows:

Day 51= 1,138.3
Day 52= 1,132.68

The actual figures were 1140.6, 1151.6 and 1168.8. The problem here is that the regression analysis is not bad for the next day, but is wrong for subsequent days. Even if the regression analysis is extended to more data points, i.e., more prices, the accuracy does not improve. The stock market is particularly difficult to analyse in any mathematical way; its behaviour over any period of time is chaotic in nature. By analysis of the prices of a particular share the most that can be said is that the trend is up or down. By using additional information such as the state of the market, the volume of shares traded in the last few days on a particular company, and finally studying the company's books, a fair idea of the expected medium-term share price might be obtained, i.e., an expert opinion on a particular share will take into account these factors amongst others.

Exercise: Make a fortune! Repeat the above analysis for a publicly quoted company of your choice.

GLOSSARY OF MAIN TERMS

Constraint A condition or requirement placed upon the solution to a problem, e.g., capacity available, market demand.

Objective function In linear programming, an equation for the objective that is to be maximised or minimised.

Optimal solution A solution that is feasible (meets all constraints) and achieves the best value for the objective function.

Shadow price The value imputed to a constraint, e.g., for a resource constraint the improvement in the value of the objective function by acquiring one more unit of the resource.

REFERENCES

Johnson, D. (1986) *Quantitative Business Analysis*, Butterworths

Saberherwal, R., and Grover, V. (1989) 'Computer Support for Strategic Decision Making: Review and Analysis', *Decision Sciences*.

Mitchell Waldrop, M. (1992) *Complexity : The Emerging Science at the Edge of Order and Chaos*, Viking.

Wagner, H. M. (1975) *Principles of Operations Research: with Applications to Managerial Decisions*, Prentice Hall.

FURTHER READING

Neelamkavil, F. (1987) *Computer Simulation and Modelling*, Wiley.

Williams, H. P. (1993) *Model solving in Mathematical Programming*, Wiley.

Pidd, M. (1992) *Computer Simulation in Management Science*, Wiley.

Willis, R. J. (1987) *Computer Models for Business Decisions*, Wiley.

Sincich, T. (1993) *Business Statistics by Example*, Macmillan.

CHAPTER 7

A management accounting perspective

Alan Pizzey

INTRODUCTION

The Management Accountant provides both information and advice when decisions are made in business. There are special techniques, thought patterns, and computations which assist business decisions in the short and long run. It is important, however, to recognise that figures presented in a costing computation are not infallible, and that the assumptions on which those figures are based must be understood before they can be used to make decisions. It is also important to realise that factors which cannot be accurately measured in monetary terms may also influence a decision. These factors are referred to as 'qualitative factors', e.g., the effect a decision may have on the morale and subsequent performance of the labour force will have an unquantifiable effect on future costs. The significance of qualitative factors is increased if quantitative analysis does not give a clear-cut answer to the problem.

Planning for the long term is a significant part of decision making in business, and budgets are a principal part of implementing a plan. The budget is usually drafted a year in advance, and subdivided to cover monthly costing periods. The annual budget is fitted to the corporate plan of the business, which shows the long-term course the directors intend to follow. A budget is a co-ordinating decision whereby the managers decide in financial terms how to achieve their objectives, and how to co-ordinate the various aspects of the business, e.g., sales, production, etc.

RELEVANT COSTS

It is important to recognise those costs which are relevant to a decision in order to exclude non-relevant items from the decision's calculations. Decisions should be based on costs which will change as a result of the decision, and non-relevant costs must be excluded to simplify the data on which the decision is based. The term 'contribution' is significant in decision making since it expresses the incremental revenue earned as a result of the decision, less incremental costs – those extra costs incurred as a result of the decision. Contribution is the surplus arising from a decision which is available to pay for the pool of fixed costs and thereby directly influence profit.

The costs which are affected by a decision must be identified. Clearly fixed costs which do not change as a result of a decision are not relevant and can be ignored when the decision is made. If, in the situation of the decision, conditions change, then some fixed costs may become variable and thus relevant, while other normally variable costs may be fixed and thus not change as a result of the decision. For example, in retailing the shop rental is normally seen as a cost fixed for the year, or indeed for a longer period under the terms of the lease. If, however, the shop is to be closed, this fixed cost becomes variable since the lease will be sold and the rent will no longer be payable.

Management accountants apply a special logic to costs when decisions are taken. The costs and revenues resulting from a decision are best measured in terms of cash flowing out of or into the business as a direct result of the decision. Revenue lost as a result of the decision counts as a cost, and costs saved consequent upon a decision can be seen as revenue. Examples of this special logic are as follows.

Sunk costs

Costs which have been incurred before the decision point is reached should not be allowed to influence the decision. A sunk cost is sometimes called a committed cost. Logically if the result of the decision, positive or negative, will not increase the amount of the sunk cost, this cost is not relevant when the decision has to be made. For example, a feasibility study concerning the installation of a computer, which is undertaken before the decision to install the computer is finalised, should not affect that decision. The cost of the feasibility study is a part of the total cost of making the decision. Likewise, a market survey used to provide evidence to assist a decision on the development of a product, is a cost incurred before the related decision is made, and should be ignored for the purposes of the decision since it will not cause cash flows in or out of the business after the decision point.

Disposal costs

If a machine is to be replaced as a result of a decision, the scrap value of the machine may be less than its carrying value in the books of the business, so that a book loss may be incurred by the disposal of the machine. This loss must not be allowed to influence the decision to install the new machine, since logically the book loss represents past profits overstated because depreciation on the old machine was inadequate. The loss on disposal is not in any way connected to the future profitability of the new machine. However, any cash received from the sale of the old machine could be treated as a cash inflow caused by the replacement decision.

Non-cash costs

Costs which allocate, or provide for, other expenses which have already been spent cannot be considered in a decision. Depreciation is a provision to spread the cost of a machine over its useful economic life, and is thus a book cost rather than a cost which concerns cash flowing out of the business. If a share of group overhead expenses is allocated to a project, this should not be treated as a cost of the project since it does not generate outward cash flows. It is merely an allocation of a central cost which would be incurred whether the decision is made or not.

Opportunity cost

This is a management accounting concept borrowed from economics, which concerns the value of a benefit sacrificed in favour of an alternative course of action. Decision making concerns the selection of one course of action from two or more alternatives, so that the opportunity cost of accepting one alternative may be the net cash flow foregone because the next best alternative is rejected. For example, investing scarce funds in Project A may mean that Project B cannot go ahead for lack of finance, using scarce resources for Project A requires the sacrifice of profits that could have been earned from Project B. The selection and measurement of alternatives and the cash flows derived from them is of course a matter of estimate.

The ripple effect

Organisations are systems and the effect of a decision may be felt in other parts of the organisation as a 'ripple' effect. For example, the effects caused by a change to costs or revenues following a decision may either harm or enhance products in other parts of the company. A decision to use a certain material in a new product may increase the quantity of that material purchased by the business so that a quantity discount is received which will in turn reduce the costs of other products which already use that material. A further example concerns the launch of a new brand which may, while gaining market share from rival products, also compete effectively with established products of the group thus reducing their sales.

RELEVANT COSTS: A CONTRACT DECISION

Materials

Material required for a special contract may be in regular use elsewhere in the business. In that case the cost of the material for the contract will be its replacement cost, not the historic cost for which it was originally purchased, since its use on the special contract will create the need to replace the material. If, on the other hand, materials which are surplus to requirement, and may be sold or scrapped, are to be used on a special contract it is the net realisable value, i.e., the cash foregone if they are not sold as scrap, which would be used when deciding if the special contract is worthwhile. Some materials are of a toxic nature and their disposal may incur costs. In this case the decision to use these materials on a special contract reduces rather than increases cost, so that disposal costs avoided will act as a revenue to the contract under decision. The historic cost at which a material was purchased is rarely relevant because it is sunk and gone and will not affect the future cash flows of the business. The use of a scarce raw material which cannot be replaced may be the profit foregone by not using the material on an alternative product, i.e., opportunity cost.

Labour costs and contract decisions

The relevant labour cost for a contract is the cash paid out for the labour used. Overtime payments are an incremental cost but if labour is already paid, and would be idle if not otherwise employed, no extra labour cost is incurred. Skilled labour is a scarce resource and the cost of using it on one project may be the profit foregone if production of another product is curtailed.

Illustration 7.1 Relevant costs for a contract decision

A specialist manufacturer of components in the electronics industry has been offered a contract by the XYZ company to supply 500 identical components over the next 6 months. The data relating to the production of each component is as follows.

The material required for each component is 8kg of A1, 6kg of A2, 2kg of A3, and 1 item of Part No. 321. Material A1 is in continuous use by the company; the current stock is 4,000kg at a book value of £12 per kilo, but it is known that future purchases will cost £15 per kilo. The company has a stock of 3,000 kilos of material A2 which originally cost £8 per kilo. This material has not been used for the last 2 years except as a substitute for material A4, but this involves further processing costs of £3.60 per kilo. The current cost of material A4 is £6.60 per kilo. The company has ample stocks of material A3 which cost £7 per kilo 2 years ago. This stock has been written down to £3 per kilo, its scrap value. Investigation shows that Part No 321 can be purchased at £30 each.

Each component would require 4 hours of skilled labour and 3 hours of semi-skilled labour. It is impossible to employ additional skilled workers but skilled employees, currently paid at £8 per hour, can be transferred from another production line. This tactic would result in the loss of 1,000 items of another product on which there is a profit margin of £2 each. A semi-skilled employee is available and is currently paid at £6 per hour. A replacement would, however, have to be obtained at a rate of £5 per hour to undertake the work which would otherwise be done by the semi-skilled employee.

The company absorbs overheads by a machine hour rate currently £30 per hour of which £10 is for variable overheads and £20 for fixed overhead. If this contract is undertaken it is estimated that fixed costs will increase for the duration of the contract by £3,000. Spare machine capacity is available and each component would require 6 machine hours. The investigatory work to develop a prototype for this component is £1,000.

The XYZ company has indicated that a price of £320 would be competitive with their present cost.

On the basis of this information should the company accept this contract from XYZ?

Solution to Illustration 7.1

Proposed contract cost (based on a run of 500 units)

			Unit cost
		£	*£*
Material			
A1 8kg at replacement cost £15		120	
A2 6kg at incremental cost of A4	6.60		
Less A4 conversion cost	3.60		
	3.00	18	
A3 2kg at £3 scrap sale foregone		6	
Part No. 321 – cash outflow			30
			174

Labour

Skilled 4 hours × 500 units = 2,000 hours			
4 hours × £8 per hour		32	
Profit foregone on other product:			
1,000 × £2 = £2,000 ÷ 500 units	4		
Semi-skilled 3 hours at £5		15	
			51

Overhead

Variable 6 m/c hours at £10	60	
Fixed – no charge for normal fixed overhead	–	
– incremental £3,000 ÷ 500 units	6	
		66
		291
Proposed selling price		320
Profit margin per unit		£ 29

500 units x £29 = £14,500 profit on the contract.

The development cost is a sunk cost and is thus not relevant because it is incurred before the decision is taken.

The contract for 500 components should be accepted at the offered price of £320 each because this is greater than the incremental costs of production. In no circumstances should the work be undertaken at a price of less than £291 each.

Among the qualitative factors which might be considered in this decision are:

(1) This contract may lead to repeat orders from this or other manufacturers. It might even be worth accepting a small order at a loss, to demonstrate the ability of the company to compete in this field and to gain sufficient know-how to enter a new market.

(2) The contract provides employment for machinery which might otherwise lie idle. Thus a contribution is made towards the overheads of the business and to the eventual profit.

(3) Stocks of raw materials consumed on this contract have been charged to it at replacement cost but, in the financial accounts, the lower historic cost would be used and the profit disclosed would therefore be greater.

(4) No extra cost has been included for managerial supervision since it is assumed that management could oversee this contract without engaging extra personnel

SHORT-TERM BUSINESS DECISIONS

When management takes decisions within the scope of a short-term planning horizon it is usually reacting to changed circumstances or attempting to improve efficiency by adjusting or tuning its present operations. Such decisions are taken within the parameters of existing production facilities, the need to maximise the return from limiting factors, and to apply the logic of relevant costs.

Cessation of operations or closure of facilities

Many businesses use full absorption costing which allocates to various products or activities the fixed costs, or central administration expenses, which will not change if the activity or product is withdrawn. Such costs, allocated on an hourly or per-product basis, may be considered as variable yet in reality they are fixed and will not be reduced if an activity ceases to take place. Thus closure decisions taken on the basis of full absorption costing may fail to consider the fact that cost behaviour may be different in the context of closure from the way it is under normal business activity. The inflow of revenue will be discontinued and variable costs will certainly cease if a product line is dropped or a shop is closed, so each of these items are relevant to the decision. Accordingly, a closure or withdrawal decision should be taken on the basis of contribution rather than on the basis of profit which may include an allocation of fixed costs which will remain after the closure has taken place. There are five basic rules for such a decision.

(1) Cost behaviour in the context of the changed circumstances must be considered. For example, the rent of a shop may be seen as a fixed cost whereas, if the shop is vacated, the lease will be sold and the rent will no longer be paid.
(2) Any activity, a product, a department, a sales area, a shop, which shows a negative contribution should in principle be discontinued. If the revenue from an activity does not cover the variable cost generated by that activity then losses are certain to be made, unless other actions can improve efficiency and turn the loss-making activity into one which has a positive contribution. However, closure is difficult to reverse and should therefore only be undertaken when management has exhausted all other possibilities.
(3) In general an activity which has a positive contribution should not be closed even though it appears to make a loss under the full-absorption costing system. The exception to this rule is when it is considered that a greater contribution can be earned from resources tied up in an activity if the activity is closed and the resources are transferred to an alternative product.
(4) The ripple effect must be considered as part of a decision to close facilities or activities, because the withdrawal of one product, or the closure of a branch, may have an effect on other products or sectors of the business.
(5) Sensitivity. In decisions which are based on forecast figures, a measure of uncertainty exists. Thus it is correct to assess the impact on the expected result of changes in estimates for costs and revenue. If a proportionally small change in one factor can have a significant impact on the final outcome of the decision, the decision is said to be sensitive to a change in that factor. Alternatively if a large difference between an estimated cost and the actual amount will have only a small effect on the outcome of the decision process, then the project is said to be insensitive to fluctuations in the amount of that factor. Sensitivity measures how far the estimated figures for cost or revenue used in a decision can be wrong before the project ceases to be viable.

Illustration 7.2 A closure decision

Bradmore Bakery Ltd operates a small plant which produces bread, cakes, pies and rolls. The Cost Accountant has analysed the activity for the next six months and has produced the following budgeted cost statement for consideration by the board. Sales are made through three shops, and a baker's round.

Outlet - shops	Keyworth		Bunny		Plumtree		Round		Total	
£000	£	£	£	£	£	£	£	£	£	£
Sales		538		910		556		308		2,312
Cost of materials	106		188		130		100		524	
Baker: labour	196		260		206		92		754	
Roundsman's salary	-		-		-		40		40	
Shop salaries	60		60		110		-		230	
Roundsman's vehicle	-		-		-		90		90	
Shop admin cost	110		122		162		-		394	
Factory overheads	80		160		120		40		400	
		552		790		728		362		2,432
Profit/(Loss)		(14)		120		(172)		(54)		(120)

On the basis of these figures the Board propose to close the Plumtree and Keyworth shops and the baker's round.

If the baker's round is extended to Plumtree, 15 per cent of the gross profit of the closed Plumtree shop could be retained.

On the basis of these figures, what advice should the Board be given?

Solution to Illustration 7.2

The information provided for the Board is drafted in terms of full absorption costing when marginal costing, which discloses contribution, should be used.

Factory overheads are not relevant to the decision since they will not be affected by shop closures.

In the context of closure, shop salaries and administration costs (rent/rates, etc.), which might be considered as fixed costs for a year, will behave as variable or direct costs.

If the round can be extended to Plumtree a 'ripple' effect must be considered.

£000	Keyworth	Bunny	Plumtree	Round	Total
Sales	538	910	556	308	2,312
Cost of sales (mat & lab)	302	448	336	192	
Gross profit	236	462	220	116	
Direct costs (salaries & admin)	170	182	272	130	
Contribution	66	280*	(52)	(14)	280
Factory overheads					(400)
Loss (The same as for the full absorption computation)					(120)

The budgeted loss remains at £120,000. If Plumtree, Keyworth and the Round are closed, contribution will still be £280,000* towards factory overheads of £400,000 so a loss of £120,000 will be made.

Keyworth with a positive contribution should not be closed. Bunny and Keyworth together have a contribution of £346,000 so the loss will be reduced to £54,000.

Ripple effect. If the Plumtree shop closes, the Round can be extended to Plumtree, earning 15 per cent of £220,000, i.e., £33,000. The Round would then have a positive contribution of £19,000 and the loss would be reduced to £35,000 for the half year.

The business is still losing £70,000 pa so a suitable decision would be to cut the factory overheads and replace the Plumtree shop with one in a better trading position.

The optimum use of a limiting factor

A limiting factor is any factor which holds back a business from achieving a further improvement in its performance. A scarcity of raw materials or of a grade of skilled labour will seriously inhibit production, as will the possession of insufficient plant capacity to provide the machine hours required to make all the products which can be sold. Other limiting factors include finance, which will in turn reduce the amount of stock and trade credit available to support a level of production, and managerial talent itself which, if it becomes a scarce factor, will inhibit the successful operation and development of a business. The optimum use of limiting factors concerns decisions to maximise the contribution from each unit of a scarce resource so that production will be concentrated on the most profitable plan of operations. Fixed costs are not relevant to this decision since, whichever course is taken, those costs will not change.

Illustration 7.3 Optimum use of a limiting factor

Bunney Bowyers Ltd operates a small factory to manufacture a range of sports bows for club archers. The modern bow is made from a mixture of materials (wood, carbon fibre, etc.) by highly skilled craftsmen and sophisticated machinery. The company has three compound bows in its range of products, namely the Champion, the Goldwinner and the AR17. These bows sell at prices of £70, £90, and £120 respectively.

The factory plans to work four 40-hour weeks in October. Eight skilled craftsmen are employed and paid at £10 per hour. Overhead costs are £6,000 per month. Other cost information:

	Champion	Goldwinner	AR17
Sales potential – units	200	280	90
Material costs	£35	£40	£55
Labour costs	£22.5	£25	£40
Maple timber used	0.4 kilo	1 kilo	0.2 kilo
Machine time	1 hour	1.25 hours	2 hours

1000 hours of machine time are available in the factory each month.

(a) Draft a production plan for October which optimises use of the resources available.

(b) As a result of the plan derived in (a) above, management decide to work a 47.5 hour week with overtime at time and a half. It is then discovered that the supply of maple has been curtailed and only 320 kilos can be supplied in October. On the basis of this information what should management do?

Solution to Illustration 7.3

(a) Machine hours required for production:
Champion, 200 × 1 + Goldwinner, 280 × 1.25 + AR17, 90 × 2 = 730 hours
1000 m/c hours are available so there is no shortfall.
Labour hours required to meet all sales potential.
Champion 200 × 2.25 + Goldwinner 280 × 2.5 + AR17,90 × 4 = 1,510 hours, but labour hours available are 4 × 40 × 8 = 1,280, so a shortfall of 230 hours exists, a limiting factor.

Unit	Champion	Goldwinner	AR17
	£	£	£
Price	70	90	120
Direct cost – material	(35)	(40)	(55)
– labour	(22.5) 2.25 hrs	(25) 2.5 hrs	(40) 4hrs
Contribution	£12.5	£25	£25
Contribution per:			
Labour hour (£12.5 ÷ 2.25)	£5.5	£10	£6.25

Ranking with labour as a limiting factor is:
Goldwinner, AR17, Champion – so Champion is the product to be cut back when the production plan is drafted.
230 hours ÷ 2.25 hours = production of 103 Champions

Production Plan

	Champion	*Goldwinner*	*AR17*	*Total*
Volume produced	200-103 = 97	280	90	
Contribution	£1,212	£7,000	£2,250	£10,462
Overhead cost				£ 6,000
Profit				£ 4,462

(b) Labour is no longer a limiting factor. Extra overtime hours at a premium of £5 per hour will cost (4 × 7.5 × 8 × £5) £1,200 – an overhead cost.

Maple required to meet all sales potential is:
Champion, 200 × 0.4 + Goldwinner, 280 × 1 + AR17, 90 × 0.2 = 380 kilos. However, only 320 kilos of maple is available so production must be concentrated on the products which give the greater contribution per unit of limiting factor. There is a shortfall of 60 kilos of maple.

	Champion	*Goldwinner*	*AR17*
Contribution	£12.5	£25	£ 25
Maple required	0.4 kilo	1 kilo	0.2 kilo
Contribution per kilo	£31.25	£25	£125

Ranking if maple is the limiting factor:
AR17, Champion, Goldwinner – so Goldwinner is the product to be cut when the production plan is drafted.
60 kilos at 1 kilo per unit of Goldwinner = 60 units

Production Plan

	Champion	Goldwinner	AR17	Total
Volume produced	200	280 - 60 = 220	90	
Contribution	£2,500	£5,500	£2,250	£10,250
Overhead costs £6000 + overtime premium £1200				£ 7,200
Profit				£ 3,050

This type of problem may also be solved by the use of linear programming (Chapter 6). The aim of the two approaches is the same – to achieve the optimum use of resources. As problems increase in complexity the Management Accountant is more likely to seek a solution through the use of linear programming.

Make or buy decisions

A decision which is frequently taken in industry is to decide whether to make a component within the business, or to buy it from an outside subcontractor. This decision must also ignore fixed costs and concentrate on the marginal cost of production (variable costs) because if a product is bought into the organisation, the saving concerns only the variable cost since fixed costs by definition will remain whether the product is bought out or made in. Thus the price offered by the subcontractor must be set against the variable cost of producing the product within the business.

Illustration 7.4 Make or buy decision

A company needs 4000 electronic switches to build into its main product. The alternatives available are to manufacture the switches at its own factory or to buy them from a specialist subcontractor at £14 each. The Cost Accountant estimates the manufacturing costs of the switch as

Materials	– A	£4
	– B	£3
Labour	– Assembly 20 minutes	
	– Machining 40 minutes	

Variable overhead is estimated to cost £1.50 per unit. Fixed factory overheads are absorbed to production as £2 per direct labour hour, irrespective of labour grade involved. Assembly labour is paid £3 per hour while labour in the machining shop is paid £6 per hour.

On the basis of this information, should the company make the switches or buy them in?

How would the analysis of the problem change if skilled machinists were in short supply?

Solution to Illustration 7.4

		£	£
Variable manufacturing cost per unit			
Materials	– A	4	
	–B	3	7
Labour	– Assembly	1	
	– Machining	4	5

Variable overheads	1.5
	13.5
Bought-out price	14.0
Cost saved by making	£0.5

4,000 units at £0.5 = £2,000 as cost saved.
A make or buy analysis must compare the bought-out price of the component with the variable cost of manufacture 'in house', i.e. fixed production overheads are ignored.

The margin per unit is narrow so qualitative factors affecting the decision may prove significant.

Making these switches takes up 2,666 hours of skilled machinist labour, which might be employed on some other product if it were released by buying out.

Contribution earned per unit of limiting factor is an important criterion when planning to maximise performance. In this case the cost saved per hour of machinists' time (50 pence for 40 minutes) is 75 pence, and it is this figure which must be set against cost saved per hour on other products which could be made by these skilled but scarce workers.

Qualitative factors affecting a make or buy decision

A number of particular factors influence the make or buy decision and may act to override the quantitative answer produced by the normal computation. The impact of qualitative factors on costs cannot be measured with accuracy but these factors can be very important when the decision is made. The major factors are:

Can the subcontractor maintain the price quoted for the supply of a component, or will he act to increase the price once the buying company has committed itself to dismantling its own production facilities? The possibility of a price increase, if the buying company becomes dependent on the subcontractor may be a reason to make a component, even though it can be purchased at a lower cost outside the business.

Can the subcontractor maintain the quality of the component over a long production run? Poor quality components built into a main product can harm the reputation of the buying company if they fail in service.

Will the subcontractor be able to meet delivery dates? Late delivery can disrupt production of the main product, perhaps even causing a stock-out which will result in lost custom. A strike or plant breakdown at the subcontractor's factory is outside the control of the buying company, but such circumstances may materially affect the activities of the buying company.

What if a rival company takes over the subcontractor after the buying company has committed itself and dismantled its own component production facilities? The company would then be at the mercy of its rival.

Product improvements or new designs necessitate close co-operation with subcontractors. Thus information concerning such developments will be passed outside the company and may become known to rivals. All production improvements require a close liaison between engineers and the production team. Such a liaison is easy if both parties are within the same company but may be difficult if engineers have to liaise with a production team in the subcontractor's factory which might be some way away.

If too much production is contracted out the main company may become just an assembler of the product. The management may prefer a strategy that ensures the company is self-sufficient and not at the mercy of subcontractors.

If a component is made rather than bought out, a skilled team of operatives will not need to be dismissed or broken up after the company has invested considerable amounts in training such a team.

LONG-TERM INVESTMENT DECISIONS

These decisions are sometimes referred to as Capital Budgeting or Capital Investment Appraisal. Company funds are to be invested at the present time in a project which will operate and continue to pay off over a period of years into the future. Funds for long-term investment are always scarce in business so the techniques of capital budgeting are designed to ensure that scarce investment resources are channelled into the most worthwhile long-term projects. Proposals for the use of the funds available to the business are identified and formulated, they must then be ranked according to their potential success. The available funds are rationed between the potentially most successful projects so that the return on investment funds available to the business is optimised. This decision largely determines the long-term survival of the business. The nature of long-term investment decisions is to consider the whole life of a project so that the accounting year, an arbitrary concept, is ignored and book costs, such as depreciation, created because of the need to account in yearly periods are seen as not relevant for such decisions.

Capital investment appraisal is significant for several reasons:

- Investment has a direct impact on profitability, and long-term investment will thus influence profits well into the future.
- Usually large sums of money are involved in these investment decisions and it may be costly to disinvest later if a mistake is made.
- Investment decisions once made will set the pattern and strategy for the business into the future and thus influence its long-term success or failure.

Management information for investment decisions

In order to appraise an investment decision sufficient relevant information must be accumulated. This information may be classified as follows:

The capital cost involved. The full amount of capital to be sunk into a project will include the cost of the hardware plus transport and installation expenses, and perhaps training costs as well. An accurate estimate of these figures will avoid budgetary overspend during the installation stage, and perhaps financial difficulty if available funds are exhausted before the project can begin to generate cash inflow. The time profile of expenditure is important since the cost of a large project may be spread over several years.

The life of the project and any scrap value to be received when the project completes its operational life. It is difficult to estimate these items since obsolescence may shorten the life of a project.

Net cash flow. Since an investment decision considers results over the full life of a project the decision must be based on net cash inflow rather than a profit figure, with the cash inflows calculated over the full life of the project to ensure that they exceed the funds invested in it. Depreciation, a non-cash cost, will therefore be ignored in an investment appraisal computation.

The incidence of income. This term means that if cash flow is spread over a number of years the return received in successive years cannot be given equal weighting when the project is evaluated. Cash flow received sooner should be more important than cash flow received in later years because it can be reinvested to earn an income, and is less subject to loss of value from inflation; also there is less risk that it may not be received at all. For this reason the profile of cash flow derived from a project is very important when that project is compared with rival alternatives.

The concept of present value is employed to enable a fair comparison to be made of cash flows in successive years. Assuming a rate of interest of 10 per cent, an amount of £909 received immediately will grow with interest to £1,000 in a year's time. Therefore the present value of £1,000 to be received in a year's time is £909. By the same token £826 when, invested at compound interest of 10 per cent will grow to £1,000 after 2 years, so that £826 is the present value of a cash flow of £1,000 to be received in 2 years' time. This simple arithmetic device enables a comparison to be made of cash flow received at different periods. The validity of the comparison depends upon the rate of discount applied in the sum. Algebraically the discounted cash flow (DCF) can be expressed as

$$\text{£}1{,}000 \times \frac{1}{1.1} = \text{£}909.1 - \text{p/v of the amount in 1 year at 10 per cent}$$

$$\text{£}1{,}000 \times \frac{1}{(1.1)^2} = \text{£}826.3 - \text{p/v of the amount in 2 years at 10 per cent}$$

The same calculation can be made for any discount rate or for any number of years, e.g.: for 15% $\frac{1}{(1.15)}$ for 1 year, or $\frac{1}{(1.15)^2}$ for 2 years or $\frac{1}{(1.15)^n}$

where n represents the number of years.

Working capital. Any investment, be it a machine or a new product, will require working capital in the form of stock and probably trade credit (debtors) to enable production and sales to take place. The investment of this working capital will gradually increase at the beginning of the project and will probably be gradually disinvested when the project ceases, e.g., as stocks are run down and debts are collected.

The ripple effect is just as important for long-term decisions as for short-term decisions.

The cost of capital. This should be the discount factor used when the incidence of income is considered. If a company can borrow funds as say 15 per cent, then investment projects should be discounted at that rate and only those projects which show a return in excess of a 15 per cent discount should be accepted. This calculation is made more complicated by the fact that businesses use funds recruited from a range of sources, e.g., share capital, long-term loans, ploughed-back profits, so it is usual for a weighted average cost of capital to be calculated. Occasionally this rate is increased to take account of the extra risk of a certain project. An investment project with a return which is greater than the cost of capital will increase the value of the firm.

Tax and government grants are a natural part of the business environment and must therefore be taken into account when an investment decision is made. Cash inflows may increase profits and therefore tax will be paid on those profits resulting in a cash outflow in the next year. Conversely, capital investment will attract many forms of government grant which may reduce the amount of tax payable. Thus taxation has a significant effect on the amount and timing of cash flows from an investment project.

METHODS OF INVESTMENT APPRAISAL

A number of methods exist to appraise long-term investment decisions but there are three methods which are widely used.

The payback method

In this case the payback is the period expressed in terms of the number of years which it takes the cash inflows from a capital investment project to equal the cash outflows. Competing projects are ranked according to the length of time it takes to repay the capital investment from cash flowing in. The project with the shortest payback period is deemed to be preferable.

The payback method

Two investment projects A and B are under consideration.

	Project A	*Project B*
Life	5 years	8 years
Cost	£200,000	£180,000
Cash flow per annum	£ 50,000	£ 36,000
Payback period	200 / 50 = 4 years	180 / 36 = 5 years

Thus project A would be selected.

This is a simple method to evaluate alternatives when long-term investment decisions are made, and is widely used in industry. It tends to concentrate investment on the shorter-term projects which pay back at an early stage and is thus good if the business is short of cash and requires rapid repayment, or if the danger of obsolescence is significant for the decision and may shorten the life of the projects. However, this method suffers from two important disadvantages. First, it fails to recognise the incidence of income and treats cash flows in successive years with equal significance. As already noted the time value of money is important. Secondly, it ignores all cash flows after the point at which payback is reached. In the example above, this simplistic method would bias the decision in favour of Project A which returns £250,000 over its life on an investment of £200,000, in preference to Project B which gives a return of £288,000 over 8 years in return for an investment of £180,000.

The net present value method (NPV)

This is one of the discounted cash flow methods of investment appraisal which is widely used in business. The technique is to discount cash outflows and inflows by a rate which represents the cost of capital of the business. If the present value of cash inflows is greater than the present value of cash outflows then the project is considered to be viable. If a choice must be made between alternatives, the project with the greatest net present value is the one that is selected. This method can account for the time value of money and give preference to a project with a cash flow profile which concentrates cash flows in the earlier years.

Applying the net present value method

Two investment projects C and D are under consideration. Although they both have the same cost (£60,000 payable immediately) and the same total cash flow (£80,000), the incidence of the cash flow is very different for them. The NPV method will apply a discount factor (the present value of £1 at the cost of capital, 10 per cent in this case) to the cash flows so that the two alternatives can be compared. The discount factor can be calculated as shown above but it is easier to read it from an appropriate discounting table, such as that in Table 7.1.

		Project C (£)		Project D (£)	
Year	P/V of £1 at 10%	Cash flow £	P/V	Cash flow £	P/V
1	0.9091	40,000	36,364	10,000	9,091
2	0.8263	30,000	24,789	30,000	24,789
3	0.7513	10,000	7,513	40,000	30,052
Present value of the inflow			68,666		63,932
Present value of the outflow*			60,000		60,000
Net present value			£8,666		£3,932

* Not discounted because the outflow is immediate

Thus both investments are viable since they give a return in excess of the cost of capital at 10 per cent, but in the event of a scarcity of funds for investment, Project C would be preferred to Project D since it has the greater net present value (NPV).

The internal rate of return method (IRR)

This is an alternative way of using discounting for an investment decision. The internal rate of return is the percentage discount rate which, when used in a capital investment appraisal, will bring the cost of the project and its future cash inflows into equality. The IRR earned by a project is the rate of discount which must be applied to the net cash flow profile to bring the present value of inflows to equality with the present value of outflows. In the event of scarce funds, the project with the higher IRR is considered to be the winner.

Applying the internal rate of return method

The facts are the same as for the present value calculation above, but the projects C and D will be discounted at increasingly higher rates of discount until a negative net present value is computed. It is then possible to calculate by extrapolation the rate of discount at which the present value of inflows and outflows are equal. This is the IRR.

	Present value of £1		*Project C (£)*		*Project D (£)*	
Year	*15%*	*20%*	*Cash flow*	*P/V at 20%*	*Cash flow*	*P/V at 15%*
* Now	1.0000	1.0000	*(60,000)	(60,000)	*(60,000)	(60,000)
1	0.8696	0.8333	40,000	33,332	10,000	8,696
2	0.7561	0.6944	30,000	20,832	30,000	22,683
3	0.6575	0.5787	10,000	5,787	40,000	26,300
Net Present Value				(49)		(2,231)

* Outflow shown in brackets

Table 7.1 Present value factors

	Percentage rate of discount															
Future years	*1*	*2*	*3*	*4*	*5*	*6*	*7*	*8*	*9*	*10*	*11*	*12*	*13*	*14*	*15*	*16*
1	0.990	0.980	0.971	0.962	0.952	0.943	0.935	0.926	0.917	0.909	0.901	0.893	0.885	0.877	0.870	0.862
2	0.980	0.961	0.943	0.925	0.907	0.890	0.873	0.857	0.842	0.826	0.812	0.797	0.783	0.769	0.756	0.743
3	0.971	0.942	0.915	0.889	0.864	0.840	0.816	0.794	0.772	0.751	0.731	0.712	0.693	0.675	0.658	0.641
4	0.961	0.924	0.888	0.855	0.823	0.792	0.763	0.735	0.708	0.683	0.659	0.636	0.613	0.592	0.572	0.552
5	0.951	0.906	0.863	0.822	0.784	0.747	0.713	0.681	0.650	0.621	0.593	0.567	0.543	0.519	0.497	0.476
6	0.942	0.888	0.837	0.790	0.746	0.705	0.666	0.630	0.596	0.564	0.535	0.507	0.480	0.456	0.432	0.410
7	0.933	0.871	0.813	0.760	0.711	0.665	0.623	0.583	0.547	0.513	0.482	0.452	0.425	0.400	0.376	0.354
8	0.923	0.853	0.789	0.731	0.677	0.627	0.582	0.540	0.502	0.467	0.434	0.404	0.376	0.351	0.327	0.305
9	0.914	0.837	0.766	0.703	0.645	0.592	0.544	0.500	0.460	0.424	0.391	0.361	0.333	0.308	0.284	0.263
10	0.905	0.820	0.744	0.676	0.614	0.558	0.508	0.463	0.422	0.386	0.352	0.322	0.295	0.270	0.247	0.227
11	0.896	0.804	0.722	0.650	0.585	0.527	0.475	0.429	0.388	0.350	0.317	0.287	0.261	0.237	0.215	0.195
12	0.887	0.788	0.701	0.625	0.557	0.497	0.444	0.397	0.356	0.319	0.286	0.257	0.231	0.208	0.187	0.168
13	0.879	0.773	0.681	0.601	0.530	0.469	0.415	0.368	0.326	0.290	0.258	0.229	0.204	0.182	0.163	0.145
14	0.870	0.758	0.661	0.577	0.505	0.442	0.388	0.340	0.299	0.263	0.232	0.205	0.181	0.160	0.141	0.125
15	0.861	0.743	0.642	0.555	0.481	0.417	0.362	0.315	0.275	0.239	0.209	0.183	0.160	0.140	0.123	0.108
16	0.853	0.728	0.623	0.534	0.458	0.394	0.339	0.292	0.252	0.218	0.188	0.163	0.141	0.123	0.107	0.093
17	0.844	0.714	0.605	0.513	0.436	0.371	0.317	0.270	0.231	0.198	0.170	0.146	0.125	0.108	0.093	0.080
18	0.836	0.700	0.587	0.494	0.416	0.350	0.296	0.250	0.212	0.180	0.153	0.130	0.111	0.095	0.081	0.069
19	0.828	0.686	0.570	0.475	0.396	0.331	0.277	0.232	0.194	0.164	0.138	0.116	0.098	0.083	0.070	0.060
20	0.820	0.673	0.554	0.456	0.377	0.312	0.258	0.215	0.178	0.149	0.124	0.104	0.087	0.073	0.061	0.051

Thus C is negative when discounted at 20 per cent and D is negative when discounted at 15 per cent but in the example above both projects were positive when discounted at 10 per cent. The extrapolation formula will show the discount rate which will give a NPV of nil. At 10 per cent discount C was positive £8,666 and D positive £3,932.

$$\textit{Bottom of class} + \left[\left(\frac{\textit{Position in class}}{\textit{Range of class}}\right) \times \left(\frac{\textit{Class interval}}{1}\right)\right] = \textit{IRR}$$

For D the IRR will be somewhere between 10 per cent and 15 per cent calculated as:

$$10\% + \left[\left(\frac{3{,}932}{3{,}932 + 2{,}321}\right) \times \left(\frac{5\%}{1}\right)\right] = 13.14\%$$

For C the IRR will be somewhere between 10 per cent and 20 per cent, but nearly at 20 per cent calculated as

$$10\% + \left[\left(\frac{8{,}666}{8{,}666 + 49}\right) \times \left(\frac{10\%}{1}\right)\right] = 19.94\%$$

Thus Project D would not be viable if the cost of capital is 15 per cent since it gives only a return of 13-14 per cent. However, Project C would be viable at 15 per cent. If a decision must be made between C and D then C would be chosen since it has the higher internal rate of return.

SUMMARY

When decisions are taken a Management Accountant can assist the process by the provision of figures, but such figures require interpretation to disclose their meaning and significance for the decision and for the assumptions on which the figure evidence is based. Decisions should only be taken in the light of 'relevant' information, and it is the Management Accountant's task to study cost behaviour in the circumstances of the decision and to provide appropriate figures. Thus, non-relevant information can be isolated and ignored and the decision takers' minds are focused on what will change as a result of their decision. The 'contribution' related to alternative courses of action excludes the fixed costs of the situation and is thus a criterion of great importance to the decision maker.

A separate decision logic has developed to recognise relevant costs so that decisions are based on appropriate facts. Qualitative information which cannot always be expressed in figure terms must also be given due weight when the decision is under consideration. Decision information is of necessity a matter of estimate and may thus not prove to be entirely accurate. The sensitivity of a decision to changes which might affect the various estimates on which the decision is based is yet another significant factor for the decision maker.

Long-term investment decisions require a decision logic of their own with consideration of the whole life of the projects which are competing for scarce investment funds. Such decisions will tie up significant amounts of the company's finance and will have an important effect on the profitability of the business for many years. Long-term decisions are important for the survival and success of the business and if management decide wrongly in such circumstances it will be a very expensive matter to disinvest from a mistaken course of action. Once again it is important to identify all the factors which will influence the decision and in this respect the significance of taxation and the amount of working capital to be tied up in the project must not be forgotten.

In a decision process which considers cash inflows and outflows over a period of several years, the time value of money and the incidence of income are both important factors. Discounting is vital to enable a comparison of the cash flow profiles of alternative projects which are competing for scarce investment funds. Recognition of this point brings the further problem of deciding on an appropriate discount rate to apply to the calculations. A further complication is that there are two methods of undertaking a discounted cash flow computation: the net present value method and the internal rate of return method. Questions concerning the cost of capital at which projects should be discounted, and what to do when the net present value method shows a result which disagrees with that disclosed by the internal rate of return method, are the subjects of more advanced studies beyond the scope of this chapter.

EXERCISE ONE: A SHORT-TERM BUSINESS DECISION

The Carreau Company Limited is employed in the manufacture of decorative tiles. Their manufacturing range covers four patterns: Willow, Cuboid, Floribunda and Nautical. Budgeted production quantities at full capacity are: Willow 30,000, Cuboid 10,000, Floribunda 8,000, and Nautical 10,000, with prices set at £3.00, £3.50, £2.50,and £2.00 respectively for each tile.

The Cost Accountant has produced a budgeted full absorption costing statement, as a result of which the Managing Director plans to cease production of the Floribunda, Cuboid and Nautical tiles. You have been contacted as a consultant to advise on the validity of this decision.

Your investigations reveal the following information:

Raw material costs per tile are: Willow 90p, Cuboid £1, Floribunda 90p, Nautical 85p.

Willow and Floribunda use the same material, and if Floribunda ceases production, then the company will lose a quantity rebate of 10 per cent of the price of that raw material.

Direct labour is paid at £5 per hour and production times for tiles are: Willow, 7 minutes 12 seconds; Cuboid, 6 minutes; Floribunda, 6 minutes; and Nautical 9 minutes.

Factory overheads are budgeted at £29,000 and are apportioned to products according to volume of production.

Separate transport facilities are maintained for each product. The cost is budgeted to be £3,000 per product at full capacity, but will not be incurred if a product is no longer made.

Administration costs are apportioned equally to the four products. The total budgeted at £8,000.

Selling costs are considered to be fixed in nature since a predetermined amount is set aside in the budget for this activity. The amounts are: Willow £14,000, Cuboid £10,000, Floribunda £4,800 and Nautical £5,000. The cost will not be incurred if a product is no longer made.

(a) Compute a budgeted full absorption costing statement to explain the Managing Director's planned decision.

(b) Compute an alternative statement and advise the Managing Director.

The Carreau Company Ltd – a solution

(a) Budgeted production statement

	Willow	*Cuboid*	*Floribunda*	*Nautical*	*Total*
Volume	30,000	10,000	8,000	10,000	
Price	£3.00	£3.50	£2.50	£2.00	
	£	£	£	£	£
Revenue	90,000	35,000	20,000	20,000	
Costs:					
Material	27,000	10,000	7,200	8,500	
Labour	18,000	5,000	4,000	7,500	
Factory overheads	15,000	5,000	4,000	5,000	
Transport	3,000	3,000	3,000	3,000	
Administration	2,000	2,000	2,000	2,000	
Selling	14,000	10,000	4,800	5,000	
	79,000	35,000	25,000	31,000	
Profit (loss)	11,000	–	(5,000)	(11,000)	£(5,000)

(b) Statement in contribution terms

	Willow	*Cuboid*	*Floribunda*	*Nautical*	*Total*
	£	£	£	£	£
Revenue	90,000	35,000	20,000	20,000	

Direct costs:					
Material	27,000	10,000	7,200	8,500	
Labour	18,000	5,000	4,000	7,500	
	45,000	15,000	11,200	16,000	
Contribution	45,000	20,000	8,800	4,000	
Less: other variable costs in context of closure:					
Transport	(3,000)	(3,000)	(3,000)	(3,000)	
Selling	(14,000)	(10,000)	(4,800)	(5,000)	
Contribution	28,000	7,000	1,000	(4,000)	32,000
Fixed overheads					(29,000)
Administration					(8,000)
Loss					£(5,000)

Advice to Managing Director:

1 If his decision is implemented, positive contributions of Cuboid and Floribunda are lost, and contribution of Willow is reduced by £3,000 (being a quarter of material cost as rebate is lost), so loss increases to £12,000.

2 Retain products with positive contribution.
Drop products with negative contribution.
Loss reduced to £1,000.

3 Seek means to improve contribution of Floribunda by cutting costs, increasing sales, or transferring demand from Nautical.

EXERCISE 2: A LONG-TERM INVESTMENT DECISION

Glapton Glassworks Ltd are investigating the suggestion that they should manufacture an artistic, moulded, glass statuette for the luxury end of the tourist trade. They have spent £25,660 on a market survey which has forecast a life of four years for the product before cheaper competitors make it unsaleable. The survey states that if price is set at £130 for each unit, the best estimate of demand is 4,000 units in Year 1, 6,000 each in Years 2 and 3, and then falling to 2,000 in Year 4. Pre-launch advertisements will cost £20,000.

Management has undertaken a costing exercise, which shows a profit per unit as follows:

	£	£
Selling price		130.00
Less:		
Costs:		
Materials	30	
Labour (10 hours at £7)	70	
Variable production overheads	10	
Direct fixed costs	12.51	

Head office costs	5	
		127.51
Profit per product		£2.49

Information revealed during the costing exercise is as follows:

1 Factory space is worked to full capacity at present, so extra premises would need to be rented at £14,600 pa on a short lease to house the production process.

2 Artwork on the master moulds for the statuette would cost £20,000. Production moulds made from the master would cost £5,000 per set, and would last for 5,000 units of production. This cost can be written off for tax purposes as a revenue expense.

3 Machinery used in the production process could be transferred from a redundant process in the main factory. This machinery costs £135,000 and is three years into an expected useful life of nine years. It would cost £6,220 to refurbish this machinery.

4 The machinery to be transferred was recently the subject of an offer from another glassworks who wished to purchase it for £80,000. This machinery is expected to be valueless in four years' time and is written down to nil for tax purposes.

5 The manager of the redundant process is paid a salary of £10,000 pa. He is about to be dismissed with a compensation payment of £7,000, but could be employed to organise production of the new product.

6 Head office fixed costs are allocated to production by Glapton Glassworks Ltd at a rate of 50p per hour.

Direct fixed costs:	£
Rent (4 years at £14,600)	58,400
Depreciation of moulds	35,000
Depreciation of plant (£135,000 / 9) x 4	60,000
Refurbishing machines	6,220
Supervision (Manager:4 yrs x £10,000)	40,000
Feasibility study	25,660
	£225,280

£225,280/18,000 = £12.51 per unit

The management approach you for advice as to whether they should proceed with this project. They have doubts as to the reliability of their estimates concerning the life of the project and the cost of capital, which they suggest is 15 per cent.

(a) List the points of principle that affect this decision and advise management as to whether to proceed with the project.
(b) Comment on the sensitivity of the project to fluctuations in the estimates of the cost of capital, and
(c) Warn management as to the limitations of your calculations, and suggest other factors that might clarify this decision.

Assume corporation tax at 33 per cent. All cash flows arise at the end of each year.

Glapton Glassworks – solution

(a) Points of principle

1 Depreciation is excluded from NPV calculation.

2 Plant transferred is accounted for at exit value – opportunity cost.
3 Compensation payment to manager is saved – the rule for incremental costs is applied – but will there be a redundancy payment at the end of the project?
4 Head office costs are ignored, not incremental costs.
5 Feasibility study is a sunk cost and should be excluded.
6 An alternative is to sell the machinery at once for £80,000, thus attracting a tax balancing charge of £26,400.

The calculation of cash flow is based on a contribution per product of £20

	Year 1	*Year 2*	*Year 3*	*Year 4*
Volume	4,000	6,000	6,000	2,000
	£	£	£	£
Contribution	80,000	120,000	120,000	40,000
*Direct costs	17,600	24,600	24,600	24,600
	62,400	95,400	95,400	15,400
Tax at 33%	20,592	31,482	31,482	5.082
PAID	Year 2	Year 3	Year 4	Year 5

£25,000 + £6,220 = £31,220 written off against taxable profit reduces tax paid by 33% x £31,220 = £10,303 + (33% of £20,000 for advertising) £6,600 = £16,902 in Year 1.

Tax allowances on Production Moulds in Years 2 and 3 reduce tax paid by 33% of the sum – £5,000 x 0.33 = £1,650 saved Year 3. £10,000 x 0.33 = £3,300 saved Year 4. Tax is offset by one year.

Year	*Cash Flow*	*Capital Expenditure*	*Tax*	*Net*	*Discount Factor 15%*	*PV*
	£	£	£	£	£	£
		(80,000)				
0	(20,000)	(6,220)	–	(131,220)	1.0000	(131,220)
		(25,000)				
1	62,400	–	16,902	79,302	0.8696	68,961
2	95,400	(5,000)	(20,592)	69,808	0.7561	52,782
3	95,400	(10,000)	(31,482)			
			1,650	55,568	0.6572	36,519
4	15,400	–	(31,482)			
			3,300	(12,782)	0.5718	(7,309)
5	–	–	(5,082)	(5,082)	0.4972	(2,527)
					NPV	£17,206

Note: outflows are in brackets

There is positive NPV so the project is viable

*Direct costs are Rent £14,600 + supervision £10,000 less compensation saved £7,000 = £17,600 for Year 1 end no compensation in Years 2,3,4.

Depreciation is ignored and refurbishing costs (£6,220) are treated as capital expenditure before the project commences.

(b)

Year	*Discount Factor 25%*	*Cash Flow*	*PV*
	£	£	£
0	1.000	(131,220)	(131,220)
1	0.8000	79,302	63,442
2	0.6400	69,808	44,677

3	0.5120	55,568	28,451
4	0.4096	(12,782)	(5,236)
5	0.3277	(5,082)	(1,665)
		Negative NPV	(1,551)

$$\text{IRR of project} = 15 + \frac{(17{,}206)}{(17{,}206 + 1{,}551)} \times 10 = 24.2\%$$

Thus the cost of capital must rise to 24 per cent before this project ceases to be viable.

$$24 - 15 = 9.\ \frac{9}{15} = 60\%$$

An error of 60 per cent of the cost of capital figure used in the calculations would be needed before the project ceased to be viable for that reason. So the cost of capital is not a very sensitive figure for this decision.

(c)

1 The volume changes over 4 years: will variable costs behave in proportion to this fluctuation and will fixed costs show a tendency to be semi-variable? For example, with labour there is no estimate for recruitment, training or redundancy costs.

2 A project such as this will require servicing by working capital in order to fund stocks and debtors. This aspect of capital employed in the project has been omitted from the analysis. A significant amount applied in Year 1 and disinvested in Years 3 and 4 after the application of the discount factor could affect the NPV calculation.

3 Uncertainty. The calculations above depend on a single estimate for factors such as materials, labour, overheads and revenues. The probability that alternative cost levels may apply should be taken into account, as should be the possibility that changes in costs may cancel each other out or may all tend in the same direction. The market survey should have produced information as to the probability of various sales volumes that may be experienced.

GLOSSARY OF MAIN TERMS

Contribution Contribution to fixed costs and overheads. The difference between the selling price per unit and the variable cost per unit.

Discounting Conversion of a future receipt or cost to a present value, recognising the time value of money.

Opportunity cost The benefits or revenues foregone by pursuing one course of action rather than another.

Payback The number of years required in order to recover funds invested.

Sunk Cost Previously incurred costs; costs that are not relevant to the present decision.

FURTHER READING

Merrett, A. J., and Sykes, A. (1973) *The Finance and Analysis of Capital Projects*, Longman.

Pizzey, A. V. (1989) *Cost and Management Accounting*, Paul Chapman.

Van Horne, J. C. (1989) *Financial Management and Policy*, Prentice Hall.

Weston, J. F., and Brigham, E. F. (1981) *Managerial Finance*, Cassell.

CHAPTER 8

Strategic decision making

David Jennings

STRATEGY

The study of strategy is probably as old as human conflict. The Greeks initially used the term *strategos* to refer to the art of the general in the command of an army. Modern use of the word has broadened away from solely referring to decisions concerning the use of military force. Today when we refer to the strategic decisions facing a business we are concerned with all those issues that have long-term implications for the organisation. The decisions themselves are of fundamental importance to the organisation and probably have consequences for other decisions that the organisation has to consider. In a business context strategy concerns all aspects of the business, the development of technological and human resources as well as products and markets, the relationship between the business and the community and the issues associated with competition.

In the last three decades there has been considerable academic and practical interest in concepts and techniques for understanding and developing strategies for business situations. Much of this literature has been concerned with the adaptation of the organisation to a changing environment on the basis of the executives of the business analysing the situation in which the organisation is operating. That viewpoint will be the basis of this chapter.

First of all, in order to understand how a company's actions can be viewed as a strategy, a short case study will be analysed, the case concerns SMH, the producers of the Swatch watch.

SWATCH

The 100 millionth Swatch came off a Swiss production line this month and straight into the private collection of its maker, Société Suisse de Microélectronique et s'Horlogerie (SMH). The cheap plastic watch, which pundits said was doomed to failure at its launch a decade ago, spearheaded the rescue of the Swiss watch industry from near-obliteration by Japanese competition, and has broken all records as the world's largest and fastest-selling timepiece. Annual sales surpassed 17m units in 1991, and SMH plans to boost output to 25m–30m this year and to 50m within five years.

Swatch's secret was a manufacturing technique that cut down the number of parts in a watch and allowed fully automated assembly, making Swatches cheap to produce even in high-cost Switzerland. It mixes that with dazzling design and clever marketing that project a 'Swatch lifestyle' – youthful and stylish.

By launching new limited collections of watch designs twice a year, Swatch has managed to combine cheapness with Swiss quality and to feed a collection mania that has seen older models fetch thousands of dollars at auctions. While sales of the basic

Swatch have remained fairly steady in recent years at 12m–13m a year, sales of Swatch variants – such as the Pop Swatch, the Flik-Flak for children and the higher priced chronograph and Scuba diving watches – are rising rapidly. A Swatch automatic, which needs no battery, comes on the market this year.

Some designs have not been successful. Sales in America went down in the late 1980s because of mistakes in distribution and marketing policy. But continuing innovation and strict cost-control (the basic Swatch still sells for its original price of SFr50, or $35) have kept Swatch on a roll that analysts think looks good for a few years yet.

Much of this is due to SMH's energetic and idiosyncratic boss, Nicolas Hayek, creator and principal shareholder of the group, which was formed in 1984 by the merger of two ailing Swiss watch firms. Creativity is fostered, he says, by maintaining a childlike openness to new ideas and by running 'an open company'.

Mr Hayek is regarded with some awe by other Swiss businessmen. But he has never won their wholehearted backing, partly because he and SMH are famously reluctant to give information. He had already built up a big engineering consultancy when he was brought in by the banks to advise on the SMH merger. Against the conventional wisdom he proposed tackling the Japanese head-on in all segments of the market, including the cheap end. When the banks wanted to quit, Mr Hayek backed the plan with his own money. In the most spectacular company turnaround in Swiss business history, profits soared, debts were erased and, by value, SMH watch sales are poised to overtake those of Seiko of Japan, the current world number one.

Swatch may be SMH's trendiest product, but it represents only a quarter of the company's SFr 2.37 billion sales last year, and only half of its 30m output of watches. SMH is one of the world's biggest luxury-watch producers, making also the Omega, Longines and Rado brands. Additionally it produces components and movements (about 50m in 1991) for assembly by other watchmakers. But with the world market for watches expected to grow sluggishly during the 1990s, SMH has cast covetous eyes towards more exciting markets where Mr Hayek thinks the Swatch formula could work. Surprisingly, he has picked as similarly 'emotional' consumer-product areas the high-cost (and high-risk) sectors of telecoms and cars.

Swatch's first foray into the telecoms market was with the Swatch twin-phone, a dual-handset telephone in Swatch-style designs. It created barely a ripple in Europe, though Mr Hayek claims SMH cannot meet American demand. Analysts said that approval problems, along with poor marketing and distribution, shared the blame in Europe. But Mr Hayek says he is aiming for production of 1m units this year, and plans to announce in June a partnership with a top telecoms manufacturer to produce not only the twin-phone but also cordless, cellular and fax telephones. Mr Hayek is even more enthusiastic about the Swatchpager, a paging watch just launched in America in partnership with BellSouth.

It is Mr Hayek's project to produce a Swatch car that has aroused most controversy. Hayek, whose consultancy, Hayek Engineering, has advised several big car manufacturers, claims SMH has the technology and design skills to come up with a cheap ecological car that has the performance and safety features of a conventional petrol-driven one. Last year he announced a joint venture with Germany's Volkswagen (VW) to develop, manufacture and distribute the car for launch in 1995. The car will be powered by an electric or hybrid electric-petrol motor. A prototype is already being tested.

Mr Hayek has calmed investors by insisting that SMH's development costs in the project will be only $10m, with VW putting in another $10m. SMH's prime target is the American market, where new pollution legislation means many cars will have to be emission-free by the end of the decade. If the launch of the Swatchmobile goes well, SMH hopes to build 100,000 a year. Too optimistic? Mr Hayek says SMH has come up with new solutions to old problems by rethinking the car concept from scratch. That kind of rethink, sceptics are reminded, was how Swatch started ticking. (Source: *The Economist*, 18 April, 1992.)

In the case, Swatch is a company that has achieved a marked turnaround in its performance by following a set of strategies; these strategies have enabled Swatch to develop a number of key abilities and to improve its competitive position. Two types of strategy may be identified from the case, business and corporate strategy.

BUSINESS STRATEGY

Most businesses operate in a situation where their products and services compete with those provided by other organisations to meet the customer's need. Competitor firms can be aggressive and act in a purposeful way to win the firm's customers. SMH had encountered such competition and it had almost driven the company out of business.

All businesses have to make a decision concerning the basis upon which they compete. If it is assumed that the firm's competitors have been careful in choosing a strategy that reflects their distinctive strengths and abilities then it may be unwise to simply respond to competition by copying the competitors' strategy. The result would be head-on competition, for example a price war which the firm could only survive through having an outstanding strength, the ability to operate on a low-cost basis, or the financial resources to endure the losses that arose from the price war longer than the competition. An organisation must compete on the basis of a strategy that, as far as possible, is unique. A strategy that reflects the firm's own particular strengths and abilities.

A range of business strategies are available to an organisation; these options are summarised in Fig. 8.1.

Following Porter's analysis there are only two routes through which a business can successfully compete and achieve superior performance. Either through becoming the lowest-cost producer or through differentiating the product/service in ways that are valued by the buyer. The firm can apply either of these strategies to a broad market, or to a narrow, focused, market. The combination of these two decisions is a business strategy. Each strategy provides a basis upon which a product or group of products might develop competitive advantage.

Swatch has established a basis upon which the business can compete and achieve superior performance. *Swatch has developed a group of products that appeal to various segments of the mass market for watches, on the basis of style.*

The products appeal on the basis of being differentiated from those produced by competitors. The product projects 'a Swatch lifestyle', youthful and stylish. The watches appeal to both a basic market and increasingly, through variations in style, to a range of market segments, including the children's market, young persons' and sporting markets. Some of the watches are even achieving high values as collectors' items.

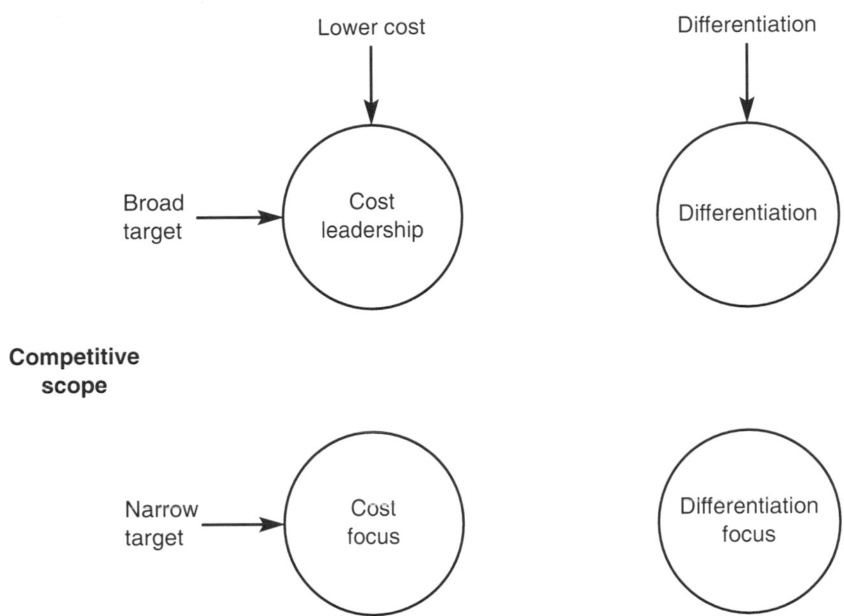

Fig. 8.1 Generic business strategies (adapted from Porter, M. E., 1985)

This aspect of the product's appeal is based upon:

(a) *Design* and styling of the Swatch watch, both to compete with other producers and to avoid saturation of the market.
(b) *Marketing* identifying and testing the opportunity for new products.
(c) The company fostering creativity, through its open *style of management*.

Swatch are able to produce stylish, mass market watches at a price that competes with the products of rival companies. At the same time the business is profitable and operates on a low-cost basis.

For Swatch low cost is achieved through:

(a) *Design* and the specification of component parts. A Swatch watch has a stylish appearance that differentiates it from competitors' products and makes it particularly appealing to the consumer, but that effect is not achieved at the expense of costs that would make the product too expensive. The issue of costs is addressed in the fundamental design of the product and its use of component parts.
(b) The high volume of production enables Swatch to achieve *economies of scale*, low unit costs in production, marketing and distribution.
(c) The accumulated volume, 100 million watches to date, has provided Swatch with an opportunity to *continue to learn new ways to improve efficiency*.

Swatch operates in a competitive market. Although it is highly efficient in the manufacture of watches, it has established its appeal to the consumer on the basis of differentiating itself from other watches that are available to the market. For Swatch, as for any differentiator, cost reduction is engaged in as a means to maintain a price level that qualifies the product for purchase by the customer and provides improved margins, it is not the primary basis for competing in the market.

CORPORATE STRATEGY

Corporate strategy concerns *the scope of the organisation and the range of activities which the organisation is engaged in.* Corporate strategy can be defined by looking at two aspects of the business: diversification, and the various activities that the company undertakes in order to provide those products and services – vertical integration.

Diversification

This aspect of strategy is concerned with the different products and markets that are served by the company overall. Swatch is only one of the product areas of Société Suisse de Microélectronique et s'Horlogerie. SMH has an active diversification strategy that covers the following areas.

(a) *The Swatch watch*, a branded mass market product.
(b) *The sale of components* and movements to other watch manufacturers.
(c) *Luxury watches.*
(d) *Telephones.*
(e) *Automobiles.*

SMH is diversified and is trying to increase that diversity in order to provide a range of products for a number of different markets.

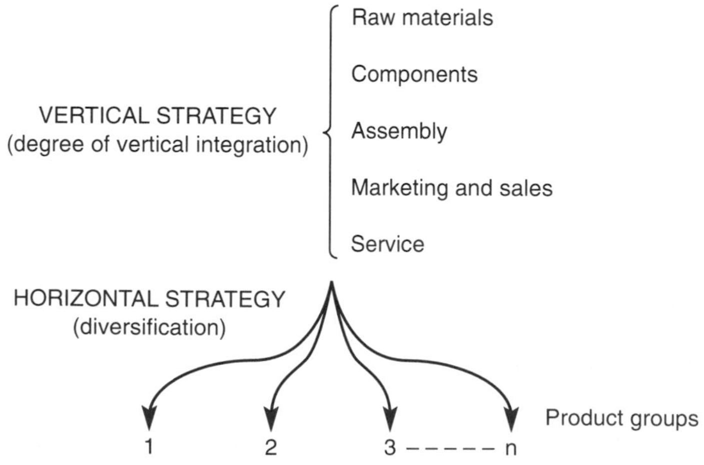

Fig. 8.2 The dimensions of corporate strategy

Vertical integration

All products require a complex chain of activities, materials and components that stretch from the ultra-raw materials from which the product will be constituted to the final customer. The vertical strategy of an organisation concerns decisions on which of those activities should be supplied in-house rather than purchased from outside the organisation. There are exceptions, for example oil companies which undertake all stages of production from exploration, through production to distribution, marketing and retailing – but in general few organisations decide to undertake all stages of the chain of activity.

For the Swatch watch SMH undertake the following activities:

(a) *Manufacture of components and movements.*
(b) *Assembly.*
(c) *Product design.*
(d) *Marketing.*

Not all of these activities need to be undertaken by a watch producer. Some manufacturers are avoiding involvement in the investment and technology required for the manufacture of components by buying-in those items from SMH. Which activities should SMH undertake? The answer to that question needs to address the same issue as business strategy, competitiveness. Does undertaking an activity make SMH's products more competitive?

Many of the components that are sold by SMH become a part of the products sold by competitors. But SMH can derive competitive advantage from supplying those components if it helps SMH to achieve even higher volumes of production in the manufacture of components, providing access to greater economies of scale and consequently lower unit costs.

Defining a company's corporate and business strategies is a necessary stage in evaluating those decisions. The two areas of strategy are not, however, separate from one another. Corporate strategy has to underpin and strengthen business strategy and the ability of the business to compete in its various product areas.

The view of strategy that arises from the Swatch case is that strategy is a complex set of decisions concerning fundamental aspects of the company. The decisions have consequences for the long-term future of the company and focus on the issue of where and how it will compete. Many of the decisions affect each other. The design of the watches partly determines the costs of their production. In turn the Swatch image and design ability form a basis for the company's diversification.

THE ROLE OF STRATEGIC DECISION MAKING

Strategic decision making is a central part of the management of an organisation. Strategic decisions and statements of those strategies serve the following purposes.

(a) Strategic decisions answer two fundamental questions. What activities should the organisation be involved in and how will it compete in it's various business areas? The corporate and business strategies of the organisation are determined by these decisions.

(b) Strategy states the fundamental means by which the organisation seeks to achieve its goals.

(c) All decisions are concerned with the future. The long-term nature of strategic decisions means that they will be implemented and will operate in a business environment which the organisation cannot fully anticipate. Strategic decisions take place in a context of uncertainty concerning the future. Consequently, when those decisions are made they need to provide contingencies with which to meet unforeseen events. In this role it may be argued that the function of a strategy is not to 'solve a problem' but to so structure a situation that the problems that will emerge are solvable. For Swatch an efficient production process would enable the business to compete on the basis of lower prices, should changes in demand or competition make that necessary.

(d) Strategy also has a purpose in relation to the internal world of the organisation and the people who make up the organisation. A shared understanding of the company's strategy helps to reduce the uncertainty experienced by the organisation's members and promotes consistency in the decisions and actions taken by the organisation. A clear understanding of the organisation's strategy enables its members to share a common view of the situation they are working within, promoting efficiency and organisational learning.

THE STRATEGY PROCESS

Strategic decisions are the most fundamental and important decisions that a business has to make. But it is wrong to assume that the strategies one sees an organisation enacting are the result of a decision process that is entirely based upon rational analysis of the situation that confronts the business. The strategy that a business enacts may arise from a number of processes.

On the basis of a literature survey, Mintzberg (Mintzberg, 1990) identified ten schools of thought concerning the strategy process, ten largely competing explanations of how an organisation's strategy originates.

Prescriptive schools

1 *The Design School*: strategy formulation is a conceptual process. A conscious process of thought, preferably a creative process centred upon the Chief Executive. Strategies emerge from this design process fully developed and ready to be implemented.

2 *The Planning School*: strategy formation is a formal process enacted by the organisation. A controlled, conscious and formal process, decomposed into steps, each delineated by checklists of matters to be considered. The process is based upon the Chief Executive and a planning staff. Strategies emerge from this planning process fully developed; they are then implemented.

3 *The Positioning School*: strategy formulation is an analytical process. It is based upon an understanding of the particular industry and competition. Analysts play a major role in the process, feeding their conclusions to management. The strategies are generic and emerge fully developed from this process. Decision is followed by implementation. The selected strategies lead organisational and functional changes.

Descriptive schools

4 *The Entrepreneurial School*: strategy formulation is a visionary process; strategies exist in the mind of the organisation's leader as a sense of vision and long-term direction. The leader maintains close personal control of implementation. The strategic vision is adapted through the use of feedback derived from implementation.
5 *The Cognitive School*: in this view of the strategy process strategies are perspectives or concepts that form in the minds of executives and managers. The decision is a semi-conscious process based upon tacit assumptions. As a result the strategy, and the assumptions upon which it is based, are difficult to change. In view of the environment's complexity the strategy is based upon restricted and biased information.
6 *The Learning School*: strategy formulation is an emergent process. Environmental complexity and dynamism require a process of learning and strategic adaptation over time. In this view of strategy, formulation and implementation are indistinguishable, thinking is retrospective following action. Strategy-making is a diffuse and emergent process. Consequently, the role of strategic leadership is not to preconceive a strategy but to manage and help to develop the strategic learning process.
7 *The Political School*: strategy formulation is a power process. Strategy is based upon the power positions and ploys of influential groups and individuals. If the process is focused within the organisation there is no dominant actor but rather a number who vie to control organisational decisions.
8 *The Cultural School*: strategy formulation is a process of collective behaviour based upon beliefs shared by the organisation's members. Strategy is rooted in intentions that may not be explicit. Culture and ideology perpetuate the existing strategic perspective rather than encourage strategic change.
9 *The Environmental School*: strategy formulation is a passive process. There is no real internal strategist; the environment dictates strategy by forcing adaptation.
10 *The Configurational School*: draws upon elements from the other schools to define the strategy process as one that varies with circumstances. The particular form of process is based upon the type of organisation, the period in the organisation's history and the kind of environment in which the organisation exists. The result is a particular form of strategy process operating for a distinguishable period of time.

A number of questions concerning the strategy process arise from Mintzberg's analysis, among which are the following.

Who makes strategic decisions? Are they made solely by the Chief Executive. Are staff involved as analysts or planners. Do politically powerful individuals and groups influence these decisions? Or is the strategy that a business actually experiences based upon the shared culture of it's members?

How are strategic decisions made? Are they the result of conscious mental processes taking the form of planning or other forms of analysis? Or are they based upon experimentation and learning, finding out which developments pay off and building upon those successes? Are strategies shared beliefs about how the organisation should be run, based upon assumptions which go largely unexamined, and of which the managers are barely conscious? Or is strategy imposed by factors outside the organisation, through the environment dictating the choices that are open to the organisation?

All the answers may be correct. There are many accounts of strategic decisions which reveal the interaction of a number of processes in the development of a decision. Many case studies, such as Swatch, imply a rational and analytical approach to decision making. A fuller account of such decisions, as they are taken, often reveals the influence of other processes.

STRATEGIC ANALYSIS

Strategies enable the organisation to adapt to a changing external world. For the survival of the organisation it is essential that the strategy is viable, taking account of the organisation's abilities as well as the opportunities and threats presented by the environment. To ensure that this is so requires analysis to be used as an input into the decision process.

> Analysis is the critical starting point of strategic thinking. Faced with problems trends, events or situations that appear to constitute a harmonious whole or come packaged as a whole by the common sense of the day, the strategic thinker dissects them into their constituent parts. Then, having discovered the significance of these constituents, he reassembles them in a way calculated to maximise his advantage. (Ohmae, 1982, p12.)

Strategic analysis is a way of perceiving and structuring a problem. It leads us to seek information about potentially important aspects of the problem and provides a way of relating pieces of information to each other in order to better understand the situation facing the business.

Over the last two or three decades business managers, consultants and academics have developed a substantial body of techniques for analysing business situations with a view to developing more effective strategies. The role of these techniques is not to 'make' the decision but to help decision makers develop an understanding of the strategic situation they are operating in.

The strategy model that is developed over the remainder of this chapter provides an analysis that is based upon:

- The *purpose* (mission, objectives and goals) that the organisation is seeking to achieve.
- The organisation's *environment*.
- The organisation's *resources*.

Each of these factors is a fundamental part of the strategic situation and needs to be taken into account when a situation is being analysed and a decision made.

MISSION, OBJECTIVES AND GOALS

Decisions are not made purely on the basis of resources and what the environment will allow. Decisions are also affected by the purpose and objectives of the decision maker. This is true for both the personal and business lives of individuals. Booking a package holiday faces the individual purchaser with a bewildering range of options and prices. There is a great deal of information in the travel brochures and the travel agent will supply more but the eventual choice, although cloaked in the uncertainties of exchange rate surcharges, aircraft delays and the possibility of doubtful claims in the brochure, reflects the preferences of the decision maker, the customer.

Fig. 8.3 Three sector model of strategic analysis

All decisions have some lack of information and present the decision maker with uncertainty, but decisions can be improved by decision makers developing a clear idea of their purpose – what they wish to achieve by this decision.

MISSION STATEMENTS

Strategic decisions have long-term implications, consequently those decisions have to be guided by a view of the organisation's purpose which is also long term.

A mission statement defines the basic reason for the existence of an organisation and helps legitimise its function in society.

A carefully constructed mission statement can provide direction for today's activities and guidelines within which future development should take place. As a part of the mission statement an organisation needs to define its business.

This requires a special type of thinking. While we can all accept that the business world is experiencing unprecedented technological and market changes, it is extremely difficult for a business to accept that its existing customers and products will have to be replaced with different customers and that new customers' needs will have to be met. Today's products and markets will become obsolete.

Business definition

Conventionally businesses have defined themselves by reference to the products and services they produce and the markets they serve. A good mission statement helps to define the nature of the business in a way that will continue to have relevance even in a changing environment. A more enduring business definition can be established by looking beyond the product/market characteristics of the firm to identify:

- The organisation's customer groups; *who* it sells to.
- Customer function; *what* customer needs the organisation is meeting.
- The technologies and processes utilised by the organisation, *how* the function is performed.

These characteristics provide a three-dimensional definition of the nature of the business.

An example can be constructed for a university.

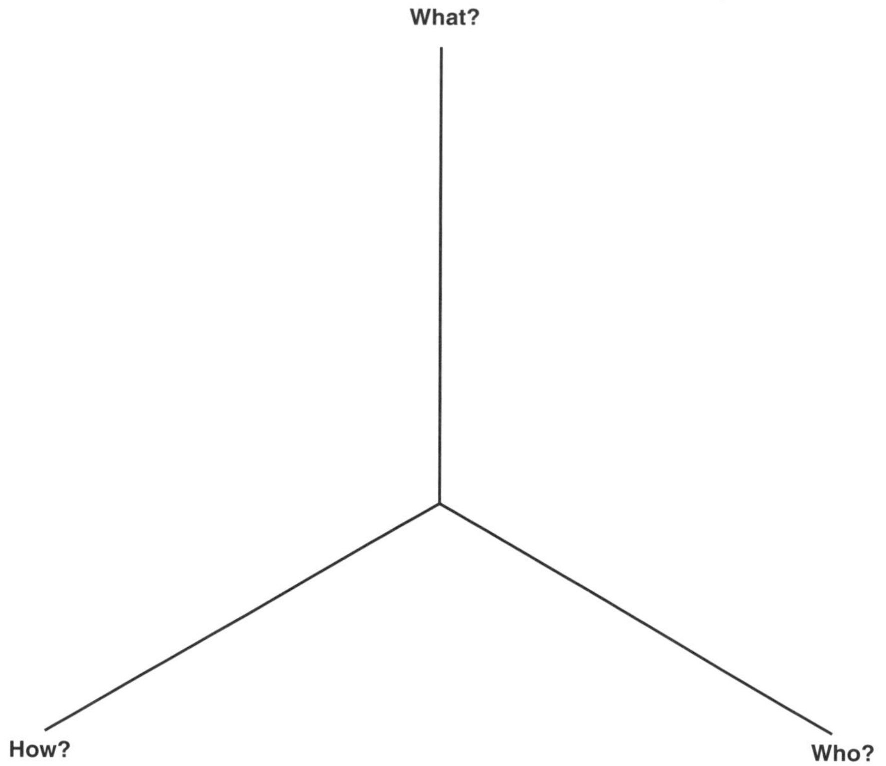

Fig. 8.4 Three elements of business definition

Who. The university has among its customers, individual students and corporate clients. The corporate clients include businesses, local and central government, and international governmental bodies, such as the EC. The university serves a considerable range of client groups.

What. The various clients receive a range of services from the university. Universities are fortunate in being legally authorised to certify degrees and other educational awards. The university also provides education and training services, consultancy and research.

How. In order to provide services the university engages in the following functions; the design of services, such as courses; the production of course and consultancy material; and the delivery of services. These activities are preceded by a search for information and the screening and evaluation of developments in the university's disciplines. In addition, there is a more specific development of the university's knowledge base, through the university's own research activities. The organisation also monitors changes in the needs of its client groups.

Defining the business of a university in terms of *who*, *what* and and *how* has two main benefits. First, the components of the business are put into perspective and their relative importance recognised. For example, most of the developments in knowledge will take place outside the university. Library services and the ability to effectively review and retrieve information will account for the greater part of the development of the university's knowledge base. The outcomes from the organisation's original research

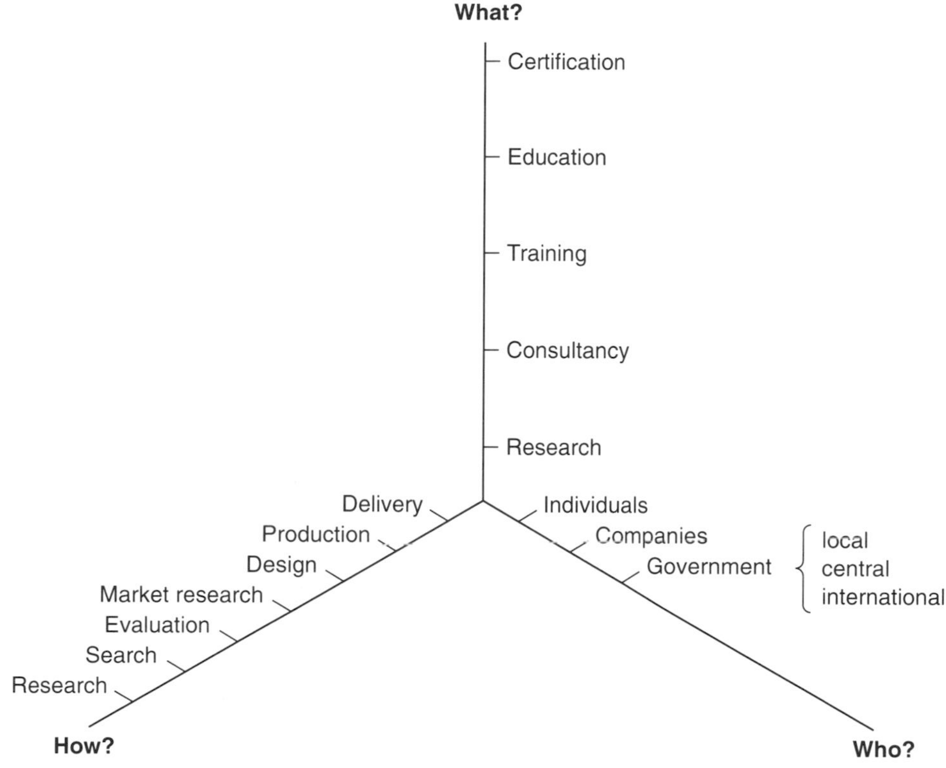

Fig. 8.5 Defining the business: a university

activities will be more specific to the university's purpose. Similarly the importance of services, such as certification, is recognised. Loss of this quasi-monopoly right would detract from the value given by employers and other groups to the university's education and training programmes. The business definition also recognises that the university serves a wide range of client groups.

The second benefit of a business definition is that it opens out the prospects for future product/market combinations that can be developed from the organisation's activities (*how*), functions (*what*) and client groups (*who*). The business definition should facilitate identification of possible future developments. For the university, examples of possible developments include:

1 The scanning and retrieval functions of the library (*how*), may provide the basis for a technical intelligence service (*what*), for a corporate client (*who*).
2 Companies engaged in in-house training could have value added to those activities through the university providing certification to improve external recognition of the training.

A business definition aims to recognise the fundamentals of the business. Over time, new functions and client groups, and ways of meeting their needs, will evolve, but a business definition provides a powerful insight into the nature of the business and helps to identify product/market developments that are accessible to the organisation.

Purpose and values

Mission statements also need to make clear the purpose and values of the organisation. This often involves identifying various groups that the organisation is trying to serve. For some organisations a single group is identified as a reason for the organisation's existence; this may be the customer or, for example in the case of Hanson Trust, the shareholder. More commonly organisations have to meet the claims of a number of stakeholder groups, for example customers, shareholders and employees. Each of these has a special interest in the organisation; they are stakeholders in the organisation. Certain groups may possess power and it will be necessary to maintain their support for the organisation. Among the more common stakeholder groups are the following:

Stakeholder	*Support for the organisation*
Customers	Sales and revenue
Shareholders	Equity finance
Suppliers	Raw material, components, equipment, energy
Managers and employees	Productive activity
Society	General support and freedom to operate

Each of the stakeholder groups may be important to the long-term prosperity and survival of a business. Failure to serve the needs of the customer may lead to those customers turning to a more suitable supplier. Similarly a company may neglect the more general needs of society, through causing unacceptable levels of pollution, failing to meet safety regulations or acting without regard for the needs of the local economy. The consequence of such actions may be the emergence of consumer and environmental groups seeking regulation of the industry, also a decline in support for the industry.

Mission statements serve an important role in communicating the purpose of an organisation to the various groups concerned, both within and outside the organisation. The aim is to clarify what is to be expected of the organisation. Mission statements need to be clear and memorable. Where a statement is in danger of becoming overlong some organisations adopt a brief statement of purpose followed by a set of supporting goals. An example, for British Airways, is provided in Illustration 8.1.

The statement by British Airways includes a series of broadly defined goals, some of which address particular stakeholder groups; these groups include:

Goal	*Stakeholder group*
Financial performance	Shareholders
Service and value	Customers
Customer driven	
Good employer	Employees

The statement also includes goals for the environment and for safety. Safety is the first goal listed in the statement. Clearly the reason for the goals' pre-eminence is that in order to be viable an airline's operations have to be safe. The issue of safety involves not just the customer but potentially everyone in society.

There are organisations that define their purpose in terms of an ideal, a principle that they wish to pursue without specific reference to a stakeholder group. An example of such an organisation has been provided by Body Shop's focus upon environmental

Illustration 8.1 British Airways – mission and goals statement

OUR MISSION
To be the best and most successful company in the airline industry.

OUR GOALS
Safe and Secure:
To be a safe and secure airline.

Financially Strong:
To deliver a strong and consistent financial performance.

Global Leader:
To secure a leading share of air travel business worldwide with a significant presence in all major geographical markets.

Service and Value:
To provide overall superior service and good value for money in every market segment in which we compete.

Customer Driven:
To excel in anticipating and quickly responding to customer needs and competitor activity.

Good Employer:
To sustain a working environment that attracts, retains and develops committed employees who share in the success of the company.

Good Neighbour:
To be a good neighbour, concerned for the community and the environment.

(Source: British Airways Company Report.)

issues. Such concerns are inspirational and may make association with the company a unique experience for its investors, customers and employees.

Making mission statements

Many organisations construct mission statements, as a part of their strategic planning, to help provide direction for employees and to enhance the effectiveness of such corporate communications as the annual report. Ideally a mission statement is brief and memorable yet expresses the fundamental nature of the organisation. Providing a useful *definition of the business* together with a statement of *purpose* and *values* implies that mission statements will often be lengthy. This may detract from the impact of the statement and make it rather too long to be memorable. A balance needs to be achieved between developing a statement that is lengthy, but provides for a depth of understanding, and a shorter statement that is more memorable yet contains less insight into the distinctive nature of the organisation. The mission statement in Illustration 8.2 is provided for the reader to evaluate and, if appropriate, re-draft.

Illustration 8.2 A university's mission statement

The mission of the University is to:

- develop a community of scholars seeking excellence in teaching and learning, and the discovery of new knowledge in the context of university education and academic freedom;
- attain national and international recognition for the quality of the teaching, scholarship and research of the University;
- provide, in an appropriate environment, a range of programmes relevant to the diverse needs of regional, national and overseas students;
- ensure relevance and value for the community in the activities and services of the university.

OBJECTIVES AND GOALS

The objectives set by an organisation need to reflect two considerations. The first is the long-term purpose of the organisation as expressed in the mission statement.

The mission statement provides a context from which to establish a set of objectives and goals for the business. The statements concerning purpose which arise in the mission statement help to identify areas in which to set objectives. The organisation's purpose in serving the shareholder, the customer, the employee and other stakeholder groups provides a basis for setting objectives for attaining that purpose.

Stakeholder	*Possible objective*
Shareholder	Growth of dividends
Customer	Service level
Employee	Stability of employment and employee development

There is a lack of agreement concerning the use of the terms 'objective' and 'goal'. In the usage adopted by Keeney and Raiffa (Keeney and Raiffa, 1976) an objective is a direction for organisational performance, for instance to increase market share or improve profitability. A goal is a level of performance, a level of achievement of an objective, for example, an organisation may have the objective of improving profitability. A goal for profitability would specify a rate of return. Similarly a goal for the objective of increased market share would specify a target level for share.

Mission statements and the objectives that support them reflect the most enduring and long-term aspects of the company, however the organisation's goals also have to take account of the more immediate circumstances of the company. In a period of recession or difficulty the returns to shareholders may have to be limited in order for the company to retain sufficient capital to maintain its facilities and market position. Similarly the objective of providing security for employees may not be achievable while maintaining the other objectives of the organisation. Adherence to the long-term objectives of the organisation have to be moderated by short- and medium-term circumstances. Goals are targets for the organisation to achieve in a specified period of time; they need to be relevant to the company and its circumstances.

The level at which a goal is set is important. If goals are set at a level which is unattainable, the result is a loss of motivation. A goal which is set at too low a level simply leaves the organisation lacking an effective target for its efforts.

So far goals have been discussed as if they should always be capable of being expressed in a quantitative form, for example as a target figure for profitability. It may be undesirable to provide quantitative goals for all objectives. Excellence in customer services may be a reasonable objective for a particular business but it is very hard fully to define all the dimensions of service. To set a goal that specifies a level of attainment may detract from management's intention of inspiring a never-ending quest for improvement. Similarly defining a goal for innovation simply in terms of numbers of innovations per year will miss the significance of innovation as a generator of future revenue and a basis for company development. There may be other dangers in over-specifying corporate goals. These arise from goals being defined so closely that they lead to rigidity in the direction of the organisation, restrict creativity and limit the organisation's ability to find suitable strategies.

ENVIRONMENT

The organisation has two tasks in relation to its environment, the first static the other dynamic.The discussion of systems theory in Chapter 2 introduced the concept of an organisation as an open system interacting with its environment. Viewed as an open system, a business is engaged in a circular flow of activity in which inputs are transformed through the operation of the business into outputs; these in turn are exchanged for further inputs.

Every organisation has to maintain the circular flow of inputs, transformation, output and exchange. If the cycle is broken the organisation will be unable to obtain the required inputs of labour, materials, components, energy and information, and the organisation will decline, its level of activity and output reduced. Under the above system's model the management of the system is a static task, an act of maintaining the flow of activity.

It would be difficult to find a manager who felt that his task was static, simply maintaining a pattern that was established in the past. The second task facing the management of an organisation is dynamic and concerns the organisation's adaptation to changes in the environment; this adaptation involves strategic change.The environment changes and is changing at an unprecedented rate. New technologies, changing consumer demands, increased competitive activity, these are factors that affect most industries. The environment provides the organisation with opportunities; it also poses threats to the organisation's continued existence. In principle the effect of the environment is so profound that it helps to determine not only the prosperity of individual businesses but also the emergence and decline of industries. Illustration 8.3 describes some of the environmental changes which led to the rapid development of the frozen foods market in the 1970s.

Illustration 8.3 The UK frozen foods market

During the 1970s there was a substantial increase in the sale of frozen foods.

Consumer expenditure on frozen foods

	£ millions (current prices)
1974	293
1975	365
1976	470
1977	550
1978	605
1979	700
1980	850

Why should the market have shown such strong growth at that time? Part of the answer lies in the entrepreneurial activities of retailers, especially Bejam, a specialist frozen food retailer. However another part of the answer is that developments in the UK had established conditions which were favourable to the growth of the industry. These environmental changes included the following social and economic developments:

- an increase in the number of working housewives and the number of households with two incomes
- increased ownership of cars
- a marked increase in the proportion of households owning a freezer or refrigerator

	percentage of households
1971	6
1973	14
1975	26
1977	37
1979	45
1980	50

Clearly these developments supported the growth in sales of frozen foods. In turn the actions of the retailers helped to further these trends.

(*Adapted from*: Kenny, Lea, Sanderson and Luffman, 1987)

Organisations can only exploit environmental changes if they have been able effectively to scan the environment and obtain information that allows them to understand the changes that are taking place. This is a complex and difficult task and it could be claimed that few organisations are entirely successful in analysing their environment. The environment is *complex*; it consists of a large number of forces influencing the organisation and many of them may interrelate in their effect. The environment is also *dynamic*; trends change and new factors emerge and assume importance. Some of the most fundamental aspects of the business environment may be difficult to predict; these include factors such as:

- The business cycle, the timing of a move from recession to growth.
- The future rate of interest.
- Changes in consumer behaviour, such as a preference for discount items.

In view of the high degree of uncertainty in predicting the environment, it needs to be considered whether it is worthwhile for an organisation to divert resources into scanning and analysing it's environment. There is empirical evidence that the more information gathered and used in strategic decisions, the more effective the performance (Grinyer and Norburn, 1975). However, organisations do differ both in terms of the environments they face and of the resources they have available to meet the opportunities and threats that the environment presents. A study by Miller and Friesen (Miller and Friesen, 1977) helps to identify the relationship between the *amount of environmental analysis a firm undertakes*, the *type of firm* and the *characteristics of the environment*. The study, based upon case study data for eighty firms, identified ten types of firms, 'archetypes'. Four of the archetypes were associated with failure, six with organisational success.

Failure combinations

The impulsive firm. A powerful and entrepreneurial chief executive entering a new environment creates, in the process, a highly disturbed environment. Environmental change is rapid and the firm lacks the intelligence system with which to keep up with the rate of change; the entrepreneur also exacerbates the situation by trying to do everything himself.

The stagnant bureaucracy. The firm does not recognise that the environment is changing radically and does not adapt its product/market strategy. Power remains centralised, the leader remains committed to the 'old ways'. There is a lacklustre intelligence effort.

The headless giant. In the absence of a strong leader the firm's subunits act in a quasi-independent manner. The diffusion of power leads to a lack of decisive action. The environment changes markedly, the intelligence effort is poor, and decisions are often muddled and misdirected.

The firm swimming upstream. Past failure has severely damaged the organisation and the environment is complex and hostile. The firm is making some efforts to recover; there is a strong leader and efforts to improve organisational rationality are being made, but environmental conditions and past damage to the organisation make a turnaround unlikely.

Successful combinations

The adaptive firm under moderate dynamism. The firm faces a slowly changing environment, which is matched by a moderate amount of environmental analysis – enough for the rate of change in the environment and more than that achieved by the failing archetypes. Power for strategy making is quite centralised; the firm is proactive and risk taking, able to beat its less ambitious competitors to the punch.

The adaptive firm under extreme dynamism. The firm faces a very turbulent environment, scanning and communication is sophisticated, decisions are subjected to a lot of analysis. The power to make decisions is not all that centralised; many individuals in the organisation are involved in intelligence activities and strategic decision making. The firm is bold and often leads in forging new product/market and technological orientations.

The giant under fire. The environment faced is the most difficult of all, a diverse environment with powerful competitors and a vigilant government. The firm has diverse products and markets, diversity has resulted in the decentralisation of power. A sizeable and concerted intelligence effort takes place in order to facilitate adaptation, which is achieved in a gradual and piecemeal fashion in the face of high environmental complexity.

The entrepreneurial firm. The firm grows primarily through acquiring other companies, and, as a consequence, the firm faces a heterogeneous environment which, fortunately, is not that turbulent. Intelligence activity is quite well developed but is carried out principally by the entrepreneur himself. Decision making is centralised and often involves substantial risks.

The dominant firm. Past success has made this firm the strongest in the market; there are few environmental changes. Decision-making power is mostly centralised, risk taking is moderate. There is less environmental analysis than with the previous four successful types, but the amount is adequate for the environment.

The innovator. The firm is very successful because it has great strength in a particular area of operation, usually product design. The environment is quite challenging but the intelligence effort is low. Power is concentrated in the hands of the entrepreneur. The firm is always rescued by another brilliant and bold innovation.

Some firms are able to succeed with little effort given to environmental intelligence; for others the situation requires an extensive and sophisticated system and the careful negotiation of difficult environmental conditions. For each organisation, considering the characteristics of its environment and the position and resources of the organisation, there is a proper amount of environmental analysis and diagnosis.

ENVIRONMENTAL ANALYSIS

Strategic analysis needs to identify and analyse the major environmental variables that are critical to a firm's performance. The environment can be subdivided to provide two levels of analysis: the task environment of the organisation and the organisation's remote environment.

The *task environment* concerns the everyday operation of the firm and the environment it operates in in order to attract inputs and market goods and services. Key variables in the task environment include the firm's customer base, its labour market, suppliers, etc. The firm routinely interacts with this environment and can exercise a degree of control over it, for example, through relationships with suppliers, or by building brand loyalty with customers.

The remote environment includes those forces that originate beyond the firm's operating situation: economic, political, socio-cultural, technological forces upon which the firm has less, or possibly no, influence. The *remote* and the *task* environments are not distinct from each other; changes in the remote environment may feed through to cause change in the task environment, for example, technological progress resulting in a changed relationship with suppliers.

INDUSTRY STRUCTURE

Michael Porter (Porter, 1980) has developed a model of industry structure that incorporates a number of the factors that make up an organisation's environment.

In this model the firm is exposed to five competitive forces. The forces are in competition with the firm in that they are pressures that act to reduce the profits available to the business. The five forces will vary in their form and effect from industry to industry. In general they operate as follows.

Rivalry among existing competitors

The intensity of rivalry between competitors; those firms that are selling similar products and services in the same market. Rivalry will be intense if a number of the following factors are present:

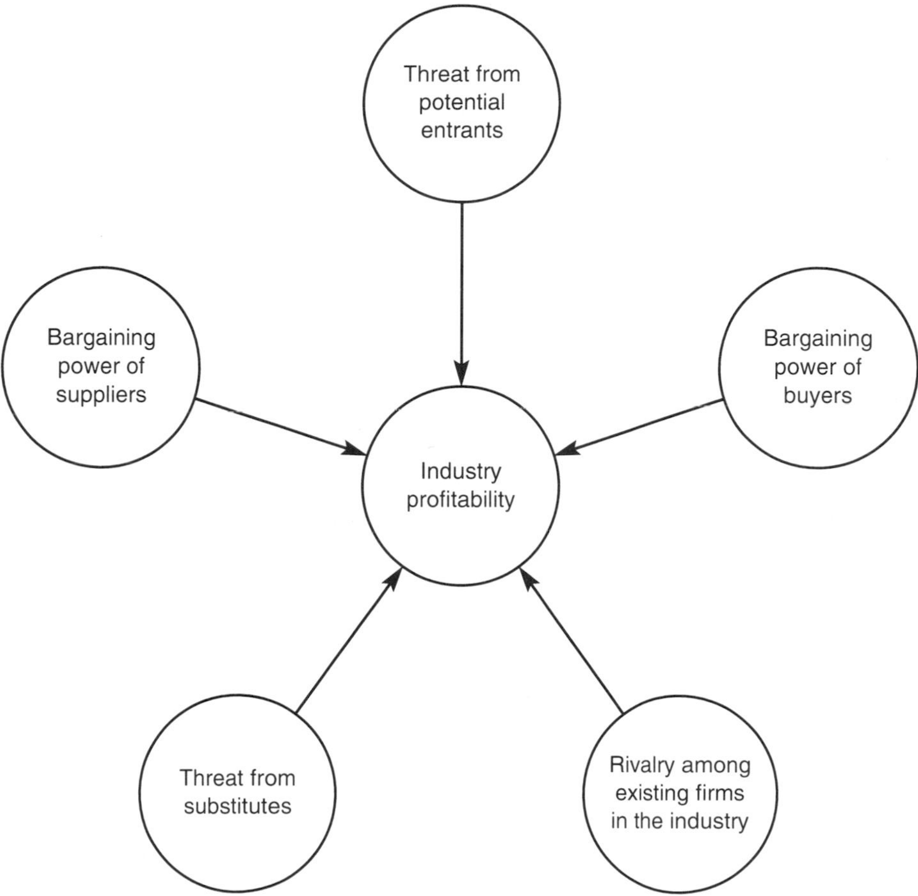

Fig. 8.6 Industry structure: the five forces model

- Large number of competitors similar in terms of their capability and size.
- Industry growth is slow, so expansion requires other firms to lose market share.
- The products and services offered by firms are very similar.
- The fixed costs of the business are high, tempting firms to increase the volume of sales by price cuts.
- There is excess capacity resulting in an imbalance of demand and supply.
- It is costly for firms to leave the industry, through selling assets or finding an alternative use for them.
- Competitors are diverse in terms of how they intend to compete and the resources they possess; as a result, rivalry is volatile and unpredictable.

Power of buyers

Many organisations face a buyer situation which puts pressure upon the firm's margins; buyers are powerful when:

- The product the firm is selling is not differentiated from that offered by other firms, or where there is a large number of potential suppliers with the buyer facing only low costs when switching from one supplier to another.
- There are few customers, their power is increased if they buy in large volumes so that each purchase may account for a considerable part of the supplier's capacity utilisation.
- The buyers themselves are facing pressures upon their margins and consequently become more price-sensitive in purchasing.
- The buyer could integrate backward to make the product rather than purchase the item.

Power of suppliers

The industry requires a range of inputs, raw materials, skills, information and energy. The suppliers to the industry may be able to raise their prices or reduce the quality of the purchased goods and services if:

- The supply industry is concentrated in a few companies and lacks competitive pressure.
- The item is unique, differentiated, or involves significant costs for buyers should they switch to an alternative source of supply for the input.
- The supplier could integrate forward into the industry's business.

Threat from substitutes

A substitute is a product or service that meets the same customer needs as the industry's output. The substitute places a limit upon the industry's price and profitability. The impact of the substitute will be reduced to the extent that the industry is able to differentiate its own product and services from the substitute, whether that is through improved product performance, quality or service. If switching to the substitute involves significant cost for the customer in making the changeover, then the power of the substitute is again reduced.

Threats from potential entrants

Industry profits act as a signal to other firms, indicating that the industry could provide a rewarding use for their assets. The new entrants cause an increase in industry capacity that leads to an excess in supply and a consequent decline in profitability. The threat of entry places an upper limit on industry profitability; the threat is reduced when:

- There are significant economies of scale, if entry would have to be on a significant scale and would require substantial expenditure (for example upon production, marketing, distribution or research) for the new entrant to be viable in the industry.
- Where the existing companies have other advantages, for example, from accumulated experience of cost reduction, or experience of customer behaviour, or advantages from being among the first in an industry, resulting in acquisition of the best locations or the development of customer loyalty.
- If the government regulates entry into the industry through its actions and policies; these include licence requirements, the setting of safety and pollution standards, the granting of patents and the existence of tariff barriers.

The industry structure model enables answers to be found for the following strategic questions.

Is the industry an attractive one to operate in? Are the firms operating in this industry able to develop high margins, through lack of pressure from customers, low threat of entry from organisations outside the industry, weakness in the position of their suppliers, or any other lack of competitive pressure from the five forces?

Even if the industry is not particularly attractive the model helps the firm to develop and evaluate strategies to maintain the desirable features of the industry structure and, if possible, improve the industry's attractiveness. A strong supplier situation may be mitigated by encouraging the development of alternative suppliers, increasing the ability to switch to alternative sources and even by developing in-house supply. These strategies have helped to build the profitability of UK supermarkets. Similarly avoidance of price wars may delay concentration of the industry into a smaller number of firms.

Illustration 8.4 concerns the competitive environment of a regional building society, Central Building Society, the case is set in 1987. The following issues may be considered.

- Is the home loans industry a good industry to operate in?
- How might the industry and it's attractiveness change over time?
- Can strategies be identified that would improve the structure of the industry for Central?

Illustration 8.4 Central Building Society

The Central Building Society was founded in 1850 to service its local shire. Since then it has expanded its branch network to two neighbouring counties and acquired a branch in London. At present the Society has over 50 branches, 160,000 customers (144,000 of whom are investors) and an asset value of £290m; as such it is the 40th largest building society in the UK.

The demand for mortgages

The Central Building Society has 16,000 mortgagors. Mortgage business is received from a number of sources: solicitors, estate agents and insurance brokers, and through a link with a major insurance company's direct sales force. Business gained 'across the counter' provides 35 per cent of the mortgage business. This figure is higher than for most societies and Central would not wish over-the-counter lending to exceed 75 per cent in case this would lead to the loss of other sources of business.

The limit to total lending is in part set by the level of risk that the society is willing to undertake. This includes the marketability of the mortgaged properties, the income multiplier allowed on borrowing, and the spreading of business over a sufficient geographic area to avoid local economic risk. To that end £60m is lent outside of the Society's home county.

A number of banks and insurance companies are purchasing estate agents but Central does not see this as a particular threat. The Chief Executive believes that customers will always want a mixture of organisations to supply their house buying, finance and insurance needs. Also, at least in the short term, the Society appears to enjoy good relationships with those agents who have recently been acquired by the banks and insurance companies.

Competition and customers

Over the last few years the building society movement has faced considerable change, and possibly the greatest of these changes has been the rise of competition for mortgage lending from the banks. It may be that building societies themselves contributed to the entry of the banks into a form of lending that had traditionally been the preserve of the societies. The disbanding of the building societies' cartel was followed by increases in the mortgage interest rate of sufficient magnitude to signal to the banks an opportunity for profitable lending. While building societies still retain 77 per cent of the mortgage market (July 1987) a large number of banks, ranging from the Big Four to a host of foreign banks, have taken an increasing share of the total.

Not only is there increasing competition; there has also been a change in the nature of the customer. In general customers are becoming more aware of the variety of financial services available and are more sophisticated in making their choices.

Central has its head offices in the region's main city. The management believes that one of the Society's strengths lies in it being the local Society, an identity which it tries to promote. The Society's branch network and its convenience for the customer is seen as a further strength.

The supply of funds

In order to lend, Central has to have a supply of funds; it is the availability of funds rather than the applications for new mortgages that at present limits the growth of the Society's lending.

Most of Central's funds are gained over the counter through the various forms of account offered by the Society. A further source of funds available to building societies is wholesale funding, borrowing on the money market. By 1987 the building societies were allowed to raise up to 20 per cent of their liabilities from this source at a rate similar to that enjoyed by the banks, nearly 3 per cent below the interest rate paid to the Society's customers.

Potentially the funds deposited with a building society have a high degree of mobility. Accounts with other societies are easy to open and interest rate structures widely advertised. The Society believes that while investors still value the convenience of well located branches they increasingly respond to interest rate differentials. In addition, the flow of funds is affected by a number of factors including seasonality and competition from National Savings and privatisation share issues.

New technology

Over the last few years the Society has developed its technology beyond the systems that deal with branch business and administration. A computer-based home banking system has been successfully introduced, attracting a group of largely new lenders into a more durable relationship than that based upon conventional branch business. The system has obvious potential for extension to include the buying and selling of shares.

The provision of Automatic Telling Machines, 'holes in the wall', is also being considered. This would also help to cement relationships with the customer. However, providing the facility through Link or Matrix would be expensive, an annual charge of £250,000 for the minimum number of five sites. The economics of the Society providing one or two ATMs for itself seem more attractive.

Appendix 1

A report on the UK housing market by the Henley Centre for Forecasting concludes that:

- every 1 per cent increase in the population in the 25–35 age group leads to an equivalent increase in house prices.
- each 1 per cent increase in real incomes raises house prices by 2.5 per cent.

Appendix 2

Building Societies, 1900-1986

	Number of Societies	*Share Accounts ('000)*
1900	2,286	585
1920	1,271	748
1940	952	2,088
1960	726	3,910
1980	273	30,636
1985	167	39,997
1986	151	40,563

Appendix 3

	UK Personal Saving £m	*Building Societies' Net Inflow £m*
1982	23,328	6,466
1984	23,186	8,572
1986	19,054	5,964

Appendix 4

Building Societies Act 1986

Under the Act provision is made for societies to convert to company (or PLC) status provided their members agree.

At least 90 per cent of a society's lending must be for first mortgages to owner-occupiers.

Societies are allowed to offer new services including money transmission services, foreign exchange facilities, provision of second mortgages and other secured loans, provision of unsecured personal loans, management as agents of land and residential property development, estate agency services, insurance broking, share dealing services, unit trust and pension scheme services, surveying and conveyancing services.

MODELLING THE REMOTE ENVIRONMENT

Porter proposes that the industry model can be used to include the effects of any variables that have not been explicitly included as one of the five forces. In the case of the home loans industry (Illustration 8.4) the effects of an ageing population may be considered through changes in customer behaviour; similarly the effects of the economic cycle may be included through considering changes in the supply of funds and consumer behaviour.

The remote environment, the factors which make up the remote environment and their interaction, need to be identified and analysed to ensure that the firm's long-term strategies are well founded. These influences can be categorised as follows.

Political
Economic
Socio-cultural

Technological
Demographic

Consideration of each of these may require a number of variables to be identified and information gained for them. For example, an analysis of Central's economic environment would include information for:

Growth in national income
Distribution of income
Taxation
Interest rates
The ratio of savings to income
The rate of inflation

Environmental analysis can rapidly become very complicated. The analyst can make the task manageable by focusing the analysis upon those variables which have the most powerful effect upon the organisation and for which reasonably reliable information can be made available. Porter's model (Fig. 8.6) provides the strategist with a flexible yet well structured model with which to analyse the environment. The analyst may have to decide if this alone provides sufficient insight into the workings and effect of the remote environment.

RESOURCES

As part of its strategic analysis, the organisation must identify and evaluate the resources that it is able to command. The resources that the organisation has access to limits its ability to adapt to and exploit the opportunities presented by changes in the environment.

Functional resource analysis

Each area of the business can make a contribution to the achievement of the organisation's strategy. Examining the business on a functional basis allows a resource profile, such as that in Fig. 8.7, to be constructed.

The profile is a record of the organisation's past expenditures and the assets they have provided. The assets are physical (buildings, plant, facilities), human (the employees of the organisation) and the systems that the organisation has created to integrate, direct and control its operations.

The organisation's assets are highly significant; they are the result of the company's accumulated expenditures and development efforts, but they are not in themselves the basis upon which the organisation serves its markets and competes. Successful organisations have strategies that reflect the competencies they have developed over a period of time. The assets and processes acquired by the organisation have to be integrated and developed to provide a distinctive competence, the basis upon which the business will compete. In the watch industry (Swatch case study) other organisations may invest in design, automated manufacturing and marketing, but would that result in the same strength of brand image and the same low unit cost as that achieved by Swatch? These are capabilities that result from the careful development and integration of the organisation's resources.

	Research	Manufacturing	Marketing	Finance	Management
Focus of financial deployments	basic research development	plant equipment inventory	sales promotion distribution market research	S.T. cash management L.T. funding	management development
Physical resources	size, age & location of R & D facilities	size, age & location of plants, degree of automation & integration	location of sales offices & warehouses accommodation	computers accommodation	location of corporate headquarters
Human resources	types, ages of key scientists & engineers	types, ages of key staff, employee skill profiles	types, ages of key salesmen & marketing staff	types, ages of key financial & accounting staff	types, ages of key managers and corporate staff
Systems	systems to monitor technological change, screen & develop innovations	purchasing systems scheduling quality control systems	market research information systems competitor analysis system	cash management system corporate financial model	planning & control systems

Fig. 8.7 A functional resource area profile

Resource conversion

It is useful to view the organisation as a system involved in a resource conversion process.

The financial resources of the organisation, arising from the issue of equity, borrowing and the retention of past earnings, are used to acquire a variety of human and physical assets in order to develop the organisation and its systems. The aim of management is to operate those resources in such a way as to add value to them through the development of distinctive features in its output of products and services. For example, the quality and cost control systems developed by Marks and Spencer provide the firm with a reputation that assures consumers that they are justified in shopping at the store and paying prices that may be higher than elsewhere for the same category of goods. Similarly, to be successful a conglomerate firm must develop a distinctive competence. The success of Hanson Trust has, in large part, been due to the company's well-known ability to reduce the operating costs of subsidiaries.

One of the most useful insights provided by strategic analysis is the identification of a company's competencies, the functions that they perform so well that they are the basis upon which the organisation's success is built. Such a competence may be transferable to new product and market situations. In the Swatch case study the company is considering diversification into the telecoms market. Swatch's contribution to that venture would be a transfer of its product styling abilities to another mass market product.

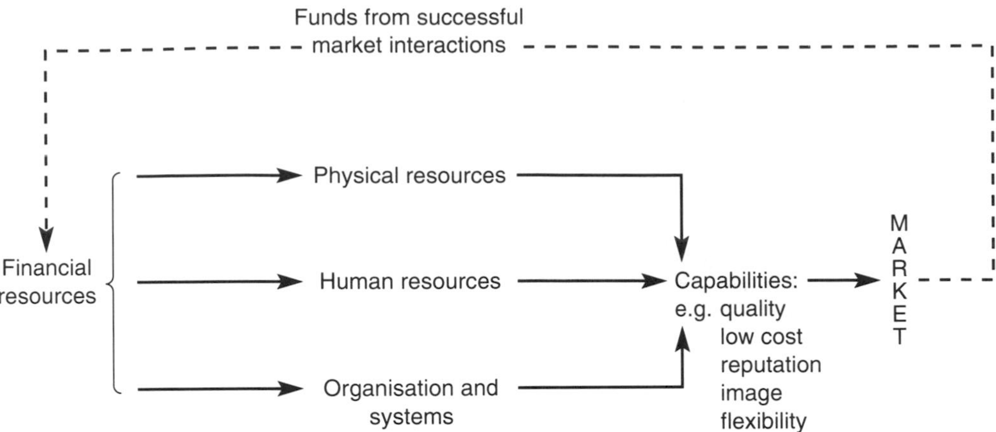

Fig. 8.8 The resource conversion process

Similarly Hanson Trust has used its capability at cost control in a variety of industries, including coal mining, house construction and foods. The transfer of core capabilities to new products and markets is an essential part of successful diversification. Such transfers can produce surprising developments. Marks and Spencer's reputation for quality and reliability provides the company with a latent ability to enter and compete in other markets, such as financial services, where the firm's outlets provide a ready-made distribution system.

Value chain analysis

Whether the firm chooses to diversify or remain in a single business the organisation's products and services must:

- Create sufficient value for the consumer so that they will pay a price that at least enables the firm to meet the cost of all of its resources, including the payment of dividends to the shareholder.
- Displace competing products and services.

These objectives can only be achieved if the organisation's resources are used to deliver and sustain competitive advantage, through achieving lower costs than those of competitors or through the effective differentiation of products and services. Each of the organisation's activities needs to be developed and co-ordinated to deliver the business strategy. The firm can be viewed as a set of integrated activities, *a value chain*. Each activity can be examined for its contribution to the firm's cost behaviour and the existing and potential sources of differentiation.

Value-creating activities are the physically and technologically distinct activities that the firm performs. The value activities can be divided into two broad types: primary activities and support activities.

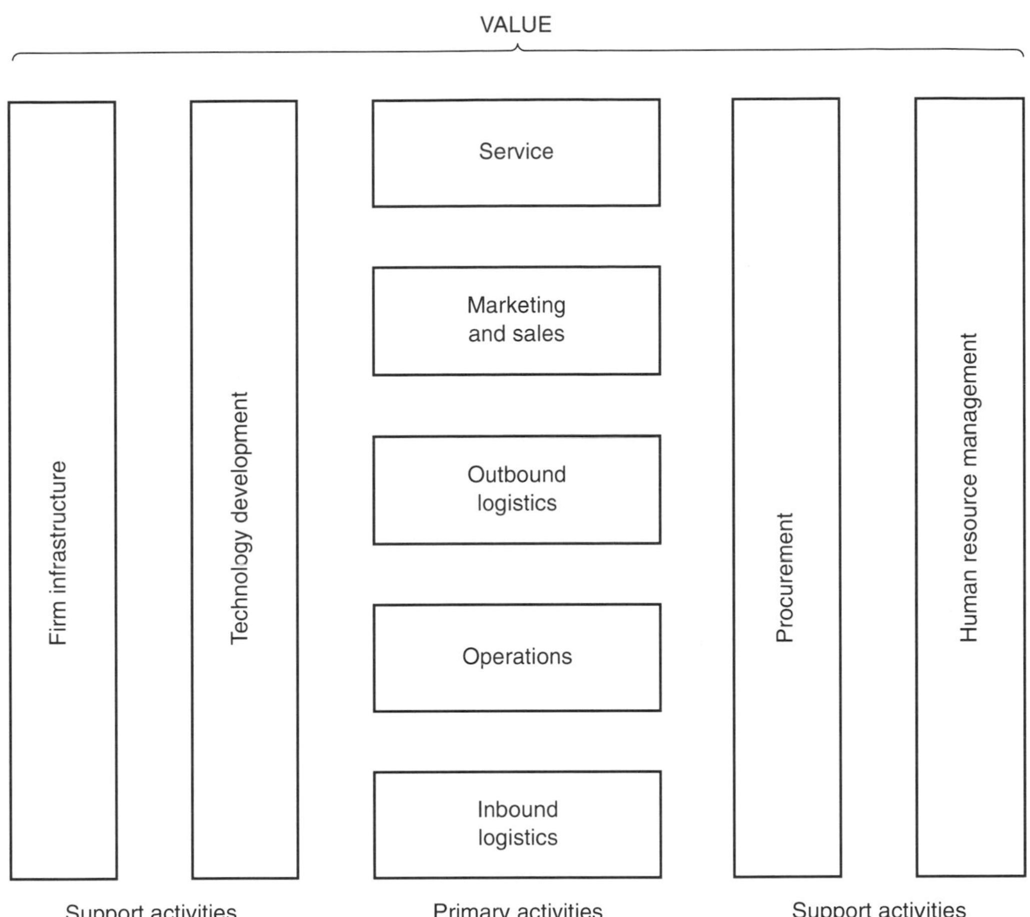

Fig. 8.9 The value chain (from Porter, M.E., 1985)

Primary activities are those involved in the physical creation of the product or service, its transfer to the buyer and any after-sales service. Primary activities may be grouped into the following categories:

1 *Inbound logistics*. Activities associated with receiving, storing and disseminating inputs to the product.
2 *Operations*. Activities required to transform inputs into the final product. These may include activities such as machining, assembly, testing, packing and equipment maintenance.
3 *Outbound logistics*. Collecting, storing and distributing the product to buyers.
4 *Marketing and sales*. Activities associated with providing a means by which buyers can purchase the product and inducing them to do so. These activities include advertising, selling, pricing, channel management and promotion.

5 *Service.* Activities such as installation, training, parts supply, repair and maintenance. Providing services to maintain or enhance the value of the product.

Each activity is a source of value that must contribute to the business strategy. The effectiveness of the primary activities is enhanced by the provision of support activities, these can be divided into four categories:

1 *Procurement.* The purchasing of inputs. This includes all the procedures for dealing with suppliers for the whole range of the firm's inputs.
2 *Technology development.* The development of 'know how', product and process improvement. These activities include research and development, product design and the development of systems and procedures.
3 *Human resource management.* The activities concerned with the recruitment, training, development and remuneration of staff.
4 *Firm infrastructure.* These activities include general management, finance and planning, estate management, quality assurance.

Each of the activities, primary and support, contribute to the ability of the business to achieve its strategy. Activities also affect each other; for instance the design of a product can reduce the cost of production and may also cut procurement costs, while enabling the product to achieve greater appeal to the customer. Similarly, a sophisticated sales and re-order system may reduce staff training costs, improve stockholding costs and customer service.

The role of all the organisation's activities and their integration to achieve a successful business strategy is illustrated by the success of Benetton (Fig. 8.10). Benetton is an international organisation, with over 7,000 shops in 108 countries and a turnover in excess of £1bn. Benetton's product may be described as brightly coloured basic garments of reasonable quality, with some styling emphasis. Their differentiation from competing products is enhanced by the strength of the Benetton brand. However, while competing on the basis of product differentiation Benetton are similar to other differentiators in that they are careful to reduce costs.

Benetton's value chain, the various activities and their co-ordination, enables the company to achieve the following competitive features.

1 An attractive and changing range of products (through marketing, design and the control of production).
2 Rapid response to customer demand; production is based upon retail demand (through use of a world wide real time information system and logistics).
3 Intensive use of Benetton resources (the use of agents and franchising provide market access at low investment cost by Benetton; in production outsourcing provides flexibility and lowers the need for investment by Benetton).

The resource-based view of the firm

When making a strategic choice, each of the three components of the strategy model needs to be evaluated, but resources, like environment, can also be seen as fundamental in driving the strategic direction of the firm. Among the numerous examples of resource-based diversifications are:

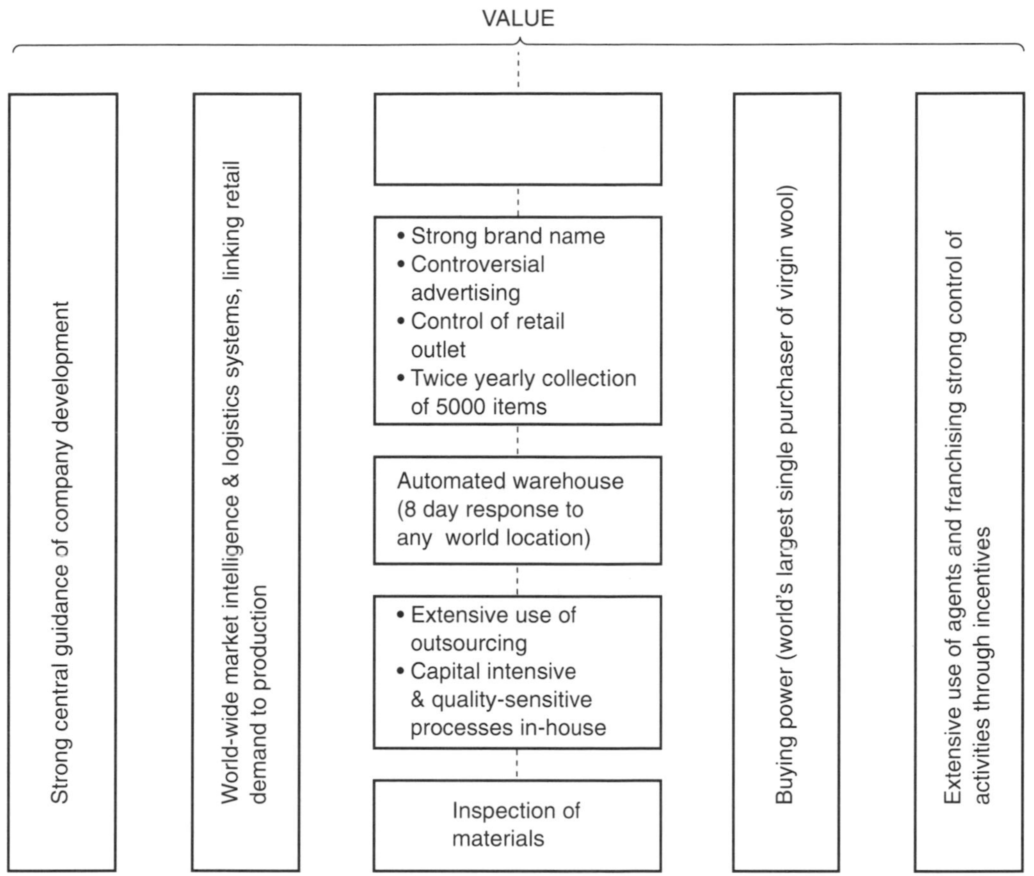

Fig. 8.10 Benetton's value chain: distinctive activities

- Retailers who successfully diversify to other areas of retailing on the basis of having developed systems and procedures for purchasing, logistics and skills in the management of product range.
- Airline operators who use their booking systems to sell additional services to the customer.

A resource-based view can be adopted for developing the firm's strategy, focusing upon the tangible and intangible assets that constitute the firm (Wernerfelt, 1984). Such resources include locations, plant and facilities, brand names, in-house knowledge of technology, employment of skilled personnel, trade contacts, procedures and systems, etc. The resources are the basis for superior current performance and may also effectively act as a barrier to the entry of other firms. The key resources, those in which the firm has particular advantage, also provide a logic for the organisation's future diversification, building upon the distinctive strengths of the organisation. Such diversifications in turn enable the organisation to sustain and further develop its key resources.

STRATEGY AS A DYNAMIC PROCESS

Decisions are about the future, yet essentially the future is unknowable. In an age of unprecedented change the strategist finds that past patterns and trends provide an unreliable guide to the context in which a selected strategy will operate. One of the roles of strategic decision making is to help position and develop the organisation so that the problems that emerge in the future, even if they are unanticipated, may be solvable. This aspect of strategic decision making can be developed in a number of ways.

Testing for robustness

All decisions are made on the basis of a set of accepted information concerning the past and its implications for the future. These assumptions should, as far as possible, be explicitly recognised and the effect of possible variations in those factors tested. The aim of this exercise is to test the robustness of the decision, to identify the set of circumstances under which another strategy would be preferable. Changes in price, variations in anticipated market growth, the possible extent of future cost reduction, the intentions of a rival firm; which of these assumptions should be tested? There is no standard list of assumptions that should be tested. For the strategic decision maker the aim of testing is to find the key assumptions that support the particular strategic choice under consideration, the variables that are open to uncertainty and have the greatest effect upon the decision to support a particular strategic option.

As with any analysis there is a need to make a trade-off between the analysis becoming over complex and unclear, and the provision of an analysis that is sufficiently comprehensive. Always the aim is to establish the essential characteristics of the situation, in this case the identification of any variables that appear open to sufficient future variation to make the proposed strategy questionable.

Testing the assumptions of a decision may identify a strategy as dependent upon a particular set of future circumstances. As a consequence a different option may be preferred or developed. But the analysis has further usefulness. Where it is found that an assumption is uncertain and affects the choice of strategy, this highlights a need for further information that could be used to develop a fuller understanding of the situation.

Testing for robustness and acquiring further information help to develop a strategic decision; however, the selected strategy must take account of a number of specific factors concerning the future.

Followers

In a competitive environment the successful organisation can anticipate that other organisations may seek to enter the industry and that rival organisations will attempt to copy the strategies of successful firms. The business that has successfully differentiated its products and services from those of other firms has to maintain its competitive position by continuing to develop its basis for differentiation. Similarly the business that competes on the basis of cost must continuously seek further cost improvement through whatever means are available, including sourcing, design, scale economies and using accumulated experience in order to produce more efficiently. The organisation that does not continue to develop the basis of its competitive advantage will have its competitive position eroded.

Outpacing

Outpacing faces the strategist with a dilemma. While it is necessary for the business to stay ahead of organisations that are followers, it also has to be recognised that the basis upon which the industry operates will change over time. The producers of computer hardware once competed through product development, reputation and service; today the industry requires a greater commitment to cost.

Products and markets develop and evolve. The product life cycle shown in Fig. 8.11 is the most commonly proposed path for this evolution. Following the life cycle a product or service may be expected at some time to pass through the phases of introduction, growth, maturity and decline. In the first phase the product has unique attributes that appeal to the consumer; the firm competes on the basis of differentiation rather than price. If the product is successful its characteristics may become standardised and other organisations may produce similar products. Rival producers and the growing choice available to the product's buyers will make price a matter of increasing competitive concern. Eventually maturity may require another phase of fundamental product innovation.

For the business to remain in the market throughout the various phases of the life cycle it has to develop an appropriate competitive ability and, if possible, develop it ahead of rival firms in order to outpace their competitive ability.

The Swatch case study describes a firm that is following a differentiation strategy, but Swatch has also achieved a low-cost basis for manufacture; the business is even able to sell components to other manufacturers. Should the time come when other producers are able to provide a watch as appealing as a Swatch, or consumers tire of the product's distinctive features, Swatch may continue successfully to compete through having developed a low-cost base.

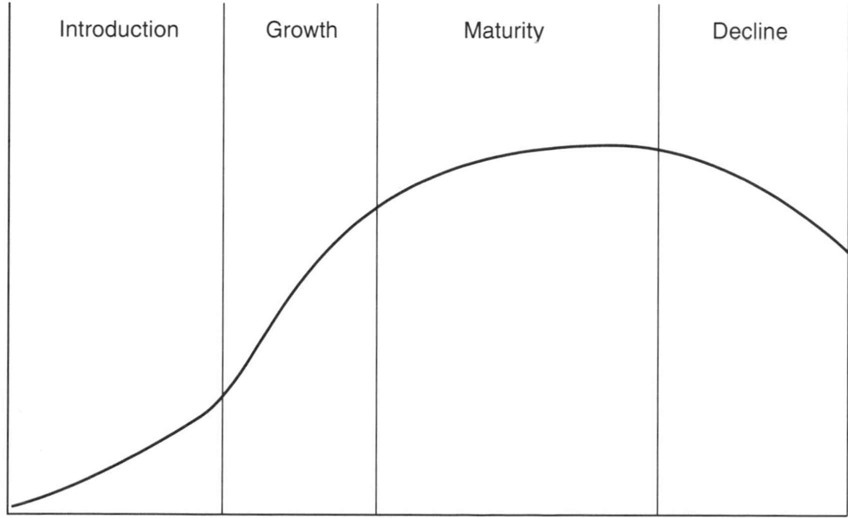

Fig. 8.11 The product life cycle

Anticipating and understanding changes in the firm's environment is extremely difficult. The evolution of the product/market situation illustrated by the product life cycle leaves open the question of when each phase will occur and the form that the life cycle will take in a particular situation. Nevertheless the strategies that organisations adopt must be capable of meeting the challenges that are presented by a changing environment.

The following exercise provides an opportunity to apply some of the ideas from this chapter. It is based upon Illustration 8.4, the Central Building Society case study.

EXERCISE: CENTRAL BUILDING SOCIETY

Using the material provided by the Central case study (Illustration 8.4), consider the following issues:

(a) Should Central develop a focused strategy? If so should that be based upon cost or differentiation?
(b) How should Central's value chain be developed in order to pursue that strategy?

Should Central:

(c) Outsource some of their activities, e.g. IT?
(d) Develop a wider range of services?
(e) Merge with another building society, if so should that be with one of the large societies, a regional building society (such as itself), or a smaller society?

GLOSSARY OF MAIN TERMS

Business definition A statement identifying the organisation's customer groups, the needs that the organisation meets and the processes utilised in meeting those needs.
Business strategy How a business, or strategic business unit, competes in a particular market.
Corporate strategy The scope of an organisation's activities.
Differentiation The provision of a product or service that is regarded by the user as meaningfully different from that offered by the competition.
Distinctive competence The abilities or skills that distinguish an organisation and are the basis of its competitiveness.
Diversification A new product market combination undertaken by an organisation.
Mission statement A clear description of the fundamental nature and purpose of an organisation.
Outpacing strategy A planned series of strategic moves, from one strategic position to another, in order to maintain competitive advantage.
Value chain The interlinked series of strategically important activities that are used by an organisation to provide a product or service.
Vertical integration Ownership of part(s) of the organisation's value system.

REFERENCES

Grinyer, P. H. and Norburn, D. (1975) 'Planning for Existing Markets: Perceptions of Executives and Financial Performance', *Journal of Royal Statistical Society*, Vol. 138, Pt. 1, 70-97.

Jauch, L. R. and Glueck, W. F. (1988) *Business Policy and Strategic Management*, McGraw-Hill.

Keeney, R. L., and Raiffa, H. (1976) *Decisions with Multiple Objectives: Preferences and Value Tradeoffs*, Wiley.

Kenny, B., Lea, E., Sanderson, S., and Luffman, G. (1987) *Cases in Business Policy*, Blackwell.

Miller, D., and Friesen, P.H. (1977) 'Strategy-Making in Context: Ten Empirical Archetypes', *Management Studies*, October, 253-280.

Mintzberg, H. (1990) *Strategy Formation: Schools of Thought in Perspectives on Strategic Management* (Ed. Fredrickson, J. W.) Harper Business, 111-188.

Ohmae, K. (1982) *The Mind of the Strategist*, McGraw-Hill.

Porter, M. E. (1980) *Competitive Strategy: Techniques for Analysing Industries and Competitors*, The Free Press.

Porter, M. E. (1985) *Competitive Advantage: Creating and Sustaining Superior Performance*, The Free Press.

Wernerfelt, B. A. (1984) 'Resource-based View of the Firm', *Strategic Management Journal*, Vol. 5, 171-180.

FURTHER READING

Dyson, R. G. (1990) *Strategic Planning: Models and Analytical Techniques*, Wiley.

Johnson, G., and Scholes, K. (1993) *Exploring Corporate Strategy Text and Cases*, Prentice Hall.

Mintzberg, H., and Quinn, J.B. (1991) *The Strategy Process Concepts, Contexts, Cases*, Prentice-Hall.

CHAPTER 9

Ethics in decision making

Paul Whysall

INTRODUCTION

The whole idea that there is scope for a discussion of ethics in business decision making is initially surprising to many people. Such people would perhaps take a view that business is solely about making profits, or that in business all the moral conventions of private life are in abeyance. The reality of the world of business shows this not to be the case, however.

Many companies make explicit reference to their ethical stances; few major company reports now appear without statements of commitment to environmental responsibilities, or concern for the welfare of employees, or involvement in areas of community benefit. Cynics may wish to see such claims as part of a marketing strategy rather than anything more fundamental, but nonetheless the adoption of such a position both distinguishes a company and has implications for all its dealings, internally and externally.

For a decision to be required, there must be a number of (at least two) possible actions open to the decision taker. Those actions must be expected to have different outcomes. Hence, decision making can be envisaged as a choice between perceived future circumstances. The decision taker has to form a perception of what is the likely outcome of each potential action (or set of actions), and select that which is most desirable.

But how can the desirability of an action be measured or evaluated? There are quantitative approaches which can help to do this, as explained elsewhere in this book. Even the most sophisticated quantitative techniques can still leave unresolved areas of personal judgement or moral worth, however. How can we compare the disadvantage of the loss of a view across unspoilt countryside with the benefits of wealth and job creation in a new industrial development? Essentially, we are likely to come down to choices which involve such imponderables as effects on the environment, changes in personal affluence, changed working conditions, impacts on other businesses, and so forth. These take us out of the realm of techniques and methods – helpful though those will still be to clarify and quantify the nature of a decision – and into the realm of ethics and morals.

The rise in ethical concerns in recent years has closely mirrored the rise in environmental awareness, and it will be shown that the environmental dimension is indeed an important part of any discussion of the ethics of business decision making; but there are other important dimensions too, such as dealings with the labour force, with customers, with competitors, with suppliers, and with government and similar agencies which are equally important. *Whenever one can ask questions such as 'Would it be right to do that?' or 'Is that fair?', we know that we are entering a field with ethical connotations.* The difficulty comes in answering such questions, since notions of what is right or fair are neither absolute nor universally agreed.

A simple introductory exercise

It may sometimes seem that discussions of business ethics are either concerned with major issues, such as global warming, or relate to large-scale businesses. Both these assumptions are untrue, as can be shown with a relatively simple hypothetical example (Illustration 9.1).

Illustration 9.1 Sam's Fashions (1)

Assume that you run a small newsagent's shop, and that your friend, Sam, runs a clothes shop called 'Sam's Fashions' nearby. Sam's Fashions sell fashion clothes with designer labels at discounted prices.

When you met Sam yesterday, she asked you as a favour if you would deliver some small handbills advertising her shop with your normal newspaper deliveries. You said you would do this, and laughed at the suggestion that she would pay you for your service, saying it was just a favour to a friend, and caused you no additional problems whatsoever.

When later you met another mutual friend, and mentioned that you had just seen Sam, he made the following comment without any prompting or probing from you:

'I don't know how Sam gets away with it. At the prices she sells things they must be either fakes or stolen! I'm sure there will be trouble soon.'

Reflect on these questions:

Does it worry you that you may be becoming involved with a business that may be, if not illegal in its operations, at least questionable in its practises?
Will you still deliver the advertisements?
Is your decision influenced by the fact that you see Sam as a friend?
Would you see things differently if you were being paid to deliver the handbills?
If you don't deliver them, what will you tell Sam?

Whatever your reaction to the above example, one can see that for some people such an apparently simple event as doing a favour for a friend could come to raise moral qualms. You may ask yourself, 'Is it right to support a business that may be illegal?' or you may be concerned about being fair to a friend. Self-interest may mean that your only concern is any possible effect on your own business. In any respect, an ethical aspect has developed in a quite simple, routine business situation. When a number of people are confronted with this problem, experience has shown that a variety of responses arise, demonstrating that ethical judgements are essentially personal, born of individual beliefs and attitudes.

How can we respond to the problem posed by Sam's Fashions? Essentially there are two approaches that tend to be taken. First, one can try to categorise the alternative actions as either 'right' or 'wrong'. If it transpired that the goods being sold were stolen, then many people would say that it is 'wrong' to help publicise the business, whether or not that implied you yourself breaking the law. From that viewpoint, it would be 'right' to refuse to distribute the advertisements and, presumably, to tell Sam why.

Many issues are not easily categorised as wholly right or wrong, though. Selling copies of designer styles may or may not seem to you a clear-cut case of right or wrong. That being so, an alternative approach may be preferred, which looks at the relative outcomes of actions. In simple terms this may simply involve asking 'What does it matter to me?' For some, if there are no adverse effects personally, then they may take a 'live and let live' approach. If, however, there is a personal risk – of legal action perhaps at an extreme but, less seriously, simply of a threat to the reputation of your business – you may not wish to get involved. More systematically, you may even try to work out a list of 'winners' and 'losers', together with their relative gains and losses, and base your decision on that.

As will be shown later, these contrasting responses are central to ethical thinking. But for the moment let us return to the matter of Sam's Fashions, in Illustration 9.2.

Illustration 9.2 Sam's Fashions (2)

While still thinking about whether or not to deliver Sam's handbills, you find yourself sitting in a café. At the next table is a group of teenagers, one of whom is proudly showing off the contents of a Sam's Fashions carrier bag.

You just listen, and hear the following:

'I know it's not the real thing... of course it's a copy. But I could never afford something this smart unless I got it from Sam's.'

'That's right. My sister says all Sam's stuff is stolen anyway, but if it wasn't for her shop, kids like us would never be able to dress well!'

Reflect on the following:

Does this affect your opinion? Had it occurred to you that what had seemed, perhaps, to be a problem was possibly, from another standpoint, a positive benefit to some people?

If you had taken the viewpoint that your decision would be based on what you felt to be either 'right' or 'wrong', then the conversation reported above would probably not change anything. Something intrinsically wrong presumably does not get justification from the additional information that another party actually seems to benefit. If, however, you had tried to work out the 'winners' and 'losers' in the situation, then this additional information may contribute to your eventual decision.

There is a problem here, though, in that the additional information we receive may be misleading or inaccurate. If we had gone to a different café, we might have heard other equally poor kids complaining that they had bought goods from Sam's that were of poor quality, had shrunk, or had faded quickly. So should we base our decision on our limited experience, or on more general principles?

Once we accept that our decision may be based on our current awareness of circumstances, and that our level of awareness is at best probably partial, the difficulty of responding to ethical problems purely on instinct and current knowledge becomes highlighted. It seems inevitable that there may be other possible consequences of our action that we have not yet taken into account or are not fully aware of, so do we need some broad rules to guide our decision?

Consider the following potential 'news stories' which might, to varying degrees, influence our opinion of Sam's operation (Illustration 9.3):

Illustration 9.3 Sam's Fashions (3)

'Cheap fakes of designer clothes ignore safety standards by using dangerously inflammable fabrics', a medical conference was told yesterday. A leading specialist in the treatment of burns described a number of horrific incidents in which young people had suffered disfiguration and worse as a consequence...'

'Leading clothes designers are protesting at infringements of their copyrights, claiming that fakes, widely sold throughout Europe, deprive them of major income as well as damaging their reputations for quality and exclusiveness.'

'A study of the textile industry has suggested that many jobs in established companies in Britain and the rest of the European Community are under threat because of a flood of cheap imports from the Far East. Several leading clothing manufacturers are said to be at risk of closure, and this could only aggravate already high unemployment levels in several British cities.'

'It has been suggested that those who buy expensive designer clothes are paying excessively inflated prices for what are sometimes low-quality products. A consumer group's researches suggests that often such goods could easily be retailed at far more modest prices. It is said that the designers prefer to keep prices high to instil images of exclusiveness in customers' minds, but that the supposedly exclusive goods have often been produced in 'sweat shop' conditions, by badly paid workers.'

Clearly one could continue to invent a number of other such stories, some or all of which could then influence any attempt to evaluate the ethics of supporting Sam's Fashions, either positively or negatively. The point, though, should be clear already that often our ability to perceive the full ethical ramifications of any decision is likely to be constrained, if only because we can never know what the future holds.

SOME ETHICAL MODELS

The example of Sam's Fashions has already shown that two fundamentally different approaches can be taken in the face of a decision with ethical aspects. First, there is what has previously been described as basically 'right' against 'wrong', but which in ethical terms is better termed a *deontological* approach. Deontology is defined as the 'science of duty', and a deontological approach is therefore one which involves doing one's duty in terms of established ethical principles. Often these principles may have a religious origin, but that is not necessary; humanitarian or socialist views also produce strong moral stances.

Some things are virtually universally agreed to be wrong – murder for example – and these are clear cases where a deontological stance tends to be adopted. In the world of business, issues which, to many, would seem intrinsically wrong, might include selling unsafe products, lying to customers, or breaking contractual obligations for sheer gain. While in these discussions the terms 'right' and 'wrong' are frequently used, largely for simplicity, many writers on ethics prefer not to use such terms, favouring less emotive or absolute words such as 'acceptable' and 'unacceptable'.

Other issues, however, tend to be far less clear cut. The long debate on Sunday trading in the United Kingdom, for example, provokes a definite deontological response from those whose religious persuasion says it is wrong to trade on the sabbath; but those who take that view absolutely for that reason are probably in the minority. Many people do shop on Sunday. Animal testing is another controversial issue on which different viewpoints clearly exist. There are those who would oppose the use of animals in the testing of products as a matter of basic principle. Others might prefer to limit such testing to products such as drugs and medicines where there is an apparently great benefit to mankind, but would not wish to see animal testing in areas such as cosmetics. There are also those who perhaps have few, if any, reservations about the use of animals in this way.

This latter example reveals an alternative to pure deontology, through an evaluation of the relative costs and benefits of a proposal. It was suggested that many people would only prefer to see animals used in tests where there was likely to be a substantial benefit to mankind. Hence the gains to the 'winners' are likely to exceed the losses to the 'losers', to use the terminology introduced earlier. There are, of course, great difficulties here in terms of evaluating the benefits to the 'winners': how serious a medical condition might be considered worthwhile for such research? Cancer research would clearly seem more meritorious than, say, temporary relief of the symptoms of the common cold, perhaps. Yet if that is a difficult area to give precision to, how could one ever seek to measure the price of animals' suffering? Even though we may seek to look at all the consequences of an action, to compare them is still likely to be difficult if not impossible.

This second approach, sometimes referred to as *teleology*, is said to be *consequential* in ethical terms, in that it seeks to inform a decision through an evaluation of the likely consequences of that decision. A consequential approach does not seek to classify choices as purely 'right' or 'wrong', then, but to evaluate the merits of the various possible outcomes of alternative choices. Even if one decides to adopt a consequential approach, however, there are many possible methods still to be chosen from.

Utilitarianism is probably the best known variant of consequentialism. Jeremy Bentham, who died in 1832, constructed a scale of values based on the 'sovereign masters' of pleasure and pain. A preferred action would be one which generated the greatest pleasure for the greatest number of people, so decisions would involve selecting actions which offered the greatest balance of aggregate human pleasure. Subsequently John Stuart Mill (1806–1873) argued that happiness should be the criterion rather than pleasure.

In the twentieth century, philosophers such as Karl Popper have offered the alternative approach of *negative utilitarianism* which contends that the principle should be less to maximise pleasure than to minimise suffering, so that if utilitarianism can be summarised in the dictum 'the greatest happiness for the greatest number', negative utilitarianism would be typified by the phrase 'the least suffering for the fewest number'.

Several other variations on the theme of utilitarianism might also be mentioned. According to *preference utilitarianism*, it is the satisfaction of people's actual wants and needs which is important. Happiness or pleasure may occur incidentally as a result of an action, but does it result from the satisfaction of a person's actual needs or wants? In this approach, then, the measure takes the form of 'the greatest number of people getting what they want'.

However, critics of this approach have said that what we want is not always what is best for us. Someone who has recently given up smoking may temporarily crave a cigarette, but is it in that person's best interest for that want to be satisfied? Hence we may distinguish between wants on one hand, and what is in our best interest on the other. From such arguments arise the notion of *interest utilitarianism*, which approximates to the idea of 'the greatest number of people getting what is in their best interest'.

The negative utilitarian approach may also be applied to generate 'negative' versions of preference and interest utilitarianism, leading to contentions such as 'the fewest number of people getting what they don't want', or 'the fewest number of people getting what is bad for them'.

However, rather than seek to explore the potentially wide range of variations which can be generated around the theme of utilitarianism, it is more useful briefly to reflect on some wider issues pertaining to utilitarianism in general.

Probably the greatest difficulty arises in trying to put a measure to concepts such as 'good' or 'benefit'. What is the scale of happiness? Can we translate levels of happiness into numerical values? How can the level of happiness gained in one respect (e.g., enjoying a good meal) be compared to that in another respect (e.g., working in a pleasant environment)?

Clearly any attempt to quantify such elusive concepts as the 'goodness' of an action, or the happiness of those affected, is fraught with difficulties and dangers. Economists have promoted ideas such as Cost-Benefit Analysis as a way of resolving decisions by reducing everything to a cost-equivalent basis, but once one enters areas of ethical concern this becomes questionable in effectiveness and dubious in meaning.

Illustration 9.4 Costs and benefits of a new airport

In the late 1960s, the Roskill Commission, inquiring into the siting of a third airport for London, used cost-benefit studies as part of its analyses of alternative locations.

The method used, however, came under widespread attack for many reasons. User benefits,for example, were calculated in terms of aggregate time saved. Aggregate time saved involved multiplying total time saved by the number of passengers making the saving. But while the saving of a few minutes by a very large number of passengers may result in the same total as a large time saving for a smaller group of travellers, are the two really equal? Then it was suggested that a value be put to the time saving on the basis of lost productive time. But from a British perspective, is it legitimate to count the savings made for foreign business travellers?

Hence the concept of utilitarianism can be seen to underlie this attempt to maximise the greatest benefit for the greatest number of people; but, immediately, problems arise. Is the creation of many small benefits able to be compared to the generation of few major disbenefits? Whose benefits should be put into the analysis?

Even were it possible to resolve these difficulties satisfactorily, another minefield lies ahead. One of the potential sites involved the destruction of a cherished wildlife area. How can a price be put on the loss of a coastal breeding habitat for birds in the same scale as time savings for travellers? Other alternatives could cause noise pollution for existing residents or local traffic problems. Again, can these be compared absolutely and objectively?

So, attempts to quantify costs and benefits within a broadly utilitarian framework seem highly problematical, if not sometimes impossible.

The example in Illustration 9.4 also points to another criticism of utilitarian approaches, namely individual rights. According to the basic principle of 'the greatest good for the most people', a decision taker seems to be justified in inflicting harm on me as an individual so long as this is outweighed by greater general benefits for others. In the airport example, the rights of residents to relax peacefully in their gardens might be subordinated to the greater benefits of air travellers. More fundamentally, there is the question of whether animals have rights too! In both cases, do established patterns of residence give any protection against change? Some rights are widely recognised, despite the absence of a reaction to calls for a new Bill of Rights in Britain. What is not always clear is at what level a right exists: in the case of residents threatened with airport development, for instance, should there be a right to object, a right to protection against disadvantageous actions, and/or a right to compensation?

A further difficulty with utilitarian approaches can be the concept of a general 'good'. If a utilitarian sets out to maximise the satisfaction of other people's needs, for example, his actions are no longer determined by his own ethical code or his own roles and responsibilities. A manufacturer might see the greatest good to the most people occurring through selling goods at cost to poorer consumers, but is that justifiable given the company's responsibilities to shareholders? Will the manufacturer be able to reward the workforce fairly with such a strategy and meet other obligations, such as a desire for his children to enjoy the best possible life-style? Most of us can envisage ourselves as having a number of roles, each of which generate groups of wants and desires. Some of these wants and desires may be compatible, such as, say, the wishes of an industrialist to reward employees well and to support the local community. Other wants and desires, though, may conflict, such as the level of commitment to the workplace and the amount of time to be spent with one's family. These are not problems that can readily be resolved, and they require individual response. The criticism of utilitarianism here would be that to allow one's personal duties to be overshadowed by the needs of others may be unacceptable. Spending more time in the office may result in the greatest good for the largest number if the company is able to pay higher wages and dividends as a result, but can this justify neglecting duties as an important member of a family?

There are many other respects in which criticism can be mounted of utilitarian approaches, some of which will emerge subsequently, but at this point it seems that we have come back to the basic distinction between deontology and consequentialism. The pure utilitarian consequentialist could argue for maximising time spent on company business; the deontologist might see it as fundamentally wrong to neglect family duties and responsibilities. An appreciation of this basic distinction is essential in order to appreciate the nature of many ethical choices facing organisations.

ETHICS AND BUSINESS: DIMENSIONS OF CONCERN

An impression could be forming that the concept of business ethics is so broad as to embrace everything in the world of business and, to some extent, that might not be a bad starting point. What is needed, though, is a framework within which to identify ethical concerns in order to help structure discussion and clarify the interplay between issues.

The *stakeholder model* of the firm, introduced in Chapter 8, provides a sound framework for an ethical exploration of the corporate challenges facing organisations. An organisation's stakeholders can be defined as all those who have a stake in its performance, be they internal or external to it. Internally, then, this will include the owners or shareholders, the management and the workforce. Externally it will include suppliers and customers, central and local government, competitors, local residents, neighbouring activities, trade associations, and so forth. Arguably, it also includes the dependants of those economically reliant on the organisation. Obviously, in terms of major atmospheric polluters for example, those potentially affected could be virtually global but, more conveniently, we can think in terms of major groups.

The stakeholder model allows us to identify those groups that may be affected, either beneficially or adversely, by any business decision. Firstly, there are the employees of the firm, although in many decision examples it may be necessary to subdivide these further. Clearly the implications of a given decision may be very different for managers by comparison with shop floor workers. Consider, for example, a decision to sponsor a major sporting event. The management position might be that the sponsorship will promote the public image of the company, allowing it to become associated with a sport that complements the company's image – be that the speed and life-style associated with motor racing, or the grace and healthy connotations of gymnastics. To ordinary workers, though, such sponsorship might be seen as the diversion of a potential wage increase to an event where the senior management of the company can indulge themselves in corporate hospitality and rub shoulders with the famous.

However, other decisions may require quite different subdivisions of the workforce to be made. Future investment decisions may set plant against plant. Product development decisions may juxtapose the Research and Development department against production staff. Redundancy decisions may differentially affect older, loyal staff by comparison with newer, younger members of the workforce. Potential subdivisions within the workforce, then, are numerous, but fundamentally there is no doubt that decisions that affect the workforce will have differential affects in such respects as job prospects, quality of working life and remuneration, all of which raise ethical concerns of fairness and justice.

Yet, notwithstanding the cases of true co-operatives, generally the company does not exist solely to benefit its workforce, and there are the rights of its owners to consider. In simpler company structures this may relate to the family firm, but more complexity occurs in relation to shareholders. Shareholders risk their assets in expectation of reward from company profits, and, as will be shown later, there is a case that their interests are paramount. Some may see differences between the interests of small shareholdings by private individuals and major corporate interests. Also, some may distinguish between the priorities and interests of speculators who only hold shares for short periods in expectation of quick returns, and others who see shares as a long-term investment over a period of many years. Thus, in making decisions about reinvesting profits into new product development, clearly the rights of shareholders to returns on investment need to be addressed, but different types of shareholders may have different priorities. The voting rights of shareholders are a means for the resolution of such differences, but is it acceptable that decisions may be dominated by a few large corporate bodies as opposed to the far greater number of small investors? Should other stakeholder groups also have a role in decision-making processes?

Externally, the company will have duties and responsibilities to many bodies.

Government agencies, at all levels from the supra-national, such as the European Community, to the local council, are important. The simplest resolution here is that it is the company's responsibility to keep within the law, but that is a narrow view for several reasons. First, the law often lags behind events, so that in areas of health and safety, for example, practices may be known to be harmful before they are actually subjected to legal restraint. Further, government policy is not always interpretable in clear terms of legality or illegality. Governments not only pass laws, they frequently issue statements and launch campaigns urging firms to mechanise, to train employees better, to reduce pollution, and so forth, as a matter of seeking wider benefits. Also, some laws can seem to lose credence over time: in Britain the issue of Sunday trading by retailers is a good example where many companies have argued that it is acceptable to break the law because public opinion no longer supports the Shops Act of 1950.

Here, we are seeing an interesting distinction emerge between government bodies and the community. A simple view of a representative democracy would be that the government's actions reflect popular opinion and the public interest, but the Sunday trading debate suggests that there may be a case for seeing public opinion as sovereign over government (in)activity. Equally, at the local level, compliance with matters such as local planning regulations on the provision of car parking around a workplace may satisfy legal responsibilities, but it could be argued that there is a more general commitment to the local community which involves other concerns such as landscaping, or limiting traffic noise at some times of the day. The community, at all levels, from the global to the local, may be seen as a set of stakeholder groups.

Other businesses can also be seen as stakeholders. Some may be party to contractual arrangements, such as licences or supply contracts. Other links may be more informal in nature, but nonetheless relevant. In some areas, responsibilities to like traders become formalised through trade associations which seek to set minimum standards. A decision to promote a product in a particular way, linking the product to certain life-styles for example, may not only affect the brand being promoted but also other competing brand images. The concept of fair competition implies that there is a morality in competition which involves such matters as not making false claims to promote a product, or unjustifiably slurring competing products. Thus even competitors may have a justified interest in the way a company conducts its business, and expect that basic standards are met. When the Hoover company ran a promotional scheme which collapsed under demand for flights to overseas destinations, other companies felt there was a threat to their own promotional plans, and the wider sales promotions industry was said to be affected.

Arguably the single most important stakeholder for a company is its customers. They purchase the firm's output, and thus permit its survival. Responsibilities to customers are obviously focused around issues such as fair trading methods and product safety. As with all stakeholder groups, ethical responsibilities do not just exist at the instant of the purchase, but have a before and after sale element. The customer has a right to know that what is being purchased is fit for the use it is intended for, is safe, is fairly priced, and is protected against early failure or malfunction. In part those duties can be enshrined in law, but most companies see the rights of customers more widely than minimum statutory terms.

If the stakeholder model starts to provide a framework for investigating the ethical implications of business decisions, however, it also demonstrates difficulties when used to interpret even relatively straightforward business decisions. Two main reasons underlie these difficulties: first, in respect of any stakeholder group there tends to be a range of concerns (e.g., economic, environmental, risk); second, any given decision tends to involve conflicting concerns within and between interested groups.

As an example of the range of concerns, consider the issues for a local community of a proposal to mine coal by open cast methods. The creation of jobs, and the additional spending that may result in local businesses are positive economic benefits. The potential for reinstatement of the site at a future date as a recreational facility would also seem beneficial to the local community. Conversely, there might be serious environmental disadvantages such as the loss of attractive countryside, adverse effects on wildlife, noise and dust pollution directly from the workings, and the environmental effects of traffic movements. Thus, for some residents there could well be a trade-off between economic benefits and environmental costs; in a single household, these issues could be perceived quite differently by different members of that household. Also, as suggested in relation to reinstatement of land, benefits and disadvantages have different time-scales. While some factors may be relative short-term considerations, say only having effect during initial site preparation, others may only occur in the longer term. Some shorter-term factors may trigger secondary impacts at a later stage or in a different location. Thus open cast mining may affect deep mines and threaten other jobs and communities.

Hence, while it is useful to employ the stakeholder model when seeking to understand the ethical implications of business decisions, this does not avoid complexity and often may seem only to highlight it. But are all these issues relevant to the decision taker who has to decide if the company should go ahead with its mining proposal?

HOW SHOULD DECISION MAKERS BEHAVE?

The idea that business decisions have ethical dimensions is in no sense new, and in seeking to understand the ethical issues of business decisions, it will help initially to consider two 'classical' articles on the responsibilities of business decision makers.

One view of ethics can be termed *relative*, which means that the decision maker accepts the prevailing ethics of his current and immediate business environment. Broadly this can be termed the 'When in Rome' approach. So, if a manager is seeking to settle a deal in a country where bribery of officials is alleged to be the norm, and is convinced that a bribe would expedite a successful completion of the deal, the bribe is seen to be acceptable, although it conflicts with 'normal' business standards in the manager's own society. Hence, according to this *ethical relativism*, what may be illegal in one country may be quite acceptable business behaviour in another. Consequently there may be few absolute 'rights' or 'wrongs'.

In fact, the idea that different ethical standards apply in different countries is only part of the wider relational argument, as a consideration of the views of Albert Carr (Carr, 1968) demonstrates (Illustration 9.5).

Illustration 9.5 Albert Carr on 'business bluffing'

In 1968, Albert Z. Carr published a controversial article entitled 'Is Business Bluffing Ethical?' Carr's main argument was put thus: 'The ethics of business are not those of society, but rather those of the poker game.' He contended that most business executives 'from time to time are almost compelled, in the interests of their companies or themselves, to practise some form of deception when negotiating with customers, dealers, labour unions, government officials, or even other departments of their companies'. Indeed, Carr suggests that any executive who refuses to take part in this bluffing – which is seen to include acts such as conscious misstatement, concealing pertinent facts, or exaggeration – 'is ignoring opportunities permitted under the rules and is at a heavy disadvantage in his business dealings'. For those who find difficulty in accepting such a view, Carr offers the advice that business 'has the impersonal character of a game – a game that demands both special strategy and an understanding of its special ethics'.

So Carr is not arguing that business has no ethics, but that it has *a special set of ethics*, which he chooses to compare with a poker game. Developing the analogy with poker, he notes that the player who breaches the ethics of the card game, by having a card hidden up his sleeve or marking the cards, for example, is thrown out of the game (or shot in the Old West, he observes!). Yet success at poker requires distrust of other players, ignoring friendships, cunning deceptions and the concealment of strengths and intentions.

Businessmen cease to be private citizens in their office environments, according to Albert Carr, and 'so long as a businessman complies with the law of the land and avoids telling malicious lies, he's ethical... A good part of the time the businessman is trying to do unto others as he hopes others will not do unto him.'

Carr sees it as illusory to suggest that businessmen can follow strong ethical principles such as are the norm in private life. Statements such as 'it pays to be ethical' are seen as actually self-serving, disguised commercial calculations since 'in the long run a company can make more money if it does not antagonise competitors, suppliers, employees and customers by squeezing them too hard.'

That there remain great psychological stresses for the executive is not denied, particularly when there are conflicts between private and business ethical codes. This only reinforces the need to behave as in a game, though, with greater objectivity and less personal and emotional involvement, as 'the major tests of every move in business, as in all games of strategy, are legality and profit... A man who intends to be a winner in the business game must have a game player's attitude.'

In distinguishing between the ethics of the home and the office, Carr adopts what now seems to be a blatantly sexist analysis, contending 'many wives are not prepared to accept the fact that business operates with a special code of ethics.'

So there is a recommended ethical stance for a businessman to succeed, but allegedly that does not mean being 'ruthless, cruel, harsh, or treacherous. On the contrary, the better his reputation for integrity, honesty, and decency, the better his chances of victory will be in the long run.'

Carr, A.Z. (1968) 'Is Business Bluffing Ethical?' *Harvard Business Review*, 46(1), 143–153.

may seem appealing, but on reflection there are serious difficulties implicit here in Carr's argument.

Argument by analogy is always dangerous, since notwithstanding many aspects of correspondence between the situation and the analogy, which we may term the positive analogy, there are usually also many differences, or negative aspects of analogy.

Here the comparison with a game is questionable in many ways. Players choose to join the poker game, but may have to work to survive. So the loser in the game knows that the risk of losing was there all along, and if he did not want to play, then he should not have joined the game. Few of us have any choice but to join the 'game' of being employed, however, nor can we decide to withdraw, as we might leave the game. Logical poker players would not risk more than they could afford, so the penalties of failure should be affordable and presumably, the same goes for one's opponents in a poker game. But the penalties of failure in business may be far more severe, both for oneself and for others who are reliant on us.

Is it really possible to appear honest and decent while being known to be deceitful and disingenuous? Carr would have us believe that everyone in business knows that the norm is to mislead and deceive, but somehow one can succeed and maintain a reputation for integrity! That seems dubious. Might it not be that many executives do maintain high standards of behaviour, and that it is the bluffers who are the exceptions? Ultimately the mechanisms of business require some degree of honesty and reliability for agreements to be worth anything, and for future plans based on them to be feasible. Without a basic level of trust, the linkages between firms, and between people, which hold business and commerce together would soon fracture. And the bluffer may not only be risking his own future livelihood, but also the future welfare of all other stakeholders and their dependants.

Ultimately, though, for many the idea of a 'law of the jungle' attitude in business is not acceptable. Simply to avoid that which is illegal or malicious is not enough. People should be treated fairly and decently, many would feel, whether that be for reasons of common humanity or religious conviction. Thus Carr's case, which appeals to many simple views of business, needs careful personal scrutiny. Ultimately, you need to make up your own mind here. Would you cheat on your workforce or let down a supplier simply to increase your own profit slightly, or do you take your responsibilities more seriously and value your esteem more highly? If you were to succeed by 'bluffing', is that a solid and sustainable basis for the future anyway?

WHO SHOULD DECISION TAKERS BE RESPONSIBLE TO?

It was suggested that one of the difficulties in the arguments of Albert Carr was that other stakeholders and innocent dependants were reliant on the outcome of the 'game player' as business decision maker. As the earlier discussions of the stakeholder model have shown, however, the potential number of vulnerable stakeholders for any significant decision could be very large. Can the decision maker realistically hope to accommodate even the majority of these groups' concerns in his decision making? How should the relative importance of the different groups be evaluated? Is there a danger that in seeking a compromise which is acceptable to many groups, few if any gain what they really want or need?

Milton Friedman has argued very strongly that businesses should not seek to satisfy goals other than the narrowest view of seeking to maximise profits by legal and acceptable means (see Illustration 9.6)

Illustration 9.6 Milton Friedman's views on business responsibility

In 1970 Milton Friedman wrote a forceful article in the *New York Times* in which he mounted a provocative defence of the profit motive and the market system, and contended that *the single social responsibility of business was to increase profit by legitimate means.*

He argued that any business executive who took another stance, such as to place emphasis on employment creation, environmental improvement, or countering discrimination, was 'preaching pure and unadulterated socialism' and such decision makers were 'unwitting puppets of the intellectual forces that have been undermining the basis of a free society'.

Friedman offered the view that businesses cannot have responsibilities, only people can. Corporate executives have direct responsibilities to their employers, the owners of the business, and 'that responsibility is to conduct the business in accordance with (the owners') desires, which generally will be to make as much money as possible while conforming to the basic rules of the society, both those embodied in law and those embodied in ethical custom.'

The executive may well have other responsibilities as an individual, and may choose to see these as social, but if he reacts to them it should only be as an individual, and not as an agent of the company. He should only expend his own time and money, not the time he is contracted to his employer for, nor the company's money. To respond to a social responsibility, such as employing other than the best qualified candidate for a job, or investing more than the legal minimum level for pollution control, is to threaten other people's welfare, and to divert other people's money for a wider social interest, since such actions will reduce returns to shareholders or raise prices to consumers.

Friedman uses the concept of taxation to explain this view. On one hand the socially responsive executive is, in effect, levying a tax on investors and customers, and on the other is spending the proceeds of that tax without accountability. This type of taxation is, Friedman argues, unjustified in principle, with taxation being the concern of democratic government within a constitutional framework which does not apply to the executive. It is also said to be unjustified in terms of the executives competence to act on behalf of wider social interests.

Central to this position is a notion of individual responsibility:

> 'the great virtue of private competitive enterprise' is that 'it forces people to be responsible for their own actions and makes it difficult for them to "exploit" other people for either selfish or unselfish purposes. They can do good - but only at their own expense'.
>
> 'In a free society it is hard for "good" people to do "good", but that is a small price to pay for making it hard for "evil" people to do "evil".'

Friedman anticipates one criticism of his arguments by contending that even the slowness of political processes strengthens his case. Responses by executives to 'social' problems are portrayed as 'trying to attain by undemocratic procedures what they cannot attain by democratic procedures'.

Friedman recognises that some apparent acts of social responsiveness act as a cloak to disguise actions that have other justifications. Hence, providing amenities in a local community may serve the purpose of easing recruitment problems or improving behaviour at work. Such acts, though, are 'one way for a corporation to generate goodwill as a by-product of expenditures that are entirely justified in its own self-interest', despite being dismissed as 'approaching fraud'; 'the use of the cloak of social responsibility... does clearly harm the foundations of a free society.'

Values and responsibilities attach to individuals, not society, in Friedman's view.

Friedman's original article 'The social responsibility of business is to increase its profits' appeared in the *New York Times Magazine* on 13 September 1970 (pp 32-33 & 122-126). It is reprinted in DesJardins and McCall (1990).

There is clearly much to appeal to many decision makers in Milton Friedman's arguments. For those who see in the field of ethics difficult trade-offs between a multitude of stakeholder groups, Friedman offers a simplifying solution: seek greater profits within the parameters of decency and legality. Business strategy tells us that there are still complexities to resolve here – as between short- and longer-term profit maximisation, or in defining acceptable levels of risk – but at least the breadth of concerns has narrowed with Friedman's stance.

Thus, if a company was approached to sponsor an outing for disadvantaged children, or to provide facilities for the handicapped, according to Friedman, the only question for the executive to ask should be 'Will it increase the profitability of the company?' The benefits which may occur to the disadvantaged or disabled are not a concern except in so far as they may generate future profits. By comparison with many other views of morality, then, which stress the merits of helping the less fortunate, this is a quite radical stance.

Several of the terms and phrases employed by Friedman may well merit discussion and reflection beyond the limited scope available here. How free are the 'free societies' which Friedman would seek to protect? What happens when the legal framework embraces principles of corporate social responsibility such as equal opportunities legislation – do we still argue for a minimalist compliance with the law or an outright pursuit of its clear objectives? Are all laws to be treated equally? Are some laws more important than others (e.g., Sunday trading laws in the UK have been widely ignored by retailers arguing a wider public interest). Can we really only attach responsibilities to individuals, and not to businesses? Don't some business decisions emerge as compromises/consensus positions which are not any individual's exclusive position? How can it be that there are only individual responsibilities when laws attach rules and penalties to companies? Is democracy so efficient that any social ill we perceive which has yet to be addressed by government is by definition therefore not a priority?

Carr and Friedman in perspective

In the literature of business ethics, the contributions of Carr and Friedman have produced a great volume of discussion and analysis, far more than can be addressed here. Both positions appear to support an aggressive, profit-chasing style of management, but in truth they are markedly different. Carr argues for a particular code of behaviour in business in which normal moral constraints are relaxed in favour of the morality of the poker player. Friedman takes a far stronger ethical line arguing a directly deontological case that it is the duty of the manager or executive to pursue profits for his or her employers, with deviation from that course being morally unsound.

The common attraction of the two approaches is their apparent simplification of complex moral challenges. Moreover, they both take strong views in terms of the potential to separate 'business' behaviour from that of the private individual, although in somewhat different ways.

At the risk of grossly over-simplifying the arguments which attend these ethical positions, perhaps one issue to confront is the extent to which behaviour in business can truly be divorced from behavioural standards in the rest of one's life. If one genuinely believes promises should be kept and trust rewarded, can one really accept the poker-playing ethic advanced for business decisions by Carr? If one honestly believes that actions should be appraised in part at least in terms of their effects on others, can it be enough simply to follow Friedman and only ask what is the most profitable course of action available to the company which is legal?

If either of these issues cause the decision maker moral difficulties, then a consideration of what is 'correct' behaviour, and of the consequences for others, seems essential in business decision making.

The rest of this chapter assumes that there is a case for companies to apply ethical standards to their decision making, and to consider the implications for other stakeholders, and will seek to illustrate the consequences of those assumptions in relation to the environmental impacts of business.

ISSUES IN THE RISE OF THE GREEN AGENDA

The extent of acceptance of environmental considerations for business in much of Western Europe and North America is now so great that it may seem surprising to some younger people that it took considerable time and effort for the environmental lobby to gain an audience. It is always dangerous to suggest a starting point for a movement such as that which has brought Green issues to the forefront, but by common consensus the publication of the Club of Rome's report *The Limits to Growth* in 1972 was an important bench-mark. Since then, it has been widely accepted that the continuing exploitation of the earth's resources may not be sustainable, that resource depletion is a real threat, and that pollution threatens our future welfare.

Thus there is in the Green agenda a strong consequential strand, whereby it can be contended that to continue as we have in the past, in industrial practices, is a recipe for disaster on a huge scale. The realisation that our patterns of consumption may be distorting and damaging the delicate balances of the earth's atmosphere, through ozone depletion, the Greenhouse Effect, and so forth, has made many people environmentally aware.

The rise of environmental conservation based on consequentialist considerations is, though, only one dimension of the evolution of the Green agenda. There is also a deontological strand which asserts that certain attitudes to our environment are intrinsically wrong. Thus conservationists will campaign for the protection of threatened species not because their survival will benefit mankind (although genetic and other arguments may be made to suggest that is so) but because we have a duty to maintain the planet's ecosystems. Even stronger are those who assert that animals have rights, and campaign vigorously to defend those rights even to the extent of violence and illegality.

Two important concepts help our understanding of the Green agenda: first is the idea of sustainable development, secondly is the notion of inter-generational equity.

The concept of sustainable development seems initially simple, so that if development is defined as a 'vector of desirable social objectives, that is, list of attributes which society seeks to achieve or maximise', which may include both quantifiable objectives, such as increased real income *per capita*, as well as more conceptual objectives, such as to protect and enhance basic freedoms, '*Sustainable* development is then a situation in which development vector D does not decrease over time' (Pearce *et al*, 1990, pp 2–3). If a form of development depletes non-renewable resources, then it cannot by this definition be sustainable in the long term. In everyday terms, what this may be said to imply is a form of development which can continue indefinitely without running out of resources, or becoming socially unacceptable.

The second concept, inter-generational equity, is simply put in terms of saying that each generation should leave their environment, even the planet, in no worse a state than they inherited it.

These two principles underpin the Green agenda, and provide yardsticks against which the performance of business and consumption patterns can be evaluated. The optimist may argue that new technologies will free us from past constraints, but realistically the legacy of past industrialisation and resource depletion seem to make that optimism seem less than justified. Those of us fortunate to have enjoyed the prosperity of a life in the developed world bear much of the responsibility for environmental problems, and are now often found in the unenviable position of counselling those who aspire to that standard of living against similarly profligate behaviour.

The ethical response to that dilemma in terms of business decision making from the Green movement is on the lines that we need to evaluate all options against their potential environmental impact, and to seek to compensate for and rectify past environmental abuses.

ENVIRONMENTAL COMPLEXITY

Yet while it is not difficult to become convinced of the merits of environmental concern, once one starts to analyse those concerns with regard to a single business decision, matters become more complex. Environmental concern can exist at a number of levels simultaneously, and sometimes what seems an appropriate course of action at one level may be inappropriate at another.

Is it necessary to seek to demonstrate that environmental impacts are complex? Perhaps not, given that we can grasp such linkages as the use of CFC aerosols contributing to ozone depletion, and maybe thereby being linked to skin cancers, biological mutations and the 'greenhouse effect'. Yet while we may be willing to accept complex linkages in connection with environmental impacts, few of us would readily portray them as simple. Indeed, simplification of such linkages could well pose a danger in itself. What we most need perhaps when facing the complexity of environmental interdependencies as a result of impacts is a means for structuring our knowledge and imposing some order on available information, both conceptually and practically.

Several conceptual models have been developed for categorising environmental impacts, notably in association with the development of environmental impact assessment (EIA) and social impact assessment (SIA), as summarised by Carley(1980). One of the more complex is the Leopold Matrix, in which 100 specified actions which can potentially impact on the environment are cross-tabulated against 88 environmental factors. For each of the resulting 8800 cells in the matrix two numerical values are to be recorded: one a representative value of the magnitude of the impact and the other a measure of the importance of the impact. Leaving aside considerations of scaling, objectivity, and the like, this seems clearly to reveal the potential complexity of seeking to portray and evaluate environmental impacts.

To exemplify the way environmental problems can be interpreted differently at differing levels of analysis, consider the contention of road hauliers that allowing vehicles on our roads to carry heavier loads will reduce the number of journeys that need to be made, relieve traffic congestion, reduce road maintenance costs, and make more efficient use of fuel supplies. Thus at that level of analysis there seems a sound environmental case. Yet to residents of villages where freight movements pose problems, such a proposal may not be welcome. At that level heavier vehicles may suggest noisier vehicles, more vibration to damage buildings, and so forth. Hence the resolution of the issue at national road policy level may be out of sympathy with local environmental concerns. To many environmentalists, though, the notion of a national road policy might be challenged, and a national transport policy advocated wherein the merits of other forms of transport, notably freight movements by rail, are emphasised. Globally, in terms of use of resources, it might even be argued that we need overall to use less fossil fuels, and thus to seek to minimise the whole need for transportation. Thus the concept of the 'greenest' solution to a problem may in some senses be conditional on the way the problem is defined and the level at which it is being analysed.

Most business decisions involve a number of conflicting ethical concerns, and raise issues at different levels of analysis. An example of this is the hypothetical Welton hypermarket example in Illustration 9.7.

Illustration 9.7 Controversey over a new hypermaket at Welton

Welton is a pleasant village a few miles outside a large city. Many of the residents of Welton drive to work in the city, and do their shopping there.

Recently it was announced that the retail chain Megasave planned to build a large new hypermarket on the edge of Welton.

A protest meeting was held by local residents who claimed the proposal would have the following disadvantages:

- It would cause a lot of traffic to pass through and around the village, creating congestion, noise and an accident risk.
- Vehicles delivering to the store would destroy the peace and tranquillity of the village, and possibly damage old properties.
- Open views across attractive countryside would be lost.
- The local shop, which pensioners and the less mobile residents of the village rely on for their shopping, would probably be forced to close.
- The building would be an 'eyesore', and the expanses of car parking similarly intrusive.
- The site would be better used as a hospital, as had been proposed before recent reorganisations in the Health Service.
- There are few areas in the locality where children can play safely, but part of the proposed site is used by local children as an informal recreation space.
- Part of the site is a small, rather overgrown pond which local naturalists claim is ecologically important as a breeding place for frogs and insects, including butterflies.
- Once the store was open, the whole area might become more attractive and new housing developments might well follow with the improved local access.

Questions

Do you sympathise with the residents? Should their views be accepted and the proposal for the store dropped? Would you seek other views? How would Friedman react?

Megasave issued a press release contesting the arguments summarised above,and stressing the positive benefits the hypermarket development would bring:

- Welton residents would not have such a long drive to good shopping, which would save them time and cost of travel.
- The new store would create around 400 jobs, full and part time, which would be especially welcome for the young of the area for whom existing employment opportunities were limited. Also, according to experiences elsewhere, many mothers might find the part-time jobs especially attractive.
- Hypermarket shopping, with a wide range of goods under one roof on a single level is particularly welcome for many, such as those in wheelchairs, who find city centres difficult to get around.
- The development would include a play area for children, a facility the local residents have been campaigning for over recent years.
- The redesigning of access to the site would improve local traffic flows, and this would be paid for by the store owners.
- There would be substantial Business Rate income to the council as a result of the hypermarket, which would allow either more local authority spending or lower Council Taxes.
- Prices at Megasave stores are significantly below the national average for grocery shops, so there would be savings for those who shop at the new store, and the increased competition is likely to keep prices down in other nearby shops as well.
- The site would be fully landscaped to minimise visual impact, and this would be a significant improvement over the currently rather untidy appearance of the land.

Questions

Are these arguments proof of the value of the proposal? How might you compare the alleged costs and benefits of the store? Are you now in favour or against the hypermarket? How would Carr or Friedman perceive the company's response?

What becomes obvious if the hypermarket example is examined is that different groups have a different set of 'gains' and 'losses' from the development. Hence, a young car-owning family with children are likely to perceive the consequences of the development differently from an old-age pensioner who relies on an ability to walk but a short distance to the local shop. Also we can see some immediate effects of the development, such as flows of delivery vehicles or the loss of the pond, and what may be secondary consequences, such as later housing developments or the closure of the local shop. There are, then, what we can call first, second, and subsequent levels of impact. Moreover the levels of certainty associated with different impacts vary, so the building of the store seems certain to mean the loss of the pond, but may or may not cause the local shop to close; the possibility of the hospital being built is unlikely to increase if the store is not built, although the loss of a potential site may make it less likely if the development goes ahead.

As with many ethical issues, there are both environmental and other considerations. Certain of the above issues are environmental, such as the loss of a wildlife habitat, traffic aspects, visual impact in the countryside, and the landscaping of the site. Others, such as low prices, may be more economic in nature. There are also social dimensions to the problem, e.g., access to shops for the less mobile. Thus, what may be taken as a substantially environmental decision by the local planning authority may not be purely environmental in nature.

Structuring environmental problems

Carley (1980) offers two approaches to structuring the environmental impacts of decisions, the *impact chain* and the *tree of impacts*. Figure 9.1 is an example of an impact chain such as might arise from clearing woodland from above a lake.

This impact chain allows us to trace through an environmental impact from the initial activity (felling trees) to its later, higher-order consequences, such as local shops losing tourist spending and possibly even closing, causing problems for remaining local residents who also used those shops. The certainty of impacts will tend to decrease at higher orders.

However, while this chain allows us to see the links between successive orders of impacts, and therefore perhaps to anticipate the consequences of environmental impacts, it is in a sense a limited view of the problem. We could have constructed a parallel impact chain from the same decision to fell trees that told us the wood was to be used in a new paper mill, which would create local jobs, raise the general well-being of the local population, and provide a basis for a revitalisation of the local economy.

Therefore, we may wish to see impacts in the form of a tree model, such as in Fig. 9.2.

Obviously this is still a highly simplified picture of the potential impacts, both in terms of the variety of impacts depicted at each level, and the number of levels presented in Fig. 9.2. Indeed the earlier example of an impact chain showed that the silting of the lake could be followed by several other phases of impact. You may care to consider successive higher order impacts which follow on from those shown in the right-hand column of the impact tree. Nor are all possible impacts shown by any means. Other primary impacts can be expected, such as the production of waste materials and effluent, which will then generate their own primary, secondary, and so forth, impacts. So there is a useful exercise here in seeking to trace through other impacts from the decision to construct a paper mill. Were we to include all these in a tree of impact, the complexity of the problem would quickly become apparent, as would the value of this form of appraisal in seeking to comprehend complex environmental consequences and linkages.

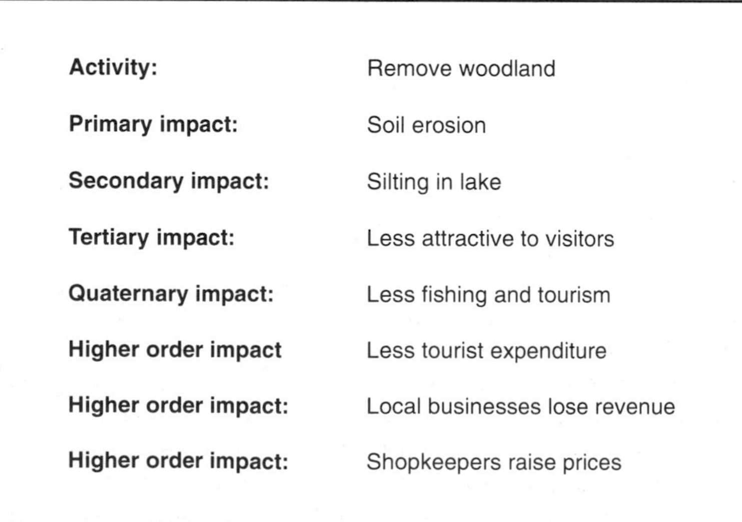

Activity:	Remove woodland
Primary impact:	Soil erosion
Secondary impact:	Silting in lake
Tertiary impact:	Less attractive to visitors
Quaternary impact:	Less fishing and tourism
Higher order impact	Less tourist expenditure
Higher order impact:	Local businesses lose revenue
Higher order impact:	Shopkeepers raise prices

Fig. 9.1 An impact chain

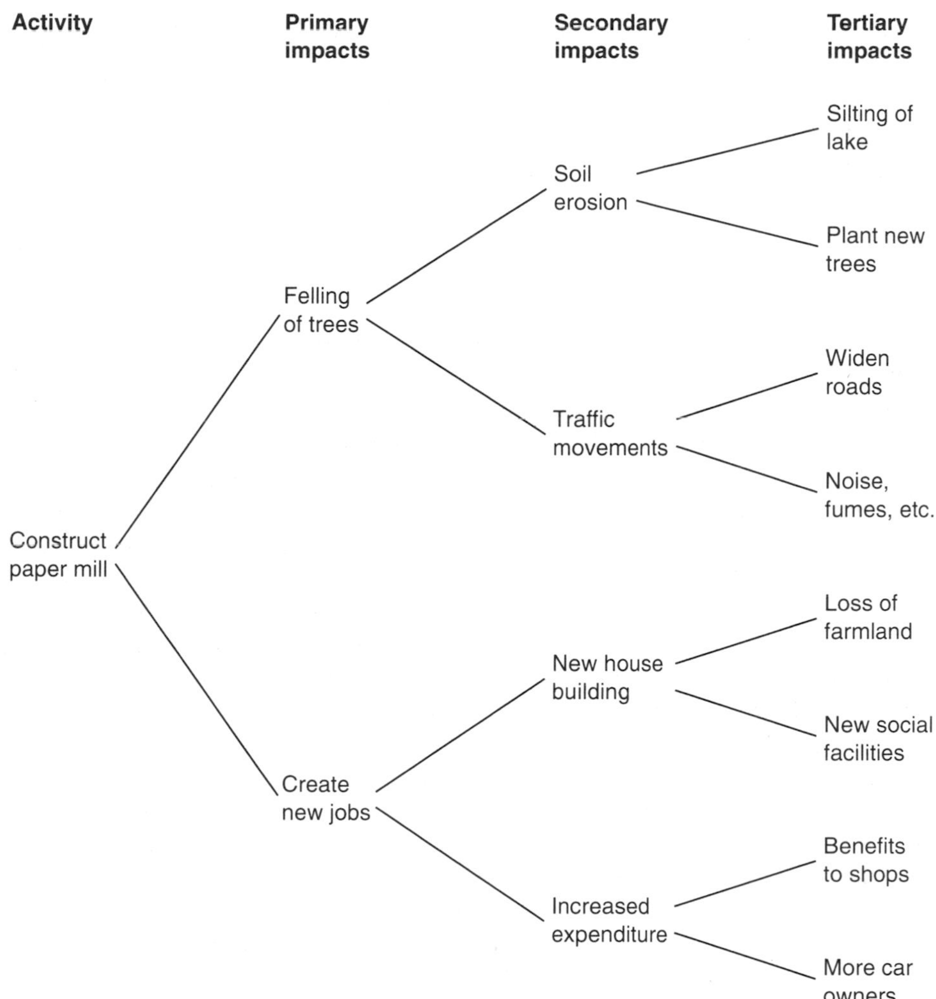

Fig. 9.2 A tree of impacts

To date the examples used have tended to be projects involving construction, as with a hypermarket or paper mill, but a wide range of strategic changes in business also generate environmental impacts, such as the change of a power source, alterations to shift patterns for workers, new packaging, or changes in product distribution. Changes that result from increased environmental concern and strengthened legislation lead to the recognition of further environmental impacts.

The wide range of environmental problems facing businesses require a variety of remedies to be considered. Should businesses be expected to pay for their own environmental improvements, or should a subsidy be offered when government demands a higher standard than previously existed? Should firms be held liable for past pollution which occurred at a time when it was quite legal to discharge those pollutants? Who should pay the price for the search for more environmentally-friendly products? What if consumers are unwilling to pay higher prices for environmentally more beneficial products? Who should pay to recycle in order to conserve resources, especially when possibly the conservation strategy may be more expensive than using new materials? Clearly there are a host of difficult ethical problems which emerge from the environmental agenda. Clearly also, as the above examples may have shown, a single issue may contain a diversity of dimensions: atmospheric, ecological, economic, social, legal, political, and so forth.

SUMMARY

The discussions in this chapter have sought to demonstrate the existence of ethical dimensions in a range of problems from small-business considerations to major industrial developments. It has also been the intention to provide some introductory ethical methods and models which may help individuals to clarify their own ethical positions in respect of business problems – and essentially ethical problems do require individual responses.

The focus of this chapter has often been on environmental issues, these being widely appreciated and perceived as important. Other areas of ethical concern for organisations and those working in them include loyalty to the firm, such as the 'whistle-blower' problem: should an individual disclose a company secret if that action was in the public interest? There are also many ethical issues concerning employment records and privacy. Worker safety is obviously a critical area, as is the safety of products. Pricing strategies can also raise ethical considerations. Hence the range of issues where business decisions may have an ethical component is extensive. Indeed it is arguable that for any problem to require a decision, there may have to be an ethical dimension to that problem, and thus decision makers cannot ignore ethical issues.

There is an ethical dimension to a wide range of business decisions. The range is wide in terms of the type of business, from small to multi-national, and in terms of many functional areas within businesses. The recent rise in concern for environmental matters has added greatly to the importance attached to ethical concerns.

Two main approaches can be identified in relation to solving ethical dilemmas. First, you may adopt a deontological approach which seeks to define alternatives as intrinsically 'right' or 'wrong' according to some code of standards or behaviour. Alternatively you may adopt a consequential approach which seeks to define the best alternative in terms of its likely outcomes, so that the preferred course of action will be the one which is likely to result in the best mix of outcomes. However, defining the best of a set of outcomes can still prove problematical, and a range of utilitarian approaches can be envisaged as variants on the initial theme of the greatest good for the greatest number. In seeking to define such a standard, the stakeholder model, by which we can itemise all those groups with a stake in the survival of the firm, can help to provide some framework for classifying 'gainers' and 'losers' from a decision. Cost benefit approaches, and other quantitative methods, seek to help such analyses, but there still often remain matters of an unquantifiable nature which require personal evaluation.

However there is another view, which stresses relative ethics, suggesting that decision makers should not seek to impose codes of conduct from outside the immediate business decision-making environment on a problem, but accept the prevailing ethical standards, be they those of a foreign country, or simply of a field of business. Albert Carr advanced a particular view of this kind in proposing that decision makers should be expected to bluff and mislead. There are, though, both practical and ethical difficulties with such an approach.

A stronger ethical position is that advanced by Milton Friedman, who contended that the sole responsibility of the decision maker was to maximise profits for the owners of a firm by legal means, hence rejecting any calls for social responsibilities. Thus Friedman would oppose any suggestion that the decision maker should seek to explore the effects of a decision on a range of stakeholder groups. Again, though, there are problems in Friedman's apparently simple solution to ethical complexities, and increasingly many companies do accept a wider responsibility for matters of a social and environmental nature.

In the particular area of environmental ethics, the decision maker may choose to consider a number of issues including sustainability. To appreciate environmental impacts requires an awareness of the complex linkages between natural and human systems, also of the ways in which impacts work in a chain of effects at successive levels.

Ultimately it is unlikely that any solution to an ethical dilemma will be resolved other than by personal means. Those with strong views of a religious or political nature may readily apply a deontological method and define which of a range of potential courses of action is preferred. For others, it will be necessary to struggle with an evaluation of the consequences of actions, and to seek some rule of desirability of outcome. Hence ethical problems are likely to provoke different, quite personal responses, so that the main contribution of a consideration of ethics in business decision making is likely to be an awareness of broad methods and approaches available in order to seek a personal resolution of a problem.

EXERCISE 1: POLLUTION CONTROL AT A POWER STATION

Flue gas desulphurisation (FGD) is a process by which sulphur emissions from a coal-fired power station can be reduced. In 1988 the Council of Ministers of the European Community agreed targets for a staged reduction of Sulphur Dioxide and other gaseous emissions from large power stations. The context of this decision was their concern that such emissions were a prime contributor to acid rain. The targets were for a reduction of 20 per cent by 1993 progressing eventually to a 60 per cent reduction by 2003, although progress to date in the UK seems to suggest some slippage from the initial timetable, and progress has been slow on agreeing revised standards.

Indigenous British coal supplies tend to be characterised by a relatively high sulphur content: at about 1.5 per cent typically, the sulphur content of British coal is almost double the levels common in imported coals. Therefore one strategy to reduce sulphur emissions would be to switch to imported coal sources. This alternative may not be wholly acceptable for a number of reasons, some political, some economic. Also, it would itself set in train a chain of environmental and social impacts such as the further loss of mining jobs, the consequences for coalfield communities, the effects of new patterns of bulk coal movement, and so forth. In the case to be discussed here, this option is not explored in more depth. The focus here will be on the FGD process which 'scrubs' wet flue gases to achieve a 90 per cent reduction in sulphur dioxide levels. The valley of the River Trent in the East Midlands of England contains a number of major coal-fired power stations. Introducing a FGD plant at one of these stations, Ratcliffe-on-Soar, set in train a series of potential impacts, the more significant of which are identified below:

(a) About 306,000 tonnes of high purity limestone will be required per year.
(b) As a result of the FGD process, some 483,000 tonnes of gypsum will be produced annually.

(c) Inevitably, higher production costs will result as the thermal efficiency of the power station is reduced.
(d) Huge, potentially intrusive, new buildings are needed to house the FGD plant.

Each of these aspects is, of course, in terms of a chain of impacts, only an initial phase of impact, and by exploring each in more depth in turn, successive orders of impact emerge.

To obtain the volume and quality of limestone supplies needed requires new sources of supply. Preferably, at least two sources would be identified in order to safeguard continuity of supply and to encourage competitive pricing. In Britain many of the higher quality limestone quarries are sited within National Parks, where there would be strong environmental opposition to any expansion of quarrying activities. Indeed, the electricity generating industry has given undertakings in the past not to use such sources. Nevertheless, major expansions of quarrying activity in some locations seem an inevitable consequence of implementing FGD.

Sites may be identifiable outside of National Parks which, in practical terms for a power station in the Trent Valley, is likely to mean a location in Derbyshire beyond the Peak District National Park boundary. Even this solution is likely to provoke opposition, however, as in some areas the Park boundary can seem a little arbitrary, and non-National Park status does not imply low landscape quality. In any case, a site proximate to the Park could well impact on the amenity value of the Park, for example in terms of visual impact or traffic generation.

Even when limestone sources have been identified the issue of transportation remains problematical. If road transport is used, as many as 61 truck loads per day are forecast as needed, with all the concomitant environmental, economic, and safety consequences they would obviously bring. Alternatively, a more environmentally-friendly solution might appear to be the use of rail transport, as is already used extensively for the movement of coal from the mines to the power stations. A similar FGD project at Drax power station in Yorkshire has provoked fierce debate about the relative proportions of road and rail movements which will be permitted. In the locality of quarries, which are not always likely to have existing or suitable rail terminal facilities, use of the rail option would entail more environmental disruption in constructing a rail facility. The total movements envisaged for the FGD, 61 limestone trucks per day and 96 gypsum loads per day, would require no more than three train movements per day.

At the power station itself, the existing road infrastructure could not safely and efficiently accommodate the envisaged levels of road movement without significant civil engineering works. Moreover as large quantities of ground limestone are to be stockpiled at the station, as is the case with rail-hauled coal at present in order to safeguard continuity of supply, problems of visual intrusion and dust could result. These are to be overcome with huge storage provisions, but of course that incurs further cost and visual impact.

The production of large quantities of gypsum could well represent a positive economic benefit, since relatively pure gypsum has wide markets in cement manufacture, wall plasters, plasterboard, and other construction materials. Nottinghamshire already has an established gypsum industry to the south of the Trent, based on local mines, and a new source of gypsum as a by-product of FGD could be seen either as a benefit or a threat to that industry. If the new source of gypsum was to be substituted for traditional sources, existing jobs in the gypsum industry could be threatened. Alternatively, it could be that the addition of new supplies creates economies of scale and acts to strengthen the competitive position of the existing industry. Possible sites for disposing of the gypsum as waste have also been considered, which would again raise various environmental concerns.

However, to transport large volumes of gypsum to existing factories would be difficult unless the gypsum were dried first. If the gypsum is totally dried, dust could again be a serious problem. Also, the water extracted in the drying process tends to contain concentrations of heavy metal ions, hence special arrangements for disposal are needed. An obvious alternative would be to site a new plasterboard factory close to the FGD plant, thus obviating the need for trans-shipment of gypsum. Environmentally this option would still need careful evaluation in terms of the traffic generation consequences (including the workforce), visual impact, and competition *vis-a-vis* existing local gypsum production and processing.

The energy demands of such a FGD plant, its capital cost (perhaps in excess of £250 million), and the cost of raw materials, cannot but increase unit costs and reduce the thermal efficiency of the station. Current practice in Britain involves the National Grid purchasing the production of the privatised electricity generating companies on what is broadly a 'cheapest first/dearest last' basis. In this way the more thermally efficient stations, which broadly means the larger ones, provide the base load throughout the day while at times of increasing demand, towards the peaks of power consumption, smaller and/or older capacity is brought into production. After FGD, this may no longer be so simple though. Ironically, a situation could be envisaged in which the effects on unit costs of reducing pollution from larger, newer generating capacity, had the effect that smaller, older, 'dirtier' capacity came into greater usage. What should the role of government be in such a scenario? Having withdrawn from a position of influence through a privatisation policy aimed at increasing the public accountability of the electricity supply industry, should government then dictate a more environmentally friendly outcome? Or should government accept the financial consequences of its historical commitments and subsidise the post-FGD stations?

Perhaps it is the case that it is the consumers who have enjoyed the benefits of relatively cheap power without the accompanying burdens of social and economic costs, both nationally and globally, who should be brought to account. Yet so long as it remains legal to produce electricity in power stations which pollute the atmosphere, and so long as consumers continue to be willing to use that electricity, is there not a case, in the style of Friedman, to say companies should produce in the way that is most profitable for their shareholders?

EXERCISE 2: POLLUTION CONTROL, SOME QUESTIONS

Several issues are raised by the pollution control case. The exercise that follows requires you to address some of these.

Assume you are employed in connection with the Flue Gas Desulphurisation plant at Ratcliffe-on-Soar power station, and in that context provide answers to the following seven questions. In each case, you should consider how you would justify your decision to a variety of groups such as your Board of Directors, shareholders, the press, environmentalists, and local residents.

1 Do you think that environmental impacts at limestone quarries are factors you will consider in deciding which sources to use?

2 Apart from price, what other issues might you consider in deciding whether to move limestone by road or rail?

3 If government was to withdraw pressures for cleaner generation, would you still use the FGD plant even though it made your product more costly?

4 If FGD plants became so efficient that required emission reductions were exceeded, would you consider burning some 'dirtier' fuels, such as orimulsion, to increase profits?

5 What criteria would govern your decisions on disposal of wastes?

6 Would you spend money to improve roads so as to reduce traffic through nearby villages?

7 How would you react if government announced it hoped to impose stronger statutory controls on polluters?

GLOSSSARY OF MAIN TERMS

Consequentialism A view by which the evaluation of the acceptability of an action is determined in relation to the consequences the action is likely to have.

Deontology Literally 'the science of duty', but in general can be taken to mean the approach by which reference to some external set of beliefs or standards provides a basis for appraising the acceptability of an action.

Environmental impact analysis Seeks to identify and evaluate all the impacts on the environment of a decision, and embraces a consideration of all aspects of the environment (e.g., physical, atmospheric, biological, social, economic, cultural, political etc.).

Inter-generational equality Each generation should pass the planet on to the next generation in a state which is at least no worse than that in which it was inherited from the previous generation.

Stakeholders All those groups, organisations and individuals who have an interest in the future of an organisation.

Sustainable development Development that does not deplete non-renewable resources nor diminish the quality of life of anyone over time.

Teleology Another term for consequentialism, which relates the acceptability of a decision to its consequences.

Utilitarianism A form of consequentialism usually defined in terms of the dictum of 'the greatest good for the greatest number'.

Interest utilitarianism A version of utilitarianism which stresses people getting what is to their benefit or in their interest.

Negative utilitarianism Suggests that rather than seeking the greatest good for the greatest number, the decision maker should seek an outcome which results in the least harm to the fewest number.

Preference utilitarianism A variant of utilitarianism which stresses people getting what they actually want or need.

REFERENCES

Carley, M. (1980) *Rational Techniques in Policy Analysis*, Heinemann Educational.

Carr, A. Z. (1968) 'Is Business Bluffing Ethical?', *Harvard Business Review*, 46 (1), 143-153.

DesJardins, J. R., and McCall, J. J. (1990) *Contemporary Issues in Business Ethics*, Wadsworth.

Pearce, D., Barbier, E., and Markandya, A. (1990) *Sustainable Development: Economics and Environment in the Third World*, Elgar.

FURTHER READING

Beauchamp, T. L. (1993) *Case Studies in Business, Society, and Ethics*, Prentice Hall.

Donaldson, T., and Gini, A. (1993) *Case Studies in Business Ethics*, Prentice Hall.

Hay, R. D., Gray, E. R., and Smith, P. H (1989) *Business and Society: Perspectives on Ethics and Social Responsibility*, South-Western Publishing Co.

Meadows, D. H., Meadows, D. L., Randers, J. and Behrens, W. W. (1972) *The Limits to Growth: A Report on the Club of Rome's Project on the Predicament of Mankind*, Earth Island Press.

Smith, D. (1993) *Business and the Environment: Implications of the New Environmentalism*, Paul Chapman.

Velasquez, M. G. (1988) *Business Ethics: Concepts and Cases*, Prentice Hall.

CHAPTER 10

Chaos and decision making

Ray Lye

INTRODUCTION

Decision making of all kinds rests on some assumptions about our ability to predict the future. Given the ability to forecast the future with accuracy decision making would become a relatively easy task. If we could be sure of the success of a new product we could decide to go ahead with production and the necessary investment with confidence. If we knew the stock market was about to boom we could buy shares with the assurance of a profit. A company can happily develop a ten-year plan if it knows what will happen in the next ten years.

Even to the casual observer it is clear that business, and indeed life in general, is not entirely predictable. Conventionally in decision-making theory this lack of predictability is explained by factors such as a lack of information or the limitations of predictive techniques, but a more recent explanation provides different insights. Chaos theory suggests that a whole range of phenomena are inherently unpredictable. As a consequence, to try and foresee the future may be a futile and wasteful activity; we may need to take decisions knowing we can never be sure of the outcomes.

A chaotic situation is characterised by the absence of regularities which prevent the accurate prediction of what will happen next. An important concept underpinning chaos theory is that of non-linearity. Many of the formal techniques of decision making rest on assumptions of linearity. Budgeting, capital investment appraisal, regression analysis and linear programming are all examples of projecting past trends to provide a profile of future events. Past and current information is used to predict on the assumption that the future is like an unexplored part of a river and, though the details may not be known, it is safe to assume the waters and the flow will directly follow on from the explored part. On the other hand Chaos theory proposes that events can be discrete and that, despite having full information about past events, the next occurrence may follow a pattern different from previous occurrences. Fundamental to the concept of chaos is the perspective that many events both in the physical and social world are complex and hence intrinsically difficult to predict with any certainty.

Before looking in more detail at the theory of chaos you may wish to carry out the small experiment shown in Fig. 10.1. Balance a pencil on a sheet of paper with your index finger. Then release your finger and note the direction in which the pencil falls. Carry out a number of trials and you should note that despite all evidence you have gathered, you still cannot predict which direction the pencil will fall on the next trial. Note the non-linearity of events and the discrete nature of each trial. A further explanation of the results of this experiment can be gained from the next section of the chapter.

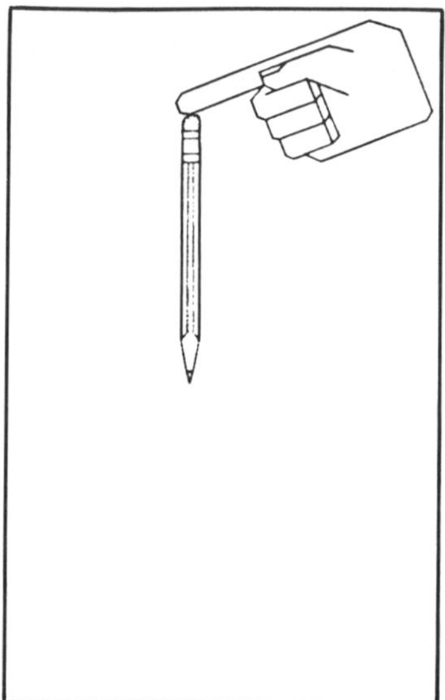

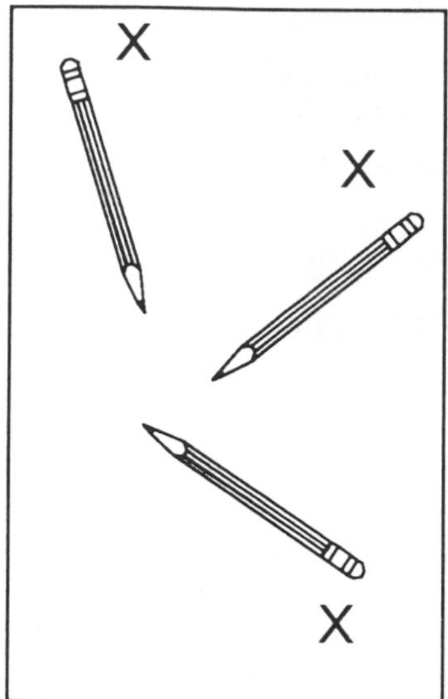

Fig. 10.1 An unstable chaotic system – a simple experiment with chaos.

CHAOS THEORY: AN OVERVIEW

Lorenz and the butterfly effect

A major figure in the development of Chaos theory was Edward Lorenz a meteorologist and mathematician. His contribution can be traced to the day when he was running a mathematical model of the weather on his computer. In order to check some results Lorenz decided to input his data and re-run the program. Taking the data from a previous printout he entered the figures into the computer and left the room while the computer performed its calculations. On returning to the room Lorenz found some surprising results. When the data was recalculated the early results were virtually identical. However, after a while the series showed a major divergence with no relationship between the first and second running of the data through the computer. These results are shown in Fig. 10.2. From nearly the same starting point, Edward Lorenz saw his computer produce weather patterns that grew further and further apart until all resemblance disappeared.

Why were the results not identical? What Lorenz had not realised as he input the data for a second time was that while the printer printed out the results to six decimal points, the computer actually calculated the outcomes to eight decimal points. Thus there were minute differences between the printed data and that which was used by the computer in its calculations. The differences at the level of six decimal points were, of course, very small (at the level of one part in 1,000,000). Such small variations might be thought to have very minor outcomes but Lorenz was able to show that very minor differences in input can have very major effects on outcomes. This is sometimes referred to as *sensitivity to initial conditions* because unless starting conditions are absolutely identical then outcomes will follow an unpredictable course. Lorenz went on to label his

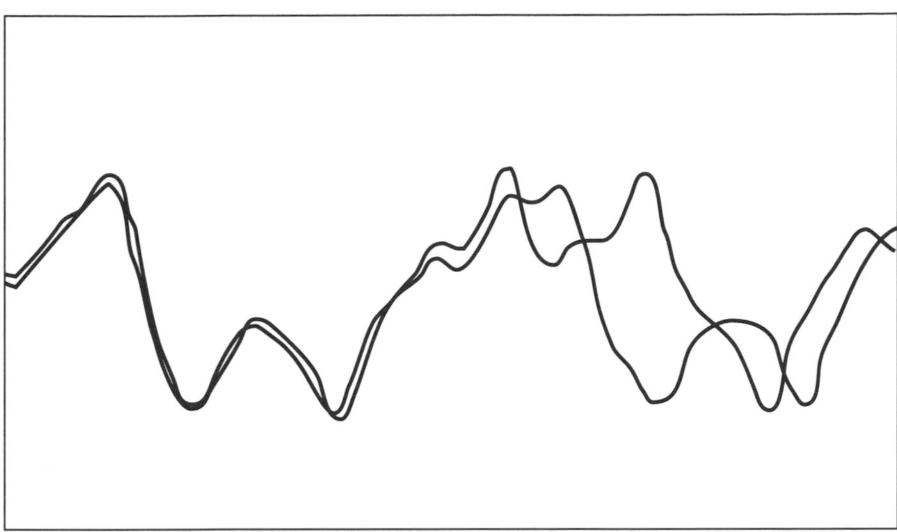

Fig. 10.2 The Butterfly Effect – how two weather patterns diverge (from Lorenz's 1961 printouts)

findings the *butterfly effect*. Since he was using a weather forecasting model Lorenz suggested that such a minor shift in air conditions as the flapping of a butterfly's wings could bring about major shifts in the future patterns of the weather. A single movement of a butterfly's wings in the Amazon jungle could alter snow conditions in the Alps.

A business example of the butterfly effect that is sometimes cited is that of competition in the UK between the rival video recording systems of VHS and Betamax. Technically the systems were comparable, the price and quality were similar and they were launched into the market at more or less the same time. Logically it might be reasonable to assume that each would obtain a fair market share but in fact the VHS system became the standard, leading to the demise of Betamax. This result is seen as due to a very minor factor which was not considered significant at the time. There were slightly more films available on VHS than on Betamax and this led rental companies to plump for VHS because it offered higher returns. This, in turn, led to even more titles being available on VHS and provided, for those who rented a video recorder, an incentive to stay with the VHS system when the time came to buy their own machine. In business, just as in weather forecasting, a very slight difference in initial conditions can have a very major impact on the long-run pattern of behaviour.

Chaos theory states that because of this sensitivity to initial conditions many events simply cannot be foretold. Because it would be impossible to know and monitor all the variations that might have a significant effect on outcomes we have to recognise and accept a high level of unpredictability. This, largely as a result of Lorenz's work, is generally accepted in the weather forecasting field, but the full impact of this view has yet to be felt in business decision making.

It is not easy to accept that so much of the effort that goes into forecasting for decision making is a waste of time and money but, as can be seen from Fig. 10.1, even a very simple system can be chaotic never mind the intricacies and complexities of the business world.

Fractal geometry and the issue of measurement

One way to deal with the problems caused by the butterfly effect might be to refine and refine our forms of measurement so that we are aware of every variation in a situation. This is an appealing and commonly followed practice but fractal geometry gives us a reason for having little confidence in the powers of measurement to make our predictions valid.

Benoit Mandelbrot, a researcher with IBM, is a major figure in the development of Chaos theory. He posed the question 'How long is the coastline of Britain?' and came up with the answer that it is infinitely long. How did he arrive at this startling conclusion? Consider how a coastline might be measured. A surveyor might measure it by walking the length of the coast with a pair of dividers set at one metre and arrive at a figure. If the process is repeated with the dividers set at half a metre one would expect the final measurement to be slightly longer as the dividers take more of the detail into account. With finer and finer measurement more detail is measured and the length of the coastline is seen to increase. If the shape is regular it is likely that a final true measurement will be arrived at but, if there are continuing irregularities in the shape, then continually refined measurement will show the length of the coastline to be infinite. In fact the shape of a coastline does show the pattern of continuing irregularity due to its fractal nature.

A fractal is any shape which, despite continuous magnification, retains the same basic geometric properties. A non-fractal shape such as a circle will, as it is magnified, look more and more like a straight line, but a coastline which looks 'crinkly' to begin with continues to look 'crinkly' however much it is magnified. Figure 10.3 shows the Koch Curve. This is a well known fractal shape composed of triangles a third of the size of the original and placed half-way along the edge of the preceding triangle. At high magnification the edge of the side of such a diagram would look like this (what Mandelbrot referred to as 'a rough model of a coastline').

Probably the best known fractal is the one named after its originator called the *Mandelbrot Set*. A simple equation, with the aid of continuous iterations by a computer, generates what has been called the most complex and beautiful pattern in mathematics. The basic shape of the Mandelbrot Set has become the icon of Chaos theory (see Fig. 10.4).

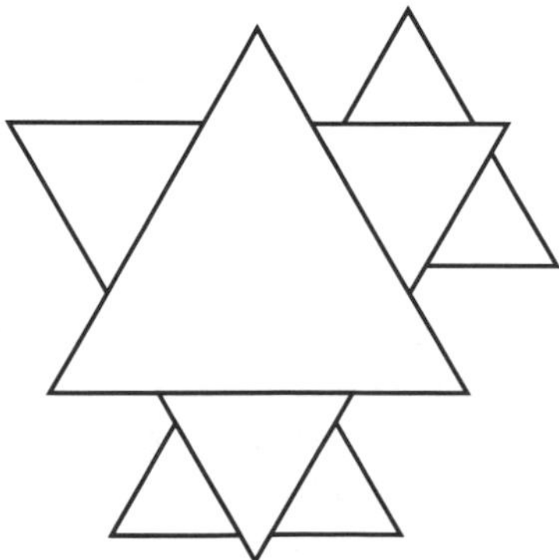

Fig. 10.3 The Koch Curve

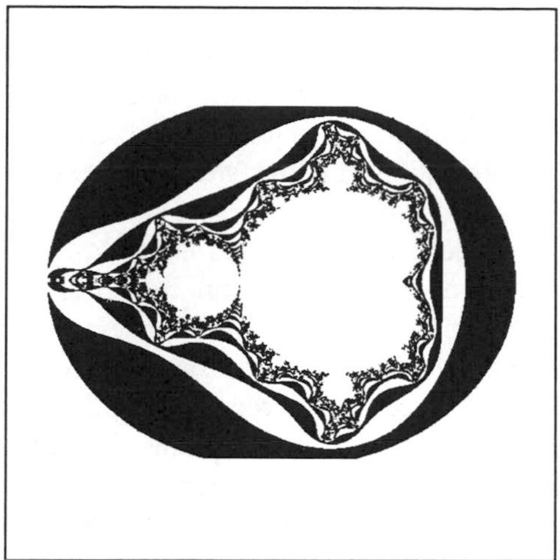

Fig. 10.4 The Mandelbrot Set

Period doubling and the onset of chaos

Imagine a dripping tap. The constant repetitive drip gives every indication of a stable, non-chaotic system. Open the tap a little wider and the regularity persists despite the drips coming at a faster rate. If the tap is gradually opened to its full extent it is possible to note a stage at which all regularity disappears and there is only a turbulent and chaotic flow. This phenomenon was studied by the mathematician Mitchell Fiegenbaum and he was able to demonstrate that it is possible to predict the onset of chaos in what appears to be a non-chaotic system. It is wrong to assume that apparent regularities in a system will necessarily continue into the long term.

The mathematical approach to understanding such events as the dripping tap is called 'period doubling' and can be applied to a diverse range of events such as demographic change or the ecology of plants. Put simply, the transition to chaos can be understood by orderly cycles of events (period doublings that will follow a regular pattern in their initial phases, such as in the dripping tap example) but will become, at a predictable stage, chaotic. Utilising a number of non-linear equations which modelled a variety of systems, Fiegenbaum was able to demonstrate common features of this descent into chaos. Rather than go into the mathematical details of his work, Fig. 10.5 shows a computerised picture of period doubling taking place. As can be seen, the highly regular initial bifurcations eventually lose all regularity as chaos takes over.

The lesson here for the decision maker is, first of all, not to be fooled by the apparent stability and predictability of a system. You may well be in for a shock! It is also important to take on board the conclusion that it might be possible to predict the onset of chaos and take appropriate decisions to cope with the emerging, vastly changed, situation.

Order in chaos: the strange attractor

Our increased understanding of chaos has some unexpected consequences. Not the least of these is that, even in a chaotic system, there are patterns and regularities to be found. The concept of the strange attractor enables the chaotic system to be described, both mathematically and graphically, to reveal such patterns. Basically defined, a strange attractor is the sequence of behaviour that one associates with a particular chaotic system, any chaotic system has its own particular strange attractor. A non-chaotic system, such as a simple pendulum or a bouncing ball, will have an attractor; the word 'strange' is added when referring to chaos. An example of the strange attractor is given in Fig. 10.6. This is Lorenz's model of the weather, a three-dimensional image where the lines never cross. Each point on the line is one weather state and the line is made infinitely long, as the various weather states develop and change. What such a diagram tells us is that, while accurate prediction is impossible, we can be aware of the range of possible weather states. Monsoon rains do not occur in the Sahara or tropical heatwaves in the Arctic. Chaos theory can be used to indicate what will not happen. For the decision maker this can obviously be valuable information. As yet there has been relatively little success in identifying the strange attractors in the business world though efforts have and are being made as can be seen in Illustration 10.1.

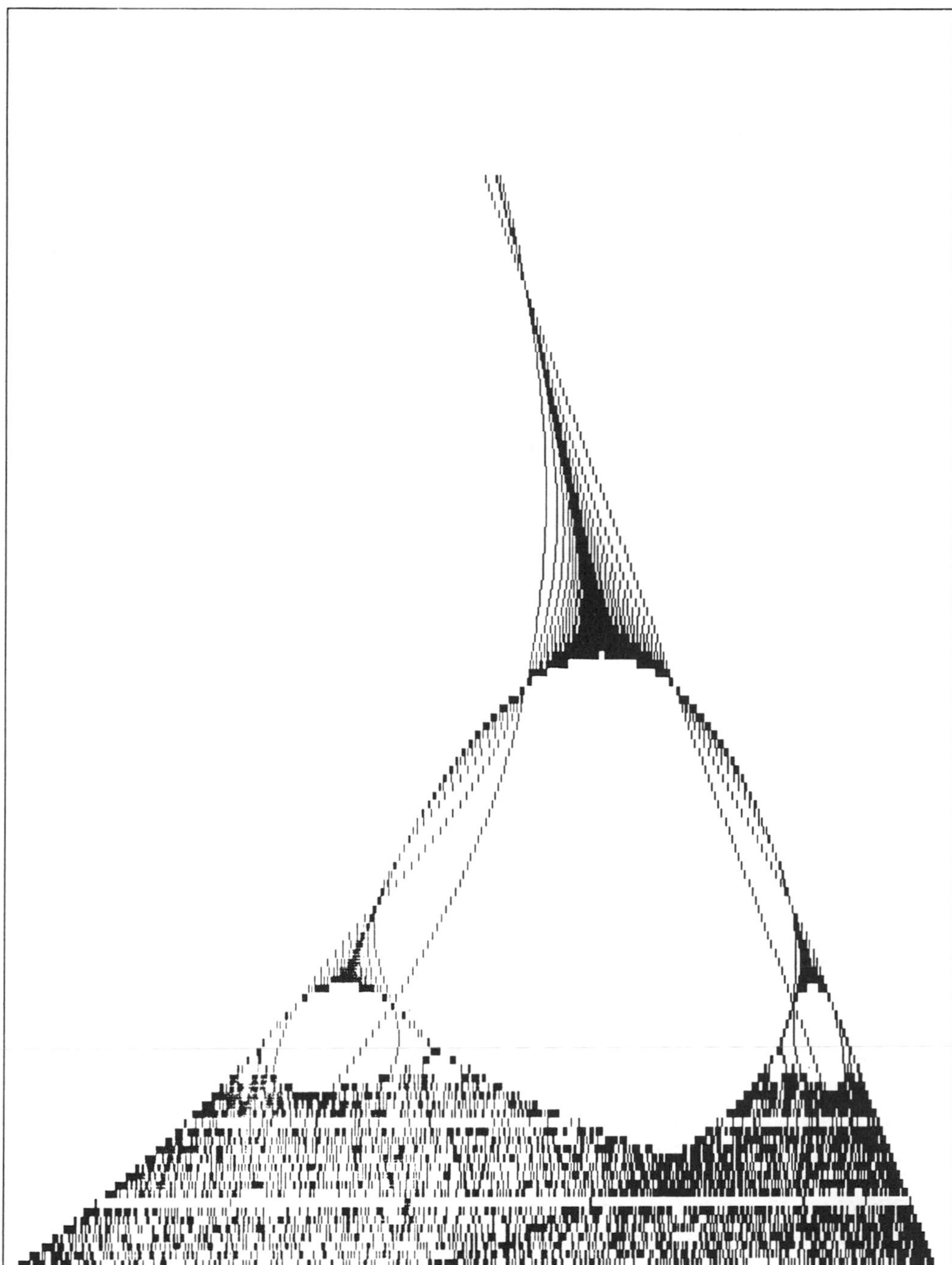

Fig. 10.5 Bifurcation

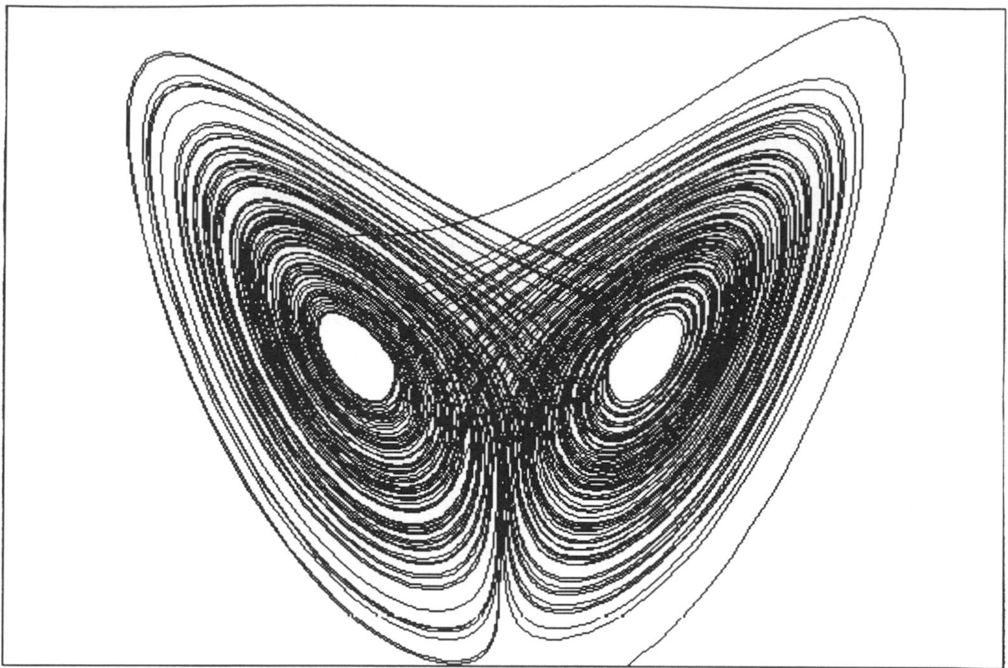

Fig. 10.6 Strange attractors

Illustration 10.1 Cash in on chaos

Intricate theory to cash in on chaos

Deep in a mathematical institute somewhere in England, a scientist is plotting to bring chaos to the stock market. Beneath a bust of Carl Gauss – "the greatest mathematician who ever lived, so of course, no one's heard of him" – a prematurely greying man stares at a computer screen. Phrases like "deterministic systems" and "Lorenz attractor" fly around the room.

This man openly admits that a multi-national oil company is funding his research but heteroclinic tangles would not drag its name out of him. "Yes, they've given us some money," he concedes but adds hastily, "but we're not the only ones working on chaos and markets." He is part of a network. An international network.

He has spent a decade working on what scientists paradoxically term the Chaos Theory and now dreams of applying it to stock markets from Hong Kong to Helsinki. His eyes twinkle at the prospect and at the billions of pounds involved.

This man, a 42-year-old mathematician whom we shall call Dr Ian Stewart of Warwick University, says he's willing to come clean about what he's up to.

He touches the keyboard. A diagram appears on the screen. It looks like spagetti flying through the air. He opens his mouth. Words come out. "Traditionally analysis of phenomena...cycles...sun spots, harvest, the stock market...chartism...scientists discounted what did not fit cycles."

The left side of my brain hurts. "Now Chaos Theory has arrived and it's getting a lot of people very excited. In ordinary language, chaos is something devoid of form. But in mathematics, chaos is something that *appears to* be devoid of form, but isn't. What were discounted as random phenomena are now recognised as part of larger, hidden patterns. Noise is now signal." The right side of my brain hurts.

"Applications are innumerable. We now know that a heart does not just misfire at random: there's a hidden pattern. If you can spot a pattern before it is fully developed, you can take appropriate action – like predicting movements in the stock market."

Light is dawning. "Chaos analysis has only to be one per cent more reliable than any current forecasting method and you'd clean up. And it certainly has the potential to be better."

What Dr Stewart is seeking is the mathematical equivalent of the Philosopher's Stone, a magical formula to turn base metal into gold. It is all too clear why oil companies are interested.

But there's a snag. It's called the Butterfly Effect.

The flapping of a single butterfly's wings can change the world's weather, apparently. Small, unpredictable, disturbances get amplified until they become large enough to alter the course of a hurricane or set off a snowstorm.

"So with markets: a five-cent fall in the price of an obscure American firm could trigger a crash."

Outside, the clouds, formless to the untrained eye, march across the sky. It is quiet, quiet enough to hear the beating of a butterfly's wing.

(Source: *The Correspondent*, 18 February 1990.)

CHAOS AND DECISION MAKING

Chaos theory suggests the need to adopt a radically new perspective on decision making. The past, rather mechanical and formal methods of taking decisions, may not be legitimate in the new framework offered by this distinctive perspective. The rational model of decision making was based on a set of beliefs about the 'clockwork' nature of the decision-making process and the general environment in which it takes place. Chaos theory describes a different world in which these views have to be discarded and the true dimensions of uncertainty have to be acknowledged. The following table contrasts the two ways of looking at the world.

Decision making

The clockwork view		*The chaos view*
Order	rather than	Disorder
Continuities	rather than	Discontinuities
Prediction	rather than	Randomness
Information	rather than	Ignorance
Stability	rather than	Instability
Measurement	rather than	Guesstimate
Logic	rather than	Intuition

Decisions are clearly easier to take if it is assumed that the prevailing circumstances are ordered and that a decision to change one part of the system will have controllable and predictable results for the whole system. Chaos theory, on the other hand, would seem to make decision making more difficult since it suggests that small changes can have major and unpredictable consequences for the system overall. The existence of the butterfly effect indicates a tendency to disorder rather than order.

Those who follow the 'clockwork' view assume the value of historical information and make future decisions on the basis that past patterns will in some way shape the future. Chaos stresses an alternative approach which emphasises the discontinuities in events, which means that decisions need to be seen as new beginnings rather than part of a continuing chain. The discontinuities must be recognised and thus a decision needs to be viewed as an opportunity to change rather than the necessary and inevitable outcome of history.

Predictability has always been a key assumption of traditional approaches to decision making. If a matter is seen as highly predictable, decisions are clear cut. For example knowing that Christmas Day is a holiday and falls on 25 December each year makes it possible to decide well in advance the necessary plans and procedures to deal with that fact. Where matters are less predictable (and chaos theory states that matters are generally less predictable than conventionally thought) it is much harder to decide. To cope with this it is necessary to have contingency plans and fall-back positions and a readiness to start all over again when plans fail.

The 'clockwork' approach to decision making makes the fundamental assertion that stability is the normal state under which decisions are made. Stability means that the past can inform the present, the impact of a decision can be accurately assessed in terms of how it changes a stable system, and the success of a decision can be judged by its effects on stability. If the chaos view is adopted then none of the above are valid. The underlying instability of a system will mean that decisions will not have predictable consequences and there must be mechanisms in place to cope with instability rather than to control and manage stability.

Measurement that is both comprehensive and accurate underpins all traditional approaches to the process of decision making. Gathering information, assessing it and using it to inform judgement requires measurement. Is factor 'a' increasing or decreasing? What is the extent to which factor 'b' is changing? How much do we wish to change factor 'c' by taking the decision? These types of questions are commonplace in decision making but chaos theory leads us to doubt many of the answers that will be given to them. Measurement will always contain elements of inaccuracy, no matter how small. From the butterfly effect we also know that very small differences in data, the sort that are inevitable because of the problems of measurement, can have a huge impact on outcomes. Over-measurement is likely to be both costly and futile in that it may still miss the important variable, however much time and effort is put into the measuring process. Chaos theory suggests that even with the most refined measuring techniques the final analysis can only approximate to a best guess. The 'guesstimate' is what decisions are really based on, not pure scientific analysis. For the organisational decision maker this is a significant view. On the one hand it can avoid an over-confident and expensive approach to measurement and on the other it should lead to a more realistic and valued view of the 'guesstimate'.

Logical procedures are built into the rational approach to decision making. The steps of decision making follow a logical sequence from the inception of the decision to the final implementation and monitoring. Chaos theory means questioning the value of always adhering to this logical process. It can only function with complete and accurate information and a view that events are logically connected. Chaos theory suggests that complete and accurate information is unattainable and events are frequently discrete and bear no relationship to what has happened previously. If logic has limitations in decision making then non-logical methods cannot be dismissed as inappropriate and ineffective. Intuitive and creative thinking, which does not follow the canons of logic, has an important role in decision making. A failure to recognise this will lead to a reliance on methods that have built-in weaknesses and decisions that are ineffective or damaging because they fail to take account of chaos.

DECISION MAKING UNDER CHAOS

The theory of chaos has profound and wide-ranging implications for business decision making. Its impact can be felt in all decisions, from high order strategic decision making to day-to-day decisions. Yet, according to the butterfly effect, even the smallest decision can have dramatic consequences, and long-term strategies are difficult to sustain in a chaotic environment.

If we accept the perspective of chaos theory then a radically different approach to decision making is required. Old assumptions must be discarded and replaced with methods and attitudes which can cope with the realities of chaos. The full implications of chaos have yet to be explored but it is already making an impact on the business world (see Illustration 10.2).

Illustration 10.2 Chaos for the City

Chaos for the City: a Midland Butterfly?

The City has habitually spent enormous sums of money on forecasting the fate of industries and companies and the future movement of the market, often with limited success. The occurrence of major changes in the movement of the market still takes many analysts by surprise. It is against this background that chaos theory is being adopted by some of the City's top firms. Among them is Midland Montague which has appointed a chaoticist to one of its research teams, the aim being to determine those situations when stability is to be expected and when conditions will become more chaotic. So far London firms are wary of applying chaos theory directly to fund management and their dealing on behalf of clients.

How many City firms will adopt chaos theory? Like all future states this is a difficult question to answer. In New York trading systems based on chaos theory have already been introduced, while in London recent chaos seminars have been met by a mixture of enthusiasm and reservations.

For decision makers, though, the implications are wider than the use of a new range of mathematical and statistical techniques. As can be seen from Stacey's (1993) analysis of the need for a change in the frame of reference for strategic management, it is clear that the significance of chaos theory is much wider (Table 10.1).

The specific implications of chaos theory for decision making in general are as wide ranging and profound as those Stacey identifies for strategy. It requires the decision maker to adopt a new and radically different frame of reference, a new perspective where the old methods and certainties are gone, and are replaced by a less secure world requiring a high tolerance of ambiguity and a capacity for imaginative, flexible and speedy responses. More directly we can identify a number of areas where chaos theory requires major shifts in our approach to decision making.

Chaos theory indicates that long-term forecasting is a futile exercise, therefore there

Table 10.1 Chaos: a new framework for strategic management

Today's frame of reference	*A new frame of reference*
Long-term future is predictable to some extent.	Long-term future is unknowable.
Visions and plans are central to strategic management.	Dynamic agendas of strategic issues are central to effective strategic management.
Vision: a single shared organisation-wide intention, a picture of a future state.	Challenge: multiple aspirations, stretching and ambiguous. Arising out of current ill-structured and conflicting issues with long-term consequences.
Strongly shared cultures.	Contradictory counter cultures.
Cohesive teams of managers operating in a state of consensus.	Learning groups of managers, surfacing conflict, engaging in dialogue, publicly testing assertions.
Decision making as a purely logical, analytical process.	Decision making as exploratory, experimental process based on intuition and reasoning by analogy.
Long-term control and development as the monitoring of progress against planned milestones.	Control and development in open-ended situations as a political process.
Constraints provided by rules, systems and rational argument.	Constraints provided by need to build and sustain support. Control as self-policing and learning.
Strategy as the realisation of prior intent.	Strategy as spontaneously emerging from the chaos of challenge and contradiction, through a process of real time learning and politics.
Top management drives and controls strategic direction.	Top management creates favourable conditions for complex learning and politics.
General mental models and prescriptions for many specific situations.	New mental models required for each new strategic situation.
Adaptive equilibrium with the environment.	Non-equilibrium, creative interaction with the environment.

needs to be a recognition of the fact that decisions taken with the long-term in view are likely to be flawed. Attention is better given to short-term forecasting and short-term decisions where chaos theory suggests that there may be a chance of 'getting it right'. Chaos theory has led to developments which provide new insights and techniques which can refine the quality of short-term forecasts. An example of this can be found in weather forecasting. While the weather system has been identified as the archetypal chaotic system the recognition of this has led to improvements in short-term weather forecasts. The new method involves looking at the general weather situation at the present moment and finding similar situations from the past. If the outcome of the past situations are more or less the same, then the weather can be said to be in a predictable mode with a high probability that the previous patterns will be repeated. If, however, the outcomes of the previous situations vary, then the weather is recognised to be in a chaotic and hence unpredictable mode. These lessons might easily be transferred to business and if long-term forecasting is pointless, then competitive edge will be gained from having the best short-term forecasts.

Recognising the unpredictability of events will enhance the importance of contingency planning. It is not enough to have a single strategy and set of tactics. To cope with uncertainties it is necessary to develop a whole set of plans and fallback positions. Organisations will already do this to some extent but chaos theory makes the activity of contingency planning more central to management's task. It cannot be regarded as of secondary importance and undertaken as a haphazard afterthought to the central planning process. Contingency planning requires the same amount of resources and skill as any other form of planning, and the message of chaos theory is that there is a high probability that organisational survival will be dependent on decisions taken in the process of planning for unforeseen contingencies.

If traditional methods of decision making placed a high priority on rational, logical procedures then decision making under chaos places an equal emphasis on intuitive and imaginative approaches. Chaos theory points up the failings of traditional approaches and suggests that any faith in them is misplaced. However, in many organisations, these methods are highly regarded and the ideas and solutions generated by such methods are afforded a higher status than those arrived at by less conventional methods. What is required is a recognition, in such organisations, of the value of intuition and creativity. Conditions need to be created to foster these skills and to reward those who possess them. These skills are not secondary or simply an addition to traditional approaches. They have a high value in their own right. Though the rational decision maker would deny it, chaos theory proposes that even decisions taken with full adherence to more traditional methods contain elements of guesswork and inaccuracy. This should not be denied and the value of the non-rational approach must be recognised and enhanced.

Organisational structures will need to change if the lessons of chaos theory are to be implemented. Structures and mechanisms to co-ordinate and control the activities of organisational members have been designed with responsibility for decision making clearly located in certain positions, together with procedures for operating consistently and logically over time. For example, a production manager will be responsible for taking decisions and following procedures defined as necessary to produce the product, the position of the manager will be relatively permanent as will the practices and procedures followed during decision making. Chaos theory requires that, given that futures are unknown and the unexpected is to be expected, organisations develop temporary systems and structures which can readily be modified as conditions change. Organisational structures and systems which stress the persisting nature of roles and procedures are likely to have problems in adjusting to change when it occurs. Decisions need to be taken by the most appropriate person or persons at a particular time. Procedures that work under some circumstances will break down as the circumstances change. There are discontinuities in organisational life and the creation of temporary structures, e.g., a project team to be disbanded on completion of the project, and temporary procedures, e.g., suspending weekly meetings in favour of daily meetings for a short period, are more likely to cope with the realities of a chaotic world.

The suggestions so far, as ways of improving decision making in the light of chaos theory, are not likely to be implemented if the prevailing culture of an organisation is shaped by the norms and values of traditional approaches. It is imperative that organisations have a culture based on the new, radical assumptions of chaos theory. Rather than a culture which stresses unity, there needs to be an emphasis on diversity and a recognition of the existence of multiple cultures in the organisation. Instead of valuing conformity, it must value creative deviance. The power of the position must not be allowed to detract from the abilities of all to contribute to the taking of decisions. The vision of a long-term desirable future state must be relegated as secondary to facing up to the current problem of coping with the challenges of a turbulent external environment. Existing values about the worth and integrity of traditional decision-making methods must be discarded in favour of values which stress the worth of novelty, conflict, imagination, intuition and creativity. Cultural change in organisations is not easily achieved. It is likely to be a matter of years rather than months before realistic results can be achieved. Nonetheless, without major shifts in culture most organisations will not be able to benefit from the insights of the chaos perspective.

CONCLUSION

The research into chaos has revealed many of the patterns to be found in chaotic systems. It is for the business decision maker to make further explorations to reveal underlying patterns in the chaos of the world of business. The suggestion is that such patterns will at least make the decision maker aware of some of the limitations in their approach to resolving problems. At best this quest may reveal pools of stability in the turbulence of the environment, allowing some decisions to be taken with a greater certainty than at present.

The main influences of chaos theory on decision making may be summarised as follows:

- The need to focus on short-term rather than long-term decision making.
- The importance of contingency planning as part of any organisation's decision-making process.
- The need to value intuitive and imaginative approaches to decision making.
- The significance of developing temporary structures and systems.
- The modification of corporate cultures to incorporate new and relevant values and norms.
- The need to look for order within chaos.

In many ways the contribution of chaos theory to decision making is negative. It says what cannot be done, what factors cannot be controlled, the limitations of prediction and the misplaced faith in measurement. While it is true that these conclusions do focus on what not to do, they should nonetheless not be undervalued. It is equally important to know the limitations of our capacities as it is to know what we can realistically achieve. However, chaos theory is more than a set of negative prescriptions. As we have seen, acting in the light of chaos theory there are many steps to be taken that will improve decision making in an organisation.

EXERCISE: RURITAINIAN STOCK MARKET

You are required to calculate movements on a stock exchange for a number of years given a magic number 0.3. This can be done on a calculator, but it is much more efficient if a spread-sheet is used on a computer. The approach below assumes that you have access to a suitable spread-sheet on a computer.

Step 1: Sign on to the computer.
Step 2: Execute the spread-sheet command.
Step 3: Display a blank spread-sheet and locate the cursor in cell A1.
Step 4: Type 0.3 and press return.
Step 5: Use the arrow to move the cursor to cell A2.
Step 6: Type +A1*A1*2-1 and press return.
Step 7: Copy the results of the calculation into cells A3 down to, say, A12.

The result is a column showing a sequence of positive and negative values which can be displayed on a graph as in Fig. 10.7.

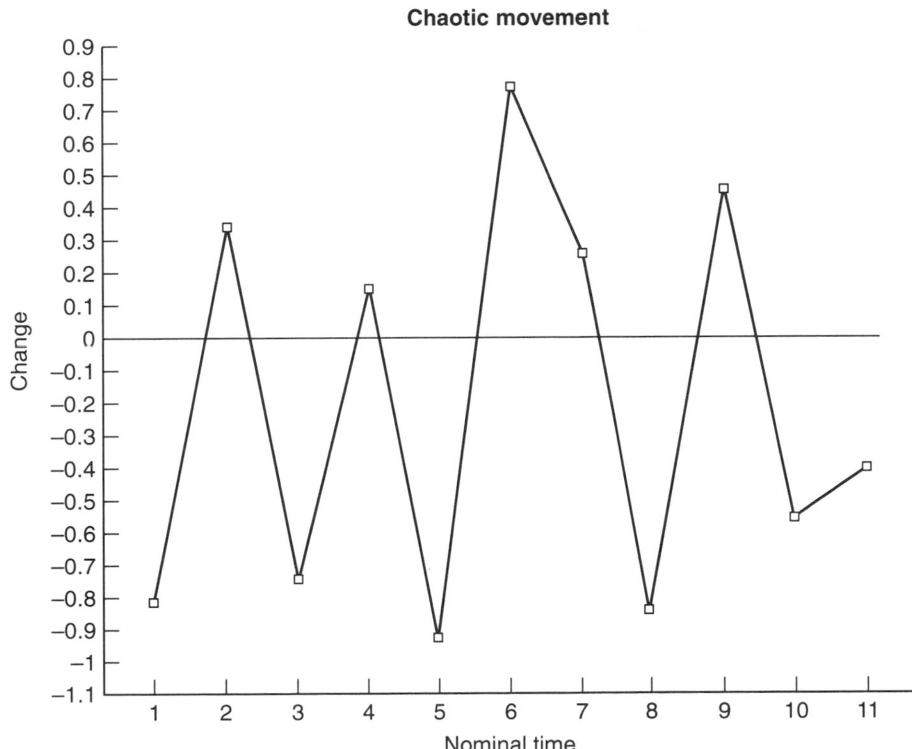

Fig. 10.7 Chaos on the stock exchange?

To calculate the effect of rumours of insider dealing use 0.3001 in cell A1 and so on.

Questions

What conclusions can be drawn from the comparisons of the sequences, and/or graphs obtained, by different magic numbers.

Do these sequences demonstrate the 'Butterfly Effect'?

What are the implications of this exercise for forecasting and decision making in the real world?

GLOSSARY OF MAIN TERMS

Fractal A shape which, despite constant magnification, retains its initial geometric properties.

Discontinuities Abrupt un-predictable changes not based on previous data.

Iteration A sequence of calculations based on prior calculations, for which the computer is particularly well suited.

Mandelbrot Set A particularly well known fractal discovered by B. Mandelbrot which consists of a computer illustration of the equation $Z \rightarrow Z^2 + C$
where Z begins at zero and C is the complex number corresponding to the point being tested. For a more detailed account and how to produce a Mandelbrot set on your own computer see Gleick (1987), pp 231-232.

Strange attractors Mathematical expressions, though frequently shown as pictures, which describe the behaviour of chaotic systems. (The picture of the mathematics shows a revolution(s) around a centre(s))

REFERENCES

Stacey, R. (1993) 'Strategy as Order Emerging from Chaos', *Long-Range Planning*, Vol.26, No 1.

FURTHER READING

Barnsley, M. F. (1988) *Fractals Everywhere*, Academic Press.

Gleick, J. (1987) *Chaos: Making a New Science*, Heinemann.

Mandelbrot, B. (1982) *The Fractal Geometry of Nature*, W. H. Freeman & Co.

Peters, E. (1990) *Chaos and Order in the Capital Markets*, Wiley.

Stacey, R. (1992) *Managing Chaos*, Kogan Page.

Stewart, I. (1989) *Does God Play Dice?* Blackwell, Oxford.

CHAPTER 11

Developing skills in decision making

David Jennings, Ray Lye, Alan Pizzey, James Stewart, Stuart Wattam, Paul Whysall

INTRODUCTION

This final chapter is based upon an extended case study. The purpose is to provide practice in applying the various concepts, theories and techniques that have been considered in the earlier chapters. The case should be read through carefully, possibly several times, and then considered from the point of each of the contexts identified in Chapter 1 (Fig. 1.7):

- Organisation and group behaviour and psychology
- Analysis and model building
- Strategic context
- Goals, objectives and ethics
- Degree of uncertainty

Taking one perspective at a time, develop your own understanding of the situation.

The case study is followed by a discussion of the decision-making issues that it raises. The chapter concludes with an examination of the rationality of the decision-making process.

HEREFORD CONTAINERS: CASE STUDY

Introduction

This case study concerns a plant manufacturing and selling corrugated cardboard cases. The plant is part of a packaging group owned by a conglomerate, Reed International, the case is set in 1986.

Reed International and the Reed Packaging Group

In 1968 Britain's biggest paper producer, Albert Reed, merged with a major publishing house, International Publishing Corporation (IPC). During the 1970s the resulting company, Reed International, pursued a policy of growth by diversification and under the leadership of Don Ryder became one of the UK's top ten companies. The growth was funded by using debt raised mainly on European markets in the form of 10-year loan stock. In the late 1960s/early 1970s corrugated packaging was a cash generator for Reed International.

In 1975/76 the paper market slumped and Reed were in trouble as profits dropped to £37m on a turnover of £lbn. A mountain of debts made all attempts at rationalisation difficult. From 1977 to 1981, under new leadership, the workforce was cut from 86,000 to 60,000 and Reed began to sell off its overseas interests.

In the early 1980s Reed's printing and national newspaper businesses were badly affected by strikes. In 1982 Mr Jarratt the new chairman sold Odhams, a troublesome and loss making printing subsidiary, to Robert Maxwell, and in 1984 Maxwell was again the buyer, this time of the *Mirror* group of newspapers, for £90m cash. Subsequent disposals have included London and Provincial (poster advertising), Spicer-Cowan (paper merchants), Crown and Sunworthy (wallpaper), Sanderson (decorative products), a paper company, and Hamlyn the book publishers. Since 1984 proceeds from disposals have exceeded £250m. This sum has been more than matched by spending on acquisitions in an attempt to reprofile the company as, first and foremost, a publisher.

Reed International

	Group Turnover		*TP/CE**
	1981/82	*1985/86*	*1985/86*
Publishing	23%	38%	31%
Paint & DIY	9%	15%	20%
Packaging	16%	18%	21%
Paper	16%	21%	15%
Other product area	36%	8%	
Turnover (£m)	1,699	1,931	

* Trading Profit/Capital Employed (HCA basis)

(Source: Company Report and General Information Booklet)

As well as the current rationalisation towards publishing there are also considerable changes occurring in the top management of the group. The present CEO is near retirement and is due to be replaced by an ex-director of Sainsburys; there is also a new financial director. Within the Reed Packaging Group the MD has been replaced by a director from the Canadian operations. The general consensus is that the new MD is ambitious and will be trying to make a name for himself within Reed International.

Reed Corrugated Cases (RCC) is part of the Reed Packaging Group. RCC consists of 12 plants, 10 of which produce conventional flute at sites located throughout the UK. Each of these plants produce a wide range of products for their local areas. The products are based upon two standards of card, 3mm (B grade) and 4mm (C grade). The two sizes account for 95 per cent of the market. The two other plants in RCC deal with the specialist end of the market, one producing heavy duty flute (A grade) and the other a fine (E grade) flute of 2mm. Together these grades account for the remaining 5 per cent of the market. The two plants service the market on a national rather than a local basis.

The UK corrugated cardboard box industry consists of approximately 300 firms. Reed are the market leaders with a 20 per cent share of the market. They are followed by three major competitors, UK Corrugated, St Regis and Bowater, each with a 15 per cent–16per cent share. The fastest growing competitor is Lin Pack which currently has 12 per cent of the market. The majority of firms are 'convertors' that buy-in board rather than having the facility to manufacture board themselves. There are about 40 'prime producers' (producers of board) in the market, including Reed.

The emergence of convertors has been the major change in the market in the past 12 years. Small convertors operate at the lower end of the market, in the 500–2,000 box range.

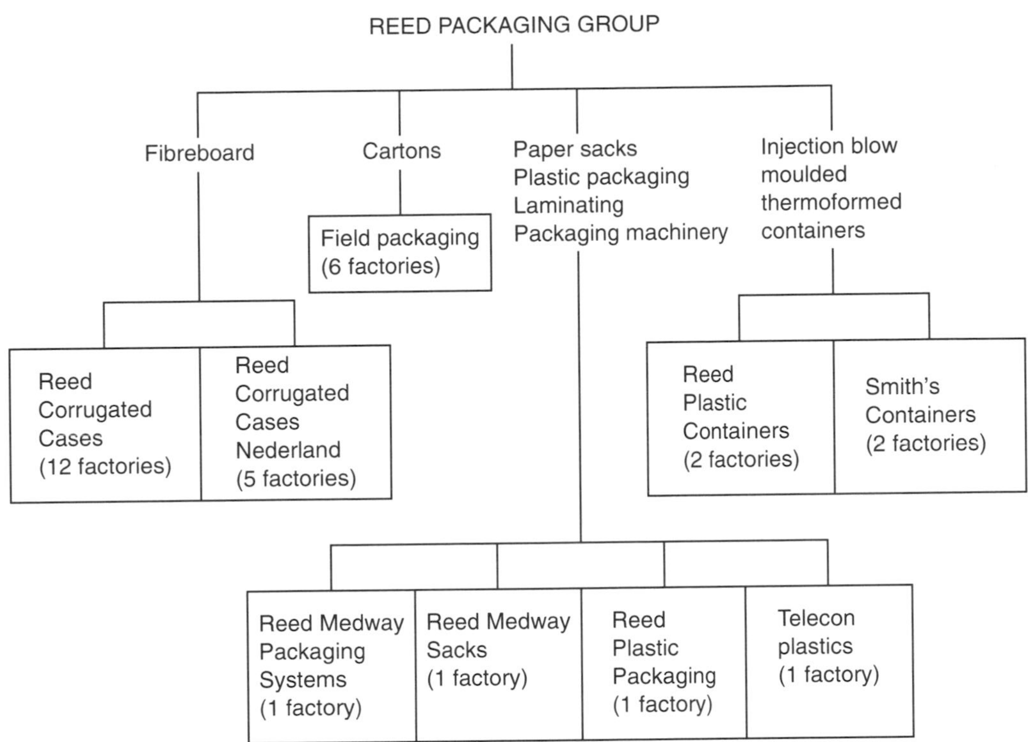

Fig. 11.1 Reed Packaging Group

They buy-in board from the prime producers and, because they do not have the manufacturing facilities and overheads associated with board manufacture, they have achieved considerable cost advantages. In addition, many of the convertors employ casual labour, paying 40 per cent below the wage rate nationally negotiated between Reed and the trades union SOGAT. The convertors can also purchase machinery cheaply from companies which have folded, indeed they often purchase equipment from companies which they have themselves operated in other areas of the country.

The Hereford Plant

The Hereford packaging plant was established in 1930 to provide boxes for the local jam factory. In 1956 the firm was taken over by Reed and benefited from Reed's growth strategy of the late 1960s and 1970s. Currently the Hereford plant employs 192 people including 53 staff. The plant is organised on a departmental basis.

The plant produces board and corrugated cardboard cases. A typical use for the cases is to provide a container for multiple packets of food product during transportation from manufacturer to store; often the cases are used in displays at the retail outlet.

Corrugated cardboard is an adaptable material and the technical properties of corrugated cases are continually being improved by Reed and other board manufacturers. Cases made with a coarse flute can provide higher impact resistance, those with a fine flute have greater strength against compression from weights placed upon them, by

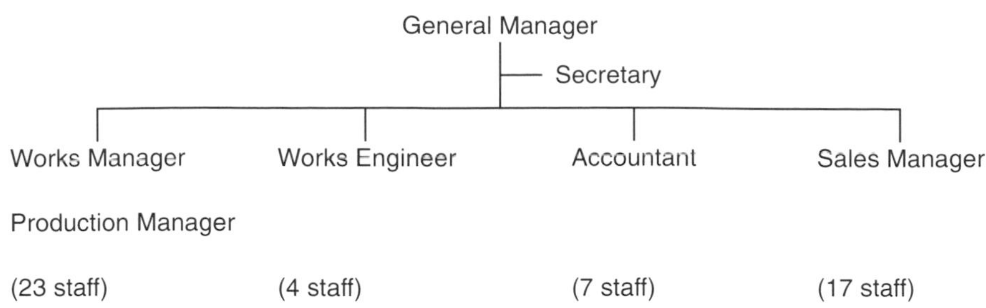

Fig 11.2 Hereford Plant: organisation

stacking, for example. If two pieces of board are combined at right angles, the result is a product with strength and rigidity equal to that of heavy-duty plywood. The surface and fluting of a case can be treated to reduce the absorbtion of moisture so that rigidity is maintained. Internal surfaces may be treated to provide a container for liquids and, within a box, a plastic bag and tap can supply a strong and convenient container for transporting and dispensing liquids. These containers range in volume from 2 to 1600 litres and are suitable for a wide variety of foods such as milk, wine, and vegetable oil, as well as industrial products, such as oil, where they have an advantage over metal drums through using up to 90 per cent less storage space when empty.

Further product characteristics can be achieved through the printing that appears on the case. While some of Hereford's customers only require a stencilled description of contents, others pay a premium to gain the particular colour tones and images that are associated with their products.

To achieve the highest quality of finish, considerable modification of the manufacturing process, is needed; this is achieved through a process called 'pre-print'. Two of the other factories in the RCC group pre-print the outer paper of the case before the paper is bonded to the board. In order that the case outlines are cut precisely to this pattern, infra red sensors, reading patterns in the pre-print, are linked to the cutting knives of board machines. This innovation, 'registered chop', has only become operational in the last few years. It is an expensive process adding 10 per cent to the costs of a case. Nevertheless the process has become popular with customers to the extent that 10 per cent of the industry's sales are now derived from pre-print, a figure that is expected to rise to about 15 per cent over the next three years.

Production

Each of RCC's plants is supplied with paper through centralised purchasing on the basis of six-month contracts entered into by Reed International.

The case production process begins with the manufacture of board, a sandwich comprised of an outer and inner card containing a corrugation (flute). The three components are welded together by starch under heat and pressure in a board machine. Before leaving the machine the board is cut and scored to produce the blank from which the cardboard case will be erected. The deckle (width) of the roll is sufficient to allow a number of different case layouts to be simultaneously cut from the board.

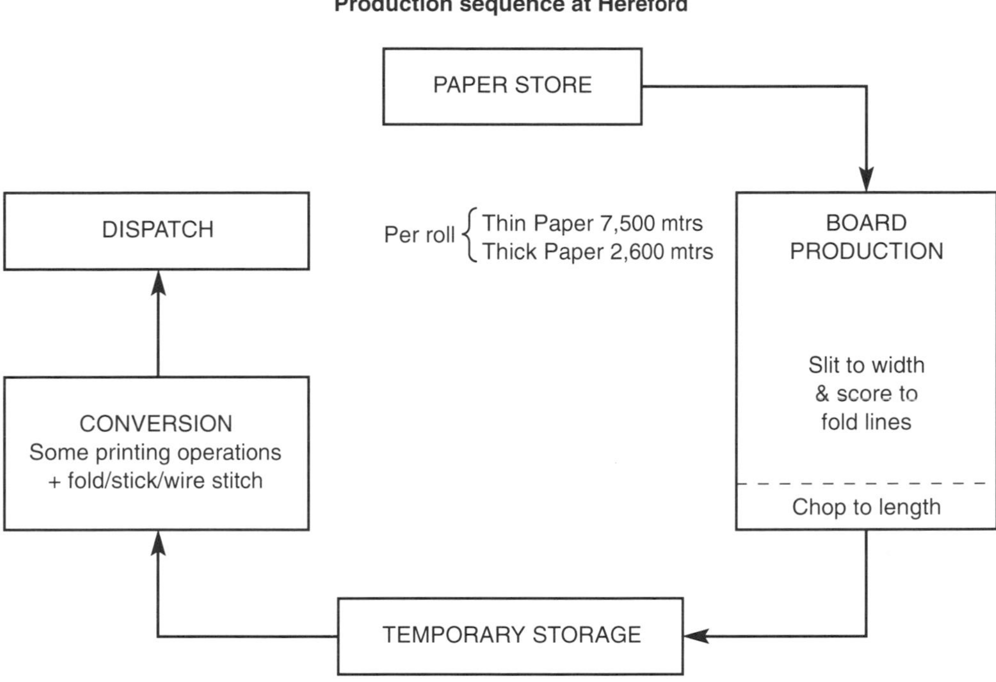

Fig. 11.3 Production sequence at Hereford

Use of capacity

The Board Machine operates on a two-shift basis, night shift and 6am to 2pm. Average run is 40–45 minutes.
Storage space, especially dispatch, is effectively at 95 per cent capacity. Conversion is operating at 90 per cent of capacity.
The greatest pressure upon capacity is caused by periods of seasonality in the food industry.

The partly finished cases are taken from the board machine to temporary storage and then to further processing and completion, by printing, folding, gluing and stitching, as necessary, before the flattened cases are dispatched.

Traditionally, throughout Reed Corrugated Cases and the industry, the manufacture of cases has followed this integrated approach, only in recent years has there emerged a growing number of small manufacturers, convertors, who do not produce their own board.

The Works Manager, Ken Bailey, has been at Hereford for over 15 years; in that time he has persistently sought to improve the efficiency of the plant. He now feels frustrated by physical and financial constraints. The Hereford factory (board machine and conversion) is housed in a 53-year-old building on a site that is bounded by a railway line and by National Trust property. The years of growth in turnover have led to a situation where space is at a premium, forcing a layout where each stage of production is distributed by pallets and ad-hoc conveyor systems. Most of these conveyors have been built in-house by engineers in what Ken Bailey refers to as a self-help policy. They provide considerable improvements in efficiency at low cost when compared to the cost of buying such systems outside. There is an acute shortage of space and, in contrast to many of the other factories in RCC, only a half a day of Hereford's production can be stored at the factory. Consequently little attempt is made to optimise distribution; production, as far as possible, is taken straight to a lorry for dispatch to the customer.

The economics of operating the Hereford plant also reflect the integrated nature of production and the age of the plant and machinery. While convertors may find it economic to produce a run of 500 cases, a company which also manufactures board has first to meet the cost of machine setting, approximately £500, and consequently, depending on the value of each case, economic production requires a minimum run of 1,000–2,000 cases. The longest runs are for 100,000 cases but are typically 2,500–3,000 cases.

The board machine was installed in 1938 and has proved remarkable for its incorporation of innovations, including the sensors for cutting pre-printed cases. Over the last ten years productivity has been steadily improved from an indexed level of 120 to the present level of 160. The most recent designs of board machine are highly sophisticated and require low manning levels. With short resetting time they provide a far cheaper output than the machines currently used by RCC. In the near future one of these machines will be installed in RCC's Newbury plant. To provide a similar level of efficiency at Hereford would require an investment of £3–4m to be spent over three years. Ken Bailey knows that approval for such investment would be dependent on the proposal meeting a required rate of return of 30 per cent. The target return on investment was introduced some five years ago when the industry ceased to produce high cash returns. Approval for sums up to £100,000 are within the scope of RCC; for expenditure up to £1m approval is required from the Packaging Group, and above £1m, approval is required from Reed International.

Besides pursuing greater efficiency, the Works Manager also tries to meet customer requirements for quality and delivery. Meeting short delivery deadlines helps Ken Bailey to cope with the lack of storage space but it typically requires production schedules to be interrupted, increasing the number of machine set-ups and detracting from an optimal layout of the patterns to be cut.

Currently Hereford is attempting to gain the British Standards Kite mark for quality. This is seen as another selling point for the customer but achieving the standard will raise the internal rejection rate of cases to 2 per cent of sales, double the plant's present figure. The remaining waste is due to trim loss (loss on cutting at the edge of the paper roll and between patterns). In a sense wastage understates the cost of quality. Generally the higher the product finish the slower the speed at which the board machine can be run. However, with a limit on the space available for conversion, the board machine's production rate is usually restricted to below capacity working.

Sales

Reed do not advertise in the general press and advertising in trade publications is kept to a minimum. Consequently, despite its size, Reed has a relatively low profile. At Hereford resources are concentrated on producing mail shots and brochures for potential clients. Peter Grundy, the Sales Manager, regards the plant's products as potentially unique to each individual customer's requirement and, until recently, sales representatives had only limited sales literature to show the customer.

Mr Grundy is deeply concerned about Hereford's sales and the plant's market share. Performance targets for sales are set by Reed International. Taken over the whole of RCC it is expected that at least a 20 per cent share of the market will be held and that growth of market share by 0.2 to 0.3 per cent per annum will occur. Hereford has a 14 per cent share of its local market, and this represents the second lowest share of the ten general producers in RCC.

The Sales Manager believes that the low market share reflects the competitive position that the Hereford plant faces in servicing its region. The local industrial base is heavily concentrated on the food and poultry industries and the vast majority of Hereford's customers are from those industries; this makes the plant particularly sensitive to certain trends.

The emergence of large supermarkets has altered Hereford's market drastically. First, large multiples are able to exert considerable pressure on food producers (major customers for Reed) in terms of pricing and delivery. This has led to a squeeze on margins and a move towards Just-in-Time inventory systems. Second, supermarkets have altered the nature of the product required. Whereas previously all food products were packed in boxes, supermarkets now insist that much of the canned produce is packed on cardboard trays and shrink wrapped. This development has greatly decreased volumes in the industry. The situation has been made worse by the growing tendency for manufacturers to undertake their own packaging, buying the board from board producers such as Reed.

The industry has also suffered from the effects of the economic recession of the early 1980s. The volume figure for Reed is still recuperating, this recovery has in part been achieved by moving into other product areas of the market, e.g., oil containers.

For prime producers, competition from convertors has depressed both price and market share. The convertors do this by offering lower prices on their (limited) range, but the customer then expects low prices from the prime producers for the remainder of the required supply. The convertors also add to the industry's severe over-capacity.

There has been a considerable change in the Sales Manager's attitude to business. In the past Mr Grundy was prepared to turn down orders which did not make a 25 per cent profit, but now he is quoting for volume business on a contribution basis. As well as competing on price, Hereford also provide a wide range of services for their customers. The services include access to the group's Packaging Advisory Centre to provide the customer with technical and design advice. The Sales Manager sees these services as often essential in getting customers to invite Reed to quote for business. In addition, to gain the order, Hereford must offer delivery to customer demand, attractive credit terms and a price that is competitive with that quoted by the convertors.

The delivery position has also changed radically from ten years ago, when a three month lead time was given on orders; it is now common practice for large customers to require delivery at 2–3 days' notice.

Food and poultry manufacturers are under considerable pressure from large multiples in terms of both when and how they deliver their products. Recently multiples have sought to play a direct role in the supply of packaging to the food manufacturers. Multiples have approached Hereford directly and asked them to quote for their supplier's business and, if the quote is accepted, to pay a rebate direct to the retailer without the food supplier, who pays for the packaging, knowing about the deal. There is little hope of legal intervention in this situation.

Despite the competitive pressures there has been an improvement in Hereford's sales and Peter Grundy has developed the plant's customer profile to a total of over 280 accounts with 85 per cent of the volume arising from 20 key accounts. This is a considerable improvement on the situation of 5 years ago when 5 customers accounted for 80 per cent of the volume.

Accounting

Reed International have established targets for debtors (7.5 weeks) and stocks (4.5 weeks); there are also targets for output per man/hour and labour costs per unit of output. In general the targets are attainable; however, it is becoming increasingly difficult to achieve the debtor figure. Reed's targets do not explicitly mention profitability, but there is a growing feeling throughout RCC that Reed International is becoming more concerned with profitability and that an explicit goal may soon be set.

Ted Cresswell is the head of Hereford's Accounting Department and, in common with his colleagues, he has concerns about the plant's performance. At a recent meeting of the management group (the General Manager and the departmental heads) he presented a briefing paper on the consequences of Hereford failing to maintain sales. The paper showed that a drop in sales volume of 30 per cent would place the Hereford plant in a position where it might not be economic to have a board machine, hence the plant would become a convertor. The paper also showed that a continuation of the pressure on margins would mean that in the coming year output would have to increase by at least 6 per cent in order to maintain the present level of profitability.

The conclusions of the paper were accepted by the meeting and a long discussion followed to identify possible courses of action, but all the managers felt that they were simply re-stating their own departmental views and that no new proposals had emerged from the meeting.

On the next pages we show the main figures and statistics relating to Hereford in 1986. Included are the Balance Sheet and Profit and Loss account to 31 March of that year.

Hereford Containers

Turnover (£m)	85/86	84/85	83/84	82/83
	8.5	8.0	7.5	6.8

Costs as % of selling price	%
Materials (inc. waste)	50
Labour (inc. all benefits)	20
Energy	2
Distribution (pure)	3
(labour)	1
Other productive materials (inks, wire for stitching, etc.)	2
Maintenance costs	3

Costings are regarded as accurate on the more standard products but may be open to 20-30% error on non-standard.

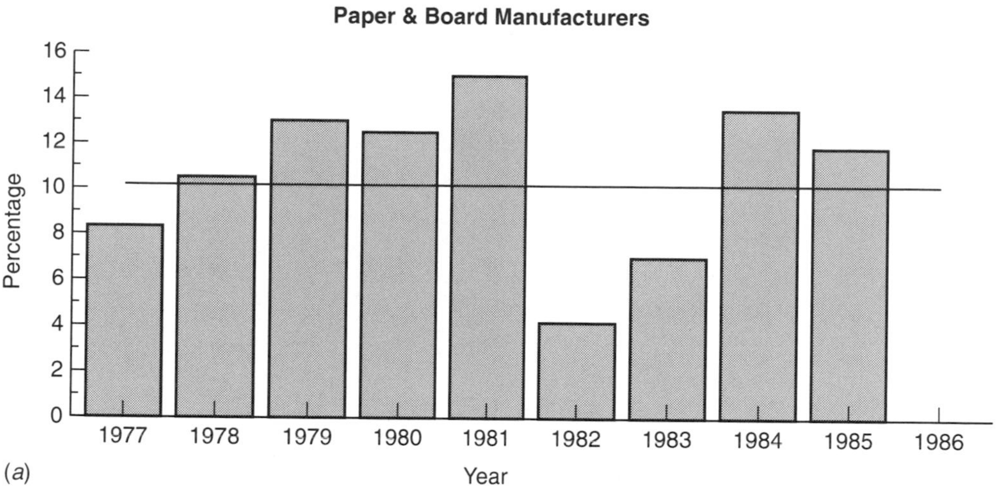

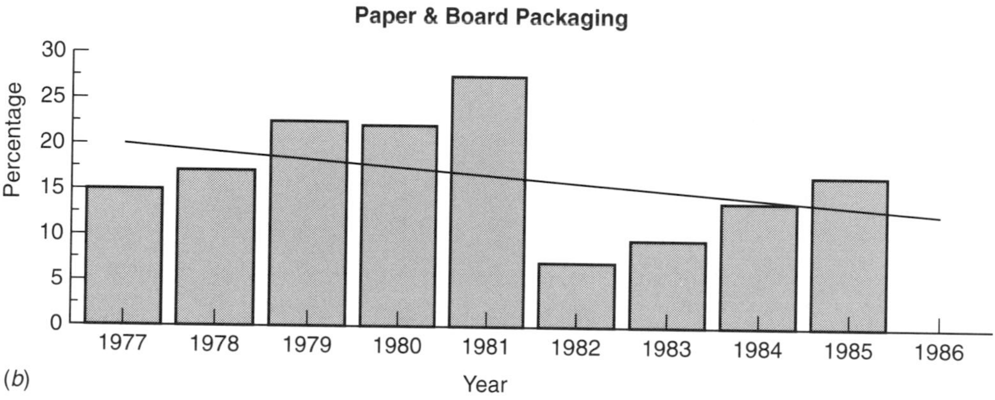

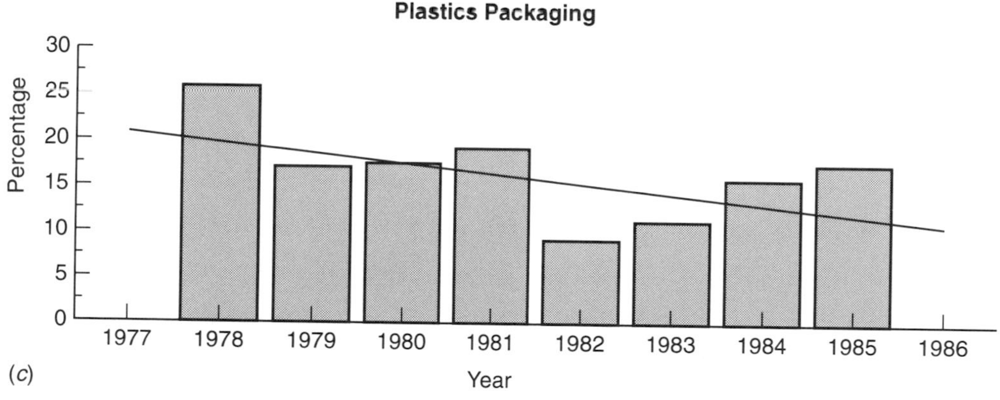

The trend line, extrapolated for one year, is shown where five years' figures are available. (Source: *Industrial Performance Analysis 1986/87 edition.*)

Fig. 11.4 Average industry return on capital (HCA)

Hereford Containers
Balance Sheet as at 31st March 1986

1985					*1986*
		Fixed Assets:	*Cost/ valuation (£000)*	*Depreciation to date (£000)*	*Net (£000)*
842		Land and buildings at valuation	874	50	824
1,161		Plant and Machinery at cost	2 ,620	1,612	1,008
2, 003			3,494	1,662	1,832
		Current Assets:			
	580	Stocks		641	
	1,292	Debtors		1,524	
	403	Cash at bank and in hand		448	
	2, 275			2,613	
		Less Creditors:			
	1,665	Amount falling due within one Year		1,865	
610		*Net Current Assets*			748
2,613					2,580
		Less Creditors: Amounts falling due after more than one Year			
	900	Loan Capital		900	
1,145	245	Other		–	900
1,468					1,680
		Financed by:			
		Capital and Reserves			
500		Called up share Capital			500
458		Revaluation Reserve			458
510		Retained Profits			722
1,468					1,680

Profit and Loss Account
For the year ending 31 March 1986

	1986 (£000)	*1985 (£000)*
Turnover	8,520	8,011
Increase in stocks of finished goods and work in progress	30	10
	8,550	8,021
Less Expenses:		
Raw materials and consumables	4,386	4,050
Staff costs	1,682	1,580
Heat, light and power	229	210
Distribution costs	398	380
Manufacturing overheads	305	302
Depreciation	225	210
Indirect overheads	822	805
Interest	300	248
	8,347	7,785
Net Profit before tax	203	236
Tax on profit from ordinary activities	58	71
Net Profit for the financial year	145	165

This case is intended to be used as a basis for class discussion rather than to illustrate effective or ineffective handling of an administrative situation. The case is based on a real life situation so, in order to provide confidentiality the location of the plant, the identities of individuals and certain data have been changed.

HEREFORD CONTAINERS: DISCUSSION

ORGANISATION AND GROUP BEHAVIOUR AND PSYCHOLOGY

Organisation and group behaviour

At Hereford Containers there is an identifiable management group consisting of the Works Manager, Works Engineer, Accountant and Sales Manager headed up by the General Manager. However, there is little evidence of the company gaining from the benefits of group decision making. The case shows a bias towards individual actions, e.g., the Works Manager's attempts, despite physical and financial constraints, to improve the efficiency of the plant. The concerns of the various managers over the profitability issue show that departmental interests are prevalent and there is little in the way of a united strategy. A recognised benefit of group decision making is an improvement in morale. In the management group at Hereford Containers, there appears to be a current lack of morale as indicated by the response to the meeting of the management group, 'all the managers felt that they were simply restating their own departmental views and that no new proposals had emerged from the meeting'.

Though we do not have full evidence we can conclude that the management are not operating as an effective group. While there is not the cohesiveness in the group to suggest the existence of groupthink, there is some of the complacency and failure to consider alternatives which go with the phenomenon.

At the general level no mention is made of employee participation in decision making and this appears to be an area where the organisation may be missing out, preferring a more traditional top-down mode of decision making.

At first glance the organisation structure of the company appears to conform to the lean-form/simple-structure recommended by Peters and Waterman. There are few levels of management and the structure is the basic line form. However, as part of the Reed International group, there is a degree of centralisation (shown in the process of getting approval for various levels of capital expenditure), and the basically flat structure of Hereford Containers is seen as much taller when viewed in the context of the group. The present problems faced by Hereford Containers appear to be more understandable as the outcome of a centralised, tall organisation than as that of the apparent decentralised, flat structure. The disadvantages of the centralised, tall organisation, noted in Chapter 3 are seen to apply in this company, namely, the problems of co-ordinating specialists, the distance between central and local decision makers, the lack of flexible responses to immediate problems and a lack of morale.

There is also evidence in the case of a lack of leadership, both from the parent organisation and within Hereford Containers. The approach to leadership in this situation is very *laissez-faire*. From the approaches to leadership considered in Chapter 3 the most suitable approach for the company is a contingency approach showing a flexibility which can cope with the special problems faced by Hereford containers at the present moment. An approach based on a traitist or style view of leadership would tend to create a situation where there is little chance of making the adjustments necessary to face up to the dynamic, constantly changing market conditions.

A final comment on organisation in Hereford Containers shows the significance of organisational climate and culture. If we try to evaluate the climate in the company it appears to be cloudy and overcast. There is little that can be described as sunny or uplifting. The atmosphere this creates for taking decisions suggests that future plans may be dogged by a degree of fatalism and pessimism which will prevent the company taking the correct decisions to remedy their present problems. Similarly, the lack of a strong culture with clearly stated and generally held values is likely to lead to a certain amount of politicking and compromise, which will mean that decisions will be taken which do not address the fundamental problems the company faces.

Psychology

The Hereford Containers case study contains a number of issues and features which illustrate the potential value of understanding the psychological aspects of decision making. The most obvious of these are described and discussed below.

Reed International was created by a merger of two large and established companies. The two businesses, paper production and publishing, are likely to have been very different in character. The types of operations and the consequent effects in terms of people suited to the separate industries will have meant that the individuals employed are unlikely to have been similar personalities. Holland's theory of vocational personality types, reviewed in Chapter 4, would support this assertion.

It is also likely that the different sets of employees will have had different sets of 'personal constructs'. These are developed on the basis of experience. Different types of experiences produce different constructs. Perhaps even totally different 'world views' were held by staff throughout the hierarchy of each original company. It is certainly likely that individual definitions of 'personal growth' and 'self-actualisation' varied across the two original companies.

All of this suggests some potential difficulties in effective communication between senior managers from different parts of the new company. This position may also be particularly acute from Hereford Containers' point of view, given that Reed International would have to approve major investment, i.e., any sum over £1m, at a time when it is deliberately seeking to re-position itself in the publishing industry.

Some specific indications of potential personality differences are also contained in the case. The new MD of the Packaging Group is Canadian. Most perspectives in psychology ascribe an important role to life experiences, especially early ones, in personality development; this is certainly true of the psychodynamic, behaviourist and cognitive approaches. It is safe to assume that life in Canada differs from life in the UK to the extent of producing different beliefs and values in their individual citizens. Thus, the new MD is likely to perceive and interpret situations differently from other managers. The new MD's ambitious nature may also affect his decision-making behaviour.

There are also different perspectives within Hereford Containers itself. The Works Manager, Ken Bailey, is experiencing considerable frustration. This is a psychological state well recognised in the psychodynamic approach as being likely to affect judgement and influence decisions and behaviour. It is also apparent that Bailey values efficiency and this may bring him into conflict with others involved in decisions who give a higher priority to alternative performance measures. The existence of such conflict is also suggested by the recent management meeting. To quote the case, 'Managers felt that they were simply restating their own departmental views'.

Other items in the case support the inference drawn from the quote. Peter Grundy is concerned about sales. He also seems to see a need to offer varying specifications to meet customer requirements. This, though, is more costly in production terms and therefore a difficult strategy in a price-sensitive and competitive market. The targeting of profitability by Reed International will produce pressure to reduce costs and this may lead to conflict between Grundy and Ted Cresswell. Such conflict will in part be the result of different interpretations of reality arising from diverse personal constructs and unique world views.

The case describes a situation in which individual decision makers come from a variety of backgrounds. Some may be from publishing and others from paper production. Additionally, a key player is Canadian and will have had different life experiences from the other senior managers. This suggests wide variation in 'learned behaviours', 'personal constructs' and 'unique world views'. The consequences for achieving mutually shared perceptions and interpretations of reality are obvious.

Particular individuals such as the MD and Ken Bailey are experiencing different though significant psychological pressures; ambition in a 'spotlight' position for one and frustration in an established position for the other.

All of these factors and more will impact upon and have consequences for the decision-making processes engaged in and for any decisions eventually taken.

ANALYSIS AND MODEL BUILDING

Soft systems analysis

The Hereford case study describes a complex situation involving a number of organisations. Soft Systems Methodology can provide a useful analysis of the situation by:

- Describing the situation as a whole, including matters of fact, value, climate and 'the feel of the situation'.
- Developing alternative ways of viewing the situation in order to diagnose problems.

Using the case study material a Rich Picture can be developed as in Fig. 11.5. The picture should be carefully examined; it can be amended and added to in order to express the reader's (the analyst's) understanding of the situation.

Figure 11.5 shows a factory that is located in a rural situation, hemmed in by trees and a railway line. The same rural context exists for the convertors, a set of 'Joe Bloggs' companies, and for the farms that are a part of the customer base. Hereford appears as an antiquated and congested site, mostly operating at near to capacity. The management group seems to be rather formal, conducting a round-the-table discussion, each of the managers retaining his/her own view of the situation. The atmosphere of the Hereford plant contrasts with that of the parent company, Reed International. Reed appears as a corporate, jet-setting organisation with a concern for improving profitability and re-profiling the group. The organisation passes down paper, new products and services, but also high wage rates. The flow of investment monies is questionable. The Newbury plant looks much more like the Reed organisation, and it receives investment. The supermarkets are shown by an entity, 'UK Groceries Ltd'; concerned with managing margins, the entity is able to bypass the Hereford plant in order to gain direct access to the farmer and convertors. Hereford appears encircled.

A number of notional systems can be proposed with which to examine Hereford's situation. Many different systems can be proposed. Examining a few of those that are based upon issues that face the plant, the plant can be seen as:

- A system for using space to generate value.
- A system to counter the power of the supermarkets.
- A system to attract investment.
- A system to develop and integrate a management team.

Taking the first of these notional systems, 'A system for using space to generate value', the sequence of activities shown in Fig. 11.6. can be specified.

Comparing the conceptual model to the 'real world' will help to generate an agenda as a basis for discussions aimed at improving Hereford's performance.

Simulation

The Hereford case throws into light the complexity of problem situations. The solution to Hereford's problems requires a set of interlocking decisions. The development and evaluation of those decisions could be aided by a number of simulations, each of which would be operated on a personal computer as a spread-sheet model.

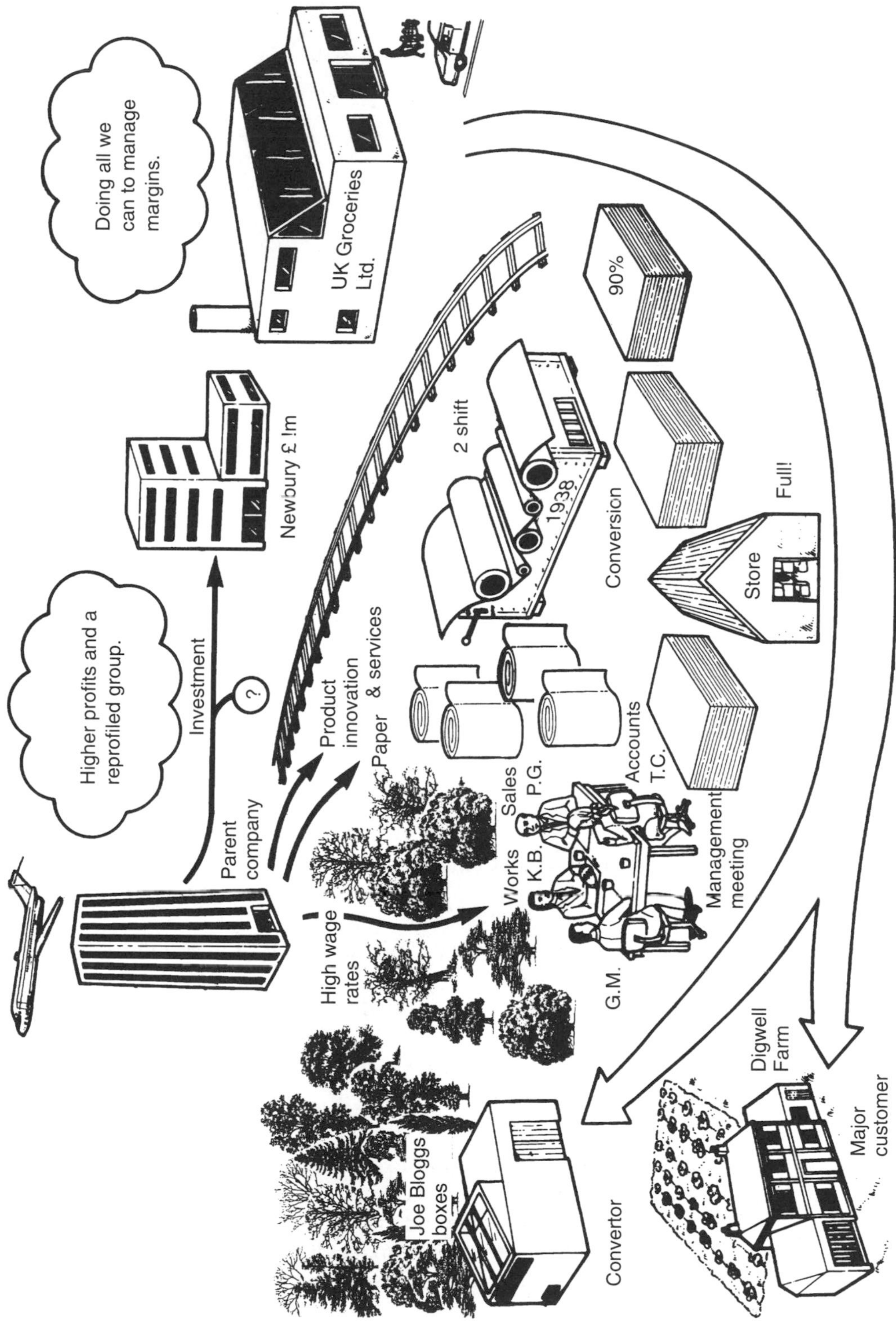

Fig. 11.5 A Rich Picture: Hereford Containers

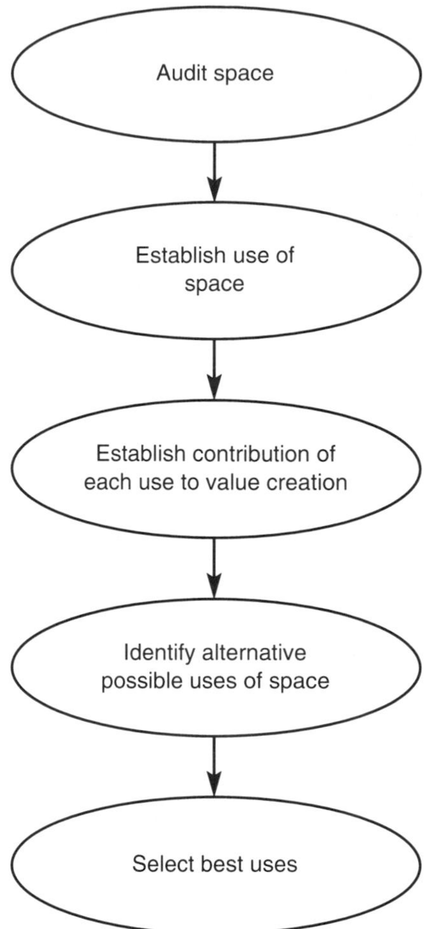

Fig. 11.6 A conceptual model: Hereford Containers

The production of cases is essential to the viability of Hereford. A simple model of the production of cartons is shown in Fig. 11.7.

The utilisation figures are given in the case and are as follows:

Production 99%
Temporary storage 95%
Conversion 90%
Dispatch 95%

These figures can be built into a simple model to assist the evaluation of plant capacity. In the model the average and minimum values consist of a set of four figures. When the utilisation factors are set against the average and minimum values, the following table is obtained; this illustrates the effect of the utilisation factors and takes into consideration the minimum, or 'break even' figures, and the average production run figures.

Hereford						
Production			*Utilisation*			
Run			*Board Prod.*	*Temp. Store*	*Convert*	*Dispatch*
Minimum	1,000	2,000	0.99	0.95	0.9	0.95
Average	2,500	3,500				
Equivalents						
1,000			1,010.10	959.60	863.64	820.45
2,000			2,020.20	1,919.19	1,727.27	1,640.91
2,500			2,525.25	2,398.99	2,159.09	2,051.14
3,000			3,030.30	2,878.79	2,590.91	2,461.36

The figures presented under Utilisation are obtained from the Equivalents. The board-production figures are calculated from the 1 per cent rejection figure given in the case. The board moves to temporary storage which can utilise 95 per cent of the production. Conversion is only 90 per cent of this figure, and so on. Therefore, the production process has a bottleneck at conversion and temporary storage. This conclusion could have been obtained from careful study of the case material but the prospective cost of the bottleneck could not; e.g., on the minimum break-even figures, the difference between temporary storage and conversion is approximately 100 case equivalents or around 10 per cent of the production. This equates to an annual cost to Hereford of approximately £85,000 (10 per cent of annual turnover). Similar amounts can be calculated from the other figures. Given the prospective investment cost of £3–4m, a new plant to improve production would not seem a good investment. From the model it appears that

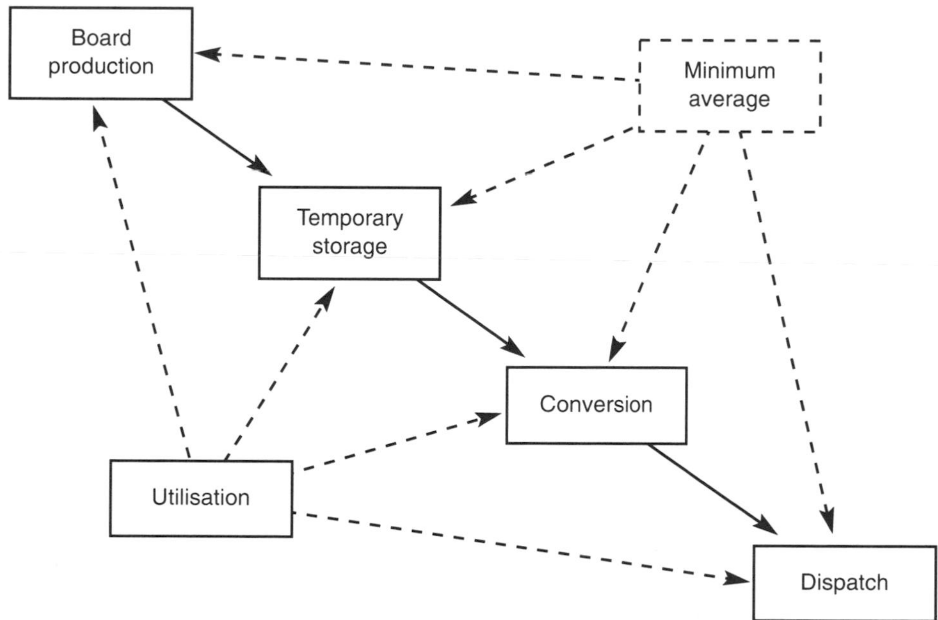

Fig. 11.7 Block diagram of model

management's efforts should be concentrated on improving the performance of the conversion process.

A second area that Hereford could model is the cost of production. The following analysis is based upon the various costs of production, expressed as a percentage of selling price, and the effect of successive increases in those costs.

Hereford

Cost of Production	*1985*	*1986*	*1987*	*1988*
Materials	0.50	0.54	0.58	0.62
Labour	0.20	0.21	0.22	0.24
Energy	0.02	0.09	0.10	0.10
Distribution (pure)	0.03	0.12	0.13	0.14
Distribution (labour)	0.01	0.08	0.09	0.09
Other materials	0.02	0.06	0.06	0.07
Maintenance	0.03	0.12	0.13	0.14
Total	0.81	1.22	1.31	1.40
(As a % of selling price)				

The greater part of costs is accounted for by materials and wages. Would total costs be significantly altered if Hereford was just a conversion plant, and paid non-union wages?

Hereford

Cost of Production	*1985*	*1986*	*1987*	*1988*
Materials	0.50	0.54	0.58	0.62
Labour	0.20	0.06	0.02	0.08
Energy	0.02	0.09	0.10	0.10
Distribution (pure)	0.03	0.12	0.13	0.14
Distribution (labour)	0.01	0.08	0.09	0.09
Other materials	0.02	0.06	0.06	0.07
Maintenance	0.03	0.12	0.13	0.14
Total	0.81	1.07	1.15	1.23

The above assumes that the production staff can be cut by 50 per cent, and that the wages will be 40 per cent lower than currently from 1986 onwards. Even doing this Hereford will still be operating at a loss in 1986, unless there are equivalent increases in selling price.

Management Science

The paper and board industry has a history of applying management science techniques to operating problems. By the mid-1960s large producers were using linear programming to optimise the use of productive capacity and to minimise waste. The Hereford plant is operating at a level of production where further increases in output are limited by resource constraints, yet at the same time the management of the plant needs to increase profitability. These circumstances, and the history of successful applications in the industry, suggest that thought should be given to the feasibility of developing a linear programming model to optimise the use of scarce capacity. The general form for such a model would be as follows.

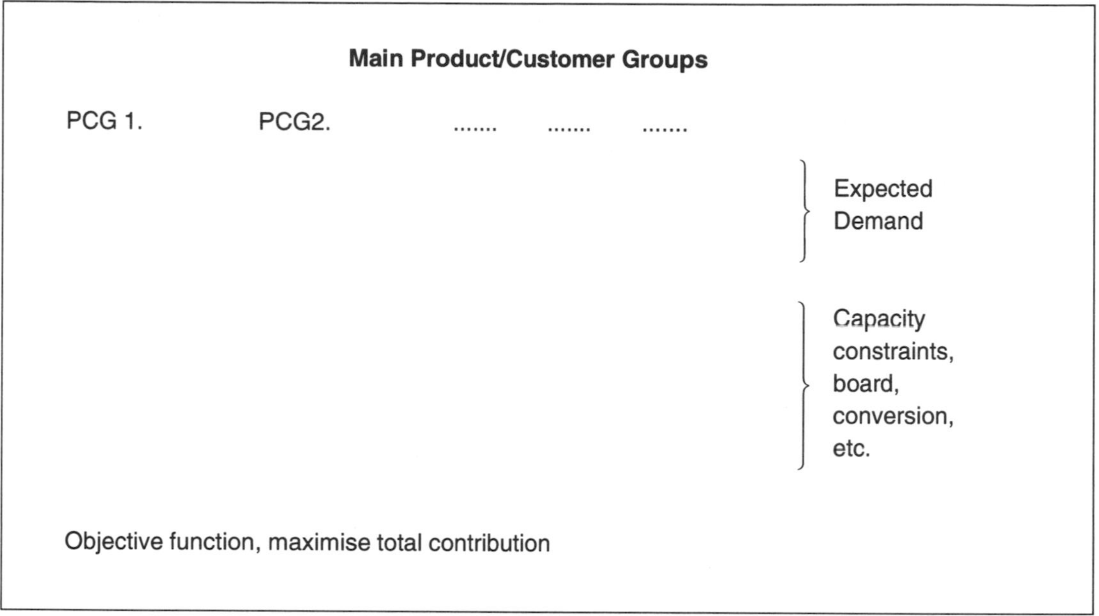

Expected demand would be estimated for each Product/Customer Group, for a given period of time. The model is assisting a short-term decision, consequently the time period would be a week or a few weeks. The same time period has to be used for measuring the Capacity Constraints. The model can be elaborated by, for example, adding further constraints requiring that the demands of key customers are met.

While this appears to be a straightforward application of the LP model, there will be problems in developing the application. The Hereford plant has a costing scheme that is accurate for standard products but may have a 20–30 per cent error on non-standard. There is a need to bring all data to a level of accuracy. Attention also needs to be given to Hereford's strategy. Hereford's managers are having to consider options that would fundamentally change the nature of the plant's operation, one of these is the possibility of ceasing to produce board to become solely a convertor. These strategic questions have to be decided before the LP model is developed.

Management accounting

Hereford Containers is a subsidiary company in a large international group, Reed International. As such its operations are funded by the parent company which raises capital on a group basis. Hereford Containers must compete with other group companies for scarce finance. When long-term decisions are made the subsidiary will have to conform to group rules as to the cost of capital to be applied as a discount factor in investment appraisal calculations. Unless Hereford Containers can advance cogent tactical reasons for the allocation of group funds, it is only logical, from the group's point of view, that projects should earn sufficient to provide the return required on the group funds tied up in them. From the case information this appears to be a return of 30 per cent but whether this is a 30 per cent discount factor or a 30 per cent return on capital employed is unclear, and whether it is 30 per cent before tax also needs to be discovered before any calculations can be made. If the group is to commit a significant amount of capital to a subsidiary to pay for a new scheme which has a 5- or 10-year life, then the returns on the whole life of the investment must be considered, after tax. Discounting is one way in which the cash flows expected to be received in, say, 5 years' time can be equated to cash flows to be received next year, when the calculation is undertaken. It is interesting to note that the Reed Group allow approval of capital expenditure of up to £100 000 at a local level and then, above that amount, larger schemes must be approved by higher echelons of group management.

Financial constraints are apparent at Hereford in that there is insufficient storage space, which causes considerable disruption to production. In a proposal to the group for funds to increase storage capacity, the cost savings through longer production runs and lower set-up costs, would be seen as cash inflows. Other benefits would be more difficult to forecast. These are the qualitative factors affecting the decision, such as the effect on sales of offering a better service to customers from stock *versus* the cost of interest on overdraft raised to finance the larger stocks which are to be held, and all the other costs of storage. The capital expenditure for a new machine would itself be phased over a 3-year period and should also be subject to discounting to show the present value of the investment.

Part of this situation, but perhaps a separate short-term decision, is the attempt to gain the quality kite mark. The extra revenue to be gained once the kite mark is achieved is almost impossible to forecast, while the cost of raising quality in terms of wastage can be estimated with greater accuracy. Slowing the speed of the machine to improve the finish is yet another cost of this plan. Management must consider what relevant costs would be saved if the machine was speeded up. This is a classic case of qualitative information *versus* quantitative information in the decision context. The weakness of qualitative information as a basis for a decision is illustrated by expectations of changes in market share. An accountant would want to check the accuracy of the assumptions on which the expected growth in market share is based before trusting to such figures.

It is noticeable that the company is using contribution as a basis on which to decide whether a contract is worth taking. However, it may be difficult to determine exactly what the contribution from an order is likely to be. This depends very much on the variable costs of the situation. The cost information given in the case shows that materials, labour and energy make up 72 per cent of selling price, thus implying a contribution of 28 per cent of the selling price to cover the other direct costs and factory overheads. Part of the labour cost may be directly employed in production, but another part of it may be indirect labour which should be classed as a factory overhead expense.

The fact that Hereford must offer attractive credit terms underlines the significance of working capital in the commercial situation. Part of the cost of accepting a contract is the interest to be paid on overdraft raised to fund the cost of the contract during the two or three month period before the customer makes payment. The balance sheet of the Hereford plant shows debtors as a major asset of the business, with one-and-a-half million pounds tied up in trade credit waiting to be turned into cash. This asset is greater than the fixed assets of plant and machinery in which the business has invested, and this underlines the significance of working capital when decisions have to be taken. It is equally significant that the Reed Group have established targets for debtors and stocks in order to encourage the subsidiary companies in the group not to waste capital in the working capital situation. However, targets for debtors (7.5 weeks) are difficult to achieve if the debtors are unwilling to pay. It would be very harmful to management morale at the Hereford plant if an unreal target was forced on them by higher management at group level.

Clearly the accountant at Hereford containers is presenting good management information to the decision makers in the company. The fact that his paper indicated that a drop in sales volume of 30 per cent would place the Hereford plant in a position where it might not be economic to have a board machine, means that the accountant is using the contribution from board sales to set against the fixed costs of that part of the operation in order to show a break-even point for that activity. The accountant can also see that output must increase by 6 per cent in order to provide the extra contribution required to meet the fixed cost increases shown by the budgets of the business.

STRATEGIC CONTEXT

The Hereford plant is owned by Reed International, a conglomerate that is attempting to improve its profitability by:

- Changing the portfolio of businesses that it owns to become first and foremost a publisher.
- Developing a greater emphasis upon profitability, leading to the introduction of explicit goals for the profitability of the corrugated case operations.

A basic strategic question concerns the corrugated case industry: has it the potential to provide a high level of profitability? The conclusions from past data are disappointing. The industry's return on capital demonstrates a declining trend. For Reed International packaging as a whole only achieves a 21 per cent return (trading profit to capital employed) as against 31 per cent for publishing. The industry's potential for sustaining good margins is based upon its structure. This can be examined by applying the five forces model introduced in Chapter 8 (Fig. 8.6) to analyse the industry.

For unsophisticated products there are few barriers to entry. Brand names do not seem to be valued by the customer, little capital or skill is required, and entry can be made on a small scale. Should the industry experience an increase in demand, the profits would be competed away by new entrants who would be attracted into the industry by its improved profitability.

Developments in the nature of the customer have had a profound effect on the industry. The emergence of large supermarkets has led to a squeeze upon the margins enjoyed by food producers; in turn this has reduced the ability of the case manufacturers to sustain their margins. In addition, the supermarkets have introduced shrink-wrapped trays, with the effect of reducing the industry's volume.

The supermarkets are a powerful force in the industry. They can exercise that power not only by negotiating with the food suppliers for lower prices but also through direct negotiation with the case manufacturers, and by introducing their own in-house packaging as an alternative to outside purchase. There are enough alternative sources of supply in the industry (approximately 300 producers) for large companies such as Reed to enjoy little market power. The product innovations and services made available by companies such as Reed do little to offset the price-sensitivity of many of the industry's customers.

If Reed is typical of the industry, advertising plays a low role in the competitive process. Technical and design advice are offered to the customer but competition in the industry is fundamentally based upon price and factors such as delivery and the availability of credit terms, items which make up the cost of supply for a customer.

The last two factors, suppliers and substitutes, do not have such an obvious role in determining the profitability of the industry.

Given that Reed International and the Hereford plant are operating in an industry that promises low margins, what can be done? There may be possibilities for improving the industry's structure. The most obvious of these is by restraining competition and entry through limiting the sale of board to convertors, although such a development would bring the accusation of operating a restrictive practice. An alternative is to attempt to offset the growing power of the customer by consolidating the supply side of the industry.

Reed International's continued commitment to the industry is becoming questionable. The Hereford management, and RCC, may soon be faced with a situation where they need to re-think their position in the industry. The company may be able to move strategic groups, probably to focus on a narrower set of customers, those with a need for sophisticated packaging. That would be a strategy based upon differentiation focus. Such a strategy may provide a reasonable match between the resources available to Hereford and the needs of the customer.

GOALS, OBJECTIVES AND ETHICS

Reed International have established goals for market share, growth, debtors, stocks and productivity. Taken together these provide some balance of long-term and short-term considerations. The goals take the form of performance targets against which to assess the various plants that make up Reed Corrugated Cases. It may be argued that some of the goals are so difficult for Hereford to achieve that they should be modified to suit local commercial circumstances. Such a development might be seen as undesirable by Reed's, blurring their abilty to direct and assess performance. In addition to the explicit performance targets there is recognition by Hereford of a growing concern for profitability. The various goals and objectives help provide direction for Hereford's decisions, but the managers still face many issues concerning the basis upon which they should assess choices and their own behaviour.

Many students approaching a business case study are likely to undertake a strategic analysis at an early stage in their thinking. Through such an analysis it is often found that a changing environment introduces both opportunities and threats and presents ethical concerns.

As was shown in Chapter 9, environmental issues will often co-exist on a number of levels. For Hereford Containers there are potentially both local and wider environmental issues.

Locally, we have been told that Reed's Hereford factory suffers inefficiencies as a result of a lack of space. To expand is difficult, although in any discussions on the future of the site a stakeholder perspective, stressing future prospects of the Hereford workforce and their dependants, could be adopted, if acceptable to the company. Also, we are told of the inefficiency of the distribution systems. An environmental audit of the plant would surely suggest that, without attempts to optimise distribution, there are bound to be inefficiencies which are not only reflected in higher costs but, from an environmental perspective, are likely to generate an unnecessarily high level of vehicle movements, with consequent environmental impacts from the movements themselves and from higher-than-necessary fuel consumption.

A Friedman-like response (Chapter 9) would be to argue for a reappraisal of the distribution system purely in terms of company profitability. So long as Reed are not infringing regulations or restrictions, they should not, according to this perspective, concern themselves with wider environmental considerations. It is quite conceivable, however, that future government action will seek to constrain road transportation, which could simply be seen as a shift in the financial context of the decision, or taken to signal an expectation that the business community reappraise their distribution strategies. Should Reed seek to anticipate such moves? There may even be direct and indirect benefits here; direct in terms of improved efficiency, indirect in terms of being able to promote the company with a Green image. Should the Green image seem attractive, though, conflicts may arise between the minimum level of environmental awareness which is needed to be shown to justify promotional claims, and a full, comprehensive, and perhaps costly commitment to environmental matters.

The whole area of packaging is rife with environmental concerns. It is conceivable that it is often in the producer's interest to provide extensive and sophisticated packaging when cheaper and more environmentally-friendly alternatives would suffice. What should Reed's attitude be to environmentalists' criticisms of the packaging industry? Should they protect their industrial interest at all costs, even if, in the terms of Albert Carr (Chapter 9), that meant adopting the deceits and misrepresentations of the 'bluffer'? Should they seek to use the shifts in attitudes to promote a Greener image, as suggested above, even if that Greening of their image was more for self-interest than ecological principles?

The case makes no direct reference to recycling, but clearly there is scope for such a discussion, even with little detailed evidence to underpin it. There are European Community initiatives requiring responsible attitudes to waste materials, and Reed may need to decide if they wish to engage in those developments purely at the level of legal minima, or to set higher standards. Friedman's views are again relevant.

Apart from the environmental dimensions of the case, several other aspects raise ethical concerns. It is intimated that new machinery could be introduced requiring lower manning levels. There are obvious ethical considerations for any company facing over-staffing. Should Reed's responsibilities to its established, loyal workforce extend beyond the statutory minima? If redundancies are to be made, on what basis should they be determined? Typically 'last in/first out' may mean the loss of younger, more adaptable employees who may prove easier to train in new work practices. Alternatively, 'first in/first out' conflicts with notions of rewarding loyalty, which may raise pragmatic as well as ethical concerns.

The whole area of costing and prices raises difficulties too. The squeezing of margins by large food multiples is a common criticism from those in the supply chain, and raises concerns about relationships between mutually dependent firms, particularly when they are of markedly different size and influence. If necessary, should Reed employ cheaper non-union labour? If competitors are unable to offer Reed's more specialised services, should Reed seek to link their strength in specialist areas to more widely available products, giving preference in some way to those who use a wider range of Reed's services?

We are told that aspects of non-price competition already exist in this sector, as in offering technical and design advice. If Reed are to be more aggressive in their search for customers, what limits should be put on such additional incentives? Need they even be linked directly to the materials being supplied? What, then, is it fair to offer as an incentive to concluding a major contract? There have been some covert deals between packaging companies and large retail customers. Reed have rejected this and lost business as a result. Is it unfair on the manufacturers to adopt this form of rebate agreement?

In resolving many of these ethical questions we may find ourselves adopting both deontological (what is right?) and consequential (what is best for Reed's?) approaches. Do we need to be ethically consistent?

DEGREE OF UNCERTAINTY

The history of Reed International demonstrates the difficulties of prediction in the paper industry. Rather than a planned, linear growth, the performance of the group shows mixed fortunes. The business strategy adopted by the group has been a series of reactions to events that have been unseen. Both the decline in the paper market and the ensuing mountain of debts suggests that the facts of the situation only became available after the event, and the organisation has not coped with the chaotic, non-linear trends in the industry. This failure has led to a series of draconian, reactive measures which have yet to prove their worth for Hereford Containers.

The problems of prediction are also apparent at the organisational level, with Hereford Containers having difficulties with market and financial forecasting. They have not forecast, or made themselves ready for, the changing demands of their customers, particularly the requirement for delivery dates of two to three days. The extent to which such events and changes are predictable is related directly to the stability of the system under consideration. It would appear that packaging for the retail trade and for the consumer products themselves is part of a complex and volatile system. Chaos theory would suggest that Hereford Containers will have to live with high levels of uncertainty and unpredictability.

To what extent is Hereford Containers, as it currently operates, capable of surviving and succeeding in a chaotic system? If we look at some of the implications of chaos theory for management decision making it is possible to identify potential courses of action for the company.

(1) *Contingency planning*. Uncertainty about the future means it is necessary to plan for a range of different futures. There is little evidence that contingency planning is a particular strength of the company.
(2) *Temporary structures/systems*. The basic organisation structure shown in the case suggests a permanent line structure which is more suited to stable conditions. There is no sign of project management or even accounts management which might better deal with pressing and unique decisions.
(3) *Short-term forecasting*. Chaos theory offers techniques which can refine short-term forecasts. What evidence we have of forecasting in the company suggests that these are not being used.

(4) *Intuitive decision making*. If there is an inherent unpredictability in a system, then decisions may be best made, not by a reliance on the formal rational methods, but by flair and intuition. Again there is little evidence of flair and the encouragement of intuitive decision making.
(5) *New values for corporate culture*. What little we know about the culture of Hereford Containers suggests that it is traditional and not particularly strong. To operate in a chaotic environment there is a need for a clear set of common values that include risk-taking and innovation.
(6) *Order in chaos*. Studies of chaotic systems suggest that there are pockets of stability and order within the general chaos. Hereford Containers might be able to find such pockets, e.g., with a particular mix of customer and product.

By applying chaos theory to this company, it appears that there is a need for significant change in the organisation and given its past performance it is not likely that this change will come from the present leadership. In particular, the necessity to develop a radically different culture suggests the need to bring in 'new-blood' and fresh ideas. The response to the meeting where the head of the accounting department presented the financial consequences of failing to maintain sales indicates a lack of motivation and new ideas amongst the present management. There is clearly a need for change.

Overall chaos theory provides useful insights into this company, though it must be said that it raises a mixture of both questions and suggestions.

RATIONALITY IN DECISION MAKING

This book has considered a wide range of material concerning the process and context of decision making. In conclusion, it is worth examining the question of rationality. How 'good' are the decisions that organisations make? As can be seen from the arguments contained in this book, there are a number of significant limitations upon the making of 'best' decisions by an organisation.

Chapter 1 introduced a normative model of decision making (Fig. 1.1) that provided an ordered series of activities, from the setting of goals and objectives, through a search for alternatives, to choice and implementation. A procedure that, if followed, would select the best alternative for gaining the organisation's objectives. However, each of the activities involved in this model is faced with practical limitations. Goals and objectives are often difficult to identify or are imprecise. Search will be limited and may develop only one solution. In the face of uncertainty the decision maker lacks complete and reliable information with which to make the decision. The process takes place in a psychological and organisational context that brings a variety of biases. Practice falls far short of the model's prescription.

A more fundamental issue concerns the assumption, implicit in the normative model, that there is a common viewpoint, shared by all those involved in a situation, as to what is the nature of the problem and what would constitute a 'good' solution. This assumption is unrealistic. Soft Systems Methodology (Chapter 2) emphasises the need to recognise the diversity of values and viewpoints that may exist in a problem situation. A similar conclusion arises from the study of ethics (Chapter 9) and psychology (Chapter 4). Following those arguments a 'good' decision is one that is acceptable to a range of actors involved in the situation.

The uncertainties concerning relevant values are paralleled by uncertainty concerning the facts of a situation. All decisions concern the future; our information is drawn from the past and is taken as a guide in assessing future situations. How can the decision maker recognise the 'best' choice when the future is uncertain or even unknowable? In some instances decision makers appear to modify their behaviour in order to cope with their lack of information, for example, by adopting an incremental approach to decision making.

However, many decisions have a short time-span. Decisions concerning an operations schedule, or materials purchasing, may address a situation that has a time span of days or weeks. In such situations the short-time horizon brings a greater degree of certainty to decision making.

Decision makers have a considerable range of techniques available to assist them and a number of those techniques have been examined in this book. How far can the techniques improve decision making? Correctly applied a computational technique, such as linear programming or investment appraisal, assists the decision maker in making a choice. The technique will identify the best alternative out of those that have been fed into the model. But that solution is 'best' in terms of the (sub)system that has been described in the model.

On the other hand, methodologies are available, such as Soft Systems Methodology (Chapter 2) and Strategic Analysis (Chapter 8), that can be used to describe and analyse a wider system. However, such an analysis may not provide an optimal solution. The decision maker may face a choice in the use of techniques.

> Model construction... has taken two directions. The first is to retain optimisation, but to simplify sufficiently so that the optimum (in the simplified world!) is computable. The second is to construct satisficing models that provide good enough decisions... By giving up optimisation, a richer set of properties of the real world can be retained in the models. Stated otherwise, decision makers can satisfice either by finding optimum solutions for a simplified world, or by finding satisfactory solutions for a more realistic world.
> (Simon, 1979.)

In Simon's view, decision making in organisations inevitably falls short of finding solutions that are truly optimal for the whole system. This conclusion should not lead to a rejection of computational techniques and analysis in general; rather it is an argument for greater realism in what we can expect from their application.

There are severe constraints on our ability to make the 'best' decision. However, the justification for this book is that if we can understand what is involved when we make decisions, then we will be more able to conduct our decision making in a way that is informed and appropriate.

REFERENCES

Simon, H. A. (1979) 'Rational Decision Making in Business Organisations', *American Economic Review*, Vol. 69, No. 4, 493-513.

FURTHER READING

Bass, B. M. (1983) *Organisational Decision Making*, Irwin.

Bazerman, M. (1986) *Judgement in Managerial Decision Making*, Wiley.

Cyert, R., and March, J. (1992) *A Behavioural Theory of the Firm*, Prentice-Hall.

March, J., and Olsen, J. (1979) *Ambiguity and Choice in Organisations*, Universitetsforlaget, Bergen.

Rosenhead, J. (1989) *Rational Analysis for a Problematic World*, Wiley.

AUTHOR INDEX

SUBJECT INDEX